PENGUIN BOOKS

ALL YOU NEED TO KNOW ABOUT THE MUSIC BUSINESS

'There are a number of books like this . . . [but] Passman's is particularly accessible because it translates the whole minefield of legal terms into common English'— David Hinckley in the *New York Daily News*

'An intriguing assemblage of advice and council . . . the book offers a wealth of information for young musicians, songwriters, and executives . . . not every artist has an attorney with Passman's clout, hence the value of his new book'—Patrick Goldstein in the *Los Angeles Times*

'A must-read for aspiring rock stars, *All You Need to Know About the Music Business* is a veritable how-to bible. With his expert knowledge, Passman details how to negotiate record deals, calculate foreign-video royalties, and handle merchandise packages (you'll have to learn to write the hits yourself)'—*Details*

'At last, a practical musician's guide that covers everything an artist needs to know . . . Before you get screwed, read Passman's primer'—Gary Cee in *Circus*

'A lucid, detailed, and frequently entertaining compendium of knowledge that lives up to its title. Written with neophyte pro musicians in mind, it covers the waterfront from how to choose one's business associates to the various ways one may be screwed by one's seemingly beneficent record company. With the artist's interests forefront, but devoid of axe-grinding, most of these kernels of knowledge are not likely to date quickly, even in a biz as mercurial as pop music. If you want a thorough education in a hurry, this is the book'—Mark Rowland in *Musician*

'If I'd had this book when I started, I'd be ten times richer and I would have saved a fortune in legal fees'—Ed Bicknell, Manager of Dire Straits

Donald S. Passman is a graduate of the University of Texas and Harvard Law School. He practises law with the firm of Gang, Tyre, Ramer & Brown, Inc., where his clients include major entertainers, publishers, producers, record companies, songwriters, industry executives and film companies. He has taught and lectured extensively, including teaching a course on the music industry at the University of Southern California Law School's Advanced Professional Program. He lives in Los Angeles with his wife and four children and lists five-string banjo, guitar, dog-training and karate among his interests.

All You Need to Know About the Music Business

FOURTH UK EDITION

Revised and Updated

DONALD S. PASSMAN

Illustrations by Randy Glass

PENGUIN BOOKS

*To my precious Shana,
and our boys, Danny, David, Josh, and Jordan*

PENGUIN BOOKS

Published by the Penguin Group
Penguin Books Ltd, 80 Strand, London WC2R 0RL, England
Penguin Group (USA) Inc., 375 Hudson Street, New York, New York 10014, USA
Penguin Books Australia Ltd, 250 Camberwell Road, Camberwell, Victoria 3124, Australia
Penguin Books Canada Ltd, 10 Alcorn Avenue, Toronto, Ontario, Canada M4V 3B2
Penguin Books India (P) Ltd, 11 Community Centre, Panchsheel Park, New Delhi – 110 017, India
Penguin Group (NZ), cnr Airborne and Rosedale Roads, Albany, Auckland 1310, New Zealand
Penguin Books (South Africa) (Pty) Ltd, 24 Sturdee Avenue, Rosebank 2196, South Africa

Penguin Books Ltd, Registered Offices: 80 Strand, London WC2R 0RL, England

www.penguin.com

First published in the U.S.A. by Simon & Schuster 1991
Revised edition 1994
U.K. edition first published by Penguin Books 1995
Revised edition 1998
Revised and updated edition published in the U.S.A. by Simon & Schuster 2000
U.K. edition first published by Penguin Books 2002
Revised and updated edition published in the U.S.A. by Free Press 2003
U.K. edition first published by Penguin Books 2004

1

Copyright © Donald S. Passman, 1991, 1994, 1995, 1998, 2000, 2002, 2003, 2004
All rights reserved

The moral right of the author has been asserted

Set in 11/13pt Galliard
Typeset by Rowland Phototypesetting Ltd, Bury St Edmunds, Suffolk
Printed in England by Clays Ltd, St Ives plc

Did You Know That . . .

- Most record deals don't require the record company even to make a record, much less to release it?

- The term 'phonograph record' in recording contracts included home video devices at least ten years before these devices even existed?

- You don't have to register in Washington to get a copyright?

- If we write a song together, and you write only the lyrics and I write only the music, each of us owns a piece of the music and each of us owns a piece of the lyrics? And that neither of us can use just the music, or just the lyrics, without paying the other?

- Prior to 1972, the United States had no law prohibiting the unauthorized reproduction of records?

- Some film music composers can't even write music, much less create the arrangements for each instrument of an orchestra?

- MTV-type videos, which didn't become popular in the U.S. until close to 1981, have been around since the early 1960s in Europe?

- A brain surgeon and a rock star have something in common?

IMPORTANT

The materials in this book represent the opinions of the author and may not be applicable to all situations. Many circumstances appear similar, but differ in respects which may be legally significant. In addition, laws and customs change over time, and by necessity of the lapse in time between the writing and printing of this book, some aspects may be out of date even upon first publication. Accordingly, the author and publisher assume no responsibility for actions taken by readers based upon the advice offered in this book. Each reader should use caution in applying any material contained in this book to his or her specific circumstance, and should seek the advice of an appropriate professional. (Author's note: Use your common sense and be careful!)

Acknowledgments

PLEASE READ MY THANK-YOUS. I KNOW IT'S A BUNCH OF PEOPLE YOU'VE PROBABLY NEVER HEARD OF, BUT THINK HOW MUCH YOU'D WANT OTHER PEOPLE TO READ IT IF YOUR NAME WAS HERE.

No creative work is ever the product of one person alone (no matter how tempting it is to believe our own hype), and I want to acknowledge and thank all the following people for their inspiration and help:

Payson Wolff and Bruce Ramer, my mentors and spiritual brothers.

Dave Dunton, editor and musician extraordinaire, who kept me in focus, and Dominick Anfuso, for taking up the baton.

Mike Ovitz and Bob Bookman, for their friendship and salesmanship.

Bea Shaw, my Mommy, who helped edit me, and who paid for my first soft-drink stand.

Snuff Garrett, for believing in me early on.

Mike Gorfaine and R. Diane McKain, for their invaluable advice on film music.

Jeff Ayeroff and Jordan Harris, for their assistance with the section on record company/distribution structures.

Rob Light, for his help with the touring section.

Ed Ritvo, for the confidence to do all sorts of things.

Lisa Thomas, for her help with publishing.

Hermione Brown, who helped lawyer my book deal so I didn't have to contradict my own advice and represent myself.

Alan Garner, for his extraordinary communication skills and advice on conversation, books, and salesmanship.

Steve Bigger and Larry Apolzon, for their help with the section on protecting the rights in a group name.

Debbie Reinberg, for help with soundtrack album deals.

Cary Sherman, for help with new media and cyberspace.

Chris Castle, for his help with the classical music chapter.

Barbie York, who has typed the original manuscript more than six times.

Kim Mitchell, my incredibly indispensable assistant.

Jules Levine and Corky, for having bulldogs.

But most especially to all the garage bands—you're the lifeblood of our business.

In addition, the following people (in alphabetical order) generously gave the benefit of their expertise: Paul Adler, David Altschul, Jill Berliner, Don Biederman, Todd Brabec, Kevin Breen, Nancy Chapman, David Cohen, Gary Cohen, Fern Cranston, Henry Droz, Bruce Eisenberg, Steven Fabrizio, Gary Ford, Dell Furano, Neil Gillis, Mark Goldstein, Lauren Gordon, Trudy Green, Peter Grosslight, Jeff Hill, Rand Hoffman, Zach Horowitz, Cathy Jacobson, Art Jaeger, Howard Kaufman, Chuck Kaye, Larry Kenswil, Paul Lenz, Peter Lubin, Jay Morgenstern, Jay Murray, Bob Philpot, Jon Pikus, Ken Powell, Peter Reichardt, Bruce Resnikoff, Jon Reynolds, Rick Riccobono, Larry Rosen, Jack Rosner, Tom Ross, Eva Saks, Joel Sill, Packy Smith, Patricia Smith, Sandy Tanaka, Joan Taylor, Lance Tendler, Ray Tisdale, Tracie Verlinde, Wayne Volat, Lenny Waronker, Ron Wilcox and Pat Woods.

I especially want to thank James Ware and Chris Organ for their extensive help with this U.K. edition, as well as Rupert Sprawson, Michelle Brown, Ed Bicknell, Steve Cooke, Terry Foster-Key, John Kennedy, and Roger La-Haye for extraordinary efforts.

The following folk (in alphabetical order) also contributed enormously to the U.K. portions of the book: Tim Bienias, William Booth, Nicholas Brown, Susannah Evans, Toby Feltwell, Ronnie Harris, Richard Jackson-Bass, Jeffrey Kaye, Jay Quatrini, David Ravden, Peter Reichardt, Richard Rowe, Luke Siddell.

Introduction to the Fourth Edition

Step right up, folks. We've got the Internet. Piracy from the wilds of Holland and Vanuatu. Digital downloads from Hollywood. Internet streaming from New York. And the horror of record companies hemorrhaging money (you must be over twelve to view this exhibit).

This is the fifth edition of *All You Need to Know About the Music Business,* and the most extensive update I've ever done. In these times of major change, the established businesses are getting very weird (it's called 'fear,' but macho record execs don't use that word). Among other strategies, the companies have started sniffing around for new ways to make money. Like taking pieces of your non-record income, such as touring, publishing, and merchandising.

Traditional record deals have also gotten more complicated. The contracts now have to cover things that don't exist in any established way (like the sale of music on the Internet, or through a cell phone). Always a lot of fun.

In this edition, I've updated all the numbers and practices for records, songwriting, touring, merchandising, films, and so forth. And for the deals with your advisors—managers, lawyers, business managers, and agents.

In addition, you'll see how the industry is reacting to the earthquakes in our biz:

- How royalties are computed in the digital age.
- Industry strategies for combating piracy.
- My thoughts on what the future will bring, and whether there will be a future. (In case you're reading this in a bookstore and thinking of buying the book, I believe there is a future. So buy it, okay?)

Now come on in, and let's have at it. The water's a little chilly, but you'll get used to it.

P.S. Congratulations if you're reading this. It means you're a real go-getter, since most people don't read the introduction to a book.

Contents

PART III

Songwriting and Music Publishing

PART IV
Group Issues

PART V
Touring

PART VI
Merchandising

I

First Steps

OPEN UP AND SAY 'AHHH'

For many years I taught a class on the music business at the University of Southern California Law School's Advanced Professional Program. The class was for lawyers, accountants, record and film company executives, managers, agents, and bartenders who want to manage groups. Anyway, at the beginning of one of these courses a friend of mine came up to me. She was an executive at a film studio and was taking the class to understand the music industry as it relates to films. She said, 'I'm here to open up the top of my head and have you pour in the music business.' I loved that mental picture (because there are many subjects I have wanted to absorb this same way), and it spurred me to develop a painless way of infusing you with the extensive materials in this book. So if you'll sit back, relax, and open up your mind, I'll pour in all you need to know about the music business (and a bit more for good measure).

HOW I GOT STARTED

I really love what I do. I've been practicing music law for over twenty-five years, and I represent recording artists, record companies, film companies, songwriters, producers, music publishers, film music composers, industry executives, managers, agents, business managers, and other assorted mutants that populate the biz.

I got into this on purpose, because I've always loved creative arts. My first show-biz experience was in grade school, performing magic tricks for assemblies. I also started playing accordion in grade school. (I used to play a mean accordion; everyone applauded when I shook the bellows on 'Lady of Spain.' I gave it up because it's impossible to put the moves on a girl with an accordion on your chest.) By high school, I had graduated from accordion to guitar, and in college at the University of Texas, I played lead guitar in a band called Oedipus and the Mothers.

While I was with Oedipus, we recorded a demo that I tried to sell to our family friend, Snuff Garrett (more about him later). Snuff, a powerful record producer, very kindly took the time to listen to the demo and meet with me. That meeting was a major turning point in my life. Snuff listened to the record, smiled, and said, 'Don . . . go to law school.'

So I took Snuff's advice, and went to Harvard Law School. In law school I continued to play lead guitar with a band called The Rhythm Method, but it was becoming apparent that my ability to be in the music business and eat regularly lay along the business path. So when I graduated, I began doing tax planning for entertainers. Tax law, like intricate puzzles, was a lot of fun, but when I discovered there was such a thing as music law, the electricity really turned on. In fact, I took the USC class that I later taught, and it got me so excited that I left the tax practice for my current firm. Doing music law was so much fun that it wasn't even like working (I'm still not over that feeling); and I enjoyed it so much that I felt guilty getting paid (I got over that).

My first entertainment law experience was representing a gorgeous, six-foot model, referred to me by my dentist. (I promised him I would return the favor, because most of my clients had teeth.) The model was being pursued (I suspect in every way) by a manager who wanted a contract for 50% of her gross earnings for ten years. (You'll see how absurd this is when you get to Chapter 3.) Even then I knew this wasn't right, and so I nervously called up the guy to negotiate. I still remember my voice cracking as I said his proposal was over the industry standards, since most managers took only 15% (which was true). He retorted with, 'Oh yeah? Who?' Well, he had me. I wasn't even sure what managers did, much less who they were. So I learned my first lesson in the art of humility.

As I began to really understand how the music business worked, I found that my love of both creative arts and business allowed me to move smoothly between the two worlds and help them relate to each other. The marriage of art and commerce has always fascinated me— they can't exist without each other, yet creative freedom and the need to control costs are eternally locked in a Vulcan death match. Which means the music business will always need lawyers.

Anyway, I now channel my creative energies into innovative business deals, and my need to perform is satisfied by teaching, lecturing, and playing guitar at my kids' campouts. (I do a great 'Kum-Ba-Ya.') Just to be sure I don't get too straight, however, I've kept up my weird assortment of hobbies: magic, ham radio, weight-lifting, guitar, dog training, five-string banjo, karate, chess, and real estate investment. I also write novels, which you are all required to buy.

BRAIN SURGERY

Speaking of marrying creativity and business, I've discovered that a rock star and a brain surgeon have something in common. It's not that either one would be particularly good at the other's craft (and I'm not sure which crossover would produce the more disastrous results), but rather that each one is capable of performing his craft brilliantly, and generating huge sums of money, without the need for any financial skills. In most businesses, before you can start earning big bucks, you have to be pretty well schooled in how the business works. For example, if you open up a shoe store, you have to work up a budget, negotiate a lease, bargain for the price of the shoes, and so forth—all before you smell that first foot. But in entertainment, as in surgery, you can soar to the heights without any expertise in the business end of your profession.

Making a living from a business you don't fully understand can be risky. Yet a large number of artists, including major ones, have never learned such basics as how record royalties are computed, what a copyright is, how music publishing works, and a number of other concepts that directly affect their lives. They don't know these things because (a) their time was better spent making music; (b) they weren't interested; (c) it sounded too complicated; and/or (d) it was too much like being in school to have to learn it. But without understanding these basics as a foundation, it's impossible for them to understand the intricacies of their professional lives. And as their success grows, and their lives get more complex, they become even more lost.

While it's true that some artists refuse to even listen to business talk (I've watched them go into sensory shutdown if you so much as mention the topic), others get interested and really study their business lives. The vast majority, however, are somewhere in the middle of these extremes. They don't really enjoy business, but want to participate intelligently in their career decisions. These artists are smart enough to know that no one ever takes as good care of your business as you do.

It was for my moderate-to-seriously interested clients that I developed a procedure of explaining the basics in simple, everyday language. With only a small investment of time, these clients got down the essential concepts, and everyone enjoyed the process (including me). It also made an enormous difference in the artist's self-confidence about his or her business life, and allowed them to make valuable contributions to the process.

Because the results of these brief learning sessions were so positive, several clients asked if we could explore the subjects more deeply. Thus the conception of this book. It's designed to give you a general overview of the music industry as it currently exists. You can read it as casually or intensely as suits your interest level, attention span, and pain tolerance. It's not written for lawyers or technicians, so it doesn't include the jargon or minutia you'll find in a textbook for professionals. Instead, it gives a broad overview of each segment of the industry, and goes into enough detail for you to understand the major issues you're likely to confront.

JUNGLE MAPS

When I was in high school, a policeman named Officer Sparks spoke at an assembly. Mr. Sparks hyped us on the life of a crime fighter, certain that we all secretly wanted to be cops. While the man didn't sway me off the path of my destiny, he did show me something I'll never forget.

Officer Sparks ran a film in which the camera moved down a street. It was a grainy black-and-white movie, only about thirty seconds long, and consisted of a camera bobbing along a sidewalk. When it was finished, he asked if we'd seen anything unusual. No one had. Apart from a couple of people bouncing in and out of the doorways, it looked pretty much like pictures taken by a camera moving along a row of shops. Mr. Sparks then said that a 'trained observer' who watched the film could spot six crimes being committed. He showed the film again and pointed out each of the incidents (there was a quiet exchange of drugs, a pickpocket, etc.). This time, the crimes were obvious. And I felt like a doofus for missing them.

Any time we learn a new skill, we go through a similar process. At first, things either look ordinary and deceptively simple, or like a bewildering blur of chaos. But as you learn what to look for, you see a world you never knew was there. To work your way through the process, and become a 'trained observer,' you need a guide to the basics—a framework in which to organize the bits and pieces. And that is the purpose of this book—to give you a map through the jungle, and show you where the crimes are.

DETAILS

There is no way one book (even one filling several volumes) could poke into every nook and cranny of a business as complicated as the music business. Accordingly, the purpose here is to give you the big picture, not all the details. (Besides, for some of those details, I charge serious money.) Also, even if I tried to lay out all the little pieces, as fast as everything moves in this biz, it would be obsolete within a few months. Thus, this book is designed to give you a broad overview (which doesn't change nearly as quickly), so you'll have a bare tree on which to hang the leaves of your own experience. Oddly, it's easier to pick up details (from trade publications, gossip at cocktail parties, etc.) than it is to learn the structural overview, because few people have the time and patience to sit down and give it to you. In fact, giving you the overall view turned out to be a much bigger job than I thought when I started. But you're worth it.

EARLY RESULTS

Since this is the fourth edition, I now have feedback from experiments using this book on actual human subjects. Of all the responses I got, I thought you'd enjoy hearing about two in particular. First, I received an irate call from a music lawyer, who was upset because he charged thousands of dollars to give clients the advice I had put in the book. Second, I received an equally irate call from a manager, who said that all the artists he'd approached lately had been pushing my book in his face.

Way to go! Keep shoving!

STAPLE, SPINDLE, AND MUTILATE

When you go through this book, forget everything you learned as a kid about taking good care of books, treating them as sacred works of art, etc. Read this book with a pencil or highlighter in your hand. Circle or star passages you think you'll need, fold over pages, stick paper clips on them—whatever helps. This is an action book—a set of directions on how to jog through the music biz without getting mugged. So treat it like a comfortable old pair of shoes that you don't mind getting dirty. It doesn't matter what they look like, as long as they get you where you're going.

UK ODDITIES

This is the United Kingdom version of this book, and a number of the practices and customs are different from those in the United States. In order to keep the book's flow, what I've done is add sections that will point out the differences between U.S. and U.K. industry practices and laws. That way, you can get an in-depth understanding of how it works in the United States, which still accounts for a nice chunk of the world's music sales and which is important even if you're signing to a U.K.-based record company. At the same time, I'll go into how the U.K. scene works, so you can have the best of both worlds.

To make it easy (particularly if your attention span is somewhere near mine), I've asked the publisher to put a snappy little Union Jack in the margin next to each section that deals specifically with a U.K. concept. That way you can bounce through the book and find them easily.

Also, at the end (on page 453) is a glossary of various U.K. organizations, suitable for framing. I've also included their addresses and phone numbers so that you can make crank calls to them.

CHOOSE YOUR OWN ADVENTURE

When my sons David, Josh, and Jordan were little, their favorite books were from a series called Choose Your Own Adventure. They work like this: You start reading the book on page 1 and, after a few pages, the author gives you a choice. For example, if you want Pinocchio to go down the alley, you turn to page 14, but if you want him to go to school, you turn to page 19 (my boys never picked school). From there, every few pages you have more choices, and there are several different endings to the book. (The boys liked the ending where everyone gets killed, but that's another story.) These books are not meant to be read straight through; if you tried, you'd find yourself crashing into various endings, twists, and turns of different plots and stories. Instead, you're supposed to skip around, following a new path each time.

This concept gave me the idea of how to organize this book. As noted below, you have a choice of reading for a broad overview, or reading in depth. The book tells you where to skip ahead if you want to do this. However, unlike the Choose Your Own Adventure books, you can read straight through with little or no damage to the central nervous system.

Here's how it's organized (there's no particular magic to the order, except that you need some concepts before you can understand others):

Part I deals with how to put together a team to guide your career, consisting of a personal manager, business manager, agent, and attorney.

Part II looks at record deals, including the concepts of royalties, advances, and other deal points.

Part III talks about songwriting and publishing, including copyrights and the structure of the publishing industry.

Part IV explores special things you'll need to know if you're a group.

Part V deals with concerts and touring, including agreements for personal appearances, and the role of your various team members in the process.

Part VI, on merchandising, tells you how to profit from plastering your face on posters, T-shirts, and other junk.

Parts VII through **IX** explore classical music, new technologies, and motion pictures. They're the last sections because you need to understand the other concepts before we can tackle them.

Now to choosing your adventure. You have four ways to go through this book:

1. **EXTREMELY FAST TRACK**

   If you *really* want a quick trip, then:
   (a) Read Part I, on how to pick a team of advisors
   (b) Get people who know what they're doing
   (c) Let them do it
   (d) Put this book on your shelf to impress your friends; and
   (e) Say 'Hi' to me backstage at one of your concerts.

2. **FAST TRACK**
   Short of this radical approach, if you want a broad-strokes overview of the business, without much detail, skip ahead each time you see the **FAST TRACK** directions.
3. **ADVANCED OVERVIEW**
   If you want a more in-depth look, but less than the full shot, then follow the **ADVANCED OVERVIEW** directions. This will give you a solid overview, plus some detail on each topic.
4. **EXPERT TRACK**
   For you high achievers who want an in-depth discussion, simply read straight through.

You should, of course, feel free to mix and match any of these tracks. If a particular topic grabs your interest, keep reading and check out the details. (Amazingly, the topics that grab your interest tend to be things currently happening in your life.) If another topic is a yawn, Fast Track through it.

So let's get going. Everybody starts with Part I.

PART I

Your Team of Advisors

2

How to Pick a Team

GETTING YOUR TEAM TOGETHER

Let's talk about the professionals you're going to use to maximize your career and net worth. The main players are your

1. Personal manager
2. Attorney
3. Business manager
4. Agency
5. Groupies

With respect to number 5, you're pretty much on your own. As to the others, let's take a look:

BUSINESS PHILOSOPHY

Before we talk about the specific players, let me share a bit of personal philosophy. (If 'share' is too California for you, try 'Let me tell you some of my personal philosophy.') Take a hard look at some facts:

1. **You are a business.**
   Even though your skills are creative, you're capable of generating multimillions of dollars per year, and thus you must think of yourself as a business.
2. **Most artists don't like business.**
   This is not to say you aren't good at it. Some artists are unbelievably sophisticated and astute in business. However, those folks are the minority, and whatever their love and skill for business, their love and skill for creating and performing are much

bigger. So even if you've got the chops to handle your own business, it's not the best use of your time.

3. **Success hides a multitude of sins.**

   This is true in any business, from making widgets to making records. If you're successful, you can get away with sloppy operations that would bankrupt you if times were bad. For example, putting all your pals on the payroll, buying lots of non-income-producing assets (such as houses, jets, raw land, and other things that cost you money to maintain), as well as an overindulgence in various legal and illegal goodies, can easily result in a crash and burn if your income takes even a small dip, much less a nose dive. You can make more money by cutting costs than you can by earning more income (see page 344 for proof of this), so the time to operate efficiently is NOW, not later.

4. **Your career is going to have a limited run.**

   Don't take offense at this—'limited' can mean anything from a year to thirty years, but it is nonetheless going to be limited. In most other careers, you can expect to have a professional life of forty-five years plus, but as an entertainer in the music business, this virtually never happens. And the road is strewn with carcasses of aging rock stars who work for rent money on nostalgia tours. So take the concentrated earnings of a few years and spread them over a forty-five-year period, and you'll find that two things happen: (a) the earnings don't look quite as impressive; and (b) you realize this money may have to last you the rest of your life.

It is certainly possible to have a long, healthy career, and to the extent you do, the need for caution and preservation diminishes radically. However, even the best entertainers have slumps, and very few truly have lengthy careers. Thus, it's best to plan as if your career isn't going to last, and be pleasantly surprised if it does. Setting yourself up so that you never have to work again doesn't stop you from working all you like—it just becomes an option, not an obligation.

HIRING A TEAM

The way you pick your professional team will either set your career and finances up for life, or assure you a place on the next Electric Prunes tour. So be very careful and pay attention *personally* to the process of assembling them. I know you don't like to deal with this stuff, but it's your career and your money, and you have to do it every now and then. If you pick the right people, you can then set your life on automatic pilot and just check up on it periodically. If you pick the wrong people and set it on automatic pilot, you'll smash into a mountain before you know what happened.

Pre-team Strategies

Since you wouldn't open a store without something to sell, before you start assembling a team, you want to be sure your music is ready for the big time. And how do you know when it's ready? You ask your tummy. Do you believe, in your gut, that your music has matured to the point that you're ready to seek a professional career? If the answer is yes, then you're ready. (Tummies are reliable indicators once we learn how to listen to them and dismiss the goblins that yell, 'You're a phony and nobody wants you.' Even the superstars have these goblins; they've just learned how to ignore them.)

The first thing is to get your music down on a CD. The people at record companies are much too busy to run around looking at live performances unless they're first intrigued by your music (or unless you have some compromising photos of the executive). The CD doesn't have to be expensive or elaborate, but the better you can make it sound, the better your chances of getting through. Most record executives will tell you that they can hear 'diamonds in the rough,' but my experience is that the more your demo sounds like a hit, the more likely that you'll get a good reception. This doesn't mean you have to go to great expense—with the advent of relatively inexpensive multitrack recorders, as well as synthesizers, you can get a very professional sound in your bedroom. In fact, a client of mine once had six record companies chasing him based on a homemade, four-track demo. The important thing is to get down your energy, enthusiasm, and drive. You know what I mean.

A word about what kind of music to make. It's simple—you make the music that moves your soul. No one has ever had a serious career by imitating others, or trying to guess what the record companies want. And I'll tell you a secret: What the record companies want is someone whose music is pure and true to themselves. So whether your music is the commercial flavor of the month, or an obscure blend of reggae and Buddhist chants, you have to put down what's in your heart. All the superstars I've known have a clear vision of who they are and what their music is.

Your CD doesn't need more than three or four songs on it. But these should be the best three or four songs you're capable of doing, starting with the primo masterpiece first. The people who listen to demos are busy, and if you don't hook them on the first song, they ain't gonna get to the second. If they're interested, they'll ask for more. But leave 'em wanting it.

So you've got a killer CD and you're ready to boogie. What's next? If you've got photographs, they're a good thing to put in the package because, in this multimedia world, record companies are interested in much more than how you sound. You have to be able to perform live, look good in videos, etc. By the way, 'look good' doesn't mean a pretty face, as you and I are both aware of successful artists who are anything but pretty. But it does mean you have to have an interesting look (or at least be presentable).

And now for a bit of a bummer. Unfortunately, the major record companies (not usually the minors) have developed a practice of not taking CDs unless they're submitted by a manager or attorney in the business. (I hate delivering bad news, but look at the bright side: I just saved you three months of waiting for a form letter that says they won't listen because it didn't come from a lawyer or manager.) The reason for this practice is that record companies can get 300 to 400 demos *per week*, and restricting who can send in CDs is one way to regulate the floodgates. However, it's also a Catch-22: How can you get your CD heard if you're not already connected in the business, and how do you get connected in the business if you can't get heard? But don't despair; I'm going to give you the key to the door. The key consists of finding yourself a lawyer or manager to shop your CD, which leads nicely into our next topic.

Who's on First?

The first person on your team is almost always a manager or a lawyer. In your baby stages, the manager is not likely to be someone already in the business; it's more likely a friend or relative with a lot of enthusiasm. While this can be a major plus (as we'll discuss in more detail when we discuss managers, starting on page 27), it may or may not get your CD into the record companies. So if you have an inexperienced manager, or if you have no manager at all, an industry lawyer can really help. Record companies prefer to deal with people they know, so your CD will get heard much faster, and by more important people, if it's submitted by an industry lawyer.

Why is it easier to get a music lawyer than a manager? Well, the time required of a lawyer is minimal compared to the time a manager has to devote. The manager is expected to help you with songs, image, bookings, baby-sitting, etc., but the lawyer only has to spend a few hours getting your CD around. It's their relationships—not their time—that count.

A word of caution about hiring a lawyer to shop your CD. Most of the lawyers consider it important to maintain their credibility with the record companies, and thus will only shop CDs they really believe in. Unfortunately, there are a few who will shop any CD that walks in the door as long as they get paid a fee. Being shopped by one of these sleazoids is no better than sending the CD yourself, and maybe worse, because the record companies know these lawyers don't screen out any of the garbage, and their CDs go to the bottom of the pile. To prevent your CD from being thrown out with the tuna cans, you should carefully check out the references of any lawyer you're thinking of using. Ask them for the names of people whose CDs they've shopped (both successfully and unsuccessfully, so they don't just give you the few success stories that slipped through the cracks), then call up the references and find out how it went. You can also check around other industry sources to see who's legit. (We'll talk more about checking references later on.)

A business manager (the person who handles the money, investments, etc.) is usually the last on board for the opposite reasons why the lawyer is first: It's expensive (in terms of staffing and labor) for a business manager to take you on, and new artists need a lot of work just to keep financially afloat. Also, very few business managers are willing to 'take a flyer' with a totally unproven, unsigned artist; the business manager's potential upside is not nearly as great as a personal manager's or agent's, and yet they have to incur substantial expense. (As you'll see in Chapter 4, business managers aren't paid as much as agents or personal managers.) But don't sweat it. Until you have some decent money coming in, you don't need a full-fledged business manager. A good accountant can take care of your tax returns and answer any questions.

The Search

Where do you find warm bodies to begin assembling your team? Well, start with the age-old ploy of asking every human being you know for a recommendation. Talk to people involved in music, even if it's only your high school choir's piano accompanist. You can lead yourself into any unknown arena by diligently following your nose, and the music business is no exception. You'll be amazed how many things fall into your life when you open yourself up to the possibilities. The only frustrating part is that the people you really want to grab don't have time for you in the beginning. (But be assured, as soon as you're successful, they'll fall all over you and say they 'knew it all along.')

The major players are almost all in Los Angeles and New York, plus Nashville if you're a country artist. That isn't to say there aren't qualified people in other places—there most assuredly are—but the music industry is centered in these three towns, and the people who live there usually have more experience. On the other hand, major managers are increasingly popping up in other places. For example, I've dealt with managers of world-class artists who live in Seattle, Vancouver, Austin, Philadelphia, and Boston. However, the better ones spend a lot of time on airplanes visiting Los Angeles, New York, and/or Nashville.

Here are some specific suggestions for building your list:

1. *All Access*

   There's a website called www.allaccess.com that has a pretty comprehensive online directory of people in the music biz. I'm told it's updated often, and it has the major advantage of being free. You'll need to register for the site (don't be intimidated by the radio station questions—anybody can register), then click on 'Industry Directory.'

2. *Hits Magazine*

   Hits is the *Mad* magazine of the music biz. It's full of current news, reported with a college-humor-magazine style, and is very funny reading. Each year *Hits* publishes an article in mid-August entitled 'Who's Got Who,' listing artists, their agents, and personal managers. You can contact *Hits Magazine* at 14958 Ventura Blvd., Sherman Oaks, California 91403. Telephone: (818) 501-7900. Web: www.hitsdailydouble.com

3. *Billboard International Talent and Touring Directory*

   The *Billboard* guide is published annually and lists hundreds of artists, together with their booking agents, personal managers, and record companies. It also has a section telling where to contact the agents and managers. For information, write Billboard Publications, 770 Broadway, New York, New York 10003. Telephone: (646) 654-4400. Web: www.billboard.com

By no means are these three an exhaustive list of sources; they just happened to be the ones lying nearby when I grabbed for something to give you. Frankly, I've been doing this long enough to know everybody I need to get to, and I don't use references on a routine basis. So don't take my suggestions as gospel. Check your local bookstores and libraries for more references, and look for ads and reviews of reference books in music magazines and online.

Use a bit of caution with published sources. Annual publications are bound to be a bit out of date by the time you pick them up. And the farther you get from the publication date, the more chance of inaccuracy. Also, I noted from a quick reading that many of them have minor errors of one sort or another (like listing a business manager as an 'agent').

Here's some more ideas on adding to your list of potential team members:

1. Read interviews with industry figures in music magazines, and note the names. The major industry trade magazine is *Billboard,* a weekly publication that's available at newsstands. Others are *Radio and Records* and *Hits Magazine. Billboard*'s and *Hits'* addresses are above. The address for *Radio and Records* is 10100 Santa Monica Blvd., 5th Floor, Los Angeles, California 90067-4004.

   Major consumer magazines (as opposed to trade magazines) are (in alphabetical order):
   (a) *Music Connection,* 4215 Coldwater Canyon, Studio City, California 91604. Telephone: (818) 755-0101. Web: www. musicconnection.com
   (b) *Spin,* 205 Lexington Ave., New York, New York 10016. Telephone: (212) 231-7400. Web: www.spin.com
   (c) *Vibe* Magazine, 215 Lexington Ave., 6th Floor, New York, New York, 10016. Telephone: (212) 448-7300. Web: www. vibe.com

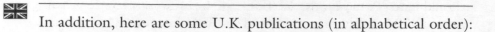

In addition, here are some U.K. publications (in alphabetical order):

(a) *Billboard*, Endeavour House, 189 Shaftesbury Avenue, London, WC2H 8HJ, www.billboard.com.

(b) *Broadcast*, 33–39 Bowling Green Lane, London, EC1R 0DA.

(d) *Music Business International*, 7th Floor, Ludgate House, 245 Blackfriars Road, London, SE1 9UR.

(e) *Music & Media*, 23 Ridgemount Street, London, WC1E 7AH.

(f) *Music Week*, 7th Floor, Ludgate House, 245 Blackfriars Road, London, SE1 9UR, www.musicweek.com.

(g) *PR Week*, 174 Hammersmith Road, London W6 7JP, www.prweek.com.

2. Watch for quotes, stories, or blurbs about music industry people in the newspapers, and on radio and TV.
3. The liner notes of CDs often list managers, lawyers, business managers, or agents in the Special Thanks section. Unfortunately, they may only list the people's names and not their roles (so you might end up managed by someone's yoga instructor if you're not careful). Still, when you're compiling a list of names, every little bit helps.
4. Some artists list the names of their professionals, together with their jobs, in their tour programs.

And here are some online places to try: Musician.com (www. musician.com), TAXI (www.taxi.com), and Tonos.com (www.tonos. com).

Anyway, using the above and anything else you can think of, write down the names and develop a 'hit list.' Just let your imagination go— follow any lead that seems promising, and keep moving forward.

Once you assemble a bunch of names, prioritize who you want to contact first. If you've heard any names from two or more sources, the odds are you are on to a person who is 'somebody,' and he or she should move up in priority. Also look for the professionals surrounding people whose music you admire and whose style is similar to your own. While this is less critical with lawyers and business managers, it's important to be sure that agencies, and especially personal managers, handle your style of music. For example, the agent who books Wayne Newton is not likely to book Eminem, and I guarantee you they have different managers. On the other hand, you may be surprised to find that acts just as diverse are represented by the same agency (with very different individual agents involved). And, the legal and business management lives of acts within the realm of popular music are not as different as you might expect. Rock 'n' rollers (like Aerosmith, the Rolling Stones, etc.) and divas (like Mariah Carey, Barbra Streisand, etc.) have similar needs in music publishing, record royalties, touring, merchandising, sponsorship, etc.

Once you've prioritized your list, start trying to contact the people on it. It's always better to come in through a recommendation, friend of the family, etc., even if it's only the person's dry cleaner. But if you can't find any contact, start cold. You can try calling people on the phone (if it's not too expensive), but expect a lot of unreturned phone calls, or at best to be shuffled off to an underling. That's okay—talk to the underling. Be sure you're brief and to the point if you get someone on the phone, because these folks are always in a hurry. It's a good idea to rehearse your rap with a friend in advance.

You can also begin mailing out CDs, pictures, hundred-dollar bills, and anything else to get their attention. If you've gotten any local press, that's a good thing to include. Use a yellow highlighter so the guy doesn't have to search the page for where you are. Be short and straightforward—good people are always busy, and you'll be lucky to get five seconds of their attention. If you can't grab 'em in that little snippet, you're off to the round file. Repeated letters to the same person help get their attention, and may even have the subliminal effect of making your name sound familiar if anyone ever asks. But expect a lot of unacknowledged letters, and don't get discouraged.

By the way, I hate to get unsolicited letters marked 'Personal & Confidential' because I have to open them myself (my office assumes they contain state secrets). Not only do I waste time fumbling with a letter opener (I've never been particularly coordinated), but I also get thoroughly annoyed that someone would put me to this extra effort for something that isn't confidential. And while we're on the subject of peeves, I also hate getting letters that are terminally cute (like 'Looking for a hit? Here's one!'). So get right to the point.

If you successfully snag someone's attention, but find out they can't get involved with you, ask who they would recommend. This is valuable for two reasons: First, you've got a lead from someone actually in the industry. Second, when you call up the recommended person, you can tell them 'So-and-so' told you to call. If 'So-and-so' is a big enough name, it should at least get your phone call returned. (Maybe.)

Someone, somewhere, will nibble, and you can parlay it into real interest by being persistent. All the superstars I've known have heaping helpings of drive and perseverance, and they'll continually hound people to further their career. So hang in there and keep following up, despite whatever discouragements get thrown in front of you. Virtually every record company in America passed on Alanis Morrisette, the Beatles, and Elton John, so don't expect people to be any smarter about your music. And don't get discouraged—it only takes one enthusiastic person to get the ball rolling.

Screening the Sharks

So you've honed your list, run up large postage and long-distance phone bills, and hopefully found two or three nibbles on your line. At this point, you should fly, drive, bus, or hitchhike to meet these people face-to-face in their natural habitat. You can't tell everything from a telephone call; you want to watch their body language, meet their associates, see if they live in a trailer, etc. Basically, use your instincts to feel how they vibe you, and don't be afraid to trust your gut. If you think you're meeting with a piece of slime, you probably are. But if they dazzle you, use even more caution—charming crooks are the most dangerous!

The fact that someone has a lot of big names is helpful, but not a final determination. There have been a lot of big names associated with disasters over the years. Here's a bit of personal history to illustrate: When we first got married, my wife and I decided to buy a vacuum cleaner. For reasons I still don't understand, we called a door-to-door salesman. This buzz-cut, square-jawed hunk bounced up to the house, all pumped up with sunshine, and fractured my pinkie with his handshake. Then Buzz picked up seven-pound metal balls with the vacuum's suction, slurped up some blue gunk that he'd poured on our carpet, and started bragging about how he'd sold vacuum cleaners to the wives of several celebrities. While he was on this roll, rattling off a list of big names, I said, 'Excuse me, but do these people know anything about vacuum cleaners?'

The point, as I'm sure you see, is that a big-name celebrity isn't necessarily a good recommendation. It may just mean the celebrity pays no attention to his or her business, or that the celebrity is an imbecile.

So how do you protect yourself? Like this:

References.   Have the potential team member give you references. And check them out carefully.

In asking for references, it's important to get people at your level of success. The fact that someone takes excellent care of their biggest client doesn't necessarily mean he or she will pay such good attention to you. Odd as it seems, some people don't even pay much attention to their big-name clients, usually because they're too busy. There's an old joke (based on truth) about a major artist who couldn't get his lawyer on the phone to fire him. Also, try to get references from someone who has been using this professional for a while, so you don't just get a report on their honeymoon period.

Although it may seem obvious, be sure this person's expertise is in music. There are brilliant real estate accountants who would be lost in the music business, just as the opposite is true. In fact, even people with extensive film, television, or literary expertise may not understand music. So be sure you're talking to someone who does.

Use Your Other Team Members.   You should consult the other members of your team anytime you hire someone, because you want their input and suggestions. Also, these people have to work together. But beware of this: Benjamin Franklin once said (and I'm too lazy to look up the exact quote, so I'll paraphrase it) that when you gather together a group of people for their collective wisdom, you also gather their collective prejudices and hidden agendas. In other words, there will almost always be a political reason your other team members do or don't want something, and this may or may not coincide with your best interests. For example, a business manager may have just referred a very important client to a personal manager. The personal manager may therefore be pushing you toward this particular business manager in order to pay back the favor, regardless of whether or not the business manager is right for your situation. (I don't mean to make you paranoid; most people are ethical and won't recommend someone unless they genuinely believe he or she would be the best person for the job, even if it's a payback. But a great deal of politicking goes on in the music business, just as in any other business, and you should be aware of it.) Thus, always ask people the reasons for their recommendation, rather than just the bottom line of who you should use. And make them give you specific, factual reasons. Facts are something you can evaluate yourself, and you should make the final decision.

Look Beyond the Sales Pitch.   Remember, everybody looks great when they're selling. When you interview someone, all the seller's attention is focused on you, and you are absolutely the most important creature on the planet. This is almost never the case when you actually get down to business; the realities of other people's needs take their toll. It's extremely difficult to know this in an interview, as 'giving good interview' can take people far in their professions.

So how do you get beyond this? Check their references very carefully. Ask the references about everything you can think of, such as their promptness in returning phone calls, how fast he or she gets work done, what's their zodiac sign, etc. It's a good idea to make a list of questions in advance, so you don't forget anything.

Don't be lulled by promises that sound unbelievably fantastic. If they sound too good to be true, they probably aren't. Many people will promise things they can't possibly deliver, just to get the job. They figure you won't fire them when they can't deliver, because they know most artists don't like to make changes in their lives. (These are the same people who will stop returning calls if your star fades.) They also figure they have to lie just to ace out the next guy, who they assume is doing the same thing. The truth is that there are no real miracle workers; the secret of success in the music business is no different from that in any other business—intelligent planning, solid work, and smart execution. Promises of 'shortcuts' usually don't come through.

Who Does the Work?   Ask exactly who is going to be involved in your day-to-day work. It may not be the person you're meeting with, and you should know that and meet the people who will. All professionals use staff people, some to a greater degree than others. With some firms the staff people divide and multiply like paramecia, in an ever-changing kaleidoscope of faces. Other places are more stable. So ask, and also ask your references.

Fees.   Never hesitate to ask what someone is going to charge you. I know it's an uncomfortable subject, but bring it up anyway—you can be in for some seriously rude surprises if you don't. And when you do raise the topic, be particularly wary of someone who gives you a vague answer. (If you really can't stomach a fee discussion, have another team member do it for you.)

Personality. It's a myth to think any one personality style is more effective than any other (assuming you don't hire a wimp). Screamers and table pounders, if they're smart and knowledgeable, can get a lot out of a deal; but no more than those who speak quietly, if they're smart and knowledgeable. Some people work with a foil, and some with a sabre, but both styles can be effective.

Remember, you're hiring people to guide your professional life, not to travel on the tour bus. It's nice if you strike up a genuine friendship with your professionals, but it's not essential. (However, with your personal manager, I think you need at least a solid rapport, if not a true friendship.) I'm not advocating you to hire someone you really dislike, or someone who has the personality of a salamander, but I am saying these folks don't have to be your pals. In fact, some amount of distance is often helpful. Just as doctors can't operate on their own relatives, one of the main things a professional does is bring some objectivity to your life.

There is a wonderful story about Genghis Khan, the great warrior and conqueror. In the midst of a pivotal battle for his empire, involving thousands of troops on both sides, an aide went into Khan's tent and was surprised to find Khan himself sitting there. The aide said, 'How can you be in your tent? The troops need your command, and the battle is at a critical point.' Khan replied, 'I found myself getting angry over a turn in the battle, and I can't think straight when I'm angry. I came in here to cool off before deciding the next move.'

Think about that. If even ol' Genghis had to be detached from his emotions to function properly, who are you and I to do any better? When I have legal problems, I hire a lawyer. This may sound funny to you, but I get emotional about my own problems (just as you do), and I don't trust my judgment when I'm too close to the situation. So I hire someone who isn't.

In sum, a bit of distance from your professionals is not a concern, but you should feel comfortable and open with your team, and have an easy communication.

Decide Now—Confirm Later. Make a decision reasonably quickly, but confirm it slowly. In other words, once you've hired somebody, continue to watch them carefully (to the extent you can stand to do it). The fact that someone came in with rave reviews doesn't mean they'll be right for you, so consider them 'on probation' until you've seen enough to merit your trust. And don't just take another team member's word that it's working. Force yourself to follow their moves in the beginning, and you will earn the right to relax later. Remember: No one pays as good attention to your business as you do.

CHANGING A TEAM MEMBER

Here's what to do if something goes wrong on your team.

Even if they never pay much attention to business, I've never met an artist who doesn't have a built-in radar that tells them when something is wrong. So if you're feeling weird, then, 'Houston, we have a problem.'

It may be that things aren't being handled right. Or maybe you just don't feel comfortable talking to one of the team members. Ignoring the issue doesn't help any more than turning up the car radio to drown out the sound of a rattle in the engine. It's like a quote I once heard attributed to Dick Gregory: 'I read so much about how bad smoking is that I got scared and gave up reading.'

So deal with problems head on.

Talk About Your Problems

I know confrontation is difficult. I have never known an artist (or anyone else, for that matter, other than a few ornery jerks that have been divorced five or six times) who enjoys confrontation. But for your team members to do an effective job, you must have an open communication with them. If you can't bring yourself to talk directly to the person who is bugging you, talk to another team member and make sure they carry the message. Fast. Nothing is worse than letting small things snowball to the point that they build into a major drama. If you discuss them when they're small, they can usually stay small, and often they are innocent misunderstandings.

If you talk about your problems frankly, and they still aren't getting solved, make a change. No one has the right to expect a lifetime contract with you. People and circumstances change over the years; those who were spectacular for you at one point in your life may no longer be interested in you (if your career has taken a nosedive, or if they've lost interest in their job, etc.). Or they may no longer be capable of handling you (if they were unable to grow with you and your career is soaring, or if you have changed careers and their expertise is in the wrong area, etc.). I respect and admire loyalty (if for no other reason than because it's so rare), but blind loyalty does no one a favor. To me, loyalty means you don't turn your head and run off with every pretty face that walks by (and as you get more successful, pretty faces come out of the woodwork to try to seduce you, literally and figuratively). But loyalty is a two-way street, meaning you're entitled to the same commitment from your professionals. You're only obligated to stick with someone as long as they're doing a good job for you. If you're not getting the service you want, then loyalty means you discuss it with them and tell them what needs to be changed. (Again, if you don't want to do it directly, do it through another team member.) If things still aren't being done right, and you're sure your complaints were clearly communicated, make a change. But do it for the right reasons, not the wrong ones.

Lost Confidence

It pains me a bit to give you this next piece of advice, but you should have it. Once you've lost confidence in someone, whether it's for the right reasons or totally wrong reasons, it's almost impossible to continue with them. It's like falling out of love—it isn't easy to fall in again. I say this sadly, because many times we lose confidence in people for the wrong reasons. It may be that someone with a political ax has buried them unjustly; it may be they are doing a terrific job, but they have the personality of a stop sign and treat you rudely or bore you to death; it may be they have just delivered bad news to you (firing such a person is known as 'shooting the messenger,' from ancient Greek times, when a messenger bringing bad news was killed); it may be they have done a terrific job on everything important in your life, but screwed up paying your bills one month, so you had no telephone or electricity and your spouse refuses ever to see their face again; or it just may be an uneasy feeling in your stomach that you don't trust them. When you find yourself in this situation, again, I urge you to talk to the person openly (directly or through another team member) and tell them how you feel. (I know this is easy for me to say, and I admit it's difficult for me to do as well. But I force myself, and most of the time I find that the problem is a simple mistake that's easily fixed. And even if it isn't, I always feel better afterward just from processing it.) If you talk things out and the situation still doesn't get any better, split.

COCKTAIL PARTY TALK

Let me say a word about cocktail party talk. In college, we used to play a kind of poker called 'roll your own.' In this game you get five cards, and then draw additional cards (like in regular five-card draw). Then you arrange your cards in any order you want before flipping them over one at a time and betting on each card. After flipping the first three cards, everybody at the table looks like they have a spectacular hand. There appear to be straights, flushes, straight flushes, three of a kind, high pairs, and every other imaginable configuration to make you want to drop out and give up the pot. However, when it comes to flipping over the last couple of cards, most of the hands are mediocre.

I've always thought cocktail party talk is the same as flipping only the first three cards. Everyone sounds like a genius; everyone has just pulled off the greatest deal since the Louisiana Purchase. The truth, however, is in the last two cards, which you never see. The $10 million deal turns out to be a $1 million deal, with the other $9 million being there only if the artist achieves success beyond anything he or she has ever had before (not that $1 million isn't a lot of money, but it ain't $10 million). Nobody talks about their losses and screwups, because self-aggrandizement is part of the dance of the sand crabs that is ritualized at cocktail parties.

The whole point of this is to say that you shouldn't take casual talk at face value. Especially if someone has an editorial point of view, like a manager trying to convince you to leave your current manager for the terrific things he or she can do for you. (Lawyers, of course, would never do such a thing. And if you buy that, I have some land in Florida we should discuss.) So make your own evaluations in the realistic light of day.

3

Personal Managers

ROLE

The personal manager is the single most important person in your professional life. A good personal manager can expand your career to its maximum potential, just as a bad one can rocket you into oblivion. When the job is done properly, a personal manager is the general manager and chief operating officer of your enterprise. (There are, of course, some artists without managers, but they are very much the exception, and they usually have one or more others on the team filling this role.)

The most important aspects of the manager's job are:

1. Helping you with major business decisions, such as deciding which record company to sign with, whether to make a publishing deal, how much to ask for, etc.
2. Helping you with the creative process, such as selecting a producer (we'll talk about who producers are on page 125), deciding which songs to record, hiring band members, selecting photographers, etc.
3. Promoting your career by hyping you to everyone the manager meets, helping you coordinate a publicity campaign, etc.
4. Assembling and heading your professional team by introducing you to lawyers, business managers, and agents, and overseeing these people's work.
5. Coordinating your concert tours by working with your agent to make the best deals with promoters, routing the tour, working with your business manager to develop and implement a budget, assembling your road crew, supervising the road and tour managers to make sure everything runs smoothly, etc.

6. Pounding your record company to maximize the advertising and marketing campaigns for your records, making sure your records are treated as priorities, screaming at them when they do wrong, praising them when they do right, etc.

7. Generally being a buffer between you and the outside world, such as fielding inquiries for commercial endorsements, personal appearances, charitable requests (both for money and for your smiling face), taking the rap for tough decisions that you make but don't want anyone to think you did, etc.

Let's first take a look at the structure of your deal with the personal manager, and then we'll talk about picking one.

For a long time, it was customary to have 'split management' in the U.K. Specifically, many artists had a main manager in the U.K. to cover the world excluding the U.S., and a U.S. manager to cover that territory. Over the last few years, however, this has dropped off, and it is now more typical for the U.K. manager to handle the world or for a U.S. manager to do the world. I think this is healthy, and, frankly, I've never seen the split management work out very well. The two managers end up squabbling over control, and they each point fingers at the other when something goes wrong. Still, with the U.S. being its own peculiar market, U.K. artists or managers sometimes engage someone with U.S. expertise.

COMMISSION OVERVIEW

Managers typically get from 15% to 20% of your gross earnings, with the majority getting 15%. These percentages are usually applied to your gross earnings, before deducting any expenses, which means:

1. If you're an individual artist, the fee is pretty much what it sounds like for songwriting, publishing, records, etc. We'll discuss some of the finer points later, but basically the manager takes 15% of what you bring in. However, when it comes to touring, the 15% means much more than you might think. You'll see when we discuss concert appearances (on page 353) that you're lucky to take home 40% to 50% of your gross in-

come. That means a manager's 15% of gross can take a big bite
out of your net. For example, if you earn $100,000 and net
$40,000 (40%), your manager's 15% of gross ($15,000) is
almost 40% of your $40,000 net.

2. If you're a group and you have more than five members, 15% of
gross equals almost the same, or more than, any one of you
earns (assuming you're dividing equally). For example, if there
are seven of you, everybody gets one seventh, that's 14.28%,
which is less than the manager's 15%. In fact, since the
manager's percentage comes 'off the top' before you divide up
any monies, you only get one seventh of the 85% left after the
manager's 15%, which is 12.14%. And for touring monies, a
manager's 15% of gross is several times the share of net each of
you is taking home.

Because artists have found it, shall we say 'uncomfortable,' to pay
managers more than the artists make, the classic '15% of gross' has
softened over the last few years. Here's what's going down:

NEGOTIATING THE MANAGER'S DEAL

Despite the powerful personality of many managers (carefully designed
to keep you in your place), it is possible to negotiate with your manager.
However, just like any other negotiation, the result depends on bargaining power. If you're a major artist, bringing in $10 million plus
per year, the managers will follow you like puppies, delighted to take
whatever you might bless them with. On the other hand, if you're
a brand-new band negotiating with a powerful manager, then you're
the doggy.

Here's the points to discuss.

Compensation. The first and most obvious issue is the manager's
percentage. You should try to limit the percentage to 15%, although
some managers argue that the risk of taking on a new band is worth
20%. They say it will be years—if ever—before they get paid for a lot of
work (which is true). A compromise is to say the manager gets 15%,
which escalates to 20% when you earn a certain dollar amount (such as
15% of the first $2 million and 20% of the excess). I've also seen the
opposite, where the manager gets 20% up to a certain level, and then
15% after that. The theory is that the manager gets a bigger percentage

when you're young and the manager can't make as much, but his or her cut drops to the 15% norm when you're successful. This seems a bit weird at first, because it looks like the manager has no incentive to make you more successful (the more success, the lower the manager's take). But it's really not true—all managers would rather have 15% of a big number than 20% of a small one.

Sometimes managers share in the net of an artist's earnings rather than the gross. This is much better for the artist—for starters, the manager won't get paid if the artist loses money, which is not the case in gross deals. In one deal I'm aware of, the manager got 20% of the net of a four-piece band, which worked out to about 8% of the gross. Another deal paid the manager on the gross for records and publishing, but on the net for touring.

When a manager has a deal on the net, they will sometimes ask for limits on the expenses. For example, artists who decide to go on the road and charter jets, throw parties in every city, put inflatable pools in their suites, etc., can easily eat up the net while having a great time. Managers don't usually enjoy these parties quite as much. Thus, the agreement might be that the manager is paid on net touring proceeds, but that the expenses of the tour can't exceed a negotiated percentage of the gross.

A variation on this theme is that the manager gets a percentage of gross, but is capped out at 50% of the net. In other words, the manager will never make more than the artist actually puts in his or her pocket. For example, if you gross $1,000, and have $800 in expenses, your net is $200. If the manager got 15% of the gross, he or she would earn $150. Under this arrangement, the maximum would be 50% of the net (50% of $200, or $100), so the manager gets $100 and the artist gets $100. Note, however, that if you're a group, you all have to share the artist's 50% of the net, which means the manager makes more than any one of you.

In a few situations, where the artist is a superstar, the manager sometimes gets 10% or less, and occasionally just a salary (no percentage). These salaries can run well into six, or sometimes even seven, figures.

Exclusions.   It's sometimes possible to reduce (or even exclude) certain types of earnings. For example, if you're a major songwriter hiring a manager to help you become a recording artist, the manager might get 15% of your earnings as an artist, but only 10% (or even 7.5%, 5%, or 0%) of your songwriting monies. Or maybe the manager gets 15% of your songwriting monies from records on which you appear as an artist, and a reduced (or no) percentage on other songwriter earnings. Another example is an established motion picture actor who hires a manager to help with his or her music career. Or vice versa. In these cases, you normally exclude (or reduce the percentage for) the area where you're already established. The possibilities are as varied as your imagination.

If you exclude any of your earnings from commission, you would of course not expect the manager to work in the excluded area (though they often do as a practical matter).

Losing Tours. You can sometimes get managers to agree that, if a tour loses money, they'll take no commission on it. (By the way, as we discussed under the compensation section, if you capped your manager's commissions at 50% of your touring profits, you already have this.) If you can't get your manager down to zero, then try for a reduced commission (meaning, for example, instead of 15%, they'd only get 7.5% on a losing tour), and at the very least, get them to defer their commission until you're more successful (meaning you agree they're entitled to a commission, but they have to wait and get paid later, when you have money coming in).

Deductions. Certain monies are customarily deducted before computing the manager's percentage, even when a manager is paid on gross. Most managers don't take commissions on these, even if their contract says they can, but some try. So it's always a good idea to spell things out and avoid any misunderstandings.

Here's the list of no-no's:

1. **Recording costs.**
   If the record company pays you monies, and you spend them on recording costs, you should not pay a commission. This is because the funds only pass through your hands (i.e., you don't keep them), and thus they aren't really 'earnings.'

2. **Monies paid to a producer.**
   The reasoning is the same as with recording costs. This includes not only advances to the producer, but also royalties. (Producers are discussed on page 125.)

3. **Co-writers.**
   When you write songs with somebody else, the manager shouldn't get paid on the other person's share of the song's earnings.

4. **Tour support.**

    This is money paid by a record company to offset your losses from touring (see page 153). Commissioning tour support is a bit controversial. Some managers argue this is money you get from the record company, and, just like any other money, they should commission it. Most of the time, however, they'll agree it isn't commissionable, because it only compensates you for a loss.

5. **Costs of collection.**

    If you have to sue someone to get paid, the cost of suing them to collect the money ('collection costs') should be deducted before applying the manager's percentage. For example, if a concert promoter stiffs you for $50,000, and it costs you $10,000 in legal fees and court costs to collect, the manager should only commission $40,000 (the $50,000 recovery less the $10,000 collection costs). Another way to look at this is to say the manager bears his or her proportionate share of the collection costs.

6. **Sound and lights.**

    It's common in personal appearance contracts for the artist to supply his or her own sound system and stage lighting. The promoter then 'rents' the sound and lights from the artist for a specified dollar amount. Customarily, the rent money is considered an expense reimbursement (as opposed to a fee paid to the artist), and so the manager isn't paid on the amount allocated to sound and lights. But you gotta ask for this one.

7. **Opening acts.**

    When you get to the superstar category, your deal for a personal appearance may also include monies you pay to an opening act. Again, since this money just passes through your hands, it shouldn't be commissionable.

Term

Historically, the term of a management agreement was three to five years. If you're an artist, you want to make it as short as possible; if you're a manager, you want it as long as possible.

The trend over the last few years is for managers to have terms geared to **album cycles,** as opposed to a specific number of years. An *album cycle* means a period of time from the commencement of recording an album until the end of the promotional activities surrounding it. Usually that means a tour, as well as promotion of all of the singles from the album. A management term geared to album cycles is fairer to the manager. If the term is simply a period of years, it could end in the middle of promoting an album and the manager could get locked out of commissions after he or she has done most of the work.

Be very careful when negotiating the term of a management deal. Many artists have lived to regret being tangled up in a long-term contract with a lousy manager. Yet there's a balancing act that has to work out for both sides. Managers don't want to put their sweat into making you happen, only to see you waltz off at the first sign of success.

The most common compromise is to say that if the artist doesn't earn a minimum amount, he or she can terminate the agreement early. For example, the deal might be for three album cycles, but if the artist doesn't earn $200,000 over the first album cycle, he or she can terminate at the end of that cycle.

I hesitate to give you specific dollar figures for the earnings, because (1) they'll probably be out of date by the time you read this; and (2) they also depend on who you are. If you're a heavy touring band, the numbers are much higher than if you write folk songs and sing in coffeehouses. But here's an example from a beginning rock artist's contract: the deal was for one album cycle, and the manager could renew for an additional cycle if the artist earned $300,000 over the first cycle. The manager could then renew for another (third) cycle if, during the second cycle, the artist earned $500,000.

The manager, if he or she has any sophistication, will also say that the earnings figure has to include offers you turn down. The theory is that you can't refuse to work and then get out of the deal because you didn't earn enough. I usually agree to this request, but require that the offers must be similar to those which you have previously accepted, so an offer to appear nude at the Moscow Circus doesn't count (unless that's your act).

Another approach is to use album sales figures, instead of dollars, as the trigger. For example, you could terminate the deal if you haven't sold X number of albums by the end of the second album cycle. The sales level varies with the type of artist involved. If you're a straight-ahead, commercial artist, you want a fairly high figure. But if you're more off center and want to build slowly, the figure would be lower. Whatever the criteria, it doesn't usually kick in until the second or third album, as the managers argue that the first album is just the beginning of a building process. Recent deals I've seen used a figure of 80,000 albums for an alternative, quirky band, and a figure of 250,000 albums for a straight-ahead, commercial artist.

Termination for failing to clear the hurdle can be done either by a letter from the artist to the manager containing legal words that translate as 'You're fired,' or it can be set up as a shorter deal that continues if the artist achieves certain earnings (for example, the term of the agreement is one cycle, but if the artist earns at least $200,000, the manager continues for an additional cycle). The only difference between these two arrangements is whether the artist has to remember to send the manager a notice.

If the manager has satisfied the criteria, the deal then continues. It's to your advantage to keep the continuation period as short as possible—say one more album cycle with a sales criteria to continue. And no matter what, a manager shouldn't have a total of more than three to four album cycles.

Earnings After the Term: 'The Gift That Keeps on Taking'

One of the most important points you have to negotiate is what your manager gets paid after the end of your deal. Even though the term may end after a few years, virtually every management contract says the manager gets paid on earnings after the term if they're generated under 'contracts entered into or substantially negotiated during the term.' This language means two things:

1. As to records made during the term of the management deal, the manager gets a commission from sales of these records occurring after the management deal; and
2. The manager is paid on records made *after* the term of your management deal, if the records are recorded under a contract signed during the term.

All of this could mean—and I've seen it happen—that a manager is still getting paid seven, ten, or more years after he or she finished rendering services. For example, suppose six months before the end of the management deal you sign a five-album deal. Under this clause, the manager gets paid forever on sales of these five albums, most of which will be recorded years after you've parted company.

I personally think this clause is way overreaching, and I've been pretty successful in cutting it back. Let's analyze the situation:

The major things to worry about are records and publishing. Unless you're in a television series or some other non-musical commitment that could run for several years, records and publishing are the only areas where you're likely to have significant earnings from activities after the term under agreements made during the term. The other contracts you make during the term, such as personal appearance engagements, may be completed after the term, but this happens in a relatively short period (although it can represent millions of dollars). And if a manager is involved in setting up a tour, it's not unreasonable for him or her to be paid something for the tour. (So if you're going to dump your manager, do it before the tour gets set up.)

Sunset Clauses. In any event, here are some of my better strategies to cut this back. These are known as **sunset clauses,** because they end the day for commissions:

1. **Records.**
   (a) The manager gets paid only on records recorded and released during the term (and not on any others). This is the best for you.
   (b) Another solution is that the manager gets a half commission (e.g., if the manager gets 15%, it's reduced to 7.5%) on records recorded during the term but released afterward. The theory is that the manager only does half the work— overseeing the recording, but not overseeing the release and promotion. (As in (a), records made after the term aren't commissionable at all.)

2. **Publishing.**
   (a) The manager is paid only on songs recorded and released during the term. This is the best for you.
   (b) The manager gets a half commission on songs recorded during the term and released after.
   (c) The manager gets a half commission on songs written during the term but recorded afterward. This at least cuts off participation in songs written after the term under contracts made during the term.

3. **Final cutoff.**
   (a) I try to have some date after which all commissions end, no matter what. Try three to five years after the term; settle for no more than seven.
   (b) Even with an overall cutoff, you can sometimes reduce the commissions while you're waiting for them to die. For example, there might be a full commission for the first two years after the term, a half commission for the next three years, then over and out.

The above three approaches are not mutually exclusive; you can creatively mix and match. For example, the manager could get a full commission on records recorded and released during the term, but only for a period of three years after the term. Or they might get a commission for a period after the term equal to the term itself (for example, if the term were three years, the period afterward would be three years; if it were four years, the period would be four years, etc.), and thereafter nothing else. The limits are only your imagination and the manager's patience.

A particularly thorny problem (and another reason you should pay so much attention to the commissions after the term) is the fact that, after the term, you'll need to hire a new manager. As you can imagine, there aren't too many managers who want to work for free, and there are even fewer artists who want to pay 15% of their gross to two managers (30%!). Thus, it's very important to limit or eliminate commissions after the term. In truth, most new managers will take reduced or no commissions on earnings that another manager is commissioning. But they're only going to do this for, say, the first album or the first tour, and they'll only do that if you're pretty successful. If they can't start making money relatively quickly, managing you isn't going to be worth their time and effort. So while you can live with paying a prior manager something on after-term projects, you should limit it as much as possible.

Key Man

Another important aspect of your management deal is called a **key man** clause (hopefully soon to be called a 'key person' clause). Although you have a relationship with a particular personal manager, your contract might be with their corporation or a partnership. Thus, it's possible that 'your person' could leave the company, and since your deal isn't with that manager personally, you can't just get up and go with them. Accordingly, you could find yourself managed by a stranger. Or an obnoxious acquaintance.

To prevent this, you should insert a clause that says the person with whom you have a relationship (the *key man*) must personally act as your manager, and if not, you can terminate the deal. If the company buys this concept (some bigger ones won't), you can easily get a clause that says you can terminate if the key man dies or is disabled, and you can sometimes get the same right if he or she is no longer employed by the corporation or partnership. Much trickier is the situation where they're alive and kicking, and still employed by your manager, but taken off your account. It's much harder to say the key man must be 'actively involved' in managing your life, because the manager begins to worry that, even if the key man is still working on your career, you'll try to use this clause to get out of your deal—you'd argue that the manager is doing a mediocre job (and thus is not 'actively involved'), and therefore the management company is in breach of your contract. (For exactly this reason, from your point of view, the broader you can make the language, the better.)

Double Commissions

If you, for tax planning or otherwise, set up a corporation to conduct your entertainment activities, you want to be sure this doesn't trigger a **double commission.** (See page 186 for a discussion of using a corporation in record deals, and page 333 for corporations used by groups.) Observe:

Management contracts say that the manager's commission is based on your earnings at the corporate level. This is perfectly reasonable—otherwise, you could easily pay the gross monies into the corporation, pay yourself only a small salary, and claim the manager gets his or her commission based on the small amount that comes out to you. (For example, if your corporation gets $100,000 for your appearance at a show but only pays you $10,000, it wouldn't be fair to pay the manager only 15% of the $10,000.) However, it's not reasonable for the manager to take a second bite at the money; once he or she has commissioned it at the corporate level, there should be no further commission when it comes out to you in the form of salary. (In the previous example, this means the manager can't commission both the $100,000 and the $10,000.) Most management contracts would technically allow the manager to do this 'double dip' (after all, the salary is your gross income), but in practice it isn't done (by reputable managers). Still, it's always a good idea to specifically say so.

Power of Attorney

Another provision to watch for is one that says the manager has a **power of attorney** (meaning the power to act for you), such as the right to sign your name to contracts, hire and fire your other representatives, cash your checks, etc. I like to wipe out most of this nonsense. You should hire and fire your own representatives, and definitely cash your own checks. The only time I let a manager sign for an artist is if (a) the deal is for personal appearance engagements, of no more than two or three nights, which will be performed within the next four to six weeks; (b) you're unavailable to sign the agreement yourself; and (c) the manager has your verbal approval of the deal. If it doesn't meet these criteria, bless the piece of paper with your autograph.

The Best Deals

Having now discussed managers' contracts at length, you're ready for a well-kept secret. Many of the top managers have absolutely no written contracts with their artists. It's all done on a handshake, and the only discussion is the percentage. Their feeling, and I respect them for it, is that the relationship is more important than any piece of paper, and if the artist isn't happy, they're free to go at any time. Also implicit in this arrangement is that the artist needs them as much as (or more than) they need the artist.

Please don't misunderstand this point. Many legitimate and well-respected managers require written contracts, and there is nothing wrong with this. But there are also a number who 'fly naked' (without a written deal), and ironically they are often the ones who keep their clients the longest.

Even with these folks, I sometimes like to do a letter outlining the terms. It spells out the percentages, states that the term can be ended by either party at any time, and deals with the post-term earnings (see the above discussion). It never hurts to make sure there's no misunderstandings.

PICKING THE RIGHT MANAGER

So how do you pick a manager? First, review Chapter 2, which applies to picking everyone on your team. Then, take a look at these specific tips on a manager.

Let's start with the absolute best. This is the yardstick to use in measuring your candidates: The absolute best manager is a powerful, well-connected person, with one or more major clients, who is wildly enthusiastic about you and willing to commit the time required for your career. If you're a superstar, you can find such a person without too much trouble. If you're not, this situation hardly ever exists. The reason is that, when a manager is powerful and successful, he or she is usually not interested in anything other than a major money-earning client. The analysis is simple—it takes as much or more work to establish a new artist as it does to service an established artist, and guess which one pays better (and sooner)? (It's true that, every once in a while, a powerful manager gets genuinely revved up over a new band. But this is rare, and you have to be extraordinarily lucky even to get such a person's attention.)

So let's take a look at more down-to-earth alternatives, which are not in any particular order:

1. A major manager with a young associate who is genuinely enthusiastic about you.
2. A midsize manager (whose artists' albums sell in the 750,000 to 1,500,000 range) who is wildly enthusiastic about you.
3. A major, powerful manager who is taking you on as a favor (either personal or professional) to somebody who is *very* important to him or her.
4. A young, inexperienced manager who is willing to kill for you.

There are of course endless combinations of the above, but these are the major categories.

Unless you can get the best possible situation described above, you'll have to make some kind of compromise. The compromise is between power and clout on one hand, and time and attention on the other. The reason a manager is powerful is because he or she has at least one powerful client who takes up most of the manager's time. This means you're going to get less of it, and thus less personal attention (although these people can often do more in a five-minute call than a newcomer can do in a week). On the other hand, a young, bright manager with no other clients will lack clout and experience, but will spend all of his or her waking hours with you and worrying about you, and will go to any lengths to promote your career. And in between lies a rainbow of choices.

I personally like young managers a lot. If they're bright and motivated, I've seen their energy overcome the lack of experience and political clout with superb results. And to help you understand why, let me give you the Passman Treatise on Managers' Careers. Managers' careers go something like this:

1. The manager is young and enthusiastic, and attaches himself or herself to a promising young act.
2. By doing whatever it takes, the manager promotes the artist into major stardom, at which point, (a) every other manager comes out of the woodwork to try and steal the act, and (b) the

manager is offered twenty-seven other acts to manage. (The people who previously wouldn't return his or her phone calls are suddenly his or her best friends, saying this manager must be a genius to have taken these obscure nobodies to stardom.)

3. The manager is now exhausted from having worked so hard on the first act (back when he or she had nothing else to do and could literally live with the band). So the manager wants to cash in on the fame and fortune while it lasts, and, accordingly, starts hiring associates and begins taking on more and more superstars.

4. This is the point at which many managers begin to lose it because they're too successful. Some of them have such huge egos that they won't take on associates of their own caliber (for fear the associates might steal the artists). So they hire less capable people and give the artists lousy service. Others hire good people, but pay them so poorly that their employees get frustrated and go out on their own (usually stealing the artists in the process). As things unravel, the manager begins to lose artists who are no longer getting the personal attention they once did. (A few managers have been able to pull off large, successful management companies, but they're the exception. They also ruin my theory, so I'm ignoring them.)

5. After these batterings, the manager feels it was a mistake to have tried to get so big, breaks up with his or her partners, keeps one or two key artists, and starts a record label or goes into the movie business.

Remember, everybody was nobody at one time. While I don't suggest that a superstar should take on an inexperienced manager, I do think many new artists are well advised to hire a bright, aggressive young manager. Obviously, you shouldn't do this if you have the opportunity to go with an established manager who is (or has someone in his or her organization who is) genuinely enthused about you. But if this is not an option, the right young manager is a real asset.

As colourful as the American music business has been (see, for example, the story about Morris Levy on page 83), the U.K. has an especially warm spot in rock history for some of its early managers. There were a number of these fine citizens who invented the practice of paying bands about £50 per week and keeping all of the artists' other earnings. Nice, eh?

4

Business Managers

ROLE

The business manager is the person on your team who handles all your money. He or she collects it, keeps track of it, pays your bills, invests it, makes sure you file your tax returns, etc.

Listen to me!!! Did you know that, in California, a person needs no credentials whatsoever to be a business manager? Contrary to popular opinion, you don't have to be an accountant (much less a certified public accountant), and you don't even have to be licensed by the state. Technically, business managers who give certain kinds of investment advice need to be 'registered investment advisors' (like stockbrokers, who are licensed by the federal government before they can sell securities to the public). However, very few are.

What this means is that you could be turning your money over to someone who has no more financial training than you do. And when you stop to think about it, that's pretty scary.

I know you wouldn't have gone into the music business if you wanted to be a financial whiz—if you were good with numbers, you'd be in some back room with a green eyeshade instead of winning your way into the hearts of millions. I also know that numbers make you nervous and may even intimidate you. On the other hand, there are parts of all of our lives that we don't like, and, while we can get other people to deal with them day to day, we have to be sure we choose good people to do it. For this reason, I urge you to *personally* spend some time investigating all of the people on your team, AND BE ESPECIALLY CAREFUL WHEN IT COMES TO BUSINESS MANAGERS. They can range anywhere from superb to slimebag, with all variations in between. And their bedside manner and office space may tell you very little of what they're really like—the bad ones can be like a shiny used car that's rotting from rust underneath a new paint job. Financial disasters can come from someone who is an out-and-out crook, or they can come from an honest person, with the best of intentions, who is just a boob. My doctor once told me a story about an orderly he had when he was in the army. One day the orderly decided to go that extra mile and do something on his own initiative. So, with the best of intentions, he sterilized all of the thermometers by *boiling* them. SO BE EXTREMELY CAREFUL!

Hopefully I've now got your attention, so let's take a look at how to find the right person.

HOW TO PICK A BUSINESS MANAGER

References

The other professionals on your team can be a great help in choosing a business manager. But remember, they may have their own agendas. For example, a personal manager may have a lot of control over a business manager because he or she handles some of the business manager's most important clients. This is a two-edged sword—it means you may get a lot of attention from the business manager, but it also means that, if you have a fight with your personal manager, the business manager may not necessarily be on your side (if the business manager loses you, it's only one account; if they upset the personal manager, it could mean their whole career). This is particularly so when the business manager also does the personal manager's work. With reputable personal managers and reputable business managers, I have rarely found this to be a practical problem, but it's worth watching.

Wheeler-Dealers

I'm leery of business managers who put together clients' money for deals in which the business manager is being paid from the deal. For example, a business manager might form a partnership to buy a shopping center for $2 million. The partnership borrows $1.5 million, and the business manager's clients put in the remaining $500,000. As compensation for putting the deal together, the business manager might get 10% to 20% of the profits of the partnership, even though he or she puts up no money.

This practice (of taking a percentage to set up the deal) is a common way for real estate operators to function. However, when a business manager is both the operator and the investors' representative, it is impossible for him or her to be objective in advising the client to put money in the deal. I understand there are advantages to it—having your own representative in there running the investment can be to your benefit—but it strikes me as a bit too cozy. (Frankly, I don't even think this is a particularly smart move from the business manager's point of view. If the deal is a success, the clients resent the business manager's taking a piece. If it's a flop, they not only get blamed for recommending the investment, but eventually get nailed for the conflict of interest. If the business manager had instead invested with a stranger, this wouldn't have been the case.)

A trend over the last few years is for business managers to farm out their investment advice to specialists, based on the fact that doing investment research can (and probably ought to) be a full-time job. Thus, if the business manager doesn't have people on staff to handle this full-time, he or she will arrange for someone else to take care of the investment advice. Also, some of them like to diversify into a number of different areas and get specialists for each area. I think this is a healthy trend overall, but you should ask how these outsiders get paid.

Family

Barring very unusual circumstances, inviting family members into your financial life is extremely dangerous. Most of them aren't qualified to do the job, and even when they are, it's difficult for them to be totally objective about you. It's something like the reason that doctors won't operate on their immediate family, because they're too involved emotionally. And not only that, (a) it's very difficult to fire your brother, and (b) if something goes wrong, Momma may stop speaking to you.

BUSINESS MANAGER CHECKLIST

When interviewing business managers, take a look at Chapter 2 again for general questions, then add these specifics:

1. What kinds of financial reports are you going to get, and how often? (You should get monthly reports.) Ask to see samples of the reports. Are they clear? Can you understand them?
2. What is the business manager's investment philosophy? Will they only keep your money in conservative, short-term paper (mean-

ing bank deposits or government notes of thirty-day to one-year duration), or in highly speculative pork belly futures? Don't settle for the gobbledygook that says 'we tailor to every individual's needs'; ask what their philosophy is for you. And why.

3. Is he or she a CPA (Certified Public Accountant)? Accountants who are certified have passed rigorous accounting exams and at least have that part of the job down. Whether they have the other skills to be good business managers is another question, but at least they're true professionals, who have trained extensively and are responsible for adhering to the CPA's code of ethics.

4. How much do they charge? (This is discussed in detail below.)

5. Find out exactly what the business manager is going to do for you besides paying your bills and keeping track of your income. Are they also going to do your tax returns? (Some charge extra for tax returns or send them to outsiders who charge.) Are they going to handle your investments or hire an outsider? In either case, how are they paid for investments? Do they do projections, budgets, and forecasts of your income? Do they coordinate wills and estate planning? Monitor your insurance needs? Oversee divorces?

6. Does the business manager want a written agreement? Some business managers require written agreements, although many don't. It isn't a bad idea, because it spells out exactly what's going on. However, don't ever agree to a deal with a term— you should be free to leave anytime you want.

7. Do they represent music clients? This may seem like a silly question, but some very talented business managers have no expertise in the music industry, and you don't want one of them. The music industry is specialized, and you need someone who understands its intricacies. For example, if they don't really understand publishing, they can't do a good job of making sure you get paid everything you should.

8. Have they handled people with your particular problems and challenges? If you're a new artist, you want to be sure they know how to watch every penny so you can survive. You also want to be sure they have time for you. If you're a superstar, you want to make sure they've handled, for example, mega tours, which require massive financial controls and records (as we'll discuss in Chapter 23).

9. Do they have **E&O** (Errors & Omissions) **insurance?** *E&O* in-

surance pays off if the business manager mishandles your affairs and costs you dough. If so, how much insurance do they carry?

10. If you live outside the United States or plan any extensive activities there, ask if they have any international experience. I probably don't have to tell you that meshing the tax laws between several jurisdictions (much less understanding the tax laws in any one of them) is a major pain, and if you have or anticipate these kinds of problems, you need someone who's been down that road before.

11. Do they get **referral fees** from any place they might put your money (such as a purchase of insurance, putting your funds in a particular bank, placing your investments through a particular stockbroker, etc.)? A *referral fee* is an amount paid to them by the people who receive your money, as compensation for referring you to them. Ideally, they shouldn't get any such fee because it could affect the advice they give you—they might be inclined to put your dough with someone who gives them a fee, even if it's not in your best interests. However, if the existence of the fee and the amount are fully disclosed up front, and if the business manager is willing to credit it against their fees, and if you get independent advice about the particular transaction, this could be okay. But put your radar up if you see it.

12. The check-signing procedure should be set up carefully, and if possible you should sign all the checks. When you get really busy—especially when you're on tour—it may not be possible to do this. However, I know some extremely successful and busy artists who manage to sign all their big checks. Most of the time, larger checks can be either signed in advance or sent to you.

13. Will the business manager object to your auditing them periodically? (An **audit** means you send in an independent person to see if the business manager has properly handled your money.) Very few people are willing to audit their business managers because they're embarrassed to do so, and think it looks as if they don't trust the business manager. In fact, the ethical business managers welcome it—they have nothing to hide and know it gives you peace of mind to find everything is as it should be. (You can figure out which ones don't want you to *audit*.) Auditing a business manager is expensive ($15,000 plus), and thus not worth it unless you earn substantial monies. However, when you get to the big leagues, an audit is important to con-

sider. If you've raised the issue up front, there won't be any hassles later on. It's surprising how few people raise this issue until it's too late.

14. Be sure the person you're dealing with wants to educate you, rather than just pat you on the head and go about their business. Most decisions can be condensed down to a fairly simple summary, and you should make all the significant decisions yourself. Be wary of someone who just wants to tell you what to do and seems offended if you question it.

FEES

How to pay your business manager varies, depending on your circumstance. The custom is for them to work on a percentage (5%), an hourly rate, a flat fee, or some combination. Some people earn great sums of money and have uncomplicated lives, and if this is you, opt for an hourly rate or a set fee. Others, who earn much less and always seem to have financial troubles, should go for a percentage. (Ironically, if your finances nosedive, you may need as much or more of your business manager's time than when you're doing well—he or she has to keep the wolves away from the door and turn pennies into nickels. This, of course, comes at a time when you can least afford to pay.)

Some business managers want a minimum fee, because they have legitimate costs just to set up their systems to service you. Unless they're willing to take a flyer on the hopes that you'll someday be hugely successful, they normally want their downside covered. Hence they charge a minimum fee, which can range from $500 to $2,500 a month, or more for superstars. Some business managers charge a minimum fee equal to a percentage (for example, two-thirds) of their hourly rate. Under these arrangements, they get a minimum that varies with how much work they do, and you get a break because they charge you less than if they were merely on an hourly rate. This discounted hourly fee isn't for everyone—if you don't like the thrill of not knowing what you have to pay until the bill arrives, stick to a minimum that's a flat amount. Whatever the minimum, it will be against (meaning a prepayment of) the percentage. If the business manager is young and hungry, or if you have a lot of clout, he or she may be willing to take a **flat fee** for all services, regardless of the amount of work.

If the charges are based on an hourly rate, spell out what the rate is, and be sure to get the rate for everyone involved, not just the top people. If the fee is a percentage, many business managers will accept a maximum fee, particularly when they're charging you a minimum. This will again vary with the amount of money you earn and the amount of work you require. Maximum fees range generally from $150,000 to $300,000 per year (which means, if the percentage is 5 percent, you are making $3 million to $6 million a year). Minimums for people in this range are roughly $30,000 to $125,000 per year.

If the business manager charges a percentage, ask if it applies to investment income. With some business managers it does, while with others it doesn't. Also, it should only apply to money *received* (not *earned*) while they are involved.

You don't have 'business managers' in the U.K., so accountants usually handle artist's money. U.K. chartered accountants are not generally allowed to charge fees on a contingency basis (meaning that they can't take a percentage), so they bill hourly. Technically, they can charge a percentage if they give you all kinds of disclosures, but it's pretty limited, and the practice isn't common. If you're interested in the details (or if you have trouble sleeping), call up the scintillating Institute of Chartered Accountants Professional Standards folks and have a go at them.

Listen again! Let me say this one more time: *BE EXTREMELY CAREFUL in picking your business manager, more than anyone else on your team.* This is the person who can make sure you have a cozy old age, or leave you playing supermarket openings in your fifties.

YOUR HALF OF THE JOB

Just as important as picking the right business manager is your own attitude. I remember seeing one of Elvis Presley's bodyguards at a press conference. A reporter asked why he didn't stop Elvis from taking drugs and destroying himself. His answer was, 'How do you save a man from himself?'

I've always felt that answer, which really hit me, was the most telling statement about an entertainer's life. If you don't care about your financial future, it's difficult for anybody else to. If someone is constantly telling you not to do something (like spend money), and you really want to do it, you'll probably get rid of them rather than listen. Remember Dick Gregory's quote (see page 24). If you're going to spend everything you make, then start spending money you don't have, you're going to end up broke. It's that simple. So don't do it, unless you subscribe to my partner Chuck Scott's philosophy of how to build a small fortune: 'The best way to build a small fortune is to take a large one and dwindle it down.'

Few things last forever, and an assured stream of earnings at your highest level is not one of them. So even the best business managers can't help you if you overspend on jets, yachts, houses, cars, and controlled substances. I know: You're reading this and saying it will never apply to you. But only you can make sure it doesn't.

5

Attorneys

Now for a subject close to my own heart, and one about which it's hard for me to be totally objective. But I'll try.

PICKING A LAWYER

Role

Attorneys in the music business do much more than just look over contracts and advise clients about the law. They are very involved in structuring deals and shaping artists' business lives.

Lawyers have evolved into one of the most powerful groups in the music industry, odd as that may sound to you. The reason is that the power bases in the music business aren't concentrated in any one group (such as, for example, the major agencies, who are the most powerful players in the film business. In the music biz, the agents are powerful but limited in their sphere of influence, as we'll see in the next chapter). Personal managers are very powerful, but the nature of their job limits the number of clients they can take. The business managers can have a lot of major clients, but they deal only in limited financial areas and are therefore not power bases. Lawyers, on the other hand, are involved in all areas, and because the time required for each client is less than that of a personal manager, they can handle a large number of clients. This means the attorneys end up seeing more deals than anyone else and therefore have more knowledge of what's 'going down' around town. Consequently, they can be influential in determining which company will get a particular deal, which means the companies want to keep them happy. They can also influence which personal manager and which business manager get a client, which means these guys also want to keep the lawyers happy. This means lawyers have power (and are happy).

Lawyers in the U.K., unlike those in the U.S., are divided into **solicitors** and **barristers**. The solicitors are the ones who deal with the public and who negotiate and draft contracts. Barristers work only for solicitors, and their job is to advise on matters of litigation (meaning disputes that are either in or heading for court). Barristers are also the ones who actually go to court to represent you, where they wear curly white wigs and say 'M'Lud' a lot. Solicitors are the ones we'll be talking about in this section of the book, since they do the deals. If you get into a legal hassle, your solicitor will guide you to a barrister.

Style

There are distinctly separate styles of attorneys in the music business. Some are into 'hanging out' and acting as if they're one of the band members, while others are more conservative and stick to the business side. There are power broker/agent types, who are good negotiators but not particularly good lawyers, and excellent lawyers who lose sight of the big picture. And of course there's a whole spectrum in between.

Using the techniques in Chapter 2, first assure yourself you're talking to a good, competent lawyer. After that, the match-up of style is mostly a matter of your personal taste in people. For example, if you like flash, you may want a flashy lawyer (although I find more often that flashy artists like their lawyers to be staid and solid). If you're honest and straightforward in your business dealings, be sure to get an honest and straightforward lawyer (your references will tell you who is and isn't). If you aren't, there are unfortunately lawyers to match you too.

Clout

It's true a lawyer with clout can get through to people that other lawyers can't (or at least faster). Indeed, one of the major things to look for in a lawyer is his or her relationships in the industry. Let me illustrate with a story about remodeling my house: Over the years I have been through a number of house remodels, always looking for the cheapest possible solution (which meant dealing directly with the workmen). I finally got sick of the whole process and broke down and hired a contractor. (This contractor was so good that, after the job was finished, I was still speaking to him. That's a serious recommendation.) During this job, for the first time, I realized the value of a general contractor. In the past, whenever I called up a tile man, electrician, plumber, etc., these people couldn't have cared less about me. They came to do the job when it was convenient for them (if ever). If my sink leaked for a few days, they didn't care because they had a lot of other customers. On the other hand, when the contractor called them, they jumped. The reason was pretty simple: If they didn't satisfy the contractor, they didn't just lose one job, they lost their next year's work.

The same applies to lawyers. Record companies can't ignore phone calls from important lawyers, nor can they afford to treat them shabbily in any particular transaction. The reason is the same as with the contractor—they're going to be dealing with the lawyers over and over, and they don't want to make enemies of them. So a lawyer with good relationships will get your deals done quicker, and, if they know what they're doing, will get you the maximum that can legitimately be had.

You should also know what clout doesn't do. There is only so much you can get from any particular deal, regardless of who is asking. If a record company doesn't like your music, they're not going to sign you because of your lawyer. If they're hot for you, you'll get a deal even if you're represented by John Ashcroft. Put another way, the real 'clout' is your musical talent. (Note that I'm not talking about a lawyer's experience and knowledge—that is truly valuable, and will indeed get you the maximum from the negotiation. But you should have a perspective on the hyped-up importance of 'clout.')

Loose Lips

Be especially wary of a lawyer who tells you about other clients' lives. Some lawyers, for example, will tell you exactly what deal they got for a specific client. Apart from the fact that this violates the attorneys' Canon of Ethics, it also means they will be telling other people about your deal. It may appear that these people trade confidential information for secrets they wouldn't otherwise have, but in fact the opposite is almost always the case—because everyone knows they have a big mouth, they're only told things that people want spread around town.

FEES

Most lawyers in the music business don't charge just on an hourly basis. For the ones that do, the rates are from $150 per hour for new lawyers, up to $600 or more for biggies. Some of us charge a percentage (usually 5%), while others do something known as **value billing,** often with an hourly rate or **retainer** against it. (A *retainer* is a set monthly fee [like the business manager's minimum fee discussed on page 46], and it is either credited against the ultimate fee, or it's a flat fee covering all services.) *Value billing* means that, when the deal is finished, the lawyer asks for a fee based on the size of the deal and his or her contribution to it. If the lawyer had very little to do with shaping the deal, but rather just did the contract, the fee should be close to an hourly rate (though I'll get heat for telling you this, because it's usually more). On the other hand, if the lawyer came up with a clever concept or strategy that made you substantial money, or the lawyer shaped or created the deal from scratch, he or she will ask for a much larger fee. If your lawyer value bills, you should get some idea up front what it's going to be, so that there aren't any rude surprises. Sometimes you can pre-negotiate the fee, based on results. At a minimum, get a ballpark range.

U.K. lawyers are prohibited from charging percentage fees, and thus their billing is typically on an hourly rate. The hourly rates for music lawyers range from about £125 to £350 per hour. It's also becoming customary for U.K. lawyers to ask for a 'bonus' based on the value of the deal, which can either be a mark-up of hourly rates, or a flat fee. Sometimes, U.K. lawyers will base their fee on achieving a particular result, meaning they'll take no fee if the deal blows, and a premium over their normal fees for success. These kinds of deals are separately negotiated each time, so there's no hard and fast rules.

CONFLICTS OF INTEREST

A lawyer has a **conflict of interest** when his or her clients get into a situation where their interests are adverse. This is easy to see, for example, when two clients of the same lawyer want to sue each other. However, it's also a conflict when two clients of the same lawyer make a deal with each other.

Lawyers are ethically required to disclose their conflicts of interest to you. Your choice is either to hire another lawyer, or you may **waive** (meaning you 'choose to ignore') the conflict, and continue to use the same lawyer.

Because the entertainment industry is a relatively small business, those of us who practice in this field are continually bumping into ourselves when our clients make deals with each other. Most of the time these situations are harmless and can be handled simply, in one of several ways:

1. Each of the clients gets another lawyer (rare unless it's a pretty serious conflict).
2. One of the clients gets another lawyer (much more common).
3. The clients work out the agreement amongst themselves (or else the manager, agent, or business manager negotiates for them), and the lawyer merely draws up the paperwork, not representing anyone's interest.

When interviewing attorneys, you should ask if they have or foresee any *conflicts of interest*. Most ethical lawyers will bring it up before you do, but you should ask anyway. For example, your lawyer might also represent your record company, your merchandiser, your personal manager, producer, publisher, etc. It's not uncommon for a personal manager to recommend his or her own lawyer, business manager, etc., and thus it's not uncommon for lawyers to represent both the personal manager and an artist. Most of the time, this isn't a problem. However, if you get into a fight with your personal manager, the lawyer will probably have to resign (or at least resign your side if the manager was there first). And you can't expect him or her to represent you vigorously against the personal manager in making your management deal.

In short, there are no hard and fast rules about conflicts. If the lawyer is straight and ethical, you can usually live with having him or her represent a few other people in your life. But if there's a problem with that other individual, you must seriously consider getting separate counsel. And if you just don't like the idea of conflicts (which is a perfectly reasonable way to feel), get someone who's independent right from the start.

Conflicts, by the way, are not just limited to lawyers. Business managers can have conflicts when they represent both a personal manager and an artist (for example, if there is a dispute over commissions). Managers can have conflicts when they act in some other capacity (such as becoming the producer of the artist's motion pictures and negotiating a fee for themselves that affects what the artist gets paid). Managers can also have conflicts when they have two artists vying for the same gig. Like I say, it's a small business. But we generally work these things out amicably.

A disturbing thing that's been happening over the last few years is that some lawyers are selling conflicts of interest as a *benefit* to their clients. For example, they might suggest that you will get a better deal with a certain record company or publisher because they also represent them. I'll give you my subtle opinion of this pitch: It's utter nonsense. For one thing, if the lawyer is being paid by a record company or publisher, it's human nature to think twice about how hard they want to beat them up and jeopardize a profitable relationship—especially for an artist who may pay them much less. Secondly, it's unethical for them to use any information they gain representing a company when negotiating against that company, and you can bet the company is neither going to like it nor permit it. So be very wary of any pitch along these lines.

As I said earlier, it is certainly possible for you to live with a conflict, if you're fully informed and are comfortable that the lawyer will be in your court. But the conflict is a reason for you to be careful, not a plus. Accordingly, the issue must be left to the tummy test. In other words, ask yourself whether your tummy feels like it's OK, or whether you're concerned about it. And, if you're concerned, get another lawyer.

In recent years, litigation over lawyers' conflicts of interest has increased. Some of the most powerful lawyers in the business have been sued over this. Hopefully, this will make everyone more cautious, including you and me. So always ask about potential conflicts of interest.

ATTORNEY CHECKLIST

Here's some questions to ask your potential lawyer:

1. Do you have expertise in the music business?
2. What do you charge? In addition to fees, do you charge for costs? (Everyone charges for long-distance phone calls, messengers, etc., but some charge for every page of photocopying, faxing, etc., while others are looser.)
3. Ask if the lawyer has a written fee agreement. In California, lawyers are required to have their fee agreements in writing in order to enforce them (a major incentive to get them in writing). Ask for a copy of the fee agreement so that you can review it.

    It's unethical in California for lawyers to have an agreement with you that can't be terminated at any time. If it's a percentage arrangement, be careful about what happens to the percentage after the term. See the discussion of this under Earnings After the Term on page 34.

You should ask if they object to your having the fee agreement reviewed by an independent advisor, preferably a lawyer, but at least a personal manager or business manager. No legitimate lawyer will object to this, and in fact they should encourage it. If it's at all possible, you should have your lawyer's fee agreement reviewed independently—especially if it involves a percentage. And, if it isn't possible to do this, make sure the lawyer explains it to you in detail, and that you understand it.

4. Ask for references of artists at your level, and check them out. Does this lawyer return phone calls? Do they get deals done in a reasonable period of time? 'Reasonable' in the music business is not going to be anywhere near the speed you would like. It's not uncommon for a record deal to take two to four months to negotiate, especially if you're a new artist and can't force the company to quickly turn around their contract drafts. Two to four months is a realistic time frame, but if it goes beyond that, someone isn't doing their job. I've always been amused by a story I heard from a new client when I was a young lawyer. He had been represented by another lawyer, and he said, 'I know my record deal is good. It took over a year to negotiate.'

5. Do you have or foresee any conflicts of interest?

6

Agents

ROLE

Agents in the music business are very different from agents in the film business. While agents in the film business are the major power brokers in the industry, controlling many aspects of it, agents in the music industry are involved almost exclusively in booking live personal appearances (concerts). Music agents are sometimes involved in commercials, tour sponsorship, television specials, and other areas, but they don't participate in (or get paid for) records or songwriting, and thus are not players of the same magnitude as film agents. This is not to suggest that agents aren't important—they are extremely so, and very influential. But their sphere of influence is limited.

FEES

Because agents aren't involved in your recording or songwriting (with the possible exception of film music, as noted on page 58), you should never give them a piece of the income from these areas. Usually agents don't even ask for this, but be careful of union forms, as noted in the next paragraph.

Agents are regulated by the unions: **AFM (American Federation of Musicians)** for musicians; **AFTRA (American Federation of Television and Radio Artists)** for vocalists and taped or live television actors and actresses; **SAG (Screen Actors Guild)** for film; and **Actors Equity** for live stage. The unions put a cap on how much the agents can charge, namely 10%. (For certain personal appearances under *AFM* jurisdiction, it can be more than 10%. However, the agents readily agree to a 10% maximum if you ask.) The AFM and *AFTRA* printed forms have a place for you to initial if the agency commissions your earnings from records. *Watch out for it and NEVER do this.*

The union regulation of agencies is called **franchising,** and unions only allow their members to be represented by 'franchised' agents, meaning those who agree to the union's restrictions. One of those restrictions is that the agency can only use contracts approved by the union, which results in each union having its own pet printed form, spelling out that union's particular requirements. So your agency contract looks like a small telephone book. Actually, it's a stack of separate contracts: three for *SAG* (one for films, one for TV, and one for commercials); one for AFM; one for AFTRA; one for *Actors Equity;* and two (called 'General Services' and 'Packaging') to pick up everything that isn't covered by a union.

Don't tell them I told you, but some agents will discount their percentage to as low as 5% for artists generating major revenues. (This is only for concerts. They stay at 10% for films, TV, etc., unless you're a major hitter in those areas—and even then, they may not budge.) Sometimes there's a sliding scale, so that as your income goes up, the percentage goes down. The industry goes through cycles as to how easy it is to get this discount, and thus you have to check the situation out when it's relevant to you.

In the U.K., the agents are not franchised by the Musicians' Union (or any other union for that matter). Thus they are free to charge whatever the market will bear. The norm, however, is 10% of gross.

DEAL POINTS

The major things to negotiate in your agent's deal are the following:

Term

The agency will ask for three or more years, and you will want to give them only one year. Shorter is better for you, because you can split if things don't work out, or squeeze their commission down if things do. The result of this wrestling match depends on your bargaining power.

If you give more than a year, you should have the right to get out after each year if you don't earn minimum levels. (See the discussion of this under personal managers' deals on page 33; agency deals work the same way, except the numbers should be lower because they don't represent all areas of your life.) If you have enough clout, you may never sign any papers at all (although some agencies can get snippy about this).

Scope

If you're involved in the film business (for example, if you're a musical artist and also an actress, screenwriter, director, etc.), and if the agency is in both the film and the music business, the trend is for agencies to insist on representing you in all areas. Thus, an agency representing you in the film business will require you to sign with them for your musical concerts, and vice versa. This may or may not be to your advantage, and it becomes more negotiable as your bargaining power increases. Some agencies have a firm policy and won't let you in the door without a full package, while others are more flexible.

Exclusions

Similar to personal managers' deals (see page 31), you can exclude certain monies from commission:

1. As we discussed a minute ago, you can exclude earnings from records and songwriting or publishing without any difficulty (if you ask). However, some agencies try to commission your soundtrack album royalties if the album is derived from a film in which they got you work as an actor or actress. I have tried to resist this, and have been pretty successful for established artists. The agencies' main argument is that, if you have no career as an actor or actress, and the agency is instrumental in making one, they should get paid on everything you get from being involved in the film. If you do agree to this, make sure it only kicks in if you're getting a major part in the film. It isn't fair for an agent to commission your earnings from musical performances (the fee for the title song, soundtrack album royalties, etc.) just because you're on screen for ten seconds to tell the doctor she has a telephone call. Your argument is that you don't need the agency to get you motion picture music work (unless, of course, you do), and that they shouldn't be commis-

sioning an area in which you already have a career independent of them. Their argument is that, if they move you into a new arena (acting), and the soundtrack album is merely an aid to doing it, they should get paid on everything. Results vary with bargaining power.

There are agencies that specialize in getting motion picture musical work for artists. In that case, of course, the agency commissions your fee for writing music and/or singing, and record royalties as well. They normally don't commission song-writer performance royalties, which are monies we'll discuss on page 236.

2. You should exclude things like commercials (unless you've specifically engaged the agency to get you commercials), book publishing (if you're so inclined), and record producing.

3. You can also exclude costs of collection before applying the commission (as we discussed in manager's deals on page 31). In other words, if you have to sue someone to get paid, you should deduct the cost of the lawsuit from your recovery before the agent gets his or her commission.

Even in excluded areas, the agents will want to be paid if they get you work. I like to say they can only get you employment in these areas with your consent. That way they don't come running in with a flood of offers if you aren't in the market, or if you just don't want them involved.

Termination of the Agency

As we discussed above, your agency deal is a stack of union forms. Each of these union agreements has a clause saying you can terminate if the agent doesn't get you work (or an offer of work) for ninety days. Since these are separate agreements, with separate terms, you want a provision that says you can get out of all these deals if you have the right to terminate any one of them. Without this, the agency would represent you in some areas but not others, because they all have different termination criteria.

This clause is a bit hard to get if you work only in the music area. Since you've never had a film career, the agency can reasonably argue that they can't be expected to produce one in ninety days. The usual compromise is to say that, if the AFM or AFTRA agreement (your area) can be terminated for failing to get you work, then you can get out of everything.

Territory

If you're a new, or even midlevel artist, it is difficult to give an agency less than worldwide rights. However, as you move up the ladder, you can sometimes exclude territories outside the United States. This is often beneficial, because you can use agents in Europe or elsewhere who are skilled in those markets. In fact, many U.S. agencies use a local sub-agent for foreign territories, and you can thus eliminate the middleman. And at a high enough level, you might even eliminate the foreign agent and deal directly with the promoters through your lawyer and personal manager (if they have the expertise).

On the other hand, the U.S. agency doesn't just sit there idly while a sub-agent does the work. The agency oversees the foreign agent and makes sure the shows are properly promoted, that you get paid on time, etc. It's also easier to deal with someone locally than to get up at strange hours and call around the world.

Double Commissions

Just like personal management deals, there should be no double commissions if you have a corporation (see page 37).

PICKING AN AGENT

If you have a personal manager, you'll have only occasional contact with your agent. You'll see him or her at your shows, and you may meet to set up your tours. The rest of the time he or she talks to your personal manager and, to a lesser degree, to your lawyer and business manager. Thus, while you should make the final decision, picking an agent should be primarily handled by your manager (since he or she deals with the agent most of the time).

If you don't have a manager, the agent will report directly to you. In this case, the criteria for picking your agent should be the same as picking a manager. So take another look at page 38.

And as always, make sure you get a good vibe from whoever you're hiring.

PART II

Record Deals

7

Broad-Strokes Overview of the Record Business

So now you've got a great team. Congratulations! Let's look at how you can participate intelligently in the work its members do for you. We'll start with records.

INDUSTRY STRUCTURE

Before we get into the various moving parts of record deals, let's first talk about how records make their way from the oven to your table. There are several designer methods to choose from:

Major Record Companies

This is the way most records are made. An artist signs a recording contract with a major label (Warner Bros., Columbia, etc.) and hands in his or her recordings. The company then turns these into records (as you'll see in a minute, the definition of a 'record' isn't so simple). It ships your records to a **distributor,** who is the wholesaler that sells your records to the stores (more about *distributors* later). The company then gears up its advertising, promotion, marketing, etc., and rockets you to stardom.

Here are the major divisions of fully staffed record companies (in no particular order):

A&R. These are the people with 'ears' who find and nurture new talent, and who work creatively with the artists (see page 125 for a discussion of A&R people).

Sales. Salespeople get your records into the stores—not an inconsequential step in having a million-seller.

Marketing. Advertising, publicity, album-cover artwork, promotional videos, in-store displays, promotional merchandise, etc.

Promotion. These folks live solely for the purpose of getting your records played on the radio. They spend their days 'jamming' radio stations, and saying 'Baby' and 'Sweetheart' a lot.

Product Management. Product managers are in charge of whipping up all the other departments (sales, marketing, promotion, etc.) and getting them to work together to push your records. This is to make sure you get propelled forward by a coordinated team, rather than torn apart by horses running in different directions.

New Media. Here one finds the species *techno-geek-us,* those folks in charge of delivering music electronically and through other strange and mysterious ways.

Production. Manufacturing, cover printing, assembling, and shipping to the distributors.

Finance. They compute and pay your royalties, bless their little hearts, and keep track of the company's income and expenses.

Business Affairs/Legal. These executives are responsible for the company's contracts, not only with artists, but with record clubs, foreign licensees, etc. Business affairs people negotiate the deals and, in conjunction with other executives, make the decisions as to what to give and what to hold. The legal department gives legal advice and drafts the contracts. Sometimes business affairs and legal are the same people.

International. As the name implies, the international department coordinates the release of your records around the world, and oversees all the functions listed above in foreign territories.

Here's a pictorial chart, suitable for framing:

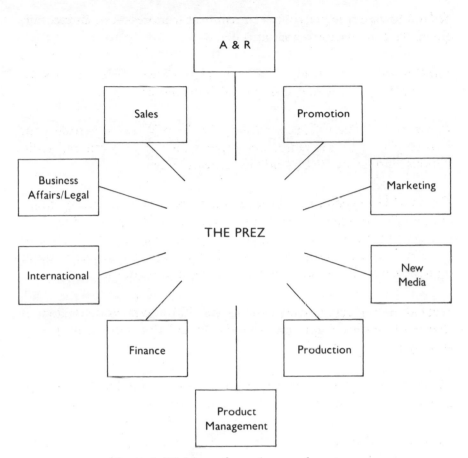

Figure 1. Divisions of a major record company.

By the way, in some companies a number of these functions are combined in a single person or department, while in other companies multiple departments handle just one of them. For example, some companies have their A&R people also act as product managers. And at larger labels, there might be separate departments for advertising, publicity, art, and video (which are all handled by the marketing department at other companies). But the above is a good broad-strokes view of the main divisions.

The major record companies are all distributed by **major distributors,** which are gigantic distribution networks that move records from manufacturing plants into the stores. And ramming these little suckers into retailers is more difficult than it sounds. You need a large network to do it, like any other manufacturing business, and it's expensive to set up and maintain the warehousing, shipping, inventory controls, sales force, etc., necessary to move goods into a marketplace. To give you some feel for it, WEA, a *major distributor,* employs approximately 1,150 people, while Warner Bros. Records (whose records it distributes) has only about 300 employees.

After years of consolidation, there are only five major distributors left, and they're all owned by the major labels (or, more specifically, by the labels' parent companies). They are (alphabetically): BMG (which distributes Arista, Jive, and RCA Records); EMI (Capitol and Virgin); Sony (Columbia, Epic); Universal (Universal, Interscope/ A&M/Geffen, MCA, Island/Def Jam, Motown); and WEA (Warner Bros., Elektra, Atlantic). The labels listed after each are only the bigger labels—all of the majors distribute smaller labels as well.

Over the last few years, several of the majors have tried to marry each other (in particular, EMI has tried to merge with both Warner Music and BMG), but each time it was torpedoed by European antitrust regulators. However, with the record biz's current difficulties, the winds seem to be shifting. So by the time you read this, someone may have managed to run off with someone else.

Mini-majors

A **mini-major** is a fully staffed company, with everything except the ability to distribute records to the stores. (And, as you now know, this is no small 'except.') So the *mini-majors* are all distributed by majors, and in almost every case they are co-owned by the major. It isn't just the expense of a distribution operation that drives mini-majors to use major distributors. It's also a question of clout: If a retailer doesn't feel like paying its bills, who will it stiff—a major record company that can keep it from getting the next Eminem album, or Fred Glump Records, which currently has a hit but next week may be in that Great Dust Bin in the Sky? (By the way, 'mini-major' is not an industry term. I borrowed it from the film industry because I didn't know what else to call these companies.)

Mini-majors can be important forces in the industry. For example, DreamWorks Records is a mini-major, distributed by Universal. There have been a number of others over the years, which have been gobbled up by majors on buying sprees, such as A&M, Geffen, Virgin, Interscope, Motown, Jive, LaFace, Chrysalis, Island, Sire, and Enigma. The gobbled companies now exist as parts of majors.

Here's a mini-major's distribution setup:

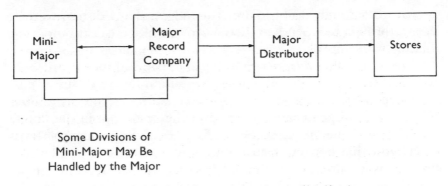

Figure 2. Mini-major record company distribution.

Independents

Independents are record companies that aren't owned by a major or mini-major, and they come in two main flavors:

Major-Distributed Independent. This is an independent entity that has little or no staff, but rather signs artists and contracts with a major or mini-major to perform all functions except recording the records. The main thing these companies bring to the party is the ability to find talent and to mercilessly beat the distributing company about the head and shoulders to make sure their product gets promoted. Product released by these companies may be on the independent's own label, or it may be on the distributing company's label (in which case the public may never even know the independent exists). This type of entity is discussed in detail on page 189, in connection with independent production agreements.

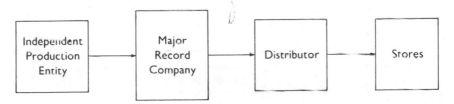

Figure 3. Major-distributed independent record company.

True Independent. A true independent has no affiliation with a major or mini-major, but rather is financed by its owners and/or investors. Examples of these labels are Ryko, Sub Pop, Epitaph, Rounder Records, Flying Fish, and SST, though some of even these companies' records go through majors. The true independents distribute their records through **independent distributors,** which are distributors not affiliated with a major.

In the past, these *independent distributors* handled the major labels. Today, all the majors do their own distribution (as we discussed), so the independents distribute only smaller labels. Accordingly, their influence has dropped substantially over the years. But in spite of all this, independents are often better for specialized product such as street music (hip-hop, rap, house music, etc.), folk music, speed metal, etc. This is because (1) specialized markets are too small to get the majors' attention; and (2) the independents are 'wired into' the smaller retailers who cater to this trade. Also, independents had a huge resurgence with rap music, which can sell millions of albums. And because independents are smaller and less cumbersome, they can move quicker. I'm told it can take ten weeks for majors to get product into their system and solicit orders, while independents can do it in just a few weeks.

The line between independent record companies and mini-majors is often blurred. You may find an independent, for example, that distributes through a major but does its own promotion and marketing, just as you may find a mini-major that lays off some of these functions on the major to whom they're married.

There is also a relatively new breed of company in the independent marketplace: independents owned by a major or mini-major record company. For example, EMI owns Caroline, and Sony owns Relativity. Even though these entities are owned by majors, they're distributed by independents. Thus they have the ability to reach specialized markets, coupled with the clout and expertise of a major.

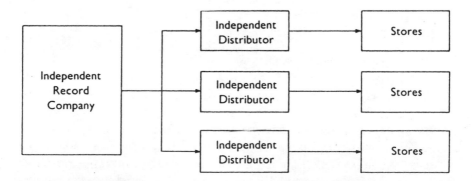

Figure 4. True independent record company distribution.

WHAT'S A RECORD?

Let's now turn to a real basic: What's a **record**?

As simple and straightforward as that question sounds, the answer is not what you'd expect. Of course, the term *record* means the device you're thinking of—a compact disc. And it also includes pre-recorded cassettes and vinyl discs (R.I.P.). However, in virtually every record agreement made since the 1960s, the contractual definition of record says a record is both an audio-only *and* an **audiovisual** device (meaning one with sound and visual images), such as videocassettes and DVDs, which play video as well as audio material. (This is particularly interesting when you remember that *audiovisual* devices weren't even invented in the 1960s! Companies anticipated their development, even though no one knew what form they would take.) The definition of records also included (and still does) any other device *now or hereafter known* that is capable of transmitting sound alone, or sound with visual images. Even more important, the current deals define records to mean *any kind* of delivery of music for consumer use, whether sound alone or with visuals. This is designed to pick up the Internet and other electronic transmissions. As you'll see later, these broad definitions in record deals can make life a bit tricky if you're a recording artist and also an actor or actress in films. Stay tuned (or peek at page 141 if you can't wait).

By the way, did you know that, originally, records were made by having the musicians and singers perform for each record sold? This was because there was no mass duplication process available, and thus the recordings were made directly onto the wax that was ultimately sold (meaning every record in a store contained a unique, one-time performance). Can you imagine how sick you'd be of a song if it sold a million copies?

MASTERS

The word **master** has two meanings:

1. The original recording made in the studio is called a *master*, because it is the master (meaning controlling entity) from which all copies are made (the machines making the copies are called *slaves*—master/slave; get it?).

   Master recordings are now done mostly on computer hard drives, tapes having become a thing of the past (although digital audiotapes occasionally pop up). These recordings are

multitrack, meaning that each instrument and voice part is recorded on a separate track or channel: the drums on one track, guitar on another, voice on another, etc. Many studios today use forty-eight tracks, and some have even more, meaning there can be forty-eight or more separate channels of information. When the recording is complete, the master is then **edited, mixed,** and **EQ'd.** As in films, *editing* means cutting out the parts you don't like and splicing in the parts you do. *Mixing* means getting the proper level for each track, so that the drums are the right volume during each particular part of the song, the voice is raised a bit on the chorus, etc. Also, the sounds may be enhanced through processes I have never completely understood. *EQ'ing* stands for 'equalizing,' and means that the bass, mid-range, and treble are each adjusted to be the right level (so that no one of them overpowers the others). The mixed *multitrack* is then reduced down to a **two-track** stereophonic master, which is ready for the duplication process.

So there are two masters—the original multitrack, and the finished *two-track* (and often a 5.1 master for DVD audio).

2. The word 'master' also means a recording of one particular song. Thus, you might say an album has 'ten masters' (meaning ten selections) on it. These individual recordings are also called **cuts,** because of the historical fact that each selection was 'cut' into vinyl.

ROYALTY COMPUTATION

Enough about art; let's talk about money. We'll start with your royalties.

Basic Concept

My brother-in-law, Jules, is in the used car business. He's famous throughout the West Valley because he'll trade cars for anything. At one point, he traded a car for a silver tea set, a set of golf clubs, and a mule. (Honest.) He then traded the mule, along with a stained-glass window of Daffy Duck, for an English bulldog named Rosie.

About that time, my wife and I were looking for a dog. It was before we had children, and we wanted to test our parenting skills on something that wouldn't use drugs if we failed. In trying to decide what kind of dog we wanted, we used to take Rosie for outings on weekends, and in a perverted way we began to think of her gnarled face and drooling as cute. Anyway, Jules decided he was going to breed her, and we wanted a puppy. So I helped by finding a stud dog, through a sophisticated referral system—the Yellow Pages. I called a place named Royal Family Bulldogs, which conjured up images of some country squire's dogs lounging on velvet pillows. Well, it turned out to be a dilapidated house in Pacoima, the most impressive feature of which was its bulldog smells. But Royal Family had a brown-and-white stud named Winston, who was a champion. So Jules hired Winston, and Rosie got pregnant.

About this time, Jules decided he wasn't interested in the headaches of small puppies. So he enlisted the help of his friend Corky. Corky's deal was that she would take care of Rosie and the puppies, and when each dog was sold, she'd get half of the sales price. Thus, if a dog sold for two hundred dollars, Jules would get a hundred dollars and Corky would get a hundred dollars.

So what does this have to do with records? Well, your record royalty is very much like Jules's share of the bulldog proceeds. In the case of records, the artist (like Jules) turns his recordings (pregnant Rosie) over to the company (Corky), who then sells the finished product (puppies). For each record (puppy) sold, the artist gets a piece of the price, and the company keeps the rest to cover its costs and make a profit.

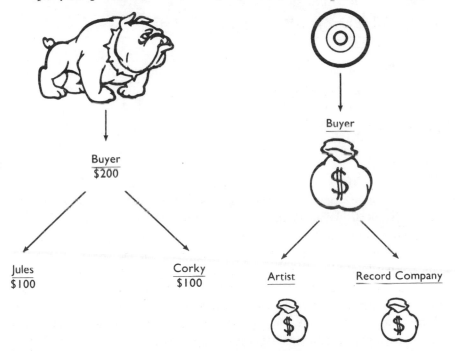

Figure 5. Bulldogs and royalties.

In case you're curious, I didn't change the example to a bulldog just for you guys—it's in the American edition the same way. And I really did want one of these little critters a few years back.

Basic Royalty Computations

For historical reasons, the division of proceeds between the artist and record company is more complicated than the puppy deal. The companies don't simply divide the money they get (that would be too easy, and I'd be out of a job). Instead, almost all of the companies compute artist royalties as a percentage of the record's **suggested retail list price** (**SRLP** to its friends). The *SRLP* is an approximation of the price received by the **retailer,** which has nothing to do with the wholesale price received by the company. (Even those few companies that compute royalties based on the wholesale price don't just divide up the company's actual receipts; there are a bunch of artificial adjustments, as you'll see.)

The U.K. companies don't use SRLP: they have a very different system, which we'll get to in a minute (on page 73).

To follow the next part we'll need to use a little math. Don't worry if numbers aren't your strong suit—I'll keep it simple and go slowly. I've explained these concepts to my cousin David, who has to take off his shoes and socks to count to twenty, and he understood them.

Here's how it works:

1. The artist's royalty is stated as a percentage of the suggested retail list price, such as '10% of retail.' I'll use retail for this example because the vast majority of the business uses it. The wholesale computation is the same as retail, except that the royalty is roughly doubled, since the wholesale price is approximately one-half of the retail price. To use simple numbers, 20% of a $4.50 wholesale price (90¢) is the same as 10% of a $9.00 retail price (90¢). (In actuality, the wholesale price is more than half of retail, so the equivalent wholesale royalty is less than twice the retail royalty.)

Note that the royalty is based on the *suggested* retail list price, which has absolutely nothing to do with what you pay at your local record store (in my experience, no two record stores ever have the same price for the same record anyway). Currently, the SRLP for the majority of newly released CDs is $17.98 or $18.98. (As I'm sure you know, you can almost always buy CDs for less than this.)

Each percentage point of retail or wholesale is known as a **point.** So if you have a 10% royalty, you have ten *points.*

2. From this price, the company first deducts a **packaging charge** (also called a **packaging deduction** or **container charge**). In *theory,* this is the cost of the 'package,' and it's deducted because the artist should get a royalty only on the record, not the package. In *reality,* it's a charge of much more than any package actually costs, and is thus only an artificial way to reduce the artist's royalty.

   The *packaging charge* is stated as a percentage of the SRLP, and the industry norm is 25% for compact discs and other 'new configurations.'

3. The result of this (i.e., the SRLP after deducting the packaging charge) is called **a base price** or **royalty base.** This is the figure against which you apply your royalty percentage.

Here's an example of a *royalty base* computation using easy (*not* real world) numbers:

Retail price of CD	$10.00
Less: Packaging (25% of $10.00)	−2.50
ROYALTY BASE	**$7.50**

Thus, in this example, if an artist has a 10% royalty, he or she gets 75¢ (10% of $7.50).

Unlike the U.S. companies, U.K. companies do not have the audacity to suggest what a dealer might charge (not that the U.S. dealers listen anyway). Accordingly, the computation of retail price in the U.K. has taken some interesting twists throughout your history.

For years, the contracts merely said that royalties were computed on 'retail' or 'retail equivalent', a term which had no real definition.

The industry practice settled into a rut whereby 'retail' came to mean the price used by MCPS (more about them later, on page 249), who negotiated with the BPI (we'll get to them, too). In English, that means an organization of the people who control the *songs* embodied in records (as opposed to the artistic performances, which may or may not be created by the same person), negotiated with an organization of record companies to determine how much they got paid for the songs. In the U.K., the songwriters got paid a percentage of retail, and so everyone had a nice, neat definition of 'retail' which had been hammered out between two powerful groups.

Under this system, retail was defined by starting with something called the **published price to dealers** or **published dealer price** (both of these abbreviated to 'PPD'), or **base price to dealers** (abbreviated as 'BPD'). I'm going to use PPD from here on so I don't have to keep saying both of them, but BPD and PPD mean the same thing—the price that the distributors charge the stores (i.e. the same concept as wholesale in the U.S.). To determine retail, PPD was increased to approximately the amount for which records were sold in the stores. The amount of the increase (called an **uplift**, because it 'lifted up' the PPD price to retail) was 131% for cassettes and 129% for CDs. Note that the mark-up in the U.K. is much smaller than in the U.S., because the wholesale price is higher than the U.S. wholesale price in proportion to retail: as noted on page 84, the wholesale price in the U.S. is about 50% of retail, whereas PPD is almost 72% of retail. (Outside the U.K., the up-lift is generally between 110% and 140%, depending on the territory.)

Here's an example:

Compact Disc Royalty	
Published dealer price	£8.00
Mark-up to approximate retail	×129%
Retail price	£10.32
Less: packaging (25%)	−2.58
ROYALTY BASE	**£7.74**

Thus, a 10% royalty is worth 77.4p.

This system moved along quite swimmingly until the early 1990s, when the MCPS and BPI beat each other in to pulp and ended up using a percentage of PPD (instead of a percentage of retail). Thus the pre-packaged, ready-to-use 'retail' definition disappeared overnight, and virtually all U.K. companies have changed their royalties to a percentage of PPD. Using PPD is infinitely more logical than using the artificial SRLP we use in the U.S. (it always ticks me off when you guys do these things ahead of us).

Now that you're educated, you can quickly figure out that a PPD artist needs to have a higher royalty rate than a retail artist in order to make the same number of pence. Amazingly, these higher rates tend to resemble the old percentage uplift of PPD. For example, if you had a 10% of retail royalty, and under the old system there was a 129% PPD uplift for cassettes, you would need a 12.9% (129% of 10%) royalty on PPD to put yourself in exactly the same position.

Here's a recap with numbers:

10% of Retail Compact Disc Royalty

Published dealer price	£8.00
Mark-up to approximate retail	×129%
Retail price	£10.32
Less: packaging (25%)	−2.58
Royalty base	£7.74
10% royalty	×10%
AMOUNT PAYABLE	**£.774**

12.9% of PPD Compact Disc Royalty

Dealer price	£8.00
Less: packaging (25%)	−2.00
Royalty base	£6.00
12.9% royalty	×12.9%
AMOUNT PAYABLE	**£.774**

In reality, these mark-ups have been squeezed, so a more realistic uplift is between 110% and 129%.

Free Goods

Royalties are paid for each record <u>sold.</u> Why do I emphasize the word *sold*? Well, before I can tell you, you need to know more about how records are distributed.

When I was ten years old, I had a soft-drink stand in front of our house. I don't mean a card table with lemonade; I mean a serious soft-drink stand made out of genuine pine (by my stepfather), with Dr Pepper and Coca-Cola signs that, if I'd kept them, would be worth more than my first car. Anyway, I stumbled on the brilliant idea of delivering soft drinks to the workmen at a construction site about a block away, using my little wagon. Instead of selling the drinks for a nickel, like everyone else, I would sell them for a dime (delivery labor, you know). But for every two drinks they bought, they would get two free. (Although I felt I was putting one over on the workmen, I have a feeling they really knew I was selling the drinks for a nickel each and using mirrors.)

My idea for a soft-drink scam, however, was taken to dizzying heights by the early record company accounting magicians. First, they figured out that selling one hundred records at 85¢ each was the same as selling eighty-five records for $1 each and giving the customer fifteen more for 'free' for every eighty-five they bought (the retailer gets one hundred records either way, and the company gets $85 either way). Then, they figured out that, because fifteen of these records were 'free,' they didn't have to pay the artist for the free records—I mean, how could you have the gall to ask for royalties on a record for which the company wasn't being paid? So by raising the price and giving away records for 'free,' the companies saved royalties on fifteen records out of every one hundred while making the same money. (Remember, the artist's royalty is based on retail, so the artist doesn't get any benefit from an inflated wholesale price.) Nifty, eh?

It took the workmen who bought my soft drinks about thirty seconds to figure out the price of my drinks was 5¢ each. But it took recording artists over twenty years to figure out that these 'free' records were hardly free, because the economics to the company were exactly the same as if all the records had been sold at a lesser price. Got it?

There are two types of 'free goods':

'Phony' Free Goods. Today, only a few companies give away 15% of the records they ship (although historically, almost all of them did this). Where it's done, these 'free' records are known as **phony free goods** because, like my soft drinks, they are nothing more than a cute way of discounting the purchase price. (Technically, they're called **normal distributor free goods.**) And in fact the companies that still use this practice charge a higher wholesale price than those who don't, and the difference (not surprisingly) is the percentage of 'free goods.' (By the way, even though it sounds like you should, you don't get

Figure 6. The author invents free goods.

more royalties from the companies without free goods, as we'll see in a minute).

Back to our example:

Retail price of CD	$10.00
Less: Packaging (25% of $10.00)	−2.50
ROYALTY BASE	**$7.50**

Using a 10% (75¢) royalty, and assuming sales of 100,000 CDs, the artist's earnings would be $75,000. However, since the company 'gives away' 15% (or 15,000 of the units in this example) for 'free,' these 15,000 units don't bear any royalties. Thus, the artist is only paid on 85,000 units, and instead of getting $75,000, the artist only gets $63,750 (75¢ x 85,000 units), which is 85% of $75,000.

Units shipped	100,000
Less: free goods	−15,000
Royalty-bearing units	85,000
Times: Royalty	× 75¢
AMOUNT PAYABLE	**$63,750**

As noted before, most of the companies have done away with the fiction of these *phony free goods*. But do you get more royalties? No; instead of free goods, they only pay you on 85% of the sales. So the result is exactly the same as it used to be with free goods. It looks like this:

Units shipped	100,000
Royalty-bearing percentage	85%
Royalty-bearing units	85,000
Times: Royalty	× 75¢
AMOUNT PAYABLE	**$63,750**

Note you could get to the same place by simply saying the artist's royalty is 63.75¢, which is 85% of 75¢, and paying a royalty on all goods shipped. But no one does this, and I'll tell you why in a minute (on page 83).

You chaps in the U.K. have always been much too gentlemanly to use the 'phoney' free goods that we have in the U.S. You simply smile and pay a lower royalty rate. However, you have always had 'real' free goods, which happen to be . . .

'Real' Free Goods.   All companies (even those who don't have phony free goods) give away **real free goods,** also known as **special campaign free goods.** This happens when a company is trying to push out large numbers of a particular artist's album. To get the stores to stock more of it, they give away 5% or 10% of all records shipped. These free goods are a very real discount of the price and are meant to encourage dealers to buy the record (which they invariably do, since the dealers make bigger profits when they sell them). And because these freebies actually cost the record company, they don't bear royalties.

Promotion Copies

Records given away for promotion, such as radio-station copies, are also *real free goods* and don't bear royalties. They are known as **promotional** or **promo** (pronounced 'pro-moe') records. These don't go to retailers and are marked 'not for sale.'

As with any number of other things in life, unfortunately the theory and reality of *promo* records don't quite converge. While these records are meant for disc jockeys, they sometimes end up being sold in record stores. And of course they're priced cheaply, for the obvious reason that whoever sold them to the store got them for free.

What is less obvious is that the people who created the record don't get paid for sales of promos. Thus, while someone is enjoying a bargain, it's at the expense of the artist, publisher, songwriter, record company, unions, etc. (I hope I'm making you feel guilty if you buy records marked 'promo-only,' since you're taking bread out of the mouths of your creative brothers and sisters.)

Some record companies—for example, Sony—have tried to solve the problem by stamping their promotional product with an official-looking statement that says the record is only licensed for promotional use, as opposed to being given away. The theory is that the record company keeps ownership of each promo record, and so any resale of it is illegal. In theory the company is absolutely right—it *is* illegal to sell something you don't own, and Sony could demand return of the record at any time. However, you can imagine how meaningful this concept is to the owners and customers of Mortimer's Used Records and Ski Shop in East Elk, Vermont. So the best cure is an informed boycott. Let's start one.

I was surprised to learn that in the U.K. not only are promo records regularly sold, but indeed they are 'collector's items'. I understand this is particularly true if the disk has different artwork or different edits, and indeed that these materials sell at a premium. However, they aren't usually sold through regular retail stores, but more through record fairs. And in any case, the artist and company aren't getting paid.

Return Privilege

To understand this next part, you need to know that records are sold on a **100% return privilege.** This means that, if a retailer orders one hundred records from RCA but can't sell them, it can bundle them up, ship them back to RCA, and get credit for (or a refund of) the price it paid. Such a practice is unlike most other businesses, because if you buy a load of plastic flamingos and can't sell them, you eat them.

The reason for this return policy is that records have to be pushed out quickly in large numbers, and the retailers simply aren't willing to take the risk of getting stuck with too many of them (especially with new artists). Thus the retailers have always said they will only stock large quantities if the manufacturer agrees to take back the stiffs. (For you sticklers, I'm aware that most companies now charge penalties for returns in excess of a set percentage of records shipped [16% to 20%, depending on the company] and they also give a discount for returning less than this percentage. For example, if a retailer buys a hundred records, and there's a 20% penalty point, it will not get a full credit [i.e., a refund of what was paid] if it returns more than twenty records. However, if it returns only ten, it gets more than a full credit [i.e., a credit for more than it paid for those ten]. The idea is to get the retailer to order more carefully, and to make it less likely those ordered will come back. However, since any given artist may have 100% of his or her records returned [the 20% applies overall, to all of the records of the company], I'm simplifying this to a pure *100% privilege,* like the old days.)

To see why this is important, let's go back to Rosie's puppies. Jump ahead to the time when the puppies have been born and are crawling all over Corky's living room. A customer comes in to buy one of the dogs, but she isn't sure the puppy will get along with her kids. So she says, 'I'll give you a check for the dog and you hold it while I take the puppy home to play with the kids. If, after a week or so, everything is going well, you can cash the check. If not, I'll bring the dog back for a refund.' Corky agrees, willing to do anything to move the little nippers out. Later the same day, she tells Jules about the deal. Jules then asks for his half of the check (which of course Corky can't yet cash), and Corky suggests he have intercourse with himself. She says he can have his share when the buyer decides to keep the dog.

Reserves

The **reserves** used by record companies work exactly the same way (usually without the suggestion for self-intercourse). Because records are sold on a 100% return basis, the companies legitimately don't know, particularly with a new artist, whether the records they shipped will sell or whether they'll be returned by the retailer at a later date. Because the records may come back, the companies (like Corky) keep a portion of the royalties that would otherwise be payable to the artist (Jules) until they know whether the sales to the retailer are final. This holdback is called a *reserve* against returns.

For example, if a company ships 100,000 records of an artist, they may only pay the artist on 65,000 of these and wait to see if the other 35,000 sell through or are returned. At some point in the future (usually within two years after the shipment), the monies are paid through to the artist. The technical term for this pay-through is called **liquidating** the reserve. Of course, if the records are returned, the reserves are never paid to the artist because the sales are canceled and the royalty is never earned.

The size of your reserves varies with how well the company thinks your *next* album will do. For example, if they think your next album will sell extremely well, they'll be less concerned about holding big reserves—if they hold inadequate reserves and overpay you, they can just take the money back from your next album. However, if you're a new artist and they're not sure there is even going to be another album, or if this is a 'one-off' record such as a soundtrack album, or if this is the last album under your deal, you can anticipate healthy reserves and a record company attitude along the lines of 'If you don't like it, tough noogies.' (As your bargaining power grows, you can put caps on reserves. See page 158 for more on this.)

Adding reserves to our computation example, and assuming the reserve is 35%, the amount payable to the artist would look like this:

Units (100,000 shipped, payment on 85%)	85,000
Artist Royalty	× 75¢
Total	$63,750
Less: 35% reserve	−22,312
AMOUNT PAYABLE TO ARTIST	**$41,438**

U.K. return allowances are much more restrictive than those in the U.S. A typical record company allowance is 5% (as opposed to 20% in the U.S.), plus defective goods. However, as with the U.S., this is 5% of the company's *total shipments*, meaning that if you create an especially distasteful bomb, most of your records could come back and still be within the company's overall 5%.

Because the return policy is stricter, U.K. reserves are smaller. New artists tend to have the largest reserves, since there's no sales history and a greater chance of the records sauntering home. Thus, a new artist might have a reserve of 20% to 25%, but note that this is still much lower than in the U.S. (35% to 50%). More established artists' reserves would be in the range of 5% to 10%, as opposed to 25% in the U.S.

An exception to this is TV advertised packages (see page 176), where reserves can be 30% to 35%.

'90% of Net Sales'

In the early days, records were made of shellac, and were therefore breakable. So the record companies developed a practice of paying the artist on only 90% of the shipment, keeping the remaining 10% to cover their breakage.

Records haven't been made of shellac for the last sixty years, but the practice of paying on 90% of net sales persisted until very recently. Today only one major record company (I won't use any names, but its initials are A&M) routinely pays on only 90%. Note this 90% computation is *in addition* to the free goods, and a wholly separate computation. There is no logical reason for this—it is a total rip-off that arbitrarily reduces your royalty by 10%. Thus, where a company pays on 90%, you are being paid on 90% (for 'breakage') of 85% (for free goods), resulting in payment on only 76.5% of shipments! Resist this with your life, or else raise your royalty rate to compensate (10% on 90% is the same as 9% on 100%).

The U.K. still has a few old dogs that pay on 90% of sales. Fortunately, it's rare, and the companies will usually raise the royalty rate to compensate (as noted above).

WHY ALL THIS WEIRDNESS?

It's late at night, and the forest is chilled with the aroma of pine. The men of the gypsy camp stand in a rough circle, blowing into their hands for warmth. The mother's hands are shaking, and she feels the stares of the camp elders as she unwraps her infant and places him on a rough horsehair blanket. The baby shivers as she lays a bag of gold on his left, and a violin on his right.

Now the crowd is quiet, watching intently. They know that if the baby reaches for the violin, he will grow up to be a musician. But if he reaches for the gold, he will be a thief. And in the rare case where he takes both, he will head the royalty department at a major record company.

So why are royalties computed so strangely? I'm convinced that these bizarre computations came from the earliest days of the record business, when artists had little sophistication (and no lawyers). We've all heard horror stories of early pop stars who received little or nothing for their music, and most of these stories are true. I'm certain a number of adult gypsy babies sat up nights trying to think of ways they could take money from the artists by doing anything other than reducing the royalty rate: 'How can I tell them they have a 10% royalty and pay them like they have 7%?' You can almost see the 'idea lightbulb' light up the green eyeshade as one of these fellows hit on the brilliant stroke that the artist shouldn't be paid for the package in which the record is wrapped, or for records 'given away' as free goods. The reality, as we discussed, is that the packaging deductions bear no relationship whatsoever to the real cost of the packaging, while the 'free goods' are just a convoluted way to pay less royalties.

Perhaps more forthright is the story told about the late Morris Levy, a music industry pioneer. Morris, a gruff guy whose voice sounded like he gargled with Drano, owned and ran Roulette Records. Ol' Morris had a tough reputation, to say the least—he was rumored to hang with some underworld types, and was under investigation for extortion shortly before his death. Anyway, as legend has it, he was negotiating with an artist who was insisting on an 8% royalty, and Morris wanted to pay him only 5%. After a half hour of arguing, Morris finally said, 'Okay, I'll tell you what. We'll put 8% in the contract, but I'm gonna pay you 5%.'

ISN'T THERE A BETTER WAY?

Yes, of course there is.

Over the years, one or two companies have tried to compute their royalties more realistically, such as using a percentage of wholesale price with no free goods or packaging. But they all abandoned it because their royalty percentages came out so much lower than the other companies that they were unable to compete. In other words, an 8.5% royalty from a company paying on 100% of its sales without free goods doesn't sound as attractive as a 10% royalty from a company that pays on 85% of sales, even though they're exactly the same. Silly as it may seem, artists want to be able to 'royalty drop' at cocktail parties, and it's easier to say you have a 16% royalty (and leave out the fact that it's on 85% of sales) than to say you have a '14% royalty with no free goods.' In fact, the 14% is a higher royalty:

At the time of this writing, BMG and Warner Music Group have announced they're going to have a very simple, straightforward percentage of wholesale price computation, presumably without a packaging deduction, free goods, and the other little hoops through which the other companies make you jump. Note this won't result in any more money for the artist—it's only a simpler way to compute royalties. And of course the royalty rates will be lower for the reasons we just discussed. Still, I think it's a healthy step, and by the time you read this, other companies may have followed.

Another way to get closer to reality is to state your royalties in pennies. But the companies don't like this because it gets too easy to compare what different companies are actually offering. So these deals are rare. And even using pennies, you still have to compensate for the free goods (which affects the number of units you're paid on, not the royalty calculation). If you ever do make such a deal (and you can with enough clout), be sure the pennies go up and down in proportion to the retail (or wholesale) price, or you'll be locked in and, in effect, have a drop in royalties every time the price goes up. For example, if your royalty is $1.00 for a $10.00 SRLP, and if it doesn't change when the price moves to $11.00, your royalty drops from 10% (the ratio of $1.00 to $10.00) to 9% (the ratio of $1.00 to $11.00).

So forget being a reformer for now, and just accept the system. Besides, I had to learn how all this crap works, so why shouldn't you?

8

Advances and Recoupment

ADVANCES: THE BASIC CONCEPT

Back to Jules and his bulldogs. Our friends at Royal Family charged him a $300 stud fee for the services of Winston. Let's suppose Jules didn't have the $300 (or at least didn't want to invest it in this particular endeavor). So Corky (who is raising the puppies in exchange for 50% of the sales price) comes up with an idea: She agrees to pay Jules the $300, or to pay it directly to Royal Family, and then take her money back from Jules's share of money from the puppies. For example, if the puppies sell for $200 each (so that Corky gets $100 and Jules gets $100 for each dog), Corky would keep Jules's $100 share of the first three puppies ($300) to get back the stud fee.

This is exactly how an **advance** works. The record company pays a sum of money to the artist (the $300 stud fee) and then keeps the artist's royalties (the proceeds from selling the puppies) until it gets its money back. So if a company gives an artist $10,000 to sign a record deal, it keeps the first $10,000 of artist's royalties that would otherwise be payable. The process of keeping the money to recover an *advance* is called **recoupment,** and we say an advance is **recoupable** from royalties. The amount of unrecouped monies is called your **deficit** or **red position** (from the accounting use of red ink to signify a business loss), since this is the amount that has to be recovered before you get paid. So if you got a $100,000 advance and earned $75,000 in royalties, you have *recouped* $75,000 of the advance, and your *deficit* is $25,000 (you are $25,000 *in the red*, or $25,000 *unrecouped*). Once you recoup, you are said to be **in the black.**

Here's another way to look at it:

When I grew up in Texas, it was a big deal to drive just outside the city and see the huge water tanks with the names of towns painted on the side. (It takes very little to make me happy.) In fact, Farmer's

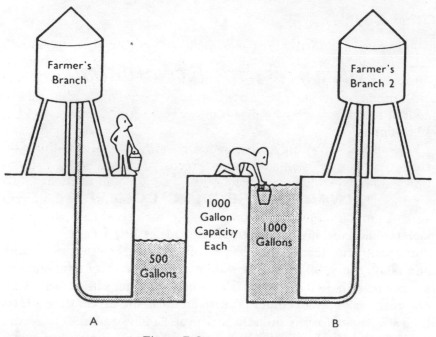

Figure 7. Separate accounts.

Branch, a city outside Dallas, had a water tower that was a major local site. (Not as big as its post office, however, because the sign there said FARMER'S BRANCH BRANCH. Honest.) Anyway, picture a water tower with a large connecting pipe that runs deep into the ground. The connecting pipe feeds into a narrow dry well that needs a thousand gallons of water to fill it up to ground level. If there were no other access to the water, you'd have to wait until the water tower filled the well up to ground level (that is, until a thousand gallons had been poured in) before you could get any water. If there were only five hundred gallons, you couldn't reach it (see Illustration A in Figure 7 above), but when another five hundred gallons was added, you could (see Illustration B).

Recoupment works exactly the same way. The water represents your sales, and the ditch is your deficit account. If you got a $1,000 advance from the record company, your account is $1,000 unrecouped. Until you earn $1,000 of royalties (i.e., until you have enough water to fill the well), you don't get anything. Just like the first thousand gallons of water have to fill the hole before you can get a drink, the record company keeps the first $1,000 in royalties to get its money back before you get any royalties.

Other Goodies

Monies paid directly to the artist are not the only recoupable monies. Recording costs are also recoupable from royalties, and so are some portion of video production costs, independent promotion (see page 150), monies paid on behalf of the artist (for example, to buy equipment or to support a personal appearance tour), and anything else not nailed down.

Recoupable recording costs include everything you can think of, which is often a page-long list in your record deal. It's not just studio time; it includes equipment rental, travel, arranging, instrument transportation, etc. It also includes **union scale** (*scale* means the minimum amount a union requires everyone to pay its members) paid to you and others to perform at recording sessions.

In addition to a specific list of recoupable stuff (like cash to you, recording costs, and video costs), almost every contract has a general provision that says all amounts 'paid to you or on your behalf, or otherwise paid in connection with this agreement' are recoupable unless the contract specifically provides otherwise. You can feel the history jumping from the pages on this one—Charlie Artist asked his company to advance the cost of a trip to see his mom, and then argued the money was non-recoupable because the contract didn't say it was recoupable. This of course is wrong, but the above broad language solution is overbearing and overkill—sort of like using a sledgehammer to squash a fly (which is effective, but messes up the kitchen). In fact, there are a number of costs paid on your behalf or in connection with the agreement that are never recouped under industry custom. These include such things as manufacturing costs, advertising, marketing, shipping, etc. In practice, the companies don't abuse this language, but I like to carve out the items I just ticked off, together with my own broad language, saying they can't recoup amounts that are 'customarily nonrecoupable in the industry.'

Risk of Loss

What happens if you don't sell enough records to get back the full amount of the advance? With very rare exceptions, advances are **nonreturnable,** which means it's totally the record company's risk. So if you don't sell any records, it will never get back its advances. (This *nonreturnable* aspect is also significant because it means advances are taxable income when you get them, as opposed to when they're recouped.)

CROSS-COLLATERALIZATION

An important concept tied to recoupment is that of **cross-collateralization.** Remember the illustration on page 86, where there are two towers side-by-side, and two 1,000-gallon wells? The water tank for one of the wells contains exactly one thousand gallons, which means the well is full and the water usable. But the other tank has only five hundred gallons, so you can't reach the water. Suppose we dug a hole in the ground connecting these two wells. In that case, the same 1,500 gallons (five hundred from Well A and one thousand from Well B) would be distributed evenly between the wells (750 gallons in each), and you couldn't reach the water in either of them (see Figure 8 below).

Cross-collateralization works exactly the same way, and it's built into every deal. Let's assume you get a $100,000 advance for album number 1, plus another $100,000 for album number 2. Let's further assume album number 1 earns royalties of $10,000, and album number 2 earns royalties of $120,000.

If the two albums were *not* cross-collateralized (the two wells were not connected), you would get nothing for album number 1 (it only

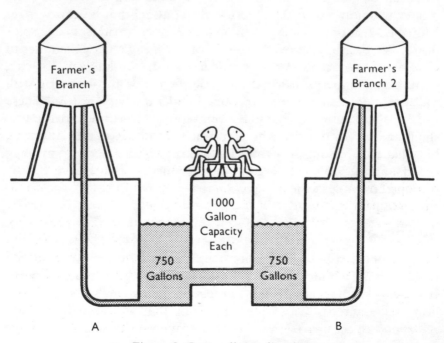

Figure 8. Cross-collateralization.

earned back $10,000 of the $100,000 advance, so it's $90,000 unrecouped), but you would be paid $20,000 for album number 2 (the $20,000 earned in excess of the $100,000 needed to recoup the $100,000 advance). However, this only happens in Fairyland. In the real world, the two albums are *always* cross-collateralized (i.e., the wells are connected), which means the entire $200,000 deficit ($100,000 for each album) is recouped from the entire $130,000 earnings ($10,000 from album number 1 plus $120,000 from album number 2). Accordingly, your account is $70,000 unrecouped ($200,000 less $130,000), and this deficit carries forward against the next album(s).

Cross-collateralization of Deals

Besides referring to royalties and recoupment on different albums, cross-collateralization can also refer to different agreements. These can be simultaneous agreements (for example, an artist signing a recording and publishing agreement with the same company), or they can be sequential (such as an artist who, at the end or renegotiation of one record agreement, signs a new deal with the same company). In either case, the concept is that advances under either agreement can be recouped from royalties under both. This is *never* good for the artist. NEVER.

Most companies include language in their form contract that automatically cross-collateralizes the deal with all other deals. Major record companies don't really try to cross-collateralize a record deal with a publishing deal, but small labels may (see page 270). However, everyone tries to cross-collateralize *sequentially,* meaning that advances under your current recording deal are cross-collateralized with royalties under past and future record deals, and vice versa. The language that does this is buried innocently in the recoupment language and can easily be missed by the untrained eye. It says that advances can be recouped from royalties payable, and royalties can be used to recoup advances paid, 'under this *or any other agreement.*' (Your eye is now trained—so don't miss it!) I've been reasonably successful in knocking this language out of artists' first deals by arguing that the issue should be discussed later, if and when there is a second contract. My argument is that there is no other deal to cross-collateralize with, and until there is, the language is meaningless. That reduces the point down to who is more likely to forget about it—the artist or the company—at the time of the new deal. (Don't worry: The company won't forget.)

9

Real-Life Numbers

OVERVIEW

Let's start to plug some real industry figures into these concepts. Before we get into specific numbers, however, you should know they are continually changing, and that they're affected by when the deal is made. Here's the Passman Theory of Record Industry Cycles:

1. The record business is a cyclical business, and by that I don't just mean they sell more records at Christmas (which they do). What I mean is that, contrary to other entertainment industries (which tend to do well in bad economic times), the music business follows the general economic cycle. When the economy is depressed, sales drop; when it booms, so do we.

2. In addition, the industry follows a cycle that it creates itself, as bargaining power shifts back and forth between companies and artists. In periods of prosperity, the companies work each other into a feeding frenzy and bid the price of artists through the roof. During this time, there are plenty of artists willing to oblige, and they negotiate agreements under which record companies have a gigantic downside risk but only a minimal upside potential. (Record companies can't be wrong about too many of these deals, because one loser can eat up several winners.) Also, during these times, new artists don't tend to do very well; when a record company has huge investments in superstar talent, you can guess where their priorities are. So new artists get ignored, despite the fact that they are the lifeblood of the business.

3. This cycle moves along swimmingly until there is an economic downturn. This can be either a general downturn in world prosperity, or simply a period of belt-tightening because the companies aren't making enough profits. At this point the limousines and parties come to an abrupt halt; the executives who

haven't been fired start flying coach; and the record company gets sold to a foreign power. Next comes a period of contraction, where artists get dropped by the carload (meaning their options aren't exercised—see page 108 for what options are), the companies stop bidding so hard against each other, and the deals move in the other direction. Ironically, this is a good time for new artists, because their deals are cheap, and cheap is in.

As with any generalization, there are always exceptions. Even when the stock market is at its worst, some company is always hitting its new high, and even in the worst of times, some artists are getting record deals (pun intended). But even these exceptions are not as rich as they would have been in good times, for the simple reason that no one is selling as many records. This is usually because consumers aren't parting with their money (since they don't have as much), but it may also be for other reasons, such as consumer dollars going into other forms of entertainment (for example, computers, video games, blockbuster movies, etc.), the current rave of Internet piracy, or the companies' putting out lousy music.

4. Following the gloom, the industry begins its recovery, and we start all over again (or, as musicians say, 'D.C. al Coda').

Despite the doomsayers when times are bad (and the doomsayers when times are good), now that I've lived through several up/down cycles, I'm certain the music business is a long-term major industry. We will go through changes—as I'm sure you know, the Internet has shaken things up to a fare-thee-well—but the bottom line is that records (whether sold as CDs or a series of squeaks over some wire or satellite) are one of the cheapest forms of permanent entertainment you can buy. Music is one of the few things that enhance other activities (as opposed to a motion picture or a book, for example, which require your total concentration), and the power of music to vividly conjure feelings, visions, and emotions is staggering. (I still can't listen to Johnny Mathis's *Greatest Hits* without thinking of slow [and close] dancing as a teenager. Am I dating myself?)

What's Your Clout?

And now, back to earth.

To discuss the range of real numbers, we have to know how strong your bargaining power is. Broadly, I'll divide it into three categories:

New Artist. This is someone who has never before had a record deal, or someone who has been signed but never sold over 250,000 or so albums per release. It can also mean an artist who was once successful but lost his or her following and is having difficulty finding a record deal (or, as one of my clients lovingly put it, someone who has 'crashed and burned').

Midlevel Artist or New Artist with a Bidding War. Either (1) an artist whose last album sold in the 750,000 to 1,500,000 range; or (2) a new artist being chased by a lot of labels. When a number of companies are chasing an unsigned artist, it's not uncommon for the deal to look like a midlevel deal, and on occasion even higher. I'm aware of one situation where an unsigned artist was offered over $1,000,000 for two albums. (Just so you don't get too jealous, that artist's records have only had mediocre success.)

Superstar. Sales from 2,500,000 into the stratosphere. (If you're between 1,500,000 and 2,500,000 your deal will be in between midlevel and superstar.)

A mid-level artist in the U.K. is someone who has sold in the range of 100,000 to 150,000 albums in the U.K., and a superstar is someone who has sold 500,000 plus. The levels are lower than those in the U.S. for the simple reason that you have fewer inhabitants. However, the quality and taste of U.K. buyers is clearly state of the art.

These categories are only rough approximations, as there are so many variables. For example, you might be a midlevel artist but have six record companies chasing you and bidding each other up, which means you'll get a superstar deal. On the other hand, you may be a relatively successful artist who is perceived as 'out of step' with 'what's happening,' so you therefore get only a lukewarm reception. But we gotta start somewhere, and this range is close enough for rock 'n' roll.

For your point of reference, a **gold album** is one that sells 500,000 U.S. units, and a **platinum album** is one that sells 1 million U.S. units (see page 90 for gold and platinum singles). The sales figures are certified by the RIAA (Recording Industry Association of America, an industry group comprised of record companies), which awards *gold* or *platinum* status. We also have an industry joke that bombs are 'certified lead.' And since we're on the topic of grading a record's performance, you may have heard the term **bullets.** Each of the major trades (see page 17 for who they are) have charts that rank records numerically based on sales and/or airplay. A *bullet* is a dot or a star next to a record's number on the chart, and it means the record is moving up strongly. The lack of one means it's weakening or on its way down. So 'Number 1 with a Bullet' is the best you can do. And of course there's an industry joke for turkeys: 'Number 99 with an Anchor.'

The determination of gold and platinum is not nearly so simple in the U.K. For starters, you have a third precious metal (silver). Here's the scoop:

1. **Albums:**
   (a) LPs and cassettes with a PPD of £3.50 or more, and CDs of £6.00 or more:

Silver	60,000
Gold	100,000
Platinum	300,000

   (b) LPs and cassettes with a PPD of £3.49 or under and CDs of £5.99 or under:

Silver	120,000
Gold	200,000
Platinum	700,000

2. **Singles:**

Silver	200,000
Gold	400,000
Platinum	600,000

ROYALTIES

Range of Royalties

Using the above categories, and bearing in mind that different record companies will have somewhat different computations (meaning these percentages will be worth different pennies at different places), the following is the current industry norm for royalties on United States album sales:

1. **New Artist Signing to Independent Company:**
   10% to 15% of SRLP. (See page 67 for what an independent company is, and page 72 for what SRLP is.) As we'll discuss on page 189, you may do a deal in which you get a percentage of the label's royalty instead of a set rate.

2. **New Artist Signing to Major or Mini-major:**
   13% to 16% of SRLP.

3. **Midlevel:**
   15% to 17% of SRLP.

4. **Superstar:**
   18% to 20% or more of SRLP (royalties over 20% are rare). Also at this level, with an enormous amount of clout, you can sometimes make an off-center deal like a joint venture (see page 198), or even a distribution deal where the artist owns the masters (see page 201).

If the company computes royalties on wholesale, you should roughly double the above figures (see page 72).

Compact Disc Royalties

You'll be thrilled to hear that the above royalty rates, and the computations in Chapter 7, are for analog (meaning non-digital) cassette tapes. This of course raises the question of what kind of weirdo spends several pages telling you how to compute royalties for a configuration that sleeps with the fishes. Well, the answer is that the dudes at record companies are even weirder than I am, and still write their contracts on the basis of cassette royalties. They then do the following for CDs:

1. The royalty rate for compact discs is a reduced percentage of the cassette rate. For example, your CD rate might be 75% to 85% (depending on the company and your bargaining power) of the cassette rate. So if you had a 10% royalty, you'd get 7.5% to 8.5% on CDs. Sometimes you can get an escalation (say to 90%) for later albums, or maybe based on sales.

2. The computation of Suggested Retail List Price for compact discs varies from company to company. Some companies use the actual SRLP, but most use an artificial price which, shock-

ingly, comes out to less than the SRLP. This is done with something called an **uplift** of the wholesale price, meaning they multiply the wholesale price by a percentage (130% for all the majors) to create what's known as a **constructed retail price.**

3. The packaging deduction on compact discs is 25%, as opposed to 20% for analog cassettes, and 10% for vinyl. (OK—you got me. I used a 25% packaging in my examples, so they weren't strictly a cassette calculation. But the royalty rates I gave you are for cassettes.)

4. At least one company charges an extra 5% of normal distributor free goods (i.e., a total of 20% for CDs, when they only charge 15% for analog cassettes); see page 76 for what normal distributor free goods are.

In researching this edition of the book, I contacted all of the major record companies and asked how they computed compact disc royalties. As it turns out, almost every one of them did it differently. They asked me not to give out the precise methods they use, but it doesn't really matter because the methods change over time, and they're subject to negotiation. Also, there are so many variables that anything you change in the equation affects the result. For example, you might have an extra 5% free goods, but the CD royalty might be a larger percentage of retail than that of a competitor. Or they may use a lesser Suggested Retail List Price, but pay you a higher royalty rate.

The real lesson is that, if you're considering signing with a company, you must sit down and make them walk you through their compact disc royalty calculations. This is the only way you can really figure out what your royalty is worth.

Here's a couple of examples:

Assuming that an artist has a 10% royalty rate, and the company pays 85% of this for compact discs (8.5%):

Suggested Retail Price	$18.98
Less: 25% Packaging	−4.75
Royalty Base	$14.23
Royalty Rate	× 8.5%
ROYALTY (ROUNDED TO PENNY)	**$1.21**

If a company uses a *constructed wholesale price*, here's the same computation:

Wholesale Price	$14.14
Uplift Factor	× 130%
Imputed Retail Price	$18.38 [*NOTE:* Less than $18.98 in prior example]
Less: 25% Packaging	−4.60
Royalty Base	$13.78
Royalty Rate	× 8.5%
ROYALTY (ROUNDED TO PENNY)	**$1.17**

As you can see, there is a difference (often even more of a difference) between the number of pennies you get for compact discs from two companies paying the same analog cassette royalty rate. So it's always a good idea to compute your royalties in pennies and give yourself a dose of reality. Also, if you have multiple offers, this is the only way to truly compare proposals—apples to apples. You wouldn't want to later find your apple was a persimmon.

As I noted implicitly on page 73, and which I'll now make explicit, you kind folk of the United Kingdom have not stooped to these shenanigans when computing CD royalties. Rather, you simply use a percentage of PPD after deducting a packaging charge, without any uplifts or reductions in rates.

Observe:

Compact Disc Royalty	
Published dealer price	£8.00
Less: packaging (25%)	−2.00
ROYALTY BASE	**£6.00**

Thus a 10% royalty would give you 60p. Clean, simple, lovely.

However, when it comes to new technologies, the U.K. companies still clip the artists for a reduction to 80% to 85% of the CD rate, for the same reasons as the U.S. folk.

Singles are typically at a lower royalty rate, on the theory that record companies make very little profit on singles (which is true). The singles rate is normally three-quarters of the album rate, but it tops out in the 10% to 12% range, occasionally up to 14% for superstars. New artists can, with some bargaining power, get to the 10% range no matter what their overall rate, and it may be possible to get escalations in your singles royalties based on sales of singles (in the United States only).

By the way, the sales of singles are shrinking substantially. Several years ago, the 'gold' award for a single was dropped from 1 million to 500,000 units, and the 'platinum' award was dropped from 2 million to 1 million. Moreover, very few records are actually manufactured as singles these days. Most of what we think of as 'singles' are merely serviced to radio and MTV. Apart from being unprofitable, the companies believe selling singles cuts into album sales—if people can get their favorite song cheaply, they may not buy the album.

Escalations

It's also common to escalate royalties based on sales of records. Typical escalations are .5% to 1% at some level between 500,000 and 1 million album sales, and another .5% to 1% at 500,000 to 1 million albums beyond that point. For example, if your royalty is 12%, it might escalate to 13% for sales over 500,000, and to 14% for sales over 1 million. The lower your royalty rate, the sooner you can expect the escalations to kick in, and in fact you may even be able to get a third bump. These escalated rates usually top out around the 14% to 15% range for new artists (10% to 13% if you're signed to an independent label), 18% for midlevel, and 20% to 21% for superstars. Sometimes, you can get the company to agree that your royalty for the next album starts at the highest rate achieved by the former one. For example, suppose your royalty was 14%, and you had a 1% escalation (to 15%) at 500,000, and another 1% (to 16%) at 1,000,000. If the first album sells 1,000,000, then the second album would start at 16%, and the 1% escalations would be on top of that (to 17% and 18%). The companies put a cap on these escalations, to make sure you don't go past the 19% or 20% range.

Escalations are based on royalty bearing units, which means (since virtually all companies pay on 85% of net sales) that only 85% of the records sold at retail, less the 'real' free goods, count toward your escalation (see page 73). Also, the escalations are on an album-by-album basis (meaning that if the first album sells 10 million, it doesn't escalate the royalty on the second), though you can sometimes get a small bump on the next record based on sales of the prior album, or based on an average of the prior two albums' sales.

These escalations only apply to sales occurring after the level is reached, and are called **prospective** escalations. For example, if you have 16% on the first 1 million units, escalating to 17% thereafter, you don't get 17% on the first 1 million. If you have sufficient bargaining power, you can sometimes get the escalations on prior sales (called a **retroactive** escalation). This is rare, and when you can get it, it is usually for stratospheric sales. For example, at sales of 4 million units, you might get an increase on the first 1 million.

Escalations apply only to full-priced retail sales, through normal retail (record store) channels. Typically, escalations are limited to sales in the United States, but as your bargaining power goes up, so does your ability to get escalations in other major territories (such as Canada and certain European markets) based on sales in those markets.

A common escalation in the U.K. would be 1% at platinum (sales of 300,000 units) and another 1% at double platinum (600,000 units).

Unlike the U.S., it's more common to get escalations for sales in territories outside your home country. This is usually for the major territories (U.S., Germany, France, Japan, etc.), and usually a territory-by-territory basis. A typical escalation might be 1% at gold, and another 1% at platinum. Sometimes you can get an escalation based on total sales outside the U.K. For example, 1% at 500,000, and another 1% at 1,000,000.

Royalties for artists in the U.K. are about the same as those in the U.S. However, since they're on PPD, you should increase the figures by about 130%.

'All-in'

The above royalties are known by the technical term **all-in,** which means the artist is responsible, out of his or her royalty, for paying the record producer and mixer. (Producers' and mixers' roles and how they're paid are discussed in Chapter 11. However, I suggest you wait till we get there before tackling how they're paid unless you're already pretty familiar with royalties.) The practice of paying artists an *all-in* rate began in the early 1970s, and is now the industry norm (excluding a few oddball situations, mostly in country music). Producers are paid a U.S. royalty in the range of 3% to 4% of SRLP. Some producers, who become 'superstars' in their own right by producing hugely successful records, can get 5% or (very rarely) 6%. Accordingly, the all-in rate is not what the artist puts in his or her pocket; that amount is the all-in rate *minus* the amount paid to the producer, which is called the **net rate.**

Partnership Deals

There's a bubbling trend in the industry, which has happened only rarely at the time of this writing, where record companies essentially become the artist's 'partner' not only in records, but also in touring, merchandising, publishing, and other sources of income. This is a completely different economic model, and we'll discuss it later (on page 96).

The range of producer royalties in the U.K. is basically the same as in the U.S., adjusted upwards for PPD by 110% to 130%, as we discussed on page 74 for artist royalties.

ADVANCES

In the 1950s, artists would go to the studio, sing their little hearts out, and have almost no other involvement in the creative process. In those days, companies paid the artist a set amount of money as an advance (for example, $10,000 for an album). The record company in addition paid the recording costs (which, remember, are recoupable from royalties, just like an advance), and everybody went their separate ways. It took maybe two weeks to do an album; three if you were a perfectionist.

Funds

Today, most recording agreements are structured as **funds.** A *fund* is a set amount of money, which includes both recording costs and any amounts that may be payable to the artist as an advance (the term *recording costs* also includes the producer's advance, which we'll discuss later). Whatever the artist doesn't spend on recording costs goes into his or her pocket. For example, if the recording fund for an album is $200,000, and the recording costs are $150,000, the artist would pocket $50,000 as an 'advance.' On the other hand, if the recording costs are $200,000, the artist pockets nothing.

Here's a rough range of recording funds:

1. **New Artist Signing to Independent Company:**
   $5,000 to $125,000. (See the discussion below for more detail.)
2. **New Artist Signing to Major or Mini-major:**
   $175,000 to $300,000, or even up to $500,000 if you're really hot.
3. **Midlevel:**
   $300,000 to $600,000, with a few particularly hot situations kicking up to the $1,000,000 range.
4. **Superstar:**
   $1,500,000 and up. It's not unusual for a major artist's fund to run into multimillions of dollars. At this level, funds are computed on the basis of past track record and future expectations, as well as on the bidding in the marketplace.

Recording funds in the U.K. tend to be higher than those in the U.S. (go figure).

1. **New artist signing to independent company:**
   £10,000 to £50,000.
2. **New artist signing to major or mini-major:**
   £100,000 to £200,000.
3. **Mid-level:**
   £150,000 to £300,000.
4. **Superstar:**
   can soar into the stratosphere, just like in the U.S., at £750,000 plus.

Unlike in the U.S., not all deals are funds. The others are a fixed advance plus recording costs (as we discussed on page 98). In this case, the range of advances is:

1. **New artist:**
   £50,000 to £75,000.
2. **Mid-level:**
   £75,000 to £100,000.

3. **Superstar:**
   £200,000+.

The company then pays recording costs in addition to these amounts.

Advances

An exception to this is the pop world (balladeers, crooners, adolescent boy-bands, and the like), where it's not uncommon for artists to have pure advances and a mutually approved recording budget. In these deals, the advances are obviously much lower, perhaps in the $25,000 to $75,000 range for a new artist, up to $125,000 to $250,000 for midrange artists. Superstars can of course be in the stratosphere.

New Artist/Independent Company Funds

Let's take a closer look at funds paid by independent labels. (See page 67 for what an 'independent' is.) When you're a brand-new artist and can't get signed to a major label (or in fact even get their attention), your best alternative to busing tables may well be signing with an independent. However, unless you're dealing with an independent owned by an industry 'biggie,' such as a major producer or manager, doing deals at this level is really shopping in the Kmart of the music biz. You're not going to get a lot of money, and your album will be recorded, shall we say, 'economically.' So, as noted above, expect an album fund of anywhere from $5,000 (for this price range I strongly suggest a kazoo chorus) up to the equivalent of what you could get from a major label. However, albums at this level typically don't exceed funds of $50,000 to $75,000.

These deals often mean you'll be working with less sophisticated studios, producers, engineers, etc. However, 'cheap' and 'unsophisticated' don't mean 'lousy.' In fact, many low-budget records have an energy that is totally lost in slick, highly produced recordings. Most people recording low-budget product are the most excited and enthused about their music, willing to make records for the devil if necessary to get ahead. (As you probably know, we have no shortage of devils in the music biz.)

Budget Problems

If your fund is $200,000, what keeps you from recording a super-cheapo album for $25,000 and pocketing $175,000? In virtually all of these deals, unless you have a lot of bargaining power, the record company has to approve your recording cost budget for precisely this reason. Well, partly for this reason. Actually, they're more worried about the other end—that you'll have an unrealistically low budget and not be able to finish your album for less than the fund. This is particularly common with new artists, because their funds are low. Albums can easily cost $150,000 or more, and this is often the entire fund. Moreover, if you're using producers of any note, this can radically jack up the budget. As we'll see when we get to Chapter 11, top producers can get advances of $25,000 or more per *master* (in addition to the recording costs for that master), and I'm sure you can see how quickly this turns into the gigantic sucking sound of a money vacuum.

So what happens when you've spent your full recording fund and have three-quarters of an album? Most of the time the record companies pay to finish the record, under the age-old business strategy of 'What the hell are we going to do with three-quarters of an album?' However, they will grumble and stomp the floor in the process, and, if they do pay, they'll deduct the excess from your next album's recording fund, from your publishing royalties (I'll explain what those are later), and from anything else they can think of. Almost all recording contracts require you to write a check for the excess, but in practice this can't happen with a new artist (who doesn't have the money), and rarely happens with a superstar (whose feathers they don't want to ruffle by asking).

Formulas

If you know enough to ask for it, a substantial number of record companies will agree to something called a **formula** for advances. This is a mechanism designed to automatically increase (or decrease) your deal if you're successful (or a flop). It works like this:

Your advance for the second album is equal to a percentage (usually 60% to 70%) of all royalties *earned* (as opposed to paid) by the first album under the agreement. The advance for album number three is a percentage of album number two's earnings, and so forth. Thus, for example, if the first album earns $1,000,000 in royalties and you have a 60% *formula*, the advance for album number two is $600,000.

The formula percentage is usually based only on earnings in the United States, or sometimes the United States and Canada. The earnings are also limited in time (usually six to eighteen months after release), so that sales trickling in over a two- or three-year period won't increase the advance for an artist who is slow in delivery. The last thing a company wants to do is reward late delivery.

Variations include delaying a formula until the third or a later album; averaging the earnings of the previous two albums (as opposed to using the earnings only of the previous one); and a limitation (or elimination) of reserves for purposes of determining the formula (reserves are discussed on page 76, and reserve limitations are on page 148).

But what, you say, if the first album is a dismal failure, and earns only $20,000? How can anyone make an album for $12,000 to $14,000 (60% to 70% of the $20,000)? Well, you can't, so this is handled by establishing a **floor** for the formula. This means that no matter how lousy the earnings of the previous album, the fund will be no less than an agreed amount (the *floor*). Not surprisingly, as soon as record companies hear the word 'floor,' they think of a concept called a **ceiling,** which means that no matter how wildly successful the prior album, the fund won't exceed an agreed dollar figure. (The prospect of owing you $4,000,000 for an album makes them nervous.)

Both the floors and *ceilings* normally escalate for later albums, varying with the bargaining power of the parties. Here's a set of floors and ceilings I got in a recent new artist deal:

LP No.	Floor	Ceiling
1	$175,000	(no formula)
2	$200,000	$400,000
3	$225,000	$450,000
4	$275,000	$550,000
5	$350,000	$700,000
6	$400,000	$800,000

Don't get excited about the big numbers for the last albums. The company isn't really committed to them, as you'll see on page 108.

The U.K. companies also use formulas, and often you can negotiate for your formula to be based on worldwide sales (not just U.K. sales). This is more advantageous than the U.S. formula, which is limited to U.S. sales. The percentage for determing the funds ranges from 66⅔% to 75%. Usually it's limited to sales during one year after release.

When artists receive an advance *(not* a recording fund), the formula percentage is of course much less, usually in the 15% to 20% range. The floors and ceilings for option years would go up in roughly the same percentages as the funds, and follow the same general formula of the ceiling being twice the floor. For example, a formula for the third album might be 15% of the prior album's earnings, not less than $125,000, nor more than $250,000.

CAREER CO-VENTURES

At the time of this writing, the music business is having a rough go. See page 90 for the Passman Theory of Record Industry Cycles, which incidentally was written long before the current dump (and will be applicable in the future as we cycle in and out of these things, despite widespread belief that the industry is finished every time we hit a trough).

At any rate, most of the major record companies are having horrendous losses, and all of them are firing people, cutting costs, and doing everything else people do when times get bad. In the search for new ways to make money, a number of companies are considering something called a **career co-venture** (that's not an industry term; I'm just grabbing one company's words for this). There has only been one of these deals signed (at least insofar as the press reports go) at the time of this writing, so the first few lines are only now being sketched on the canvas, and it's hard for me to give you any real idea what these deals will be. The basic concept looks something like this:

We, the record company, give you more money under your record deal, in exchange for which you give us a piece of your earnings in areas we've never before shared: songwriting, touring, merchandising, advertising, sponsorships, etc. I'm sure they'll also be looking for film, television, book publishing, and perhaps a share of your harmonica collection as well. The company then gives you an advance (hopefully larger than you would get under a record deal) against all these sources of income.

The percentages are all over the place. I know some companies want to be equal partners, meaning they'll give you 50% of their record profits, and take 50% of your earnings. Others have offered a smaller percentage (say 35%) of their profits on records, and asked for a smaller percentage (say 20% to 35%) of your other areas. (Don't take these percentages as gospel; as I said, I'm not aware of the specific terms of any deal that's been done. I've just heard these numbers bandied around). Still other companies want to pay a higher royalty on records (meaning you get a bigger traditional royalty, not a share of the profits), and take an even smaller percentage of your other earnings.

In addition to the percentage split, there are a lot of complicated issues to work out. For example, since the deal isn't just based on records, can the company exercise its option to extend the term if your records are a failure but you make huge money touring? Or writing songs for other artists? How much control does the company have over your other activities? Can they decide which agent or manager or lawyer you should hire? When and with whom you can tour? How much you're allowed to run up in touring expenses (it's their money, too)? Which merchandising deal you should take? Which publishing agreement? Does the record company have a right to approve the terms of these non-record deals? How long does the record company share in earnings other than records? Presumably it's for the same period as the record deal, but what about a tour for which contracts are made during the term of the record deal, yet is performed afterward? Or a publishing or merchandising deal made during the term that continues for years afterward?

At present, this is still such a new widget that no one knows the answers. And we have quite a few miles to go before these deals form any kind of industry custom, if in fact they ever get there.

However it shakes out, this is a very serious marriage, clamping serious restrictions on an artist's life. So enter it cautiously . . .

LOOK HOW MUCH YOU ALREADY KNOW

A few years ago, I got a call from a television producer. She was doing a special about the music business, and had stopped people on the street to ask how much they thought an artist made from a gold album (sales of 500,000 units). The guesses ranged from $500,000 to over $2 million, and the producer wanted to know the real answer.

Now you know enough to answer the question the same way I did. Here's what I told her:

If a new artist has an all-in royalty of 14%, an 85% rate on CDs, a 3% producer, recording costs of $300,000, and tour support of $50,000, his or her royalty for sales of 500,000 albums looks something like this:

Suggested Retail Price	$18.98
Less: Packaging (25%)	−4.74
Royalty Base	$14.24
Royalty Rate (14% all-in, less 3% for the producer [11%] × 85% for CD [9.35%])	× 9.35%
Royalty	$1.33
Royalty × 500,000 units	× 500,000
	$ 665,000
Less 15% 'free goods factor'	−99,750
	$ 565,250
Less: Recording Costs	−300,000
Less: 50% of independent promotion	−100,000
Less: 50% of video costs	−75,000
Less: tour support	−50,000
TOTAL	$40,250

As you can see, it's nowhere near the numbers that people on the street believed. And remember that the artist doesn't get a check for this all at once; the company holds back a reserve of at least 35% to 50% in case the records boomerang (see the reserve discussion on page 80). This reserve percentage is applied to the *gross* royalties (i.e., the $565,250 in our example, which is the gross before deducting costs), meaning the artist gets zippo on the first statement.

> If you're on the *Fast Track*,
> go to Chapter 11 on page 125.
> Everyone else, forward ho . . .

IF YOU DON'T UNDERSTAND THE WORDS IN THE BOX, IT MEANS YOU SKIPPED PAGES 7 AND 8. IT ALSO MEANS YOU NEVER READ THE DIRECTIONS WHEN YOU BUY A NEW STEREO.

10

Other Major Deal Points

The other major things you'll want to know about your record deal are 'How much?' and 'How long?' The 'how much' part of this doesn't mean royalties and advances, which we already discussed, but rather the number of albums you have to record. The 'how long' sounds pretty straightforward, but has taken a strange twist over the years.

AMOUNT OF PRODUCT

Pay or Play

Did you know that most record deals don't require the company to even make a record? This is not only true for new artists, but also for midlevel and even superstars. Almost all contracts contain a provision whereby the company, instead of recording the album, can merely pay the artist a sum of money equal to (in the first draft of their agreement) minimum union scale for an album or (after negotiating) the difference between the recording fund and the cost of the last album, or a prenegotiated, set fee. This is called a **pay-or-play** provision, meaning, as the name implies, that the record company has the option either to allow you to 'play your music' or to 'pay you off.'

Apart from beating them up for the most money, be sure that, once they pay you off, the deal is over. This shouldn't be hard to get, but it isn't in any form agreement, and without it the company could in theory hold you without making records. (On the other hand, since they don't want your records, they probably don't want you around either. But it's cheap insurance to add language making sure.)

Options

Record deals are traditionally structured with the company having the smallest obligation that it can negotiate, while keeping the option to get as much product as possible. For example, a company may commit to record one album of an artist and have the option to require an additional five to seven albums, each one at the company's election. Albums to which the company is committed are called **firm** albums. The others are called **optional** or **option albums.**

In the hip-hop world, it's not so uncommon for companies to commit to only two or three masters, which they'll release as singles before deciding whether to go forward with an album. In these deals, the company has the *option* to acquire the rest of an album, then options to continue for an additional four to six albums.

Options in New Artist Deals

With new artists, companies like to commit to only one album, or sometimes only two or three masters (as we just discussed). However, they insist on the right to get a total of five to seven albums over the course of the deal. This is an improvement over recent years—companies used to insist on options for eight to ten albums.

Optional albums might be one at a time for the second and third albums, but thereafter I make the company take at least two albums at a time (or else they have to let the artist go). In other words, the company can opt out of the agreement after the second, or perhaps even third album, but if the deal continues beyond that point, the company must commit to both the fourth and fifth albums before it can again opt out. (If there's one extra left over at the end, they of course only have to commit to that one album.)

Another trend in recent years is for companies to commit to two albums at the beginning of the deal (called **two firm** in industry lingo), but take the right to bail out if the first album tanks. For example, if the first album sells less than 150,000 units in the United States, the company is no longer committed to the second album. Stated another way, the second album is really optional, but the company is required to exercise its option if the first album sells more than 150,000 units.

As we'll discuss in a bit, I'm talking here about the number of newly recorded studio albums you'll have to deliver. This does not include live albums (see page 120), greatest hits albums (see page 118), or the like.

Farm Teams

In baseball, when you're not quite ready to play in the majors, they send you to a minor-league team called a *farm team*. The major teams all have affiliated farm teams (so named, I think, because they use them to grow their players from seeds into turnips, or whatever). In the minors, the scouts watch you in real-game situations, and as soon as you're good enough, they move you up to the majors.

Record companies over the years have developed a similar system. Their farm teams are **demo deals** (sometimes called **development deals**). Under this arrangement the record company gives you some money ($500 to $5,000, sometimes a bit more) to go into a studio and record demos. The term 'demo' is short for 'demonstration recording,' which is less than a full-fledged master but gives the company some idea of what you'll sound like on a professional record. They listen to the demo and then decide whether they want to sign you. If they do, the deal will be along the lines we just discussed for new artists. (We're going to discuss how to protect yourself in *demo deals* later, on page 138.)

Options in Midrange and Superstar Deals

With a midrange artist, or an artist who's the subject of a bidding war, the company typically commits to two albums *firm*, and gets additional options for one or two albums each. It's rare that a company doesn't have the right to at least four albums from this type of artist, and five is the norm. At the superstar level, deals of only three albums are possible, though the norm is four, with two or three of the albums being firm. A few artists (for example, the Eagles and David Bowie) have made deals for one album only, but this is very rare.

Options Aren't Good for You

I remember a friend of mine from the high school choir who came in one day, jubilant, because she had signed a 'ten-album deal' with Capitol Records. In reality, it turned out to be a deal for one single only, and she had merely given Capitol the option to require up to ten albums. While my friend has faded into obscurity after recording that one single, her attitude is not unusual. Many artists still think of record company options as being good for them (the numbers are so high at the end!), but in fact this is never the case. If you're a flop, you'll never see the money; if you're a success, it will probably be less than you're worth. So train yourself to think of options only as the chance for the record company to get out of your deal. They are never good for you.

Making the Best of Options

Despite my high-minded speech, the reality is that you have to live with options at all but superstar levels—this industry custom is too well entrenched to buck. However, since you're giving the company a chance to drop you after each album or two (in other words, to protect their tushies if there's no success), I think you're entitled to more goodies if they keep you. This can be done in two different ways:

Royalties.   For optional albums, you should get increased royalties. Typically, the increase is around .5% to 1%, both in your basic rate and in any escalated rates. For example, I recently did a midlevel deal that looked like this:

LP No.	Royalty on Sales of 0–500,000 Albums	Royalty on Sales of 500,001– 1,000,000 Albums	Royalty on Sales of 1,000,001– 1,500,000 Albums	Royalty on Sales of 1,500,001– 2,000,000 Albums	Royalty on Sales of 2,000,000+ Albums
1	17%	17.5%	18%	18.5%	19%
2	17%	17.5%	18%	18.5%	19%
3	18%	18.5%	19%	19.5%	20%
4	18%	18.5%	19%	19.5%	20%
5	19%	19%	19%	19.5%	20%
6	19%	19%	19.5%	20%	20%

Under this deal, if any particular album achieved an escalation, the next album would start at that escalated level. For example, if album one sold 2,000,000 units, album two would start at 19%, then would escalate ½ point at 500,000 units, etc. However, there was a cap of 20% on the overall royalties, no matter what the sales were.

Funds.   You should also get increased recording funds for optional albums. Page 103 cites an example of a new artist deal, and here's the numbers from a midlevel deal:

LP No.	Floor	Ceiling
1	$300,000	(no formula)
2	$300,000	$600,000
3	$350,000	$700,000
4	$350,000	$700,000
5	$400,000	$800,000
6	$400,000	$800,000

Don't the numbers look delicious in the later option periods? What a great deal! What a genius negotiator! DON'T BE FOOLED! OPTIONS ARE *NEVER* GOOD FOR YOU!! They only mean you'll get dropped if you're not worth the price, or you'll get too little if you're a smash. So repeat after me: 'OPTIONS ARE *NEVER* GOOD FOR ME!!!' Now write it on the blackboard twenty-five times.

HOW LONG?

Term

How long the record company keeps you under an exclusive agreement is called the **term** of your deal. Record deals used to be for a *term* of one year, with options to renew for additional periods of one year each. The artist was usually obligated to deliver two albums each year. This worked terrifically in the days when records were banged out like pancakes, since most of the time the artists just showed up, sang, then went back to the beach. As we discussed, in those days it was not unusual to make an album in two weeks (three if the artist was a prima donna). But all this has gone the way of the dinosaurs.

Every contract is a history lesson, and the clauses dealing with the length of deals have had a particularly colorful past. Behind each clause is a story that ends with 'I'm going to write language so that, if this ever happens again, I won't get shafted.' And unraveling these bits of history can be fun, so let's take a look.

Late Delivery of Albums

As artists took more creative control, albums began to take longer to make. Indeed, the more successful the artist, the longer (with rare exception) the recording process. Today, periods of years between albums are not at all unusual for superstars (or for flakes at any level).

Many reasons for this are legitimate—if an album is successful, you need to be out touring and promoting it, which means you can't be in the studio. In fact, the more successful it is, the longer you'll be out touring and promoting, and the record company won't even want you to start the second album.

However, many of these delays don't have such a noble purpose. I'm convinced (but can't prove) that one of the reasons for delay is that artists, particularly following a major success, are a bit frightened to put out their next record. When it's actually released, they have to find out whether it's as successful as the prior one; until then, it's only speculation and their track record stays intact. So, they continue to fine-tune, tweak, poke, rerecord, ponder, rethink, etc., which delays the day of reckoning. And second albums are particularly troublesome. It's interesting to realize that someone's first album can actually be ten years or more in the making. This is because they were accumulating songs for a long time before they ever got a record deal, and thus had a huge catalog to choose from in making the first album. However, when the artist gets to the second album, all the cherries have been picked, so it's a matter of writing new material or going into the second tier of old stuff. And this process now has to take place within a year or two, as opposed to the unlimited time that preceded the first album. So there is much more pressure.

Record companies historically solved this slow-delivery problem by having the right to extend the term of the agreement if an album wasn't delivered on time. In other words, if your album was six months late, the current one-year term of your deal was extended by six months. This worked terrifically until Olivia Newton-John filed a suit against MCA Records seeking termination of her agreement. (The case cite is 90 Cal.App 3d. 18 [1979], for you technical freaks who like to read court cases.) In this case, she argued that her deal should be limited to the actual number of years stated in the contract, without regard to any extensions. In other words, since her contract was for a two-year term with three one-year options (a total of five years), she argued that MCA could not enforce the deal beyond five years from the start date, even though she had not given them all the product due. To everyone's surprise, the court (sort of) agreed. It reduced the duration of MCA's injunction (meaning the order saying she couldn't record for anyone else) to the five years, rather than allowing any extensions. However, I say 'sort of' because the five years weren't over at the time of the case, and so the court technically didn't deal with the issue in full. Nonetheless, the case's language was strong enough to make all the companies nervous, and it forever changed the way record contracts are drawn.

Nowadays, the terms of record deals are not stated in specific time periods like one or two years. Instead, the contracts say each period ends six to nine months after delivery of the last album required for that period, and can be no less than a specified time period (e.g., eighteen months). For example, if you have to make two albums, the period might start upon the signing of your deal and end six months after delivery of the second album, but no sooner than eighteen months after signing.

This language nicely solves the Olivia Newton-John problem, but the companies had to add additional provisions to deal with these little snippets of history: In 1970, Dean Martin signed an agreement with Warner Bros. Records. The agreement was unusual for those days (although it is the norm today) because the term continued until delivery of all the albums. Approximately six years later, after everyone had forgotten about him, Dino came in and announced he was about to start recording a new album (for which he expected the substantial amount of money specified in the contract). This sent Warner into a tizzy, since Mr. Martin's star was not of the same brightness as when he signed the agreement, and they began scrambling to find a way out. So Dino sued them. Ultimately the case was settled, but it taught the companies a lesson—that contracts shouldn't be geared only to delivery of albums, or else they can go on forever. Accordingly, you will now find provisions stating that, if the artist has not delivered an album within a certain period of time after delivery of the previous album (usually nine to eighteen months, depending on bargaining power), the company can get out of the deal.

At the other end of the spectrum comes a history lesson from Frank Zappa. Also picking on our friends at Warner Bros. Records (so that they could have the distinction of being clobbered with both ends of the same stick), Mr. Zappa showed up one day with four albums under his arm. He said he was delivering all the remaining product required under his deal, and thus was free to sign elsewhere. As you can imagine, this didn't go over much better than Mr. Martin did.

The Zappa lesson is now handled by stating that you can't start recording an LP until you have delivered the prior album, and that the new album can't be delivered sooner than six months after delivery of the prior album. Record companies have a legitimate point in saying they don't have to take more than one album at a time, on the basis that (a) they can't reasonably market more than one album at a time;

and (b) if they put an album on the shelf for later release, it may not be in touch with the trends in the music business (which, in case you haven't noticed, change hourly) at the time of release.

MEGA DEALS

Background. Over the years, there have been a number of 'mega deals' in the music business that I'm sure you've read about. Mariah Carey, Janet Jackson, R.E.M., Robbie Williams, Michael Jackson, Prince, Madonna, U2, etc., have all had multimillion-dollar extravaganzas.

What's the truth behind all of these? Well, first you need to know about what happens to an artist when you reach superstardom.

Remember, as we discussed before, the record company takes options on new artists for up to eight albums (see page 108). Putting this together with how long it can take superstars to record a new album, you realize that the more successful you are, the longer it takes to fulfill the commitment. The other reality is that most new-artist deals have low royalties and advances or, at best, are in the midrange (and then only if there were wolves snapping at the door when the deal was made). So as soon as an artist has any success, they show up at the record company's door and ask for more substantial advances and royalties. And what do you suppose the record company wants? You got it—more albums.

All of this adds up to the fact that record companies continue extending their deals, and artists rarely end up in a position to change companies. This is why artists tend to spend their entire career at one company. They would rather get better terms on their next album (which is for sure) than live out a mediocre deal on the hopes that they'll be as hot when it's over.

On the other hand, artists do occasionally get free, and if they're important at the time, they can set new benchmarks in the industry. They don't even have to get completely free to do this—there are people out there who will make a deal with them that doesn't begin until they deliver one or two more albums to their current record company (for example, Aerosmith did this). And the fear of this can sometimes cause the current record company to come to the party in a big way.

The other reality is that, when one artist is able to raise the standard in the industry, all of the other superstars go back to their record companies and ask for similar treatment. And in fact the rash of mega deals a few years back was triggered by just such a frenzy.

The Deals.   So what makes a deal 'mega'? Several things:

1. *Advances*
   The advances are in the multimillion-dollar range. At this level, the deal becomes a banking transaction—the record company makes its best guess as to what the artist will sell and then computes its potential profit versus risk.
2. *Royalty*
   Superstar royalties tend to be over 20% of retail.
3. *Product*
   The amount of product in a mega deal has two aspects:
   a. There will be many more firm albums—at least three or four—and there may be only one option, which is normally for more than one album (e.g., two or three firm);
   b. The total amount of product tends to be less. This is less applicable in the case of the superstar who owes a lot of product to the existing company, but if the deal is with a new company, or if there are only a few albums left, the company will get fewer albums than a normal deal.

The Hype.   Some of these mega deals are nowhere near what's reported in the press. Not that they aren't substantial deals, but they aren't all of the magnitude that the public is led to believe. Also, a number of the deals (such as Madonna's and Michael Jackson's) were multimedia deals, involving not only a record deal but also a record label (i.e., funding a company to sign other artists), publishing company, film projects, and perhaps merchandising (see page 373 for what that is), books, etc.

Note also a key distinction (which the public, and indeed the press, have never fully understood) between an artist who is re-signing with his or her own record company versus an artist signing with a new company. When re-signing, the company has its entire catalog of old product from which it can hedge its bet against the future. If the deals are cross-collateralized (see page 88 for what that is), and they often are so the artist can push up the advances, the company's risk is substantially different from the risk of a new company that has no catalog against which to get back its money. Now you know something that very few people, even many in the industry, understand.

I'm often asked whether the industry has lost its mind in making these mega deals, and whether I think they'll continue. As to the first part, there are sophisticated business players on both sides of every mega transaction. Also, if an artist is free, there is always more than one company willing to step to the line on these deals. Thus, I see it more as a question of dividing up the pie of profits, and I don't think anyone has lost their mind. I use the analogy of what happened to the L.A. Kings hockey team when they signed Wayne Gretzky—their season-ticket sales went up substantially, and this paid for much (if not all) of the deal. And there is also an intangible 'trophy value' to having these artists, not to mention how it attracts new artists who want to be on the same label as their heroes. These aspects are impossible to measure with precision, but can be worth quite a bit.

Whether these deals will continue is a question of when and how many superstars become available or get in a position to renegotiate. There will always be people willing to throw money at them. On the other hand, not all of these deals have worked out successfully, and that can make the companies gun shy. You also have to factor in whether the companies are in an expansive or contracting mode (see my theory of industry cycles on page 90). Over the last few years, these deals have slowed down radically.

DELIVERY REQUIREMENTS

Apart from the number of recordings, contracts also talk about the kind of recordings you can deliver. **Delivery** is a magic word, because it means more than dumping the stuff on their doorstep. It means the company has to accept the recordings as complying with your deal, and the contract will specify what standards the company can use in deciding whether to accept. What the standards are depends on your bargaining power. The extremes are:

Commercially Satisfactory

If your contract says you must deliver **commercially satisfactory** recordings, it means the record company only has to take recordings it believes will sell; in other words, recordings it finds satisfactory for commercial exploitation (translation: recordings it likes). If your contract has this language and they don't like your record, then (a) at best, they send you back to the studio (at your expense); or (b) at worst, they take the position that you haven't delivered an album as required by the deal, and thus you're late and they can terminate the contract.

Technically Satisfactory

If you only have to deliver **technically satisfactory** recordings, then as long as a recording is technically well-made (without hissing and warp, not made in a karaoke bar, etc.), the company has to take it.

Technically satisfactory is very rare today because of abuses that I'm sure you can imagine (for example, one of my record company clients got an album which was supposed to be a secret group of superstars, but turned out to be a previously released flop from an unknown group). Newer artists can expect to live with *commercially satisfactory*. Midrange/bidding war artists may get a *technically satisfactory* standard subject to the company's approving the songs and the producer, plus the same limits described in the next two sentences. Superstars can expect an even more favorable version of technically satisfactory: the company may not have any approvals, but it will have language saying the recordings must be of a 'style' (and perhaps even a 'quality') similar to your previous recordings. They will also exclude any 'specialty' or 'novelty' recordings, so you can't give them a children's record, Christmas record, the Ella Fitzgerald songbook (unless, of course, you are Ella Fitzgerald), polka records, Gregorian chants, etc.

Other Delivery Criteria

The other requirements for your recordings (regardless of your level) are that they must be:

1. Studio recordings (as opposed to 'live' concert recordings—see page 120 for a discussion of 'live' albums).
2. Recorded during the term (to keep you from pulling out those old garage tapes).
3. Songs not previously recorded by you (I'm sure you can figure out the history lesson behind this one).
4. Recordings that feature only your performance (to keep you from bringing in the kids and your aunt Sally as guest soloists).
5. Not wholly instrumental selections (unless you're only an instrumentalist).

6. Material that doesn't cause the company any legal hassles, such as infringing somebody's copyright, defaming someone, or using obscene language (to the extent that's still possible).
7. Songs of a minimum playing time (usually two minutes).

CONTROLLED COMPOSITIONS

One of the most important provisions of your record deal is the **controlled composition clause,** which limits how much you get paid as a songwriter. However, to understand it you need a pretty extensive knowledge of publishing, which we're going to discuss later. So let's put it off until you have the background. (If you really can't wait, flip ahead to page 227. Don't forget to come back.)

If you're on the *Advanced Overview Track,* go to Chapter 11 on page 125. *Experts,* straight on . . .

GREATEST HITS

A **Greatest Hits** (also called a **Best of**) album is a compilation of songs from your prior albums, perhaps with one or two new songs. (I've always been amused by the term *Greatest Hits,* since the album is sometimes neither.) Traditionally, releasing a Greatest Hits album was a record company's way of blowing taps over an artist's career that had passed away. However, in the 1970s, Elton John released a Greatest Hits album at the height of his career and sold eight gazillion copies. Suddenly everyone rethought their position, and today a Greatest Hits album is common at any point in an artist's life cycle.

If you don't say anything, the company will put out as many as it likes, whenever it likes, and pay you no advance. While some things about Greatest Hits albums aren't negotiable—for example, no company will count a Greatest Hits album against your delivery requirements—you can fix other issues if you know what to ask for. These are:

Limits

From the midrange level and up, and sometimes at the new artist level (depending on the company and your bargaining power), you can often limit the number of Greatest Hits albums a company can compile from your material. (Incidentally, don't ever assume there's a practical limit if you don't have one contractually—I've heard of one company that managed to put out eleven different albums of an artist who only recorded two albums' worth of masters in their entire career!) The usual limit is that the company can release no more than one (or two) Greatest Hits album during the term, plus one (or two) after the term.

Greatest Hits Advances

You should be able to get an advance for your Greatest Hits albums. The amount will depend on your bargaining power, and typically it will be reduced by the amount of your deficit if you're unrecouped (see page 80 if you don't remember what a 'deficit' is). You want the date of determining the deficit to be as late as possible, so you can get in the maximum sales to reduce it. The date of release of the Greatest Hits album is the best.

A typical Greatest Hits advance for a new artist signed to a major label might be $75,000 less the unrecouped deficit. So if the artist is unrecouped by $25,000, he or she would receive $50,000 ($75,000 less the $25,000 deficit). Independent labels will pay nothing, or perhaps $10,000 less the deficit. For a midlevel/bidding war artist, the number is closer to $150,000 (again, less the deficit); and for a superstar, $250,000 to $500,000 and up (less the deficit).

Midlevel and up deals often have a 'floor' on the Greatest Hits advance, regardless of the deficit. For example, I did one artist's agreement that had a Greatest Hits advance of $400,000 minus the unrecouped deficit, but in no event less than $150,000. Here's how this advance would work under different circumstances:

1. If the artist was recouped, the advance would be $400,000.
2. If the artist was unrecouped $100,000, then $400,000 minus the $100,000 deficit equals a $300,000 advance for the Greatest Hits album.
3. If the artist's deficit was $350,000, then $400,000 minus the $350,000 deficit equals $50,000. But the floor is $150,000, so the artist would get a $150,000 advance.

4. Can you figure the advance if the artist was $200,000 unrecouped? How about $600,000 unrecouped? (Answers on page 124.)

In the U.K., you don't get any Greatest Hits advances until you're mid-level or above. Then, you can get a Greatest Hits advance of around £50,000, often reducible by your deficit (see page 119). As your fame rises, this could be increased to a range of £100,000 to £125,000 (sometimes less the deficit), and often it can go much higher for superstars, though not usually more than the highest advance you've gotten for a prior studio album.

New Songs for Greatest Hits

It's becoming more and more common for companies to require two new songs for Greatest Hits packages released during the term (not after, since you'll be signed to someone else). This is in the best interests of all concerned, because a hit single pumps up the sales of the Greatest Hits album (it's the only place to get the song). At a minimum, the record company should agree to pay the recording costs of these new masters even if you're unrecouped (but don't assume the form agreement will say so), and you should also get a higher advance for Greatest Hits albums with new tracks.

LIVE ALBUMS

A **live album** is recorded during a live concert (with lots of screaming and applause), rather than in a studio. Don't assume a live recording is inferior just because it isn't made in a studio; there are mobile recording trucks that rival the highest-tech equipment in town. These trucks are simply backed up to the auditorium, and the concert is recorded with a quality that isn't noticeably different from a studio.

Live albums go through periodic ups and downs (sort of like outerspace movies). They were historically something a company did to keep the artist happy, because they didn't really make any money. Then, in 1976, Peter Frampton broke all the rules with an album called *Frampton Comes Alive!,* which was not only a live album, but also a *double* live album (double albums are a traditional handicap at retail).

This album sold in multimillion numbers that blew out all the traditional wisdom. After the predictable glut of live albums following Mr. Frampton's, the popularity again faded. Currently, live albums sell reasonably well, but are no great shakes.

Unless you have a lot of muscle, record companies won't let you deliver a live album (or even one live cut on a studio album) without their consent. On rare occasions, superstars can get the right to deliver one live album during the term of their deal. But it will usually be for a reduced advance, both because of live records' dicey sales history and the fact that most of the material will have been previously recorded.

GUARANTEED RELEASE

Very few form record contracts guarantee release of your records. Indeed, as we discussed on page 107, very few even build in an obligation to record, much less release.

With only moderate bargaining power, however, you can get a **guaranteed release,** and you should always ask. But this clause will never obligate the company to release your product; rather, it will only say you can get out of the deal if they don't. With more bargaining power, you can sometimes get the right to buy back an unreleased album. After all, if the company doesn't think enough of it to put it out, why not let you take it elsewhere and get its money back?

Guaranteed release clauses basically turn you into a notice factory. If, within a certain period after delivery (usually 90 to 120 days) the company hasn't put out your album, you have earned the right to give it a written notice saying, 'You haven't put out my album.' After receiving this shocking news, the company has another period (usually sixty days) within which to actually put out the album (if they feel like it). If they don't, you now have the privilege of sending a second notice, usually within thirty days after the sixty days (and if you're late, you lose your rights). This notice says the company still has failed to put out your album; that you really meant it when you said you wanted them to; and that you are now terminating the deal. At this point you can say good-bye. (But note that the company still doesn't have to put out the record.)

By the way, the period after delivery in which the company must release is usually extended if any of it falls between October 15 and January 15. This is because no one other than the most super of superstars can release product after October 15. Beginning in early December, the radio stations start thinking about Hawaii or Aspen, and they 'freeze' their playlists (meaning they add no new records until after January 15). In response, the record industry closes up around the middle of December. And since a record by an artist who is not well known doesn't have time to make its climb before the December shutdown, everyone has to wait until next year. Thus, the record companies want to extend their release commitment period to make way for this phenomenon. And their vacations.

Guaranteed release clauses only let you out of your record deal if the company doesn't release in the United States. As your bargaining power increases, as well as your international fame, you may be able to negotiate a similar release provision for foreign territories. Certainly you should try to get this in the 'major' territories (see page 164 for what they are) and anywhere else where you sell big numbers. Normally you can't get out of the entire deal for failure to release outside the United States—you can only terminate for the particular territory where they blew it, and only for the specific album not released (so you can get another distributor to release that album in the territory). If you keep pushing, the company may agree that, if it fails to release two consecutive albums in a particular territory, you can have back that territory for the rest of the deal. While this is not likely to be meaningful (if you're that much of a stiff in the territory, odds are no one else will want you either), it's better than a sharp stick in the eye.

Guaranteed releases work exactly the same way in the U.K., although, not surprisingly, the territory that allows you to get out of the deal is the U.K., as opposed to the U.S. With enough clout (or if you happen to be big in the U.S.), you can also get a guaranteed release in the U.S., and perhaps other major territories as well (for example, Germany, France, Canada, or Japan). However, for territories outside the U.K., you won't get out of the deal if they don't release your record there. Instead, you'll get a wanky provision that says, if they don't put out your album, you can force them to license that album to another company. Whoopee. Sometimes, if they don't release two consecutive albums, you can get back that territory for the rest of the deal.

DEAL PECULIARITIES FOR INDEPENDENTS

When you're recording for an independent who is not a 'true independent' (see page 67 for what all that means), you have concerns in addition to those we just discussed.

Distribution

When you sign to an independent, you have to ask whether this company can get anyone to distribute your album. Remember, these companies aren't distributors, and thus they have no way to get your records into the stores unless they contract with someone else to do it. So here's how to cover yourself:

1. First of all, put a clause in your contract that says the independent must enter into an agreement to distribute your product within a certain period of time. Ideally you should get six months after either execution of the contract or completion of your album, but I've gone as long as nine to twelve months. If the time period is measured from completion of your album, be sure you have some outside date—otherwise, if the company never records you, the date will never arrive. For example, you might require a company to make an agreement within six months after completion of your album, but in no event later than twelve months after execution of your deal.

2. If you have a bit more muscle, you should say that the company must enter into an agreement with a major distributor. If you don't, you may find your records shipped out in Uncle Herbert's U-Haul. The best way to handle this is to get approval of the distributor. If the independent agrees, it will say you must be 'reasonable' in your approval, so you can't use this clause to get out of the deal when some prettier face dangles more money in front of you. (You wouldn't do that, would you?) And by the way, when I represent the independent, I insist that the artist pre-approve all the major distributors (which I then list).

3. Watch out for this one: Suppose your deal with the independent is for two albums firm, but the distributor drops the company (and you) after one album. How do you make sure the company doesn't hold you for the second album even though they have no way to put it out? Part of your protection is a

guaranteed release—if they don't put your album out, you can terminate the deal (see page 121). However, as you'll remember from page 107, companies don't even have to make a record to hang on to your contract. And if they don't record any product, the guaranteed release never comes into play. Knowing this, various sleazeballs in our business have sunk their teeth into an artist and not let go if they smelled that somebody might pay them for the privilege. So the way to cover yourself is to say that the independent has six to twelve months after a distribution deal lapses within which to get a new deal, or else you're out.

The Great Publishing Grab

Independent companies are the ones most likely to try to take your publishing (your earnings as a songwriter, as opposed to your earnings as a performer on records). Since we haven't discussed publishing, I want to defer the ins and outs of this until we do. The way to protect yourself is on page 272 if you want to look ahead, but I suggest you do it only if you understand publishing pretty well.

Answers to quiz on page 119:

If $200,000 unrecouped: $200,000 advance ($400,000 minus the $200,000 deficit).

If $600,000 unrecouped: $150,000 advance ($400,000 minus the $600,000 deficit is less than zero, but the floor is $150,000 no matter what).

11

Producer and Mixer Deals

WHAT'S A PRODUCER?

A record producer combines the roles of director and producer in the motion picture field. He or she is responsible for overseeing and bringing the creative product into tangible form (a recording), which means (a) being responsible for maximizing the creative process (finding and selecting songs, deciding on arrangements, getting the right vocal sound, etc.), and (b) taking care of all the administration, such as booking studios, hiring musicians, staying within a budget, filing union reports, etc. (The mechanical aspects of administration—actually calling the musicians, doing the paperwork, etc.—are often handled by a **production coordinator,** whose life purpose is these chores.)

History

As we discussed earlier, artists in the 1950s were mostly people who only showed up to sing, then left to 'do lunch.' My friend Snuff Garrett, one of the most important producers of the fifties and sixties, considered it burdensome if it took him more than five days to record an album (and the artist wasn't even there all that time). Using this technique, Snuff produced records for Cher, Sonny and Cher, Gary Lewis and the Playboys, Bobbie Vee, Bobby Vinton, and a host of other successes, including such strange choices as Telly Savalas and Walter Brennan.

Snuff started out (as did all the early producers) as an **A&R** man (the letters stand for 'Artists and Repertoire'). *A&R* men (in those days there were no A&R 'persons') were executives of record companies whose job was to find, sign, and guide talent, including matching songs to singers and running recording sessions (in other words, doing almost exactly what producers do today). A&R executives still exist, and indeed are among the most important industry people. But today most of them don't actually produce the recordings (although many of the better ones come quite close to producing). They are responsible for finding and signing talent, as well as finding songs, matching producers and artists, and generally overseeing projects.

Anyway, Snuff began working for Liberty Records, which was then run by its founder and chief executive, Simon Waronker (the father of DreamWorks Records' current president, Lenny Waronker); its president, the late Alvin Bennett; and its chief recording engineer, Theodore Keep. (Do the first names of these gentlemen sound familiar? Do they remind you of a recording artist on Liberty? See page 137 for the answer if you can't guess.) Snuff (who is one of the smartest businesspeople I have ever met, but hides behind this country cornpone) figured out early on that he was making millions of dollars for Liberty while drawing a generous but small salary in comparison to what he was generating. So he summoned up all his courage and asked Alvin for a royalty of 1¢ per record. This was considered outrageous, if not treasonous—the radical idea that a guy instrumental in creating product could get a royalty—and Snuff was almost fired in the process. But due to his value to Liberty, he held out and won the point. And in so doing, he started a trend that is the reason producers get royalties on records today.

ROYALTIES

We talked before about the range of royalties for producers, on page 98. However, there are some major distinctions between artists' and producers' royalties, and some fine points that will bite you in the butt if you don't know about them. For whatever historical reasons, *producers' royalties are computed more favorably than artists' royalties.*

'Record One' Royalties

The biggest difference between artist and producer royalties is that producers, at some point, are paid for *all* records sold, meaning recording costs are *not* charged against their royalties. (As you know, recording costs are always charged against artists' royalties). These are called **record one** royalties, because they're paid from the first record

('record one') that the company sells. (All producers, of course, have to recoup any advances they have received, but if you think of these advances as a prepayment of royalties, this is the same as getting a royalty on all records.)

Most producers' royalties are paid **retroactive to record one** after recoupment of recording costs at the **net rate.** What this means in English is that (a) recording costs are recouped at the artist's *net rate* (the *all-in* artist rate after deducting the producer's royalty—i.e., the artist's rate 'net' of the producer's royalty); (b) before recording costs are recouped, the producer gets *no royalties* at all (just like an artist); but (c) once recording costs are recouped, the producer gets paid on *all* sales made, including those used to recoup recording costs. In other words, once recording costs are recouped, the producer is paid from the first record sold (*record one*), and this payment is *retroactive* because the company 'goes back' and pays on sales previously made that didn't bear royalties at the time of sale.

This is easier to see with numbers. Suppose an artist's 'all-in' royalty (artist and producer combined) is 60¢ a record, and the producer's royalty is 10¢ a record. Assume the producer gets a $10,000 advance, and that the recording costs (including the producer's advance) are $120,000. (These numbers bear no relationship to reality but make for easy math.) Here's what happens at sales of 200,000 units:

Producer's Recording Cost Recoupment Computation		Producer's Royalty Account	
Units Sold	200,000	Units Sold	200,000
'Net' Royalty	× 50¢	Producer Royalty	× 0
	$100,000		0
Less: Recording Costs	−$120,000	Less: Advance	−$10,000
DEFICIT	**−$20,000**	DEFICIT	**−$10,000**

Since recording costs are unrecouped, the producer doesn't get any royalties, because 50¢ × 200,000 equals only $100,000, which is short of the $120,000 needed to recoup the recording costs. However, once the artist sells a total of 240,000 units, the costs are recouped (50¢ × 240,000 = $120,000), and the producer is paid on all the units sold (i.e., retroactively to record one). At this point, the producer gets $24,000, which is 10¢ × 240,000 (less of course the $10,000 advance):

Producer's Recording Cost Recoupment Computation		Producer's Royalty Account	
Units Sold	240,000	Units Sold	240,000
'Net' Royalty	× 50¢	Producer Royalty	× 10¢
	$120,000		$24,000
Less: Recording Costs	−$120,000	Less: Advance	−$10,000
DEFICIT	**$0**	NET PAYABLE	**$14,000**

For you sharp-eyed purists, I'm aware that the $10,000 producer's advance would not be included in recording costs to determine the artist's royalty once it's recouped from the producer's royalty—if it were, the company would be getting it twice. But for simplicity, I've ignored this in the examples, because it's an issue in the artist's deal and doesn't bear on the producer's royalty computation.

Producers are sometimes paid **prospectively** after recoupment at the **combined rate,** which means that, once the recording costs are recouped at the *all-in* rate (i.e., the *combined* artist and producer rate—60¢ in our example), you get paid on sales *after* that point (but not retroactive to record one). This means you'll get paid sooner, but it's only a better deal if record sales die after the point where recording costs recoup at the combined rate, but before recoupment at the net rate. Otherwise, under the normal 'retroactive-at-the-net-rate' deal, you're way ahead when you get to recoupment at the net rate—at that point, you're not only paid on those sales between the level of combined recoupment and net recoupment, but also on all the records sold *before* recoupment.

Here's an example, using our same assumptions, but for a producer paid *prospectively* after recoupment at the combined rate:

Producer's Recording Cost Recoupment Computation		Producer's Royalty Account	
Units Sold	240,000	Units Sold (in excess of recoupment)*	40,000
Combined Royalty	× 60¢	Producer Royalty	× 10¢
	$144,000		$4,000
Less: Recording Costs	−$120,000	Less: Advance	−$10,000
RECOUPED	**$24,000**	NET PAYABLE	**$0**

*It takes 200,000 units at the combined 60¢ rate to recoup $120,000 of recording costs. So on sales of 240,000, only 40,000 bear royalties.

Contrast this (only $4,000 earned against the advance, meaning you get zero) with getting $14,000 on top of the advance in the prior example, for the same number of units. (If there were no advance, you'd get only $4,000 instead of $24,000.)

This prospective deal is only better than a retroactive-at-net deal if the record sells 239,999 copies and drops dead. In that case, you'd get paid on 39,999 copies under this formula, as opposed to zero under a net rate deal (239,999 times the 50¢ net rate is 50¢ short of the $120,000 needed to recoup recording costs). However, once you sell one more copy, you're way behind, as you just saw. And if, as in our example, your advance is more than the royalties on the sales between the combined rate and net rate recoupment points (the 39,999 in our example), you're always worse off under a combined deal. This is because you won't get paid on those extra units even if you never get to a net recoupment, since you already got those royalties in the advance.

Historically, U.K. producers were paid from record one, without regard to recoupment of recording costs (see the discussion on page 126). This was much more favourable than for U.S. producers. However, U.K. companies also figured this out, and thus there has been a trend towards making the producers wait until recording costs have been recouped (as discussed on page 127). However, U.K. producers with some clout can usually resist this and get paid from record one.

Other Royalty Computations

Except for the record one aspect, producers' royalties are customarily calculated in exactly the same way as the artists' (home video is also different, as noted in the next section). This means they get the same packaging deduction, the same 'free goods' reduction, and (as we'll discuss in Chapter 13) the same proportionate reduction for foreign, budget, midprice, etc. For example, if an artist gets 75% of his or her U.S. rate in England, the producer will get 75% of his or her U.S. producer rate in England.

Historically, U.K. producers were not reduced for foreign territories. In other words, their royalty might be 3% for every territory in the world, as opposed to a U.S. producer who might get 3% in the U.S.

and then a proportionate reduction for other territories. However, this practice has eroded over the last few years, and the norm now is for producers to take reductions in the same proportion as for the artist.

In situations where the artist gets a percentage of the company's net receipts (such as a license to use a recording in a motion picture, where the artist gets 50% of the fee paid by the motion picture company), the producer gets a pro-rata share of the artist's earnings, based on the ratio that the producer's royalty bears to the all-in rate. For example, if the artist's all-in rate is 12% and the producer gets 3%, the producer would get three-twelfths (one-fourth) of the artist's receipts. So if the record company gets $20,000 to use a master in a film, and pays $10,000 to the artist, the producer would get $2,500 (three-twelfths of the $10,000), and the artist would get $7,500 (the remaining nine-twelfths). (By the way, I've simplified this example by omitting any special market fee, which we'll discuss on page 169.)

Home Video Royalties

For home video devices, producers generally get half of their otherwise applicable rate. The theory is that the master is only half of the product (the video portion is the other half). Accordingly, in the above example of 3% and 12%, instead of getting 25% (three-twelfths) of the artist's video monies, the producer would only get 12½%.

ADVANCES

Producers, like artists, also get advances. These advances are re-coupable from the producer's royalties, regardless of how the producer's royalties are calculated. The range is something like this:

1. **New Producers:**
   Anywhere from nothing to $2,500 or $3,500 per master ($25,000 to $35,000 per album).
2. **Midlevel:**
   $3,500 to $5,000 per master ($35,000 to $50,000 per album).
3. **Superstar:**
   $10,000 to $15,000 plus per master ($100,000 to $150,000 per album). If a major producer is doing a major artist, advances in the $150,000 plus range aren't uncommon.

U.K. producer advances are in the range of £1,000 to £10,000 per track, with the norm being £4,000 to £10,000 for mid-level producers. Superstars can push up to £25,000 per track, and newer producers are of course squeezed below the usual levels.

A distinct category of producers are those people (today mostly in the pop and the urban areas) who are considered by the industry to be as important as (and in some cases more important than) the artist. These folks often write the songs as well. For their services, the mid-range producers can get up to $7,500 per master. At the superstar levels, advances can run $75,000 to $150,000 per *master*, and sometimes even more.

Some producers, at all levels, like to do 'funds.' That means the producer gets a chunk of cash that includes recording costs and the producer's advance (just like the artist funds we discussed on page 99). This is especially so with producers who own their own studios. The important issue with funds is to allocate how much is treated as recording costs, and how much is the producer's advance. The higher the recording costs, the worse for the artist—remember, from page 126, only the advance is charged against producer royalties, since the royalties are payable from record one after recoupment of the recording costs. So this should be spelled out in the contract. I've found that the reality of the recording costs has little to do with this discussion (as noted above, many of these producers own their own studios, so the actual costs are minimal). The negotiation is really about how much gets charged to the producer's royalties.

WHO HIRES THE PRODUCER?

At one time, record companies routinely hired the producers. That was in the days when one producer did an entire album (a concept that has almost vanished, as today most albums have multiple producers). As the trend became four, five, or more producer deals per album, the companies realized their in-house lawyers were spending so much time negotiating producer deals that it was clogging up their other work. So they hit on the brilliant idea that the artist should hire the producer, which has not only shifted the paperwork burden to the artist, but has also shifted the financial burden to you. Let's analyze the issues separately.

Who Actually Hires (Contracts with) the Producer?

The question of who does the paperwork to hire the producer is really a question of whether you or the record company bear the legal fees for negotiating the producer's deal. Can you guess which arrangement is better for you? Can you also guess which one is very hard to come by?

Who Pays the Producer?

Remember, in an all-in deal, you are responsible for the producer's royalties, regardless of who actually contracts with him or her. This is a much more serious issue than it may appear at first glance. For reasons we'll discuss in a minute, the producer may be entitled to royalties before you are recouped under your deal with the record company. This means you could owe money to the producer at a time when the record company doesn't owe you anything. This means you could have to write a check to the producer from your own pocket. This is not a good thing.

A MAJOR POINT—PAY ATTENTION

In case you've been dozing, now's the time to wake up. I'm going to talk about something that can mean a lot of money out of your pocket if you don't do it right. This is true whether you're an artist or a producer, even though it concerns the same point.

Using our earlier assumptions (see page 127), suppose you only sold 150,000 albums:

Units Sold	150,000
Producer Royalty	× 10¢
	$15,000
Less: Advance	−10,000
NET PAYABLE	**$5,000**

Notice the producer is owed $5,000, but 150,000 units times the artist's 60¢ rate is only $90,000, meaning the $120,000 recording costs have not been recouped. Now remember that we talked about how the artist is responsible for paying the producer's royalties in an all-in deal (see page 98)? If you put these two points together, you'll see that the artist is obligated to pay $5,000 to the producer, but the artist is getting no money because he or she is unrecouped. A major bummer.

And the situation can get much worse. Catch this Parade of Horribles: The artist may have received substantial advances in which the producer did not share. For example, if the artist spent $120,000 on recording costs (as in our example) and got another $100,000 as an advance, the artist won't get any monies until both the recording costs and the $100,000 advance are recouped. Meanwhile, the producer (who didn't share in the $100,000 advance) is owed royalties.

Artist's Account		Producer's Account	
Units Sold	300,000	Units Sold	300,000
Royalty	× 60¢	Royalty	× 10¢
	$180,000		$30,000
Less: Recording Costs	−$120,000	Less: Advance	−$10,000
Less: Advance	−$100,000	NET PAYABLE	$20,000
DEFICIT	−$40,000		

If the $20,000 number doesn't impress you, try adding a zero to make it $200,000. Do I have your attention?

This is one of the times when success can kill you, because the more records you sell, the deeper in the hole you go! (In a sense, I'm misleading you. First of all, at some level of success the artist will recoup and earn enough royalties to pay the producer off. Secondly, part of the reason the artist isn't getting royalties is because of an advance, which is in his or her pocket. Thus, if you think of advances as prepaid royalties, the artist has really received these royalties and is only required to pay a part of them to the producer. However, unless you're very different from the artists I know, you won't be setting money aside for your producer. And much of this problem is caused by the fact that recording costs have not been recouped, which is not money sitting in your bank account. So you can't put that aside to cover the producer even if you want to.)

Think that's the worst of it? Nah; we're just getting warmed up. Here's how the above example can get truly miserable:

Suppose the deal we just discussed was the artist's first album, which ultimately sold only 50,000 units. This means the album didn't recoup its recording costs, and the producer didn't recoup his or her advance. So far, the artist doesn't owe the producer anything, and everything is fine (from the point of view of our example, that is—the artist's career is of course in the toilet). When it comes time to do a second album, the artist ditches this turkey and hires a new producer. Let's assume the second album also costs $120,000, and let's assume the artist's recording fund is $200,000 for both the first and second albums, so that the artist pockets $80,000 (the difference between the fund and the $120,000 recording costs) on each album. Also, assume the second album sells 500,000 units, so that it recoups its recording costs and the producer of album number two is entitled to retroactive royalties. This means he or she is owed $50,000 (10¢ × 500,000 units), less the $10,000 advance, or $40,000.

Let's look at how the accounts stack up. First, the artist's account with the record company:

Artist's Account with Record Company

	Royalty Earnings	Charges Against Royalties	Net Due Artist (or Unrecouped Amount)
Album 1	+$30,000 (60¢ × 50,000 units)	−$200,000 ($120,000 recording costs and $80,000 advance)	−$170,000
Album 2	+$300,000 (60¢ × 500,000 units)	−$200,000 ($120,000 recording costs and $80,000 advance)	+$100,000
TOTAL	+$330,000 ROYALTIES	−$400,000 CHARGES	−$70,000 NET DEFICIT

Now here's the computation of Album Number 2's producer royalties (Album Number 1's producer is not owed any royalties):

Album Number 2 Producer's Account with Artist

	Royalty Earnings	Charges Against Royalties	Net Due Producer
Album 2	+$50,000 (10¢ × 500,000 units)	−$10,000 (advance)	NET PAYABLE +$40,000

As you can see from the above, the producer of Album Number 2 is owed $40,000, and yet the artist is unrecouped by $70,000. If you add a few more unsuccessful albums prior to the big hit, and/or add a few zeros after these dollar amounts, you have the makings of a 10 on the artist's Richter scale. And the producer ain't gonna be much happier when he or she doesn't get paid—instead of having a nice solid record company to send out the producer's royalty checks, he or she now has to chase Fred Flake the artist, who may be vacationing in Venezuela for the next five or six years. If either of these people is you, take two Valium and call me in the morning.

So what happens in real life? Any producer who has the slightest idea what they're doing will insist on the record company paying his or her royalties. Any artist who has the slightest idea what they're doing will insist on the record company paying the producer's royalties. Any record company that knows what it's doing (and they all do) will avoid this obligation like the plague.

It's simple enough to get the record company to pay the producer after the artist is recouped. This is because there are royalties from which it can deduct the producer's royalties. This is also relatively meaningless, because the artist then has the money anyway. (It is, however, still better than not having the record company on the hook at all.) It's when the artist doesn't have the money that this issue is critical.

If you have a reasonable amount of bargaining power (or if the producer does and requires this in the producer's agreement), you can get the record company to pay the producer and treat the payments as additional advances under your deal. In our example, this means the company would pay the producer $40,000 and you would then be $110,000 in the red (the original $70,000 plus the $40,000 paid to the producer). This makes you further unrecouped, but it's vastly superior to taking the money from your own pocket (few things aren't). If the company does agree, it will insist on approving the producer's deal, so that the amount it has to pay while you're unrecouped can't get out of hand. Interestingly, they'll want to keep the producer's royalty low, and the producer's advance high. Can you figure out why they want a higher producer advance? (See the answer at the end of the chapter if you can't guess.)

As your bargaining power declines, the sources from which the record company can get back pre-recoupment producer royalties increase geometrically—not only will the company take them back from your royalties, but it will also want to take it from:

1. **This album's budget,** meaning they'll hold back part of the money until either (a) the producer earns it; or (b) you flop so bad that it becomes obvious the producer will never get it. For

example, out of a $250,000 recording fund, they might hold back $50,000 in anticipation of paying producer's royalties before the artist is recouped. If in fact the producer gets $50,000 in royalties, the artist never sees this money. If, after a period of time from release of the album it becomes clear that the record is a turkey, and the producer will never be entitled to the royalties, the artist gets it (more specifically, the artist gets the portion of it not earned by the producer).

2. **Your mechanical royalties** (we'll discuss what these babies are on page 212).
3. **The next album's budget** (assuming there is a next album).
4. Some record companies attempted to take **first-born children,** but this practice died out in the late sixties.

If you don't have much bargaining power, you're going to end up giving the company anything it wants in exchange for an agreement to pay these royalties. Whatever it is, though, it beats the hell out of writing a check or selling your prized squeegee collection, so I suggest you take it. But fight valiantly, don't let them know I said so, and burn this page after you read it.

MIXERS

Closely akin to producers are **mixers,** who we briefly discussed earlier (on page 70). Basically, these folks take the multitracks and throw them into a blender to produce a mystical potion of sublime music. Great *mixers* can make a huge difference in the success of a record, and thus they are paid handsomely. Meaning top rock mixers can get $10,000 to $12,500 per track, while the lower-level folk get more like $4,000. Often this is a one-time payment, meaning there are no royalties. If there are royalties, the monies paid to lower-level mixers are often a **fee,** meaning they're not recoupable from royalties. For the higher-paid folk, usually 50% of their up-front money is recoupable.

Recoupable from what? Royalties are usually ½% to 1%, paid exactly like a producer—retroactive to record one after recoupment of recording costs at the net rate.

When we enter the hip-hop world, however, we walk through the looking glass. The top hip-hop mixers get $40,000 to $50,000 per remix, and sometimes more. When they also get royalties (and a lot of them do), it can be more than 1% (as high as 2%). As with rockers, because they're so highly paid, half their fee is an advance, and half is non-recoupable. However, at these levels, it's hard to earn enough royalties to ever recoup. A lot of remixing is done only for singles or specific genres (like a dance remix of a pop song), which means the cut isn't on the album (or, as we discussed in connection with singles in general, might not be commercially released at all—just serviced to radio). So the royalties aren't that significant, unless an album of remixes is later released.

If you're on the *Fast Track,* go to
Part III (Chapter 15) on page 207.
Everyone else, read on . . .

Answer to question on page 126:

The Chipmunks

Answer to question on page 135:

Record companies want you to pay a higher producer advance so that the producer isn't owed royalties until as late as possible, after which you've hopefully recouped more of your deficit.

12

Advanced Record Deal Points

ADVANCED DEMO DEAL NEGOTIATION

If you're making a demo deal (see page 109 for what that is), read this section. If you're going right into a full deal, you can skip to the section on exclusivity on page 142, or read this section just for the thrills and chills.

First Refusal

Suppose you make a demo deal and record a spectacular demo. Can you thank the company very much for their help, and then go shop the demo to other companies, thereby running the price of your deal through the roof? Not very likely. The company that paid for the demo attaches the following strings:

1. In exchange for the company's giving you demo money, you have to give it a period of time after it gets the demos (about thirty to sixty days) before it has to decide whether or not it wants you. You're sitting in limbo while the company decides—you can't go to another company during this period—so the shorter it is, the better for you.
2. If the company decides it wants you, one of two things happens:
   (a) Many companies, in their demo deals, spell out the terms on which they have rights to your services if they go forward. (These terms will be within the parameters of new artists deals, which we've already discussed.) So if they want you, the deal is all set;
   (b) Some companies don't spell out the terms in the demo deal, but instead just require you to negotiate with them

and try to make a deal (called a **first negotiation** right). If you make a deal, everything's great. If you don't make a deal, however, the company gets a **first refusal** (also called a **last refusal** or **matching right**). This means that, if you get an offer from another company, you can't just accept it. Instead, you have to go back to the original company and give it a chance to match your offer.

Here's an example of a *first refusal*:

After making a demo, you *first negotiate* with the record company making the demo (let's call them the Demo Company). You insist on $200,000 for your first album, but the Demo Company only offers $125,000. You say you're insulted and, in a beautifully choreographed fit of righteous indignation, you walk away to shop your deal around town. Finally, another company offers you $150,000. In steps the Demo Company, saying, 'Not so fast, Charlie.' Under the first refusal, you have to go back and offer the deal to the Demo Company at $150,000. If the Demo Company wants it at that price, you have to sign with that outfit; if not, you're free to go elsewhere (although you can't sign for less than the other company's offer—in this case $150,000—without giving the Demo Company a chance to match that deal. I'm sure you can figure out why the Demo Company insists on that).

Here's some goodies to negotiate in your first refusal:

1. You only have to come back to the Demo Company if the other offer is less than the last offer that the Demo Company made to you. So in our example, since the Demo Company only offered you $125,000, you wouldn't have to come back if somebody offered you $150,000 (it's more than the Demo Company's last $125,000 offer). This is pretty hard (read 'next to impossible') to get. Remember, when you're making a demo deal, you haven't got a lot of bargaining power (if you did, you'd be making an album deal).

2. You only have to come back if the offer you get is less than the last offer *you* made to the Demo Company. Note this wouldn't change anything under our above example. Since the new company offered you $150,000, and you last offered the Demo Company $200,000, you'd still have to come back (the $150,000 is less than the $200,000 you offered the Demo Company). This provision is a bit more possible to get, but the

Demo Company may still insist on your coming back with any offer, higher or lower.

3. However you end up under point 1 or 2, you should limit the time within which the Demo Company can accept or reject your offer. From your point of view, the shorter the better. Ideally, I like to get five business days, but more realistic is ten or fifteen business days. ('Business days' are Monday through Friday, excluding holidays. So ten business days is two weeks if there are no holidays.) Companies may want as long as forty-five to sixty days (regular 'calendar days,' not business days), which is an outrageous amount of time to hold you in never-never land. You could sit around all this time only to discover that (a) they decided not to take you; and (b) your other deal has gone away. Try never to go beyond thirty days—after all, the company heard your demos a long time ago.

Cost Reimbursement

If the Demo Company doesn't want you after you do the demos, or if it passes on your deal when you come back under a first refusal, you're free to go elsewhere. Yippee. When you do sign with another company, however, the Demo Company will want its demo money back. Not so Yippee. Since you're not likely to be in a position to write them a check, the Demo Company will want it from your new record deal.

Most record companies 'second in line' (meaning the ones that follow the Demo Company) are willing to reimburse the cost of demos. (After all, sometimes they're the Demo Company, and they want their money back too.) This cost, of course, will be recoupable from your royalties, and thus it's ultimately your money. However, it still beats smashing your piggy bank.

Here are a couple of things you can do to protect yourself:

1. Provide that the Demo Company should *only* get its money back *if* you make a new record deal. *Period*.
2. There should be a time limit. Otherwise, five years later you might get a deal based on totally different music and owe money to the Demo Company. Try a year or so.

Non–Record Company Demos

Record companies aren't the only places that may be willing to fund your demos. I've seen deals where demos are funded by recording studios, producers, engineers, rich people who want to be in rock 'n' roll, poor people who want to be in rock 'n' roll, rich people who became poor people trying to get into rock 'n' roll, etc. Indeed, one of the more bizarre stories I came across was a guy who funded an entire album, but would never tell any of us where the money came from. He lived in a walled estate and always paid in cash (I have my guess about his occupation; how about you?). Ultimately, after the album was finished, this guy disappeared, and we haven't heard from him in years. It would really round out the story to tell you this was a hugely successful album, but they still don't have a record deal. (Sorry.)

Since non–record company sources can't actually make and distribute records, their contracts don't look anything like the demo deals offered by majors or independents. Also, because these aren't mainstream deals, there's basically no rules, and I've seen them run all over the map. Here's some of the more common arrangements:

1. If and when you get a record deal, you reimburse them the cost of the demos, and the demo funder (let's call them the Funder) gets a 1% or 2% of retail royalty on your records. This royalty is known as an **override,** because it rides on top of your deal. However, the record company will take it out of your royalties, under the age-old theory of 'It's your problem, not mine.' Sometimes funders also get a proportionate share of advances paid to the artist, in the ratio that their *override* royalty bears to the all-in rate. For example, if the artist has an all-in rate of 10% and the Funder has a 2% override, they would get 20% (two-tenths) of the advances.

2. You want to limit the participation to as few records as humanly possible. The minimum is where the Funder gets an override only on the specific demo recordings that are finished into masters on your record. Your argument is that the other demos didn't interest the record company. I've also seen deals where there is a smaller override if a song in the demo is re-recorded, as opposed to the demo being turned into a master. For example, the Funder might get a 2% royalty if you fix up and use their actual recordings, versus a 1% royalty if the same song is re-recorded.

3. At the other extreme, the Funder may ask for an override on every record under your deal, which I think is overreaching. If you agree to this, you'll be married to this yutzo forever, in exchange for their relatively small investment in your career.

Ideally the override should only apply to the first album, but perhaps you can throw in a couple more if it's necessary to make the deal. Another compromise is not to limit the number of albums on which the Funder gets an override, but to say they only get the override until they get back twice (or three times) their investment. So if the Funder puts up $10,000, they only get an override until they receive $20,000 (or $30,000).

4. If the Funder only gets a royalty based on the use of specific recordings or songs, then be sure to specify their royalty is **pro-rata** (see page 170 for a discussion of *pro-rata*).

5. The Funder's royalty should only be payable after recoupment of the amounts charged to you in connection with the records on which they have a royalty, such as tour support, videos, etc. (Note this is recoupment at your rate, not from the Funder's royalties.) It's not fair, however, to charge the Funder for recording costs of records on which they don't get an override, nor should they be charged for advances they don't share in.

6. If you make one of these deals, you should thoroughly understand the discussion on page 132 concerning payment of producer's royalties when you have no royalties from which to pay them. The exact same thing can happen here on the override—you could owe the Funder money before you are recouped. Ideally, when you make your record deal, try to get the company to pay the override obligation even though it's taken out of your royalties (in the same manner as discussed on page 135 for producers).

EXCLUSIVITY

I'm sure you won't be shocked to learn that every record contract includes a provision stating the deal is **exclusive.** In other words, during the term of the agreement, you can't make records for anybody else. However, there are some related clauses and subtle side effects you should know about:

Re-recording Restrictions

All contracts say you can't re-record any song you recorded during the term of a deal for a certain period of time *after* the term. This is known as a **re-recording restriction.** When you think about it, it's perfectly logical—without it, you could go out the day after your deal is over and duplicate your albums for somebody else, and/or put out your own Greatest Hits album. The usual period is five years from the date of recording, but with a minimum of three to five years from the end of the term. The minimum keeps you from re-recording an album delivered in year one of a six-year deal immediately after the term, even though it is more than five years since recording it. The five years from recording is pretty much carved in stone; you can almost always get the period after the term down to two years.

Re-recording restrictions used to apply only to 'records,' which meant there was no restriction on re-recording for motion pictures, commercials, etc., which fall outside the definition of records (see page 69 for the definition). However, the companies realized that their artists were re-recording songs for commercials and movies instead of using the master, for which the record company could charge a fee, so now most forms provide that the re-recording restriction applies to these as well.

Recently, most companies have taken to saying you can *never* re record your songs to sound just like the masters you've given them, for records, commercials, or any other purpose. This came out of the occasional practice of artists essentially duplicating their old company's masters to create a Greatest Hits album for a new company, or re-recording the songs for movies or commercials (to keep all the money, as we just discussed). So nowadays, after your re-recording restriction expires, you can only record a wholly different arrangement of the songs.

By the way, the world's record for re-recording restrictions belongs to Decca Records, who structured a deal under which Bing Crosby had a *perpetual* re-recording restriction for the song 'White Christmas.'

Motion Picture and Television Soundtracks

Exclusivity clauses apply to all 'records' made during the term, and most companies now define 'record' so broadly that the term includes motion picture and television soundtracks. Thus, the companies can stop you from recording for motion pictures and television without their consent (and giving them a nice piece of what you make), even where there's no phonograph record involved.

You can usually negotiate some slack in these, if you know enough to ask. The most common compromise is to allow you to perform one or two songs in a film with a laundry list of restrictions, such as keeping the size of your name the same as other artists, requiring a credit to the company, etc. With more leverage, you can do more songs as long as you aren't on the soundtrack album.

But what about a soundtrack album, you ask? You've seen lots of artists with recordings on soundtrack albums, often on different labels. Now that's a real sticking point.

Record companies don't want you freely dropping recordings on others, for the legitimate reasons that (a) they want to be exclusively identified with you; and (b) they don't want someone else releasing a record of yours at a time that would conflict with one of your own singles or albums (incidentally, neither should you, as you normally make a lot less on a soundtrack album).

So how do people get on soundtrack albums? Well, it's handled one of two ways in your record deal:

Forget It.   At some record companies, this is an absolute 'religious issue' ('sacred cow,' 'irrefutable principle,' etc.—you get the idea), meaning you have no right to let anyone else put out a soundtrack album with your recording on it. In these cases, the artist throws him or herself on the mercy of the record company each time a film company asks them to perform a song in a movie. The record company either agrees to let the artist perform (with restrictions—see below), or it refuses and the issue is closed (unless your manager can yell loud enough to reopen it). The other choice is to force the film company to give the soundtrack album to your record company, because then there is no conflict. If you're important enough, you can do this, even if you're only on one track.

If your company allows you to go elsewhere, and provided there's no conflict with your own product, then the album can be released on another label. Companies historically have been much more reluctant to allow a single to come out on another label, but this is changing as singles become less and less profitable items. If you can do it, it's best to get the single released by the same company that's releasing the soundtrack album. This is because their incentive is greater—they make money on the album even if they lose on the single, and the single helps sell the very profitable album.

Contractual Exclusions.   *If you have clout,* you can negotiate an automatic contractual soundtrack exclusion in your record deal with some companies (or even with the sticklers if you're King Kong). These typically have some or all of the following laundry list (which will also apply if you have no exclusion but the company consents):

1. You can't perform on more than one (or two at most) selections for inclusion in the album.
2. You can't do more than one of these during any one-year (or two-year) period of the term. Sometimes it's an overall limit, such as a maximum of three cuts over the term.
3. You must not be late in delivery of your product at the time.
4. All the royalties and advances must be paid to your record company. (Note that here we're talking about advances against your royalties, as opposed to a fee that you may get for performance in the film [which, as you'll see on page 410, is normally not fully recoupable from royalties]. Some companies also attempt to grab part of your fee for performing, but I think this is wrong and I slap their hands.) After the company gets your royalties or advances, it will want to keep 50% of them for releasing you from the exclusivity and allowing you to go elsewhere. The other 50% is credited to your royalty account, which means (if you're unrecouped) you won't see any of it but it will reduce your deficit. If the soundtrack album is being released by your own company, you should be able to get 100% of the monies credited to your account (to reduce your deficit), or paid out if you are recouped. If you really have a lot of bargaining power, you can get 50% or more of the royalties paid to you even if you're unrecouped, on the theory that this recording is in addition to the product they're entitled to get under your deal, and thus should be handled separately.
5. The company having the exclusive contract must receive a courtesy credit in the film and on records, such as '[Artist] appears courtesy of Atlantic Records.'
6. You must try to get the right to use the recording on one of your albums, and perhaps also on a Greatest Hits album. The film company, if it gives these rights, will ask for a holdback period before you can do so. (This is discussed on page 417.)

Websites

Back when websites were strange and unknown creatures, the companies began registering the website names of all their artists without bothering to ask. And without regard to the fact that most of their record deals, which were made before websites existed, didn't give them the right to do this.

After the predictable shouting, tugging, and gouging, most deals now provide that, during the term, the company will have an exclusive license to set up the artist's website, and the artist is allowed to set up an 'unofficial' website. After the term, the rights go back to the artist, although companies keep the right to have an artist section on their website.

I've also started seeing companies recoup the costs of creating and maintaining the artist's website. It's hard to make this go away, but you can usually limit the amount they can charge, to say $25,000 over the life of the deal.

Webcasting, TV, and Radio Broadcasts

Webcasting is essentially a broadcast over the Internet, and there are two kinds:

1. Music played by self-declared DJs, and by regular, over-the-air radio stations that put their signal on the Internet (we'll discuss this kind of *webcasting* later, on page 308); and
2. Artists who broadcast their concerts over the Internet.

Number 1 really doesn't have much to do with your record deal, and even though it's gotten a fair amount of press in recent years, it's not terribly significant to artists (yet). Number 2, however, gets immediately into your pocketbook, as people will sometimes offer money to put your concert on the Internet.

As we discussed earlier, record companies have now made their exclusivity provisions so broad that they cover all transmissions of a concert, whether over the airwaves or the Internet or any other means. This is because the contracts define 'records' to include *any delivery* of music to consumers, whether it's a CD or a package of electrons. Thus, a webcast, television, or radio broadcast of your music is a 'record' (since it delivers music to consumers). And since your company has the exclusive right to distribute your records during the term of your deal, you have to go to them (meaning get their permission and, more specifically, pay them a chunk) if you want to do a broadcast. With superstars, you may be able to negotiate some exceptions, but record companies have become increasingly touchy in recent years.

Sideman Performances

Isn't it nice how all the superstars seem to be playing instruments and singing background on everybody else's records? These nonfeatured appearances are known as **sideman** performances, and there is hopefully a trend toward calling them **sideperson** performances. Now that you're educated, don't you wonder how this is possible? Doesn't it violate the exclusivity provisions of the superstar's agreement when she sings background for her pals on another label?

The answer is that there's a strong custom in the industry (and indeed you can have the provision inserted in your contract just by asking) that *sideman* performances are permitted, on the following conditions:

1. The performance must be truly a background performance, without any solos, duets, or 'stepping out.'
2. Your exclusive company must get a 'courtesy credit' in the form of '[Artist] appears courtesy of —— Records.' (Before I started in music, I always thought they did that just to be nice.)
3. You can't violate your re-recording restriction (see page 142) for any selection, even as a background performer.
4. If you're a group, no more than two of you can perform together on any particular session. This is because your record company doesn't want your distinctive sound showing up on another label.
5. Some companies require you to get the other artist's label to give up a sideman clearance in exchange for letting you go (sort of like a future draft pick).

This is usually handled with an exchange of correspondence between the record companies in each specific instance, and it's usually just a 'rubber stamp' process (unless one company is having a fight with the other about something unrelated to the sideman). After all, if one of the companies makes an issue of it, they won't have such an easy go the next time that other company's artist shows up as a sideman on their label. The process is something like porcupines dancing carefully with each other.

VIDEOS

Promotional videos are the ones you see on MTV and (if you're over a certain age, physically or mentally) on VH-1. They're paid for by the record company to promote the sales of your records, and all the provisions concerning them are in your record deal. On a good day, a company can spend ten to twenty pages of its form agreement talking about these suckers, which have yet to break even (with extraordinarily rare exceptions), much less make a profit.

History

Did you know that music videos (which only became popular in the United States when MTV started in 1981) have been around since the 1960s in Europe? They were invented because it was cheaper for artists to make videos than to tour Europe. But videos have an even longer history than that. There are some great treasures that came from something called a 'Scopitone' (pronounced 'scope-ih-tone'). This was a jukebox that played videos on 16mm film, and it enjoyed a brief life in the late 1950s and early 1960s. Today the Scopitone videos are collectors' items, and they include a number of color videos from such artists as Sonny and Cher, Neil Sedaka, Dion, Nat King Cole, Bobby Darin, etc. And if you really want to delve into the past, there are black-and-white videos that were shown in cinemas in the 1940s and 1950s, with such artists as Fats Waller, Louis Jordan, Lena Horne, Bing Crosby, Spike Jones, and many others. But back to today.

Commercial Market

At the time of this writing, and probably for the foreseeable future, there is little (if any) profit in single-song (MTV-type) videos. This is because most of the uses are promotional (read 'free') or for a nominal charge (which covers only duplicating and shipping), to gain exposure for the record. So far, you only get monies for home video sales (DVDs and videocassettes) using music videos, either as (1) a **compilation** (meaning a program 'compiled' from a number of individual video clips, of the same or different artists); or (2) occasionally a video plus a 'making of.' (For the royalties from both of these, see page 165.) However, with rare exception, these usages don't generate huge income, so neither you nor the company can expect to make much on videos. On top of this, MTV has stopped playing very many videos, as they've found kids don't watch them as much as they used to. So, when you put all this together, companies are making fewer videos, and for a lot less money than in days past.

Now to the issues you need to cover in your deal.

Is the Company Going to Make a Video of Your Song?

This is the first question, because if the answer is no, there's not much else to talk about. Until you have quite a bit of bargaining power, the record company, totally by itself, decides whether or not to make a video. As your bargaining power increases, you can require the company to do one or two videos per album. But even in this case, almost every company will say they only have to make videos for as long as they're doing it for artists of a stature similar to yours. Their concern (with justification) is that videos may someday not be a useful means of promoting records, and I usually agree to this request—if videos don't help sell records and aren't profitable, who cares?

Control

Control concerns two areas: (1) the content of the videos; and (2) the manner in which they're exploited. Unless you have an enormous amount of bargaining power, you generally can't control the commercial exploitation of your videos. This is because the company wants every opportunity to get its money back, and it doesn't want you stopping them over some silly concept like artistry. You may get the company to agree it won't commercially exploit a video if you repay the cost of it, but this isn't of any practical value unless you're an extremely rich prima donna. More realistically, you may be able to limit the exploitation a bit. For example, you can (with some clout) prevent the company's putting your videos in a home video package that also contains videos of other artists.

The creative controls, when it comes to the content of videos, tend to be very limited. Except at the highest levels, you get only a bare bones approval of the story, song, director, and perhaps producer. Companies don't want to be in the position of having spent $150,000 for your video merely to have you say the 'vibes' don't hit you right and you don't approve. That would mean they're stuck with a turkey they can't unload. If you have serious bargaining power, however, you may be able to pull off approval of all elements and the final edit, or indeed take complete creative control of making the video.

Budget

Budgets for shooting a video will normally be either designated or approved by the company, but as your stature grows, you may be able to put in a minimum amount. Today, it's difficult to make a video of more than garage quality for less than $50,000 or so, and the majority of new artists spend $125,000 to $150,000. Midlevel videos are in the $250,000 to $500,000 range, while superstars routinely spend more like $500,000 to $750,000, and there are occasional forays that take people into the $1,000,000 plus range (I think the record is $3,000,000). When you go upscale like this, you get a video that can compete with *Lord of the Rings* (or *Waterworld*).

Recoupment

Typically, the record company charges 50% of the cost of videos against your audio royalty, and 100% against your video royalties. One of the things you want to make sure is that they don't double-up—in other words, once they charge 50% against record royalties, they can't take the same 50% against video royalties, and vice versa.

Once a video budget has been approved, record companies get very touchy about your running over the limit. Sometimes they flatly refuse to pay, and the artist (only superstars can afford this 'luxury') actually writes a check. Other times they grudgingly, grumblingly, bitchingly pay the excess, but charge it against anything they can grab—future advances, mechanicals, etc. And, of course, 100% of the excess is recouped from your audio and video royalties.

Most companies have a 'bright line' beyond which they'll charge 100% against your audio royalties, even if the costs are within an approved budget. For example, a contract might say that if an approved video budget exceeds $150,000, they'll charge 100% of the excess against audio royalties (as well as of course against video royalties).

INDEPENDENT PROMOTION

There is an important phenomenon known as **independent promotion.** Promotion people (as noted on page 64) get records played on the radio, and they have relationships with station programmers to help ensure this. Some of these people are independent of record companies; they work for themselves and are hired by the companies on a project-by-project basis. They are cleverly called *independents*, to distinguish them from record company employees who also do promotion.

The independents are paid handsomely for their services by a record company (in most cases) or by the artist (in others). And by handsomely, I mean the costs for multiformat promotion (meaning promotion to pop, rock, Adult, R&B, etc.) can run $350,000 to $700,000 *per single*. As I write this, there's a record company revolt against the expense of independent promotion, so those numbers may tumble, but that's what the companies are paying today, despite the squeezes and cutbacks. Whatever they do spend will be 50% to 100% recoupable from your royalties.

It's almost impossible to get companies to commit in your contract to pay for independent promotion, but it's always worth asking for. Whether they commit or they don't, however, it's a great idea to ask for a **cap** (meaning a maximum limit) on how much they can charge you for independent promotion. Without the cap, it's a blank check out of your royalties.

Here's some compromises I've seen:

- You can't be charged more than $250,000 for independent promotion of any particular album. (Note, if you're only charged with 50% of the company's spend, they would be spending twice this amount.)
- You can only be charged $50,000 per single.
- The company can recoup up to $50,000 for the first single, but there's no cap after that.

It's worth putting up a fight to keep the company from recouping more than 50% of independent promotion costs. If they're charging 100% to you, they don't have the same incentive to reduce spending as they do when 50% comes out of their own pockets.

It's also worth noting that promotion has taken a new twist over recent years, with what are known as **radio-promoted concerts.** I'm sure those of you in the larger metropolitan areas have seen local radio stations promote gigantic concerts with all kinds of name acts. These acts are paid much less than their normal fees to show up. They do it to generate goodwill with the radio station (who makes a large profit on these concerts). So, in essence, the artists are paying for promotion of their own recordings.

MERCHANDISING RIGHTS

Over the years, some record companies have tried to take artists' **merchandising rights.** These are the rights to put your name on a T-shirt, poster, etc., and we'll discuss them in great detail in Chapters 24 and 25. (Note that I'm not talking about the rights to put out promotional posters, T-shirts, etc., which are distributed free to promote records, and for which all record companies have the rights. This section is about record companies wanting the right to sell merchandise at concerts, in stores, etc.)

If the companies get *merchandising rights,* they pay you the royalties we'll discuss in Chapters 24 and 25 if they exploit the rights themselves, or else they pay you 50% of their receipts if they license the rights to a merchandiser. They will also try to cross-collateralize the merchandise earnings with your record deal (see page 88 for what that means).

This is something you should resist if at all possible, since these are valuable rights and you don't want your record company's sticky fingers grabbing them. The practice has mercifully died down over the last few years (not coincidentally, I suspect, with a lot of major companies selling off their merchandising divisions). At the time of this writing, the only major still doing this is the Warner Music Group (Warner Bros. Records, Elektra, Atlantic), as their parent company owns Giant Merchandising, one of the major merchandisers. However, other companies may try to get into this pie, simply to take the rights and sell them off elsewhere. So it's a good idea to say that your company only gets the right to match a merchandising deal if they have an affiliate actively engaged in the manufacture and distribution of merchandise.

If you can't knock this provision completely, try to get one of these:

1. The company gets no merchandising but keeps a matching right. This means that you can go out and shop around all you like, but you must come back and give them a chance to make the deal on the same terms as your best offer. (We discussed the details of a matching right in connection with demo deals, on page 138.) This system isn't ideal: The requirement to come back makes your shopping more difficult because bidders aren't interested in negotiating a whole deal if someone else can waltz in and take it away. But it's better than giving away the rights.

2. Some record companies not only want a matching right, but

also want a discount. For example, they may want to pay only 80% of what someone else offers. So if you had an offer for $10,000, they would be able to take the deal for $8,000. And in case you didn't figure it out, this is not good for you. If you must give a matching right, it should be at 100%.

In the real world, when the record company has a matching right, you usually go to them first and, if they're interested, just make a deal. If they're not interested, sometimes they'll let you go and forget about the matching right. But under the contractual language, they don't have to.

3. If all else fails, and you have to give up merchandising rights, make the best possible royalty deal (see Chapters 24 and 25), and don't let them cross-collateralize merchandise earnings with your record deal. You can usually knock out the cross-collateralization just by asking.

TOUR SUPPORT

And now for a bit of my personal finances. Remember my soft-drink stand (on page 76)? Well, here's that summer's take: 250 drinks, at 5¢ each, equals $12.50. Not bad for sweating in the sun for seven days a week over ten weeks, eh? But here's the real coup: I convinced my mother to pay for the drinks, so it was *all profit*. (I hope you're impressed.) If she hadn't, the drinks would have cost me $6.25, and the lumber for the stand was $18. So the expenses were $24.25, and I took in $12.50, resulting in a loss of $11.75. If it hadn't been for Ma, I'd have had to file bankruptcy.

This is not unlike the situation of a new band going on tour. As we'll see in more detail later (on page 358), it's virtually impossible for a new artist to go on the road and do anything besides lose money. Even assuming the band members only have a 'share of profits,' and you therefore don't have to pay salaries to the players, the costs of rehearsal and putting together a show, travel, hotels, agents, managers, etc., are more than any band can earn in their baby stages. Indeed, even by the time you're midlevel, you'll be doing well to break even on the road.

This raises the question of why you should tour under these circumstances. (As the joke goes, if you buy widgets for $1 and sell them for 50¢, how do you make a profit? Answer: Volume.) The reason, of course, is to become better known, build an audience, sell more records, play bigger concerts, and generally further your career. The question, then, is, 'Who's going to pay for the loss?' The answer is one of two possibilities: (1) A rich relative; or (2) A record company. Guess which one happens more often?

Monies that record companies give you to make up tour losses are called **tour support.** *Tour support* used to be much easier to come by than it is nowadays. Record companies are more and more skeptical about whether an artist really sells more records by going on the road, and it also depends on the type of artist you are. If you're a heavy metal band, being on the road sells records better than anything else—in fact, you may never even get on Top 40 radio (Top 40 is today called **CHR,** standing for 'contemporary hit radio'), but there will be a direct relationship between your appearing in a town and the sales of your records in that town. If you're more the ballad type, it's much harder to convince the company you should go out. If you fall in between, the amount of your tour support will depend on how well your manager does the Tijuana Two-Step.

Tour support is defined as the actual amount of your loss (you'll be required to give accountings to the company), but of course it has a maximum limit, usually in the range of $30,000 to $50,000 per tour. They've also gotten more sophisticated: for example, some companies won't let you charge a management commission in computing losses, on the theory that the manager shouldn't get paid when everyone else is breaking even. Also, if you use any of the money to buy equipment, the company wants to own the stuff.

Tour support used to be nonrecoupable. For a while, the record companies bought the argument that it was 'promotion' of their records, and wrote it off just like any other advertising and promotion expenses. But those days are gone with the wind. Today, tour support is always 100% recoupable (if you need it, your bargaining power usually ain't so great).

Many record companies are reluctant to commit to tour support in the contract, but are pretty good about doing it when the situation seems appropriate. If you can get it up front, it's a great thing to have; if you can't, go in and pound the table when you need it.

Tour support is easier to come by in the U.K. than in the U.S., for the simple reason that they want you to tour in the United States and other territories, and they know that you can't afford it. In the U.S., we figure the earth stops at our boundaries.

Whatever tour support you get, it will be 100% recoupable.

If you're on the *Advanced Overview Track*,
go to Chapter 13 on page 161.
Experts, read on . . .

TERRITORY

For United States artists in the new-to-midrange category, the **territory** of your recording agreement (i.e., where the company can exclusively sell your records) is almost always the world. In fact, the *territory* is usually defined as 'the universe,' because our early thinking was that someone might argue satellites weren't covered by a contract that only said 'the world.'

This 'universe' wording was the cause of one of my most bizarre negotiations, as well as my initiation by fire to the music business. I had only been practicing entertainment law a few months when a label I represented signed a jazz artist named Sun Ra. This guy said he was a reincarnated Egyptian, and had recorded records in the pyramids (for real). Anyway, his lawyer called me up to say that it was unacceptable to grant the universe, and that our territory must be limited to the Earth Zone. At first I thought he was kidding, so I said I would give him everything beyond our solar system, and maybe Neptune and Pluto, but that the Moon and neighboring planets were mine. I also asked if we had to pay him in Earth money. The lawyer, very seriously, said this was not negotiable and would blow the deal. So I added 'satellites' to the territory of 'the world' and caved in on the rest. (That lawyer owes me one.)

More routine negotiation of the territory comes at the superstar level, or when the artist is not based in the United States. In this case, the artist may divide North America (United States and Canada) from the rest of the world, thus making two separate recording agreements. The advantages of this are (1) the fact that these two territories are not cross-collateralized (meaning unrecouped amounts in North America aren't offset against foreign royalties, and vice versa); and (2) you can always get a higher royalty outside of North America because you're eliminating the U.S. company's share of it. The disadvantages are (1) the advances may be lower (because there is no cross-collateralization); and (2) it's a pain for the artist to deal with two record companies. Dealing with two companies means shipping two sets of master tapes and artwork, 'schmoozing' (hanging out) with two sets of executives, and most importantly, coordinating releases. If one territory releases prior to the other, you may (and you will, if you're an important artist) find records manufactured in one territory exported to the other, much to the dismay of the company with the exclusive rights in that territory. These deals are also much more complex, as you have to work out how the two companies will share the costs of artwork, videos, etc.

In recent years, more and more companies have been refusing to sign you for anything except the entire world. So this type of deal is getting harder to come by.

UNION PER-RECORD CHARGES

It's important that you not be charged with any union payments based on the sales of records, as these are customarily borne solely by the record company. (This is different from union scale—see page 87 for what that is—paid to you for recording sessions, which has nothing to do with sales and is due even if the recordings are never released. Session scale payments are always recoupable as recording costs, as we discussed on page 87) The most significant per-record union charges are payments made to the AFM (American Federation of Musicians) Music Performance Trust Fund (MPTF) and the AFM Special Payments Fund. Through various computations, these currently total about 5.6¢ per CD, for worldwide sales during (a) the first five years after release for the MPTF portion of these monies (28%); and (b) ten years after release for the balance. These royalties aren't paid on the first 25,000 albums or on any singles. There are some reductions of these amounts built into the record company/union deal over the next few years, but these monies can still add up to a chunk of change.

There is also an AFTRA contingent scale compensation based on record sales, which is much less money. This is only payable if you have nonroyalty background singers, and it has a ceiling (meaning it stops after the union gets a certain amount). The ceiling is currently five and one half times scale for a one-hour session, and you hit it at 3 million units. One-hour scale is currently $162.50, so the maximum AFTRA contingent scale is $893.75 per singer.

There is also a requirement that record companies pay AFTRA $900 each time they sign a new artist. That's the good news. The bad news is that AFTRA also bills the artist (you) $1,040, of which $40 is the first quarter's dues, and $1,000 is a one-time new member fee. The $1,940 provides you with one year of health benefits.

The British equivalent of the AFM and AFTRA is one union, called the Musicians Union (MU), and it doesn't have a per-record charge. Accordingly, unless you record in the United States or use members of the AFM or AFTRA on the sessions, you won't be subject to union per-record charges. This is a substantial saving for the record company, and if you are making a deal with a U.S. company, you should tell them you want a higher royalty because of it.

ALBUM COVER ARTWORK

At almost any level you can usually get some involvement in your album cover artwork, but you have to ask for it.

'Involvement' at lower levels means they tell you what they're doing, then go ahead and do it whether you like it or not. This process is called **consultation,** which means they talk to you but don't have to get your approval. *Consultation* is actually more valuable than I'm making it sound, because you can at least make your feelings known before the horse leaves the starting gate, and many companies will actually listen to you.

The next step up is **approval,** which means you can approve the artwork the company prepares. When you have *approval* rights, the company has to please you or you can stop them from using it.

Top of the line is the right to create your own artwork, subject to the company's approval. You can get this as your bargaining power grows. If you're a superstar, the company's only approval rights may be as to legalities, obscenity, and other major grossness—otherwise it's your show.

When you get the right to create artwork, the trick is to make sure you have an adequate budget, or your creative juices will be severely hampered. So build in a set figure and escalate it over time (for inflation). I hesitate to give you specific figures because they may be out of date by the time you read this, but as of now a normal (no particular frills) artwork budget is in the range of $20,000 to $25,000. Contractually, it's hard to get this much for new artists; maybe you get around $12,500 or so. On the other hand, companies will usually spend a reasonable amount even if it's not in your deal (but may charge the excess against your royalties if the contract permits).

CREATIVE, MARKETING, AND OTHER CONTROLS

There are a number of controls you should ask for, some of which you may actually get. These are:

1. Consent to coupling (see page 170 for what this is and the details on controlling it).
2. Consent to usage of your masters in commercials.
3. Consent to licensing your masters for films or television.
4. Approval of your photographs and biographical materials used in advertising and promotion.

If you can't get approval of any of these, at least try to get consultation rights (see the prior section for what those are).

RESERVE LIMITATIONS

When you're a midlevel to major artist, you can often get a limit on album reserves, usually 35% to 50% of the records shipped. (Reserves are discussed on page 80.) You won't get a limit for singles, because the market is so weird, as noted on page 97.

At midlevel and up, you can also force the company to liquidate the reserves over a set period of time, usually two years. Try to make the liquidation **ratable,** meaning they have to pay an equal amount each time. For example, if the company has to liquidate your reserves over two years, that means four six-month accounting periods. If they must liquidate ratably, they have to pay you one-fourth of the reserves in each of the four periods. If you don't say this, they could pay you a small percentage in the first three periods and hold the bulk of your money until the end.

As a newer artist, the best you normally get is contractual language saying reserves must be 'reasonable.' This is helpful in banging on your record company to release monies held in reserve, but as you can imagine, it leaves a lot of room for argument. Also, the amount of reserves a record company holds will be larger if you're a new artist. When you're new, they hold more because there's no history to judge whether your sales will stick or bounce back like little rubber balls.

On the other hand . . .

SOUNDSCAN

A company called SoundScan, which began in 1991, measures how many records are sold at *retail*. They do it by reading the register tapes of reporting stores, thus measuring records that walk out the door with consumers. (In the past, the companies only knew how many records were shipped *to* the stores.) SoundScan's data is used for *Billboard*'s charts and is also sold to record companies and other users.

SoundScan isn't 100% accurate—they get exact information from a substantial portion of the retail market, then statistically extrapolate the rest. For mainstream records, I understand it's a very good snapshot of the marketplace. However, I'm told that records which sell primarily in independent stores and other outlets that aren't measured by Sound-Scan may be reported low. Still, it's the most accurate measure we have.

Sometimes companies will agree that reserves will not exceed the SoundScan numbers or SoundScan plus 10% or so. This is definitely worth asking for.

SPECIAL PACKAGING COSTS

Most record companies believe that, other than massaging an artist's ego, printed inner sleeves, special inserts (Alice Cooper once included a pair of girl's panties with each copy of an album), inflatable ducks, etc., add little, if any, to the sales of records. With vinyl discs disappearing, this has become virtually a nonissue, because CDs and cassettes don't lend themselves to this kind of abuse. However, there is still an issue over things like special inks, oddball packages (cardboard, gold leaf, diamonds, etc.), and extra panels in CD booklets. If you print your song lyrics, add 'special thanks,' write a letter to your mom, etc., you may need more than the standard sixteen-page CD booklet, (i.e., four sheets folded and stapled in the middle). At superstar levels, you can negotiate for more than the normal allowance, but if you don't have it in your contract, most companies charge artists with the excess that the fancy stuff costs over a standard package. And this can be significant money out of your hide. Since the variations are so infinite, and costs change quickly over time, it's hard to put any real parameters on them. But this provision could reduce your royalty by 5¢ to 10¢ or more per unit, which is serious money if you sell millions of albums. So be aware that this attack of ego could happen to your pocketbook.

ACCOUNTINGS

When do you get your royalties? Twice a year, within sixty to ninety days after the close of each calendar six-month period (except for some companies that use weird, non-calendar six-month periods).

Objections

Your contract will say that each accounting becomes 'final' (meaning you can no longer argue it's wrong) within a period of one or two years after the statement is sent to you. If the companies didn't say this, you'd have until four years after the statement (in California) or six years thereafter (in New York) within which to sue them. That is, of course, precisely why they say it.

You can increase the objection period to two years, and often three years, with minimal clout. Always do it, because it's uneconomical to audit unless you can do two or three years at once. What's auditing? Funny you should ask . . .

Audit Rights

Closely following the accounting clause is an **audit** clause, which says you can *audit* (meaning send in an accountant to verify) the record company's books. This is a way of assuring that you're getting a fair reporting, and if you have any success you should do it. Audits are expensive ($25,000 to $50,000 or more), so you'd better be recouped before you start. (There's not much joy in proving to the record company that, instead of being $1,000,000 unrecouped, you're only $900,000 unrecouped.) Most reputable auditors will give you an indication of whether an audit is worthwhile before you engage them. They do this by looking at your accounting statements and contracts, and knowing what the various record companies do.

Nowadays almost every record contract has a built-in right to audit, although in the past you had to ask for it. The audit clause will also say you can't audit more than once in any twelve-month period; that you can't examine any particular accounting statement more than once; and that you have to audit before the period to object has expired (see the above section).

13

Advanced Royalty Computations

DISTRIBUTION METHODS

Before we can get deeper into royalties, you need to know a little more about distribution. Records are distributed by four major methods: wholesale distribution entities, one-stops, rack jobbers, and licensees. Here's a brief look at each.

Wholesale Distribution Entities

Record wholesalers are by far the major means of distributing records. They're just like wholesale distributors in any other business—they buy from the manufacturing company (like Warner Bros., Epic, Universal, etc.) and sell to retail stores. (These are the major and independent distributors we discussed on pages 65 and 68.)

One-Stops

One-stops buy from the major distributors and then sell to 'Mom and Pop' record stores, who buy quantities too small for the majors to bother with. The one-stop buys in bulk (like a big retailer, so the majors will sell to them), and then sells onesies and twosies to the stores at a markup (which makes the price higher to Mom and Pop than to the chain stores).

Rack Jobbers

Rack jobbers are people who lease floor space from department stores and put in 'racks' of records. Although it looks like Sears and Target are selling your records, in fact they only turn the space over to someone who decides what product to carry, delivers it to the racks, pays rent to the store, and keeps the profits. (After all, could you really expect the shoe buyer at Wal-Mart to decide how many Marilyn Manson records to buy?)

Licensees

Records are also distributed by **licensees.** A *licensee* is someone who signs a 'license agreement' with a record company, which allows them to *actually manufacture* and distribute records, as opposed to merely buying and distributing goods manufactured by the record company. Typical examples of licensees are:

1. Foreign distributors of U.S. recordings;
2. Record clubs (you know, the ones you signed up for in college so you could get ten records for a penny and then move out of that dormitory before you got the bill for the next six at full price); and
3. Television-advertised packages (such as *Psychedelic Hits of the Sixties, The Best of Slim Whitman,* etc.), which are packages advertised on television and usually sold through direct mail ('Not Available in Any Store!'). These are still referred to as 'K-Tel' packages, after a company named K-Tel that was the biggest in this field; the name stuck even though K-Tel is now a much smaller player. (A friend of mine accurately observed that you know you're getting old when you watch commercials for the *Great Love Songs of the Nineties* and you want one.)

In addition to these four major methods, there are a variety of other weird ways to get records to the public. None of these are particularly meaningful at this time, but we'll touch on them because companies include royalty computations for most of them in their deals. They are things like direct mail by the record company (which almost never happens), distribution through armed forces post exchanges, and sales to educational institutions and libraries. There are also a host of new technologies, such as the inevitable delivery of records via Internet, satellite, or cable to your home, which we'll discuss on page 166.

So how does all this affect your royalties? To paraphrase George Orwell in *Animal Farm,* some record sales are more equal than others. Royalties for the exact same record can be quite different, depending on how and where it's distributed. For example, a record that sells in a U.S. record store at full price will bear a higher (substantially higher) royalty than the same record when it's sold through record clubs, or outside the United States, or through other assorted methods. It's especially fun to watch how new technologies (such as compact discs and the emerging electronic transmissions) go through predictable patterns of royalty shifts as they work their way from obscurity to the major way we deliver music. (See page 166 for an in-depth discussion of these patterns.)

Now you're ready to get into advanced royalty discussions. Let's take a look.

ROYALTIES FOR UNITED STATES SALES

We'll start first with United States sales, because, if you're signing to a U.S. company, all other sales are based on (i.e., a reduced percentage of) the rate for the United States.

The royalties we discussed in Chapters 7 and 9 are for records that meet *all* of the following criteria.

1. Sold in the United States; *and*
2. At full price (meaning, today, $17.98 or $18.98 for CDs. Some superstar CDs are priced at $19.98); *and*
3. Through normal retail channels (record stores); *and*
4. By the company's normal distribution channels (meaning the customary wholesale distributor—remember that some television advertised packages, for example, occasionally turn up in record stores, but these are sold by the television marketer's distributors [not the company's], and the royalty computation is totally different).

Sales that comply with 1 through 4 are known as **United States normal retail sales,** or sales through **USNRC,** meaning **U.S. Normal Retail Channels.** The royalty rate for these sales is usually defined in record deals as something like the **U.S. basic rate.** For simplicity, let's assume that your *U.S. basic rate* is 10% of retail; this makes the percentage reductions easy to follow.

FOREIGN ROYALTIES

The royalty reduction for sales outside the United States varies widely from company to company, and artist to artist. As a broad rule, companies usually give a higher rate in territories where they have an ownership interest in the foreign distributor (note—today the majors all have worldwide operations). Conversely, they give a lesser royalty where they are only licensing their product to a wholly independent third party.

Let's look at the most common patterns.

Canada

Canada seems to have evolved into 85% of the United States rate with most companies, although some still treat it as just another 'major' foreign territory (see the next paragraph). Using our example of a 10% U.S. basic rate, an 85% rate means you get 8.5% of retail for normal retail sales in Canada.

Majors

There are a number of markets in which American product sells particularly well, and these are known as the 'major' territories. They of course vary from artist to artist, but in general they are (in no particular order): United Kingdom, Australia, Italy, Japan, Holland, Germany, and France. (By the way, France is one of the strangest record markets on this planet. Records that are total dogs in all other territories can be gigantic smashes in France, and vice versa. France is also the only country in Europe to have a television system totally incompatible with the rest of Europe, as well as with the United States. Go figure.) The remaining EU countries (Western Europe) and Scandinavia can be treated as 'majors' if you have enough clout. The royalty for major territories again varies for the reasons set forth above (ownership versus licensing, and artist clout), but it's generally 70% to 75% of the U.S. basic rate, or 7% to 7.5% of retail in our example.

As you probably know, in 1993, Western Europe opened its borders and became one big, happy economic community. Since then (with clout), it's become a little easier to treat all of these territories as majors.

The foregoing of course also applies when signing to a U.K. company, except that the United States is considered a 'major territory'.

R.O.W.

R.O.W. stands for **rest of world** and includes the grab bag of countries left over, which I'll leave to you and your atlas to name. The royalty for these generally runs around 50% to 66⅔% of the U.S. basic rate, or 5% to 6% of retail under our assumption.

Having stated the general rules, let me also say that if you're an artist with a huge following in any particular foreign territory, you can usually negotiate a better royalty for that country. Superstars can also get better royalties than others, but the top for an artist signed to a U.S. company is around 16% to 17% for the major territories and 14% to 15% elsewhere, unless you have extraordinary bargaining power.

An interesting aspect of foreign royalties is that, in U.S. deals, they are almost always based on SRLP (see page 72 for what that is). That sounds logical, until you learn that virtually no other territory in the world has an SRLP. What really happens is that the companies **uplift** the wholesale price to create an SRLP, in a way that is identical to some U.S. companies' *uplift* for CD royalty computations (see page 95). For example, if the wholesale price is $10 and the uplift is 130%, the SRLP is deemed to be $13. The actual uplift percentage varies from territory to territory (depending on local pricing), from a low of 107% to a high of 140%, but the companies usually build in a set percentage, such as 127%.

Incidentally, foreign territories don't use the term 'wholesale.' Instead, they say **Published Price to Dealers** or **Published Dealer Price** (both of which are abbreviated as **PPD**), or **Base Price to Dealers** (abbreviated as **BPD**). There is a trend for some companies simply to state foreign royalties as a percentage of *PPD* (after a packaging deduction), and in this case your royalty should be uplifted to compensate for the fact that the base is lower. My guess is that, in time, all of the companies will move to a royalty that is a percentage of PPD or *BPD*, because it's simple, logical, and avoids any dispute about the proper percentage for uplift.

If you are signing with a U.K. record company, royalties for other territories will be a reduction of the U.K. rate. In this case, the U.S.

royalties will be less than if you signed directly with the U.S. company, but of course your U.K. royalties will be higher. The reason is pretty simple: the company you are signing with is taking a piece of the royalties in the other territories. How much less? About 2% to 4% of PPD for major territories, and another 2% to 4% for minors. You can sometimes get the same U.S. royalty as you get in the U.K. if there's a major buzz about you in the United States. And even if you're not so hot in the U.S., if the bidding is furious, you can sometimes jam up the U.S. rate with brute force. Sometimes you can also get the same rate in major European territories.

NEW TECHNOLOGIES, ELECTRONIC TRANSMISSIONS, AND THINGS THAT GO BUMP IN THE NIGHT

The next generation of music delivery will be an **electronic transmission** of some sort. This means little packets of digital joy will speed their way to you over a wire, satellite, or other gizmo not yet invented, so you can listen to it on demand (that is, hear any song, any time you want it), or burn it into a CD, or capture it on your computer or iPod or some other device coming down the pike. We'll talk more about the big picture of this area when we get to the laws on digital thingies (in Chapter 20) and the savage new electron frontiers (in Chapter 27).

Even as things careen around, the royalty structure for this coming era is starting to take form. We'll discuss what's happening after I give you:

The Passman Theory of Technology Cycles

There are predictable patterns that take place every time a new technology hits the record industry. It goes something like this:

1. The record companies scramble to see what their contracts say about these devices. Since they didn't exist when the deal was made, the contract either doesn't deal with them at all, or if it does, it usually pays a royalty that proves to be too high now that the fantasy is a reality.
2. Because the technology is so new, no one (including the record companies) really understands its economics. Also, when it's

first introduced, the thing is expensive, because it's a small market.

3. The result is a grace period during which royalties on these newbies are not particularly favorable to the artist. This is to give the technology a chance to get off the ground, and to help the record company justify the financial risk.

4. Invariably, this grace period carries on far beyond its economic life, during which time the companies make huge profits and the artist gets a smaller portion of them than he or she gets on the dominant technology.

5. As artist deals expire or are renegotiated, the rate goes up.

6. Finally, an industry pattern develops and royalty rates stabilize.

Electronic Transmission and New Technology Royalties

Right now, we're still in the 'what the hell is happening?' phase, but there are patterns developing. Before we discuss them, here's some terminology (which is evolving as I write this, so it may be out of date by the time you read it):

1. **Digital downloads.** A *digital download* is a transmission to the consumer (via Internet, satellite, cell phone, mental telepathy, etc.) that allows the buyer to record music for later use. In essence, it's the sale of a record electronically—instead of purchasing a physical copy, you buy the packet of information and record it yourself. (In other words, what you're getting right now through various pirates.)

   In the eyes of record company gurus, there are two different kinds of downloads:

   (a) **Tethered downloads.** *Tether,* which is a fancy word for 'leash,' means the record company doesn't give you complete control over the download. For example, you could download it to your computer, but couldn't copy it onto a CD. Or you could make two or three copies of it, but no more. Or you could make copies, but the copies would be encoded so you couldn't copy those. Or you could play it for thirty days, after which it self-destructs. Or you could listen to it but not hear anything (these are the cheapest).

   (b) **Untethered downloads.** As the name implies, you can copy it, burn it, stomp it, or do anything else your little heart desires.

2. **Streaming-on-demand.** This means you can call up and listen to any songs in the database, any time you like. Essentially, it's a virtual jukebox (the industry term is **celestial jukebox**), meaning you never have to carry your music collection around with you anymore. However, you're not allowed to copy; just listen.

The royalties for downloads and streams have yet to take a consistent pattern, but most companies are doing the following:

1. Where these rights are licensed to a third party (and by the way, the major record companies have conveniently created Music Net and Pressplay, entities owned by the majors, to act as a 'third party' for these purposes), you get a share of the money paid back to the record company (i.e., the license fees). The artist's percentage of these monies ranges anywhere from a high of 50%, down to as low as the artist royalty rate (which, as noted above, could be 12% or so). Big spread, huh? And the 50% companies are pushing their percentages downward as you read this.

   One company pays 50% for streams and tethered downloads, and pays the royalty under number 2 below for untethered downloads. Others are trying not to structure anything as a license, arguing in effect that they're 'selling' the digital rights to a third party just like they sell records to a retailer. Thus, they pay everything under number 2 below.

2. Where music is sold by the company directly to consumers or to a middleman (as noted in the last part of number 1 above), you get anywhere from 70% to 80% of your otherwise applicable royalty rate, based on the price received by the record company. They also take a packaging fee of 25%, and only pay on 85% for 'free goods.' This, of course, for a sale in which there is no package, and there are no free goods . . .

By the time you read this, things may have changed several times. For example, Universal Music Group (the largest of the major record companies) recently took the step of paying a full royalty rate (no CD reduction) on untethered downloads, based on 100% of a constructed retail price (130% of universal's receipts), with no packaging deduction, and no free goods. As of this writing, we're still waiting for the others to fall in line. Hopefully they'll have done so by the time you read this. If not, help me pound them.

Here's a sample calculation: If the consumer pays $1 to download a single song, and Universal receives 65¢ from the download store, your royalty would be computed as follows: 65¢ times 130% equals 84.50¢ as a royalty base. If you have a 15% royalty, Universal would pay you 15% of the 84.50¢ (i.e., 12.68¢). Other companies pay you 15% of the 65¢, which is only a royalty of 9.75¢. And some even pay you 80% of that rate (taking a 'new technology' reduction, which reduces the 15% royalty down to 12%), then further deduct 25% for packaging (meaning the 12% is applied to a base of 75% of 65¢, or 48.75¢), so your royalty is only 12% of 48.75¢, or 5.85¢. Thus, the royalty for the same download could range from 12.67¢ to 5.85¢. Big difference, huh?

U.K. royalties for downloads are just about as messed up as those in the States. In general, the companies try to treat downloads as if they're sales of physical records, even though there's obviously way less cost.
   Here's an example:

1. The customer pays £1 to download a track.
2. The distributor takes about 20%, and pays 80p to the label.
3. The label uses this 80p as the royalty base, so it takes off 25% for packaging (that doesn't exist). Some labels try to reduce another 25% to 30% on the theory that (a) it's a new technology, and a lot of contracts allow a new technology deduction; or (b) it's a way of converting a retail price to a PPD; or (c) we're a big record company, and you're not, so we can push you around.
4. The company then applies your artist royalty against whatever's left over.

At the time I'm writing this, things are still moving around like the stairways in Harry Potter. Stay tuned for late breaking news.

MASTER LICENSES

When masters are licensed out, like for motion pictures, television shows, commercials, etc., record companies historically credited the artist's account with 50% of the net receipts. Over recent years, however, a fee for handling the license has crept into agreements. All of the majors have what's called a **special markets** division, which basically means people who take existing recordings and figure out ways to squeeze money from them. For example, they promote the use of their masters in motion pictures, put together compilation records (which we'll discuss in a minute), etc. To cover the cost of these special marketing divisions, companies like to get a fee of anywhere from 15% to 25% of the receipts, which comes off the top before splitting with the artist. In other words, if they got $100 for a license, and took a 20% fee, they'd take off $20 for special marketing, then credit the artist with 50% of the remaining $80 ($40). With enough bargaining power, you can squeeze down this overhead fee, and sometimes (rarely) eliminate it.

Now, speaking of those compilation packages . . .

COUPLING AND COMPILATIONS

The practice of putting your performances together with those of other artists is known as **coupling,** and albums with a bunch of different artists are called **compilations.** Samplers (see page 183) are a form of *coupling,* but the practice also exists at a much higher end of the scale. It includes television-advertised *compilation* albums (*Texas Punk Bands of the Sixties,* etc.); soundtrack albums from motion pictures with diverse music (*O Brother, Where Art Thou?; Austin Powers; The Bodyguard;* etc.); and any other marketing device the record companies can dream up. Something called the NOW series has radically changed the face of U.S. compilations, by including major artists and major hits relatively soon after their popularity. The practice started in Europe (where these kinds of compilations have been common for quite a while), and spread to the U.S. a few years back. NOW CDs can sell multimillions of copies.

Royalties

The royalty on coupled product sold by your record company is pretty much what you would think—if there are ten cuts on the album and you've done one of them, you get one-tenth of your normal royalty; if you've done two cuts out of ten, you get 20%, etc. This process is called **pro-ration,** and you are said to have a **pro-rata** royalty (meaning your royalty is in proportion to the number of cuts on the album). (Every once in a while *pro-ration* is based on the playing time of your cut versus the total playing time of the record, but this is pretty rare. It's almost always based solely on the number of cuts.)

The royalty on coupled product that's licensed to someone else by your record company is usually 50% of the company's licensing receipts, less an overhead fee, as we just discussed. For example, if a record company licenses your song to a TV-packaged album and gets 10¢ per master (these deals are often done in pennies rather than as a percentage of retail), and your company charges a 20% fee, they pay you half of 10¢ less 2¢ (i.e., half of 8¢, or 4¢). Remember, in an all-in deal, your half includes the producer's royalty (the producer's share of this is discussed on page 129).

Control

You should always try to control coupling, both for (1) the artistic reason that you don't want to be on a record with someone you hate; and (2) the financial reason that you don't want to be the major cut selling an album of dorks when you only get a small part of the royalty. With moderate bargaining power, you can control this completely during the term of your deal. With more bargaining power, you can control it after the term if you're recouped, and with massive clout, you can control it forever. Restrictions normally are only for the United States, unless you have really strong bargaining power. These compilation albums are major sources of revenue in foreign territories, and the foreign licensees tend to do whatever they feel like, regardless of what your contract says. Also, even if you have ultimate control, companies will insist on the right to couple for in-transit uses (such as in-flight programs for airplanes) without your consent—they view these as promotional.

Even as a new artist, you should at least be able to get a limit on the number of couplings. A common provision is to say the company can't couple more than two of your selections per year, and can't put you on more than two albums per year. Note the difference between these two concepts: If the company's only limit is two selections per year, they could put one of your hits on 37 different compilation albums.

JOINT RECORDINGS

A close cousin to coupling is a **joint recording**. A *joint recording* is where more than one royalty artist gets together on the same song, such as a duet.

Royalty

The most common arrangement is for the royalty to get split among the artists in proportion to their numbers, so that if it's a duet, each gets half; if it's a trio, each gets a third; etc. While this is usually pretty straightforward, there are a couple of twists:

1. If you do a duet with a five-piece group, be sure that the group only counts as one entity. Otherwise, the company might say there are six royalty artists instead of two (you and the group), and you'll only get one-sixth of the royalty instead of one-half.
2. Whose royalty gets divided, yours or theirs? If you're the star, be sure your price is a share of your royalty. If you're new and singing with a star, try for a piece of theirs.
3. A lot of times, joint recordings are done on a 'trade-out' basis. In other words, if Sally records a duet on Fred's album, Fred agrees to record a duet on Sally's album, and neither one pays anything to the other.

Control

It's easy to get control over joint recordings. Just ask and the record company will readily agree. The reason why is pretty simple—no one goes into the studio with someone he or she doesn't like.

'GREATEST HITS' OR 'BEST OF'

The royalties on Greatest Hits albums (see page 118 for what a 'Greatest Hits' album is) are pro-rata royalties (see page 170), based on the album they come from. For example, if your first two albums were 12%, and the others 13%, and if half the Greatest Hits album was from the first two albums (12%) and half from the others (13%), your royalty on the Greatest Hits album would be 12.5% (50% times 12%, plus 50% times 13%). But these calculations are trickier than they look at first glance.

For example, suppose that some of the albums from which you take the selections had escalations because of sales success (see page 97). Which royalty do you use? The initial release royalty? The escalated royalty? And do you also get an escalation based on sales of the Greatest Hits album itself?

The answer is usually one of three:

1. You get the lowest royalty for the album from which each selection is taken (i.e., the royalty before any escalations based on sales of that album), and then a negotiated escalation based on sales of the Greatest Hits album. Under this formula, the starting royalty is pro-rated based on non-escalated rates.
2. You get the highest royalty rate achieved by the album from which the selection is taken (i.e., the escalated rate based on sales of that album) with no further escalations for sales of the Greatest Hits album. These rates are then pro-rated the same way we did it in the first example.
3. You get the lowest possible rate and no escalations for anything. This is what you get if you don't ask.

Let's look at examples of the first two:

1. Suppose a Greatest Hits album contains ten selections, consisting of three selections from the initial term, when your rate (before escalations) was 10%; two selections from the first option period, when your (non-escalated) rate was 11%; and five selections from the second option period, when your (non-escalated) rate was 12%. Under the first approach (no escalations count), the result would be the following:

Masters	Album Royalty
3 Masters recorded during initial term: These masters are ³⁄₁₀ of the album (30%), because 3 of the 10 selections on the album are at this rate. Thus, the royalty for these cuts is 30% of 10% (the initial period royalty):	3.0%
2 Masters recorded during first option term: 2 of 10 (20%), at 11%:	2.2%
5 Masters recorded during second option term: 5 of 10 (50%), at 12%	6.0%
TOTAL ROYALTY ON ALBUM	**11.2%**

This 11.2% royalty might then escalate based on sales of the Greatest Hits album. For example, you might get an additional 1% (to 12.2%) at 1 million units, and another 1% (to 13.2%) at 2 million.

2. Now let's look at the second method (where escalated royalties are pro-rated). We'll use the same figures as the first example, but assume the royalties on early albums escalated because of sales, to 12% for the album made in the first option period, and to 14% for the album made in the second option period. (Assume there are no escalations for the initial term album.)

Now here's how the royalties look:

Masters	Royalty
Initial Term: 3 of 10 (30%) at 10%:	3.0%
First Option Term: 2 of 10 (20%) at 12%:	2.4%
Second Option Term: 5 of 10 (50%) at 14%:	7.0%
TOTAL ROYALTY ON ALBUM	**12.4%**

As noted above, under this method there are no escalations for sales of the Greatest Hits album.

MULTIPLE ALBUMS

The **multiple album** has gone through an enormous change since vinyl disappeared. Originally, it meant an album that couldn't fit on one vinyl disc, since vinyl discs were limited to a maximum of fifty some-odd minutes of playing time. Since CDs can hold substantially more than this, it takes a lot of material to require two CDs. Thus *multiple albums* (in the classic sense of a two-CD package) are rare. (Box sets of three or four CDs are a special category, which we'll discuss in the next section.)

These two-in-one sets don't sell as well as single albums, if for no other reason than because they're more expensive (at the time of this writing, a double CD package costs around $24.98). Because of this, and serious mechanical royalty issues (we'll get to that on page 234), every form contract says you can't deliver a true multiple album without the company's consent.

If the company does consent, your royalty may be reduced. The reduction works like this: Your royalty is adjusted downward in the ratio that the selling price of the multiple album is less than two times the price of a single-album price. That's not as confusing as it sounds if we use numbers: For easy math, assume a single-album CD price is $10. That means you'd only get a full royalty for a multiple album if its retail price were doubled to $20 (i.e., if the company were getting the full price of two single albums). If the price of the double album is $19, that is only ¹⁹⁄₂₀ths (or 95%) of $20. Accordingly, you'd get 95% (¹⁹⁄₂₀ths) of your normal royalty, applied against the $19 price. So if your normal royalty is 10% of retail, you'd get 9.5% (¹⁹⁄₂₀ths of the 10%) for a $19 multiple-album set.

If a single album has more than fourteen selections, some form contracts consider it a multiple album. But, if it only consists of one CD, it's priced the same as, or perhaps a dollar more than, a single album. Your royalty shouldn't be reduced for a single CD album just because it has a lot of tracks, but a lot of forms do. And because the price is not increased (and thus is nowhere near double that of a single album), the formula in the prior paragraph could cut your royalty in half. So watch out for this. (Mechanical royalties are greatly reduced for these babies, as we'll see on page 234).

Regardless of how you define it, and no matter how your royalty gets computed, all record companies treat a multiple album as only one album for purposes of your delivery commitment. Accordingly, if you thought you'd knock out your obligation to deliver two albums with a multiple album, they got there ahead of you. Sorry.

Note here I'm discussing multiple albums that are sold through retail stores. The multiple albums sold through TV campaigns are an entirely different story, as we discussed on pages 170–71.

BOX SETS

Box sets are a collection of three, four, or sometimes more CDs sold in a single package, usually with an expensive booklet, and for a very high price. Most often these are retrospectives of an artist's career, and may contain unreleased cuts, alternative versions of well-known songs, compromising photos, etc. They can also be a retrospective of a company (for example, Capitol or Motown) or a genre (the Blues, the Definitive Polka), etc.

The royalties on *box sets* are always negotiated at the time, and are very specific to the deal. They'll depend on the price, the number of selections (which affects the mechanical royalties—we'll discuss those later), the size of the artist's original royalty rate, and your leverage. Unfortunately, there are no real guidelines since each deal is made separately, except that there's almost always a reduced mechanical royalty, and usually a reduced artist royalty as well.

TELEVISION ADVERTISING

A number of years ago, record companies figured out (only in Europe at the time) that they could sell a lot of records by doing short bursts of television advertising. And, in fact, this worked swimmingly. However, television advertising is very expensive, and the companies said they couldn't do it unless the artist gave them some kind of a break. What kind of break? Funny you should ask:

Companies want to reduce your royalty on the advertised album to 50% for as long as they can get away with. They love to get two years, and I love to give them much less. Here are some things to ask for:

1. Get approval of the campaign before they can deduct anything.
2. Try to keep the reduction to the semi-annual accounting period during which the campaign is launched, and the following period (maybe a third if you have to). The idea is to keep it close to the campaign, so the reduction is only on those sales generated by the TV ads.
3. The total amount taken from your royalty shouldn't exceed half of the cost of the campaign.
4. Make certain that they can only reduce the royalties in those territories where the campaign is running—you'd be surprised what their little forms say about taking reductions everywhere.

This practice quickly spread to the United States, so the idea of taking a royalty reduction for TV campaigns is alive, well, and thriving on American soil.

DVDS, VIDEOCASSETTES, AND OTHER HOME VIDEO DEVICES

DVDs that are *purely audio* are treated as CDs, except the royalty is usually 70% of the full (cassette) rate. If there is a substantial video component (e.g., the entire album plus promotional videos), some companies prorate the royalties (see page 170 for discussion of proration) between audio and video, meaning they pay your audio royalty on a portion, and your video royalty on a portion. In other words, if there's thirty minutes of music, and ten minutes of video, you would get three-fourths of your audio royalty rate (thirty minutes over forty minutes), and one-fourth (ten minutes over forty minutes) of your video rate.

If it's purely audio/visual, like a concert or collection of promo videos, the royalties are:

Manufactured Units

If home video units (both DVD and the disappearing VHS) are manufactured and distributed by your record company, you get a royalty which falls in the 10% to 20% of wholesale range for U.S. normal retail top-price sales. You can sometimes knock out the packaging deduction on videos, and most companies vary their royalty depending on the retail price. For example, the royalty might be 10% for a retail price of less than $15, 15% to 17.5% for a retail price of $15 to $20, and 20% for a price of more than $20. Foreign royalties tend to be around 10% to 15% of wholesale, and all royalties are reduced for budget line (usually to a one-half royalty) and for free goods (only real ones). (Budget-line records are discussed on page 180, and the same idea applies to home video devices.)

Licensed Sales

While the major companies don't do this for their mainstream sales, smaller record companies may license someone else to manufacture and distribute home video. In this case, that company pays a royalty to the record company, and the company pays you 50% of its net receipts. 'Net receipts' are what's left after the company takes its gross receipts and deducts the following:

1. **A distribution fee** for the record company, which is a percentage of gross and therefore taken first. This is a key lesson in computing fees: If you get a percentage of something, always take it first so that it's against the biggest possible dollar amount. The *distribution fee* is to cover the company's overhead in handling the licensing, and it ranges anywhere from 10% to 25%, depending on your bargaining power. It can sometimes be eliminated (if you're the ruler of a moderate-size nation).
2. **Distribution expenses,** meaning the costs of duplicating, shipping, etc., necessary to distribute the product.
3. **Third party payments** to unions and guilds, though many companies now try to charge these against the artist's 50%.

The result of this is net receipts, and you get 50% as your share.

All-in Video Royalties

When you have an all-in record deal (see page 98), then you're responsible for these little goodies out of your share of the dough:

1. All copyright royalties payable for songs used in the videos. (See page 235 for what these are.)
2. All third-party payments, which include the *audio* producer of the master recordings used in the video, the unions, and anyone else entitled to a royalty.

Recoupment of Video Costs

All the costs of making videos go into a pot, to be charged against your video royalties. Half of these costs are also charged to your audio record royalties, under the theory that 'we're a big record company, and you're not, so we can do this.' When you make your deal, be sure you don't end up getting charged twice for the same cost—in other words, once the costs have been taken from your audio record royalties, the same amount shouldn't also be taken from your video royalties, or vice versa. Many record company forms would technically allow this, although I'm not certain it's intended, and I've never seen them do it.

So now we have a pot with chargeable costs in it. The company next takes your video royalties and throws them into this pot. When these monies equal the costs charged, the excess royalties are paid out or credited to your audio royalty account if you're unrecouped (in the same way that audio record royalties are paid or credited after recouping recording costs). Of course, if you're unrecouped, you won't see any of the dough, because the monies are gobbled up by the black hole of your deficit.

Because it's so hard to ever see video royalties, you can sometimes get the company to pay an advance for a home video release—after all, you're giving them something beyond what's in the deal. And sometimes you can even get them not to cross-collateralize the home video with your record deal, so that you at least have a shot at seeing royalties.

MID-PRICE RECORDS

After a record has had its initial run in current release, it is known as a **catalog item,** meaning it's listed in the company's catalog of available titles, but isn't being currently promoted. Some *catalog items* are issued at **mid-price,** meaning a reduced price that's designed to encourage consumers to buy older titles. Today, a typical *mid-price* for a CD originally released at $17.98 would be $11.98. The contractual definition of a mid-price record (with slight variations from company to company) is one 'with a suggested retail price between 65% and 80% of the price for newly released top-line records.' Some companies also say it's a record with a price at least two dollars below the new release prices, so that if it fits either category, it's considered mid-price. And some companies have no mid-price, which means everything under 80% of the top price is defined as a 'budget' record (which we'll discuss in the next section).

Royalty

The royalty rate for mid-price is usually 75% of the U.S. basic rate (7.5% if you have a 10% royalty). Note this is a double whammy —not only is the royalty rate lower, but the retail price on which it's based is also lower. The record companies justify this because their wholesale price is lower, and accordingly so is their profit margin. Their thinking is that the lower price will generate extra sales to more than make up the lost revenue.

As you gain clout, you can negotiate a period of time after initial release before a record can be sold at mid-price (usually twelve to eighteen months), or perhaps even a flat prohibition without your consent. This provision used to be easier to get than it is today, because in recent years it's become routine to issue catalog items at mid-price, and also because of the 'developing artist' prices we'll discuss in a minute.

If you do get restrictions, it will only be for the U.S. This is because, in some foreign territories, mid-price is customary for the first release. Presumably, your interests and the record company's are the same, since they want to maximize their profits in that territory. Thus they won't put something out at mid-price unless they believe the reduced price will promote the sale of enough additional copies to justify the lower profit margin.

BUDGET RECORDS

The next step down from mid-price is **budget,** which means a record the company doesn't think it can sell unless it knocks the price way down. These are the ones stuck in bins (with a handwritten sign saying 'Big Savings!') selling for $9.98 or less. The contractual definition of budget records is one with a price of less than 65% of the top-line price, but (as noted above) sometimes there is no mid-price definition and the contract says everything under 80% of the top-line price is a *budget* record.

Royalty

The royalty on budget records is usually 50% of the top-line royalty rate, or 5% in our 10% example. With some clout, you can hold back budget records for a period after initial release. Because being on a budget line is a statement about what the company thinks of your career, you can usually get a longer holdback than you can for mid-price. For example, in the United States, the company might agree to wait eighteen months to two years after initial release. Again, foreign markets have their own peculiarities, and there will be little you can do unless you're a major artist in a particular territory.

As your muscle increases, you may be able to get a flat prohibition against budget, at least during the term of your agreement. And, if you can't get the right to consent to budgets after the term, a compromise is to say they can't do it as long as your account is recouped. The idea is that, if they've lost money on your project, they can do whatever they want to get even, but otherwise they must keep you off the budget line.

Over the last few years, this has been harder to get, as companies are insisting on flexibility in pricing. One reason is:

NEW AND DEVELOPING ARTIST PRICES

There's been a growing practice of releasing new artists at what's known as 'new and developing artist prices.' The theory is that folks will fork over a few bucks to try something new, but will balk at a steeper price. So a number of debut albums are released at mid-price. Because this works pretty well in pushing new artists, the companies have gotten tougher about controlling pricing, and it's harder to get limits in your deal.

Some companies take this to the extreme and put out radically discounted CDs (like at $5.99) to get a buzz going on the artist, pump up initial sales, etc. If your company wants to do that, they'll ask you to give up your royalties on the cheapies—they make no money at these prices, and it's really just another form of marketing. As long as it's for a limited run (say 150,000 units or so), I would go along because this can only be good for your career.

RECORD CLUBS

Record clubs are mail-order 'clubs' that you join by agreeing to buy a certain number of records. (We touched on them on page 162.) Royalties for record-club sales are the *lesser* of (a) half of your top-line royalty rate, or (b) 50% of your company's net licensing receipts from the record club (remember, these sales are licensed to *record clubs,* who manufacture and distribute the records, and pay license fees to your company). Usually by asking, you can get a straight 50% of the company's net licensing receipts. However, since the company doesn't get such a high rate from the club, this is what you'd get anyway (half the company's net is usually less than half your royalty rate).

The companies say lower royalties for record clubs are justified on the grounds that the marketing cost is higher (advertising, shipping, etc.) and there are a lot of 'bad debts,' meaning people who don't pay for records they've ordered. Also, the companies say they make less on these sales than if they sold the records themselves, and so they only do it because they believe these are sales to people who wouldn't buy at retail (and thus the sales are gravy). Not everyone agrees with this . . .

Record-club free goods are also a lot of fun. Guess how many records they can give away for every hundred they sell? Remember (from page 77) that the norm for retail sales is 15%, or fifteen free albums for every eighty-five sold. With clubs, it's a bit more. What's your guess for each hundred sold? If you said one hundred, you're right— the company's contract with the club only limits them to giving away *100%,* meaning one free for every one sold! In other words, out of every two hundred shipped, one hundred can be free!

So you should ask for a limit in your contract of one free record for every sale, right? Wrong. The one-to-one limit is for the company's *entire catalog,* which means they might give away more of your records and less of someone else's, as long as the *total* doesn't exceed one to one. At superstar levels you can get your own one-to-one limit (the companies have the right to do it for a few artists, but they don't like to tell you this). Even with your own limit, however, they only 'settle up' the difference between one to one and whatever they did to you every couple of years.

Unfortunately, without a lot of clout, you'll have to live with this nonsense. As your leverage grows, you can sometimes control the company's right to put your records in clubs, or at least delay the club release (the idea is that, if you hold back record clubs until, say, six months from release in stores, club sales won't compete with retail sales during the hottest period).

CUTOUTS, DELETES, SCRAPS, AND OTHER FOOD FOR BOTTOM FISHERS

Every company publishes a catalog of records it currently offers for sale. **Cutouts** and **deletes** are records that have been taken out of the company's catalog, and this isn't done until a title is pronounced dead, stiff, and buried. When a company finds that an album isn't selling at mid-price or budget, either because nobody cares about it or because the company has over-manufactured and/or had gigantic returns, it deletes the title and looks for a way to bail out for whatever it can get. These leftovers are sometimes sold as **scrap,** to be broken up for their component parts. If not, they're sold as **schlock,** which means they're put in the bins where the prices are 99¢, $1.50, etc. (I've always felt it adds insult to injury when these bins sit on the sidewalk in front of a record store, because it shows they don't even care if people steal them.) Artists get no royalties whatsoever for these, as the company says (correctly) that they're sold at cost or below, just to get rid of them. With negotiating power, you can provide the company can't schlock your records until they're deleted from the catalog, and in any event not within twelve or eighteen months after initial release. (Note you can do this for *schlock,* not *scrap.* You can't restrict their ability to sell as scrap because the public never knows about this; schlock, however, tells the world that your records are fit for lining parakeet cages.) You can also get the right to buy these records at the best price offered to the record company, but I've never felt this is of any practical value. You're not likely to be able to sell them at a better price than the company, and what are you going to do with 100,000 dogs?

PREMIUMS

Send in a Wheaties box top and get the latest Eminem single. Records sold this way are called **premiums,** which means they're sold in conjunction with a product or service, typically at a very low price. The royalty is correspondingly low—usually at half rate—and is based on the price at which the record company sells the record to the advertiser (also very low). (There may in fact be no other price, because the records are often given away or sold at less than cost to the public.)

If you know enough to ask, even with very little bargaining power, you can prohibit *premiums* without your consent. This is because they really constitute a commercial use of your name, likeness, and voice (by tying you into the product of the people offering them).

SAMPLERS

Virgin Records once put out a record called *The Tape That Ate My Brain,* consisting of one track each from a number of new bands it had signed. This is a **sampler,** meaning it gives you a 'sample' of a number of different releases. *Samplers* are typically sold at a low price (like $7.98 for a CD), and they bear no royalties because they're promotional (not profit) items. Rather than limit them for a new band, I've always thought it would be fun to *require* the company to include you, but so far no one at the record companies appreciates my sense of humor. While there is potential for abuse (sometimes they include a major artist to get people to buy the sampler and listen to the minor artists), they're pretty harmless. In fact, they're almost nonexistent these days.

DART, DIGITAL PERFORMANCE, AND WEBCASTING MONIES

Recording artists are entitled to monies payable under the Audio Home Recording Act of 1992, also known as the DART Bill (standing, I think, for 'Digital Audio Recorders and Tapes'). Also, in 1995, Congress added a right to be paid for the digital performance of masters, and in 1998, the right to be paid for webcasting. All of this, of course, sounds like gibberish because I haven't given you any background to understand what it means. The reason is that I want to do it after we've discussed copyright, publishing, and a few other concepts. So use a little of the patience that driven musical artists are so famous for, and hang on till we get there.

As a preview, the important thing to know is that with each of these, the artist is *paid directly* by the user of rights, meaning the monies don't go into the record company's tight little fist, and therefore can't be used to recoup your deficit. This is a spectacular thing, except for the fact that, at present, these are insignificant monies. And the fact that, as you read this, companies are trying to figure out how to grab them.

If you are paid directly, your record deal will say that you're not entitled to share in the company's monies. In other words, if whoever collects webcasting monies pays you and the company separately, you won't share in each other's dough. What you want to add is that, if anyone pays all the monies to the record company, you get 50% of those. And try to say that the company can't use these monies to recoup your deficit. Your argument is that they didn't expect to have them for recoupment in the first place.

FOREIGN PUBLIC PERFORMANCE OF MASTERS

In many countries, the *record company* is paid a royalty every time a recording is played on the radio. (This is different from public performance royalties that are paid to a *songwriter and publisher* of the *musical composition* when a recording is played on the radio, and which have always been paid in the U.S., as we'll discuss on page 237.) Public performance monies for recordings didn't exist in the U.S. until 1995, and the law enacting them is so narrow that it means very little today (as we'll discuss in more detail on page 304).

In foreign territories, these monies not only exist, but are substantial. Record companies don't like to share their foreign public performance royalties, on the theory that the artists can get their share by directly applying to the foreign performing rights society. The problem is that most U.S. artists aren't allowed to collect foreign performances under the local rules, and while this should move the companies to tears, somehow it doesn't. They simply dig into the position that they don't have to give the artist any part of the record company's share, and this is an extremely difficult point for the artist to win.

14

Loan-out, Independent Production, Label, and Distribution Deals

LOAN-OUT DEALS

Loan-out Corporations

As you begin to get more successful, you will undoubtedly want a **loan-out corporation.** Everybody on the block has one. It's called a *loan-out* because the corporation (not you) enters into the deals, and 'loans' your services to others for recording, concerts, etc. This is the entity you see people naming with cute little phrases (two of my favorites are 'Disappearing, Inc.,' and 'I Want It All'). As the tax laws have changed over the years, particularly in the pension area, it's questionable whether it makes sense to have a loan-out company. I personally think it's marginal whether the expense of maintaining such a corporation is worth the benefit, but it has to be looked at in each individual case. Consult your accountant, lawyer, or bartender.

Anyway, for record deals it works like this: You sign an exclusive recording contract with your own corporation, on a form that looks like the record company deal. (I'm using the term 'corporation' for simplicity, but in fact it can be an **LLC** [a **Limited Liability Company,** which is something that looks and smells like a corporation, but is treated for tax purposes like a partnership], a general partnership, a limited partnership, a partnership of corporations, a cluster of worms, etc.) Once you sign with your own corporation, the record company signs a recording agreement with that entity, which agrees to supply your services. It looks like this:

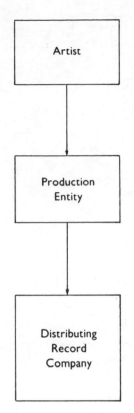

Figure 9. Loan-out deal structure.

In the U.K., because of the international flavour of European life, as well as the fact that the U.K. has various tax treaties and intricacies that don't exist in the U.S., loan-out companies may have very important tax planning aspects. In particular, since a substantial amount of money may be generated from touring and record sales outside the U.K., this type of tax planning becomes critical when you hit the superstar levels. The details of this are beyond what I would inflict on you at this stage of your quest for music biz knowledge, and I also can't think of any reason to educate the Inland Revenue by spelling them out. Just know that when you get to the big leagues, you need some tax planning.

Over the last few years, loan-outs have become less important. Also, I'm told Irish songwriters can avoid all taxes if they don't incorporate. Shall we knock out some Celtic hits?

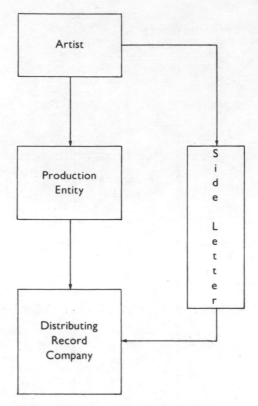

Figure 10. Loan-out deal with side letter.

Inducement (Side) Letters

As you can see, this means you have no direct deal with the record company. So what's to keep you from walking out on your own corporation (after all, you could fire yourself, or quit), and then thumbing your nose at the record company? You personally have no deal with the company—only your bankrupt corporation has a contract, and its secretary/treasurer is now in Lithuania with the masters.

Well, you know the companies won't let that happen, so they have you sign something known as an **inducement letter** or **side letter**. This is simply a piece of paper saying that if your corporation doesn't perform by delivering recordings, you will deliver them directly to the record company. So the real picture looks like Figure 10.

The side letter is an integral part of an independent production deal. It's like an emergency detour. If the highway is flooded, the company sends a Jeep down a back road to haul your butt back in.

Structure of Loan-out Deals

Loan-out contracts are very similar to contracts directly between the record company and artist (known as **direct agreements**), except that:

1. The parties, of course, are the record company and the corporation, instead of the company and you;
2. The corporation agrees to supply your services and recordings;
3. There are additional legal clauses, which are basically assurances that the corporation has the right to your exclusive services, that it has the right to deliver your recordings, etc.; and
4. You have to sign an *inducement letter* saying that the loan-out is really a phony, and if you or it try anything cute, you'll perform directly for the record company as if the loan-out didn't exist.

INDEPENDENT PRODUCTION AGREEMENTS

An independent production agreement is what a major-distributed independent label (we discussed these companies on page 67) signs with the major. These deals are just like loan-outs, except that the artist doesn't own the corporation in the middle (let's call the corporation the 'production entity,' because it 'produces' the recordings). Typically, the production entity is owned by a producer or other record mogul whose 'magic ears' have found you. It then signs to a major or mini-major (let's call it the 'distributor') to deliver the artist's recordings. As we'll see in a minute, under these deals, the inducement letter is even more critical.

There are two basic types of these production deals:

1. **A single-artist deal**
   is where the production entity makes an agreement with the record company for one specific artist. Note, by the way, that the production entity may have signed more than one artist; we're talking only about the deal between the production entity and the record company.
2. **A multi-artist deal,**
   sometimes called a **label deal,** is where the production entity supplies recordings of various artists, many of whom (or perhaps all of whom) have not yet been signed by the production

entity. As you can imagine, this type of deal is much more complicated than a single-artist deal. So let's start with the simpler one.

Single-Artist Deals

A single-artist deal is basically the same as a loan-out deal, but because the production entity isn't owned by the artist, there are a couple of differences:

1. The deal between the artist and the production entity is now a real, arm's-length transaction, as opposed to one the artist makes with himself or herself. This means there is a true negotiation—i.e., where the parties are at 'arm's length' from each other—and the artist asks for most of the things he or she would get from a record company, like guaranteed release, approvals, etc. (When you sign to a production entity, there are some points you should get in this type of deal that you don't need from a record company. We'll discuss these in a minute.)
2. There is a possibility that the artist can get into a fight with the production entity. This means it's more likely that the record company will exercise its rights under the inducement letter, and thus the terms of the inducement letter are critical.

Why Do It?   So why should an artist make a deal like this? Wouldn't it be better to have direct contact with your record company? Well, the answer is 'maybe.' A production deal has its pluses and minuses compared to a direct deal, and whether it's better for you depends on your specific situation.

Here are the negatives:

1. The production entity in the middle takes some of the royalty. Traditionally its deal with the record company provides a higher royalty than direct artist deals (by 1% to 2%) for precisely this purpose. But you still normally get less of a royalty than under a direct deal, and this is especially so when you're successful. The reason is that, with success, the production entity's deal with the record company 'tops out' and leaves no room for them to keep anything without getting it from you.
2. It may be harder for you to coordinate marketing, promotion,

etc., if you and your manager have no direct contact with the record company.

3. There may be problems auditing the distributor directly (see page 160 for what auditing is). In its contract, the production entity has the right to audit the distributor. But the distributor doesn't want two different people (you and the production entity) doing the same audit, and since it has no direct contract with you, it doesn't have to let you in at all.

4. Production entities are more likely to ask for your publishing and/or your management at the same time they make a record deal, and this is rarely to the artist's advantage.

5. The production entity might go south with your money.

On the positive side:

1. The production entity may be owned by someone who really brings something to the party. For example, there are production companies owned by major producers who will only work with a new artist if the artist signs to his or her entity. Other production companies are owned by important managers, promotion people, or industry people with good track records (translation: they have a lot of clout).

2. You may be able to get the same calculation of royalties that the production entity gets (meaning the same reduction for foreign sales, free-good limits, reserve limits, etc.). If you're a new artist and they're an established company, this can be more favorable than you could get on your own.

3. And I saved the best for last: Nobody else may want to sign you.

On balance, this is not your ideal choice (barring very unusual circumstances, like a great producer), but it can be a very desirable alternative to flipping Big Macs.

Artist Deal Points. If you're making a deal with a production entity, you want to be sure that, in addition to all the other items we talked about for record deals (guaranteed release, advances, approvals, etc.), you get the following:

1. You want the same computation of royalties that the production entity has (for packaging, free goods, foreign, budget, CD,

etc.). Indeed, you may want to ask for a percentage of the production company's receipts. It's not uncommon to structure an agreement whereby the artist gets 75% of the production entity's royalties (with the artist paying the producer from his or her share), or maybe 50% or 60% (with the production entity paying the producer from its share). This percentage should also apply to advances in excess of recording costs.

2. Try to get direct accountings from the record company. This may or may not be possible, depending on the production entity's own deal. Your worry is the situation we talked about on page 132, where a producer is owed money by an artist and no royalties are payable, but in this case the roles are reversed: You're the one due money, and the production entity may not have any royalties coming in. This can easily happen to your production entity—especially if it has signed several artists (as you'll see in excruciating detail on page 195).

Production Deal Points.   Now, let's jump over the table and get the production entity's point of view. (Come on—it will make you a better-rounded person.) Here are two major areas of concern:

1. Remember how the artist wants the same computation of royalties as you? (See paragraph 1 of the previous section.) In representing production entities, I've rarely found it worthwhile to recompute the royalties. First of all, it's difficult, complex, time-consuming, and usually given to a low-level bookkeeper who doesn't quite understand what to do. So half the time they end up paying more than you would if you just used the same computation. Second, even when done correctly, the advantage you pick up is often minimal. Third, if and when the artist finds it out (which of course will only happen if there's a great deal of success), you look like a pig, which is not usually good for artist relations.

2. Make sure you don't give the artist any rights you don't have in the first place. I remember a situation where one production company gave the artist approval of coupling, approval of album cover artwork, guaranteed release, etc., when they didn't have those things from the record company. If you fall into this trap, at best it will be embarrassing, and at worst the artist could walk away from your deal when you don't deliver. (Note the artist isn't going very far—if he or she succeeds in

walking away from you, they'll still have to record for the record company under their inducement letter. However, this doesn't do you any good—the record company won't pay you any royalties if you lose the artist because of your screw-up. This position is known in show biz as 'sucking rocks.')

Multi-Artist (Label) Deals

A **multi-artist deal,** as the name implies, is one where the production entity has a deal with a record company to sign and deliver a number of artists. It is sometimes called a **label deal,** as nowadays the production entity usually has its own label on the product. Sometimes, however, the producing entity has no identification on the records, and the public doesn't even know they exist.

Differences from Single-Artist Deals. A multi-artist deal between the distributor and the production entity looks a lot like a single-artist loan-out deal, but:

1. In addition to paying a recording fund for each album, there is often some form of overhead payment to the production entity. This is usually an advance (although it can at times be non-recoupable, at least in part) and it's used to pay the entity's rent, payroll, phone, light bills, etc. For bigger deals and mini-majors, it will also cover marketing, promotion, etc.
2. The term of the deal is usually two or three years firm, with the distributor having options for one or more additional one-, two-, or three-year periods.
3. The number of artists the production entity can sign, and whether the distributor can approve these artists, is a matter of major negotiation. A new production entity will maybe get the right to sign one, two, or three artists over the term, but a more established company may get to sign two or three artists per year. More and more, the distributors want to approve the artists before signing, but if you have a lot of bargaining power, you may be able to negotiate (a) no approval (very difficult today); or (b) for each one or two approved artists, you have the right to sign an artist that isn't approved.
4. The minimum and maximum number of albums the production entity can deliver is also pre-negotiated, both in terms of the overall number per year, and the number per artist.

Normally, the distributor doesn't want you delivering more than one album per artist per year without its consent.

5. And speaking of albums, how about this great idea (see if you can find the history lesson): You are a production entity in the last year of your deal with a distributor, and you suddenly have the opportunity to sign a hot new band. So six months before the end of your term, you deliver an album of this band and say, 'Please make these guys into superstars so that, six months later when my deal ends, I can (a) beat you to death in a renegotiation; or (b) better yet, take them to another company, leaving you with a gigantic deficit from any prior flops, while I take the royalties from this band and buy that little farm I've always wanted.' Sound too good to be true? Of course; the deal will provide that you must deliver the distributor a minimum number of albums for each artist—usually three or four—even if the term is over. (Note this will put you in the position of having your deal expire for some artists, but continue for others.)

6. The recording funds for the artists are spelled out up front. If you're a new entity, you'll probably have to live with something like $150,000 to $250,000 per album. You may be able to negotiate a pre-approved formula for artists with previous track records (for example, a fund of $300,000 to $350,000 for an artist who has sold 200,000 albums or more). To exceed these figures, you need the company's consent on each specific deal. This means, if you have the chance to sign a major artist, you must sit down with the distributor and work out a special arrangement. (It happens, on occasion, that the production entity and the distributor are both bidding for the same artist. You can imagine, since the distributor approves how much the production entity can spend, which one is likely to come out the winner. In this case, unless there's a personal relationship or some other good reason why the artist would rather sign to you, you can pretty well kiss them off.)

7. It's sometimes possible, although difficult, to get ownership of the master recordings under a label deal. Even in this situation, however, you normally wouldn't own the recordings during the term. (In fact, other than for tax planning, you probably wouldn't want to own these suckers at all. One of the fringe detriments of ownership is the joy of showing up in places like Fargo, North Dakota, to testify against record counterfeiters.

This is because the judge requires the copyright owner of the master to be at the trial. See page 319 for more information on the copyrights in sound recordings.) So even if you win this point, the distributor usually owns the masters and assigns them to you some period after the end of the term (usually seven to ten years or so). The distributor may insist on your being recouped before they'll assign; if this is the case, you should get the right to pay back the unrecouped deficit for an immediate reassignment.

Cross-collateralization. Remember our story about the two different producers being entitled to royalties from the same artist, and how the artist went further in the hole with every success? (See page 132.) Well, when you get to a multi-artist deal, this scenario gets to be a high-speed drilling rig. It is entirely possible (even easy) to have two or three real losers, together with one smash, but not get any royalties because the record company is recouping the losers' deficit from the winner's royalties. Here's an example:

Suppose a production entity has signed three artists. Assume the following (*the numbers bear no relationship to reality;* they're just for easy math):

Multiple-Artist Deal

All-in Royalty to Production Entity:		60¢
Royalty to Artist A:		50¢
Royalty to Artist B:		50¢
Royalty to Artist C:		50¢
Recording Costs:		$60,000/album
Advance for Production Entity's Operations		$100,000
Sales:		
	Artist A:	Album 1: 60,000 units
		Album 2: 40,000 units
	Artist B:	Album 1: 20,000 units
		Album 2: 40,000 units
	Artist C:	Album 1: 60,000 units
		Album 2: 500,000 units

Under these assumptions, let's look at everyone's accounts:

Artist A's Account with Production Entity

	Charges (Recording Costs)	Earnings	Balance
Album 1	− $60,000	+ $30,000 (50¢ × 60,000 units)	− $30,000
Album 2	− $60,000	+ $20,000 (50¢ × 40,000 units)	− $40,000
TOTAL	**− $120,000**	**+ $50,000**	**− $70,000**

Summary: Artist A is *in the red (unrecouped) in the amount of $70,000* (the $120,000 deficit less the $50,000 earnings), and is thus owed nothing.

Artist B's Account with Production Entity

	Charges (Recording Costs)	Earnings	Balance
Album 1	− $60,000	+ $10,000 (50¢ × 20,000 units)	− $50,000
Album 2	− $60,000	+ $20,000 (50¢ × 40,000 units)	− $40,000
TOTAL	**− $120,000**	**+ $30,000**	**− $90,000**

Summary: Artist B is *in the red (unrecouped) in the amount of $90,000* (the $120,000 deficit less the $30,000 earnings), and is thus owed nothing.

Artist C's Account with Production Entity

	Charges (Recording Costs)	Earnings	Balance
Album 1	− $60,000	+ $30,000 (50¢ × 60,000 units)	− $30,000
Album 2	− $60,000	+ $250,000 (50¢ × 500,000 units)	+ $190,000
TOTAL	**− $120,000**	**+ $280,000**	**+ $160,000**

Summary: Artist C is *in the black (and owed) $160,000* (the $280,000 earnings less the $120,000 deficit).

Production Entity's Account with Record Company

	Charges (Recording Costs)	Earnings	Balance
Overhead	− $100,000		− $100,000
Artist A	− $120,000	+ $60,000 (60¢ × 100,000 units)	− $60,000
Artist B	− $120,000	+ $36,000 (60¢ × 60,000 units)	− $84,000
Artist C	− $120,000	+ $300,000 (60¢ × 500,000 units)	+ $180,000
TOTAL	**− $460,000**	**+ $396,000**	**− $64,000**

Summary: The production entity is *in the red (unrecouped) $64,000* (the $460,000 deficit less the $396,000 earnings), and is thus owed nothing.

Grand Summary

Artist A:	Unrecouped and not entitled to royalties.
Artist B:	Unrecouped and not entitled to royalties.
Artist C:	Owed $160,000.
Production entity:	Owes Artist C $160,000, but is in the red $64,000 and thus not entitled to royalties.

Owing $160,000 and having no royalties due you is certainly the fuzzy side of the lollipop.

So how do you get out of the box? Well, if you have enough clout, you make the distributor pay the artists' royalties without regard to cross-collateralization. Thus, if you and Artists A and B are deeply unrecouped, but Artist C is recouped, they'd have to pay Artist C's royalties. In other words, they can't cross-collateralize any artist's royalties with either your or any other artist's deficits.

If you don't have enough bargaining power for this, then at minimum you should require the distributor to pay the recouped artist's royalties and to treat these payments as additional advances against your share of royalties. In the above example, that would mean the record company would advance the $160,000 owed to Artist C, and the producing entity would then be $224,000 in the red (the $64,000 original deficit plus the $160,000 paid to Artist C). You wouldn't make any money under these circumstances (until you have an awfully big success and eventually recoup), but at least you won't be breaking your kids' piggy banks to pay the artists.

JOINT VENTURES

A **joint venture** is the same as a multi-artist or label deal, except the production entity doesn't get a royalty. Instead, the production entity and the distributing record company are in effect 'partners.' This means they take all of the income which comes in (the gross wholesale price) and put it into a pot. Then they take all the expenses of operations out of the pot, and whatever is left over is split between the two entities. Historically, the split was 50/50, but over recent years this has become increasingly difficult to get. Record companies are shying away from joint ventures altogether, and when they do them, they're trying to pay less—40%, 30%, sometimes even lower.

In fact, these agreements aren't usually true 'joint ventures' or 'partnerships' in the legal sense. A true partnership or joint venture means one partner can commit both of them to legal obligations. For example, if one partner signs a bank loan for $200,000, both partners can be sued if it isn't paid back. And neither you nor the record company wants this, so the agreements sometimes specifically state they aren't legally partnerships or joint ventures. Thus, the name 'joint venture' is not technically correct; it just describes a multi-artist deal where the profits are shared as if a joint venture existed.

Computation of Profits

The economics of a joint venture look like this:

Income Side.   Gross receipts are the wholesale price received by the record company, which is easy to compute if the distributor is independent. However, as we discussed on page 65, all the major distributors are owned by the major record companies. This means you need a different definition of gross receipts when the joint-venture distributor is a major. Why? Well, if the same person owns both the distributor and the record company, they can set any price they want between the two of them. To use an absurd example, the distributor might charge $10 for a record and only pay $2 back to the record company, simply to hose you.

The companies are very straightforward about this calculation. Gross receipts are usually defined as the price paid by the dealers (i.e., the price paid to the distributor, not to the company), less a charge for the distributor's operating expenses and profit. Typically, the companies reduce the price the distributors charge to the dealers by 10%, and the 90% balance is treated as the joint venture's gross receipts. For example, if the distributor's wholesale price to a dealer is $10, the joint venture's gross is $9 ($10 less a 10% [$1] charge for the distributor).

Income from licenses is all treated as gross.

Foreign income is treated as license income, and the venture usually gets the same royalty paid by foreign distributors to the company for its entire catalog. In other words, if they get a 30% of PPD royalty in Guam, that would go into the pot as gross receipts and therefore be used for determining profits.

When the foreign distributor is owned by the same company that owns your record company, they establish an **intra-company rate**, meaning the rate at which the U.S. company is paid by the foreign distributor. Usually it's somewhere in the mid-20% range if it's based on retail, or proportionately higher if on PPD. For example, Capitol's English licensee might pay Capitol 24% of retail (I'm making up the rate) for sales of Capitol's artists in England. This rate is in place even when there is no joint venture, as it's used by the U.S. company to compute its profits and losses in reporting earnings to the parent company (and in determining executive bonuses based on performance, so you hope the executives are greedily trying to keep this number high).

The result of this foreign licensing practice, however, is that a joint venture only shares profits for U.S. sales. On foreign sales, there's simply a sharing of the U.S. company's royalty.

Expenses. From this gross, the joint venture deducts its expenses and charges. These consist of the following:

1. The first thing deducted is a **distribution fee** for the record company. (We already discussed this concept in the context of home videos, on page 178. And remember the rule we discussed there: If you're getting a percentage, take it out first.) The *distribution fee* is a charge to cover the cost of the record company's overseeing the distribution of records, meaning the accounting, invoicing, manufacturing, etc., of the venture. (Note the difference between this and the fee charged in computing gross income, which was for the distributor's expenses. The fee here is for the primary record company's expenses in overseeing the distribution.) More and more, the fee includes the charge by the distributor we discussed above, so there's

only one distribution fee, and this will run somewhere in the 15% to 20% range. It's also possible to reduce this fee as volume increases, usually on a yearly basis. For example, the fee could be 20% of the first $5 million each year, 19% of the next $5 million, and 18% thereafter. At the beginning of the following year, the fee would start again at 20%.

All the labels are responsible for their own profit centers. Thus, they have a deal with the distributor for all their records (not just those subject to the joint venture). For example, RCA Records is charged a distribution fee by BMG Distribution, even though they're all owned by the same company. With enough clout, you can get the same distribution fee they are charged, which is usually in the 12% to 14% range.

2. The record company may also charge an **overhead fee,** sometimes called a **services fee.** This is for services the label supplies in addition to distribution, such as marketing and promotion. The more they supply, the higher this will be. It can range anywhere from zero to 4% or 7%. Often this is combined with the distribution fee discussed in point 1, so that there's one percentage including both distribution and services/overhead.

3. Next come all the costs of operation. In addition to the costs you would normally expect (recording costs, advances, etc.), there are a number of things that aren't charged under royalty deals. These include:
   (a) Manufacturing
   (b) Shipping
   (c) Advertising and marketing
   (d) Mechanical royalties (we'll discuss these later, on page 212)
   (e) Per-record union payments (for a definition, see page 156)

4. Lastly, the record company takes back payments it has made to the production entity, such as reimbursements for promotional and operating expenses of the company. It's a matter of negotiation whether these are charged 'off the top' of the venture (so that each party bears 50%), or whether they're charged solely against the producing entity's share of the profits.

Profits.   The amount left after the above calculation is the profit, and the agreed split goes to each party.

The international aspects of a joint venture deal are quite interesting. Contrary to what you might believe, you don't actually get to compute profits in each of the territories. Rather, each foreign territory reports back a royalty for sales in that particular market, and those royalties constitute the 'gross receipts' of the joint venture. The royalty is usually the same as it paid to your joint venture partner, but you should always make certain that's the case—shocking as it may seem, they will occasionally pay a lower royalty so that they have to split less money with you. And remember, in any event it may be a royalty paid from a foreign company wholly owned by your company, so the money is going from one pocket to the other and there's no particular incentive to maximize it.

Royalty Versus Joint Venture

So how about the key question: Are you better off with a joint venture or with a royalty arrangement? To answer this requires a crystal ball. If you're extremely successful, you're better off with a joint venture. With modest success, you're better off under a royalty arrangement. (If you're a turkey, it really doesn't matter.) Here's why:

As we discussed, you're charged for more costs in a joint venture than you are under a royalty deal, and thus with only modest success, you're behind. However, many of these costs are not 'per unit,' meaning they're only paid at the beginning, as opposed to 'per-unit' costs that are incurred for each record ('unit') made. (Examples of per-unit costs are costs of manufacture, mechanical royalties, union per-record charges, freight, etc., which must be paid to manufacture and ship each unit. Costs that are not per-unit are such things as artwork, videos, promotion, marketing, and advertising, which are unrelated to specific units.) Thus, with a great deal of success, the non-per-unit costs are eaten up by the first dollars that come in, and thereafter the profit per unit is far greater than any royalty arrangement is ever likely to be.

PRESSING AND DISTRIBUTION (P&D) DEALS

If you are truly a record company in your own right, then this is the deal for you. It gives you the most autonomy and control of your life, as well as the highest profit margin.

A **pressing and distribution agreement** (or **P&D** deal) is exactly that—the company agrees to manufacture records for you (although in some situations this isn't even so; the product is manufactured elsewhere), and then to distribute them solely as a wholesaler. This means you sell the records to the distributing entity for a wholesale price less a negotiated distribution fee (which covers the distributing company's overhead, operations, and profit). The distribution fee ranges in the 18% to 20% range (less if you're a big label), and the balance of the monies is paid to the production entity. For example, if a CD wholesales for $10, under a deal with a 20% distribution fee, the production entity gets $8.00 per unit ($10 less 20%). Out of this, the production entity pays manufacturing, mechanicals, artist royalties, promotion, overhead, salaries, and everything else.

This arrangement is not for the weak-hearted:

1. In these deals, the entire risk of manufacturing falls entirely on the production entity. Remember how records are sold on a returnable basis (see page 79)? This means that, if you guess wrong, the returns come back home to roost. So not only are you losing your potential profit on the sale, but you're also coming out of pocket and losing the cost of manufacturing and shipping a record you can't sell (although they make passable doorstops). Many deals also require you to pay a distribution fee even if the record is returned, adding injury to insult.

2. The distributing company typically offers no services whatsoever in terms of marketing, promotion, accounting, etc. You really are on your own. (You can sometimes make a deal to get some of these services from the distributing company for an increased distribution fee. For example, they might help with marketing, sales, or promotion, and charge an extra 2% or 3% distribution fee.)

3. You may well be treated as a second-class citizen. This is because the distributing company will favor its own product over yours; they make a bigger profit on their own stuff, and they have a bigger investment in it.

These types of deals can be made at the highest level (for example, A&M Records was distributed by BMG under such an arrangement for many years), and the true independent record companies (see page 67 for what those are) make these deals with independent distributors.

P&D deals can also be made at a more modest level by anyone insane enough to want to try, or anyone desperate enough to get their records out when no one wants to pay them for the privilege. However, unless you're a real record company, with a full staff, I strongly recommend against this type of deal.

If I haven't talked you out of this, and you're still reading, you've probably struck out around town, and are looking to put out your own records on a modest basis (maybe press up a thousand or so and throw them out there). In that case, I understand there are a couple of good books on how to release your own records independently. Because I haven't read them, I can't recommend any one in particular. But if I can't force you off this road, at least educate yourself with one or more of these. And don't invest money you can't afford to lose.

PART III

Songwriting and Music Publishing

15

Copyright Basics

Before you can understand what songwriting and music publishing are all about, you have to understand how copyrights work.

When you deal with something intangible like a copyright (which you can't see, feel, or smell), it's a challenge to nail it down. Copyrights are a tremendous amount of fun—they're squiggly little critters that, every time you think you have a handle on them, take an unexpected turn and nip you in the butt. Moreover, many of the concepts have been around for close to a hundred years, yet remain unchanged; always a challenge in today's world. But don't worry. I'll guide you through the maze.

The following section on copyright is a description of the United States' copyright laws for the simple reason that I know them much better than I know the U.K. copyright law. You'd be amazed how few of my clients come in and ask me what their rights would be if they were English. However, this discussion is important because you will need these concepts in dealing with your U.S. rights. Also, I've managed to pump most of my U.K. friends for information on copyrights (making it appear as though it's all my genius, of course), so there are nuggets of info scattered throughout.

As you might imagine, the copyright law in the United Kingdom is very different from that in the U.S. However, while a number of the particulars differ, the basic concepts are surprisingly similar. (Well, maybe not so surprisingly since you guys colonized us.)

The U.S. law is more important to you than you might think; the United States is still the largest single music market, and all U.K. contracts seek to limit what you get paid for the use of your songs in the U.S. So you'll need to know this stuff in order to protect yourself. The most important section is the controlled composition clause (on

page 226), but you need the other concepts before we get to it. So let's
dig in.

BASIC COPYRIGHT CONCEPTS

When you own a copyright, it's like playing Monopoly and owning all
the properties on the board. But unlike Monopoly, you're not limited
to the rents printed on the little cards. (As we'll see later, there are
some pre-set rents, but for the most part you can charge whatever the
traffic will bear.)

Definition of Copyright

The legal definition of a copyright is 'a limited duration monopoly.'
Its purpose (as stated in the U.S. Constitution, no less) is to promote
the progress of science and useful arts by giving creators exclusive
rights to their works for a while. As you can imagine, if you created
something and everybody had the right to use it without paying you,
not very many people would go the trouble of creating anything (including you and me).

What's Copyrightable?

To be copyrightable, the work has to be original (not copied from
something else) and of sufficient materiality to constitute a work.
There's no specific test to cover this; it's decided on a case-by-case
basis. For example, the five notes played by the spaceship in *Close En-
counters of the Third Kind* are copyrightable because of their originality, even though they're just five notes.

How to Get a Copyright

Under United States Copyright Law, as soon as you make a **tangible
copy** of something, you have a copyright. *Tangible* simply means
something you can touch. If the work is a musical composition, for example, it can be written down (if you write music, which many creative
people don't these days), or just sung or played into a recorder. Once
this tangible copy exists, you have all the copyright you need.

Many people think you have to register in Washington to get a copyright. Not true. There are some important rights you get from registering, but securing a copyright isn't one of them. (More on this later.)

So it's that simple. If you sing a song in your head, no matter how completely it's composed, you have no copyright; if you write it down or record it, you have one. If you'd like to take a few minutes right now and copyright something, I'll wait.

In the U.K., as in the U.S., a copyright is secured when something is fixed in tangible form. Unlike in the U.S., there is no need for registration, and in fact there is no registration procedure.

WHAT ARE ALL THESE RIGHTS YOU GET?

When you have a copyright, you get the following rights at no extra charge. These rights are **exclusive,** which means that *no one* can do these things without your permission. (For you technical freaks, the rights are listed in Section 106 of the Copyright Act.)

You get the *exclusive* right to:

1. **Reproduce the work.**
   Keeping with a musical composition as our example, this means no one can record your composition, publish it as sheet music, put it in a movie, or otherwise copy it.
2. **Distribute copies of the work.**
   Apart from the right to reproduce your song, there is a separate right of *distribution* which you also control. Note the difference between making a copy of the work (for example, recording it or manufacturing records of it), which is one use of a copyright (it's a reproduction, as we discussed in point 1), and the *distribution* of this copy (for example, selling records to the public), which is another, separate right. One illustration of this would be a record company that hires a plant to manufacture their CDs. The plant gets the right to reproduce the songs, but not the right to distribute copies of them.
3. **Perform the work publicly.**
   With a song, this means playing it in nightclubs, on the radio, on television, in amusement parks, supermarkets, elevators

(you know your career is either soaring or history when you hear your song in an elevator), or anywhere else music is heard publicly. It doesn't matter whether the performance is by live musicians or a DJ playing records, you get to control this right. (If you're wondering how you could ever police this or get paid, stay tuned.)

4. **Make a derivative work.**
   A **derivative work** is a creation based on another work. In the music industry, an example is a parody lyric set to a well-known song (like what Weird Al Yankovic does). The melody may be a copyrighted original work (say 'Gangster's Paradise'), but with parody lyrics (like 'Amish Paradise'), it constitutes a new work. This new work is called a *derivative work* because it's 'derived' from the original.

   This concept is even easier to see in the motion picture area. Any film made from a novel is a derivative work (the novel is the original work). And *West Side Story* is a derivative work based on *Romeo and Juliet*. Anyway, you get the idea. (By the way, the original doesn't have to be copyrighted. If it isn't, the only parts of the derivative work that are protected are the newly created ones.)

5. **To display the work publicly.**
   This really doesn't apply to music; it's the right to put paintings, statues, etc. on public display.

EXCEPTIONS TO THE COPYRIGHT MONOPOLY

As we discussed before, the copyright law gives you an absolute monopoly, which means it's your bat and ball, and you don't have to let anyone use your copyright. If you want to write poems and throw them into the sea, so that no human being can ever make use of them, that's your prerogative. You may be cold and poor in your old age, but you will have entertained a lot of fish.

Compulsory Licenses

On the other hand, there are six major exceptions to this rule, and they're known as **compulsory licenses.** The term *compulsory license* means that you *must* issue a license to someone who wants to use your work, whether you like it or not. The six compulsory licenses are:

1. **Cable television rebroadcast.**
   This was originally designed for areas that had poor television reception. Cable companies set up a big antenna to receive weak signals and send them along to the homes in the area. The cable television compulsory license requires the local broadcasting stations to allow the cable company to retransmit their signals in exchange for payment of set fees. Without this license, the rebroadcast would be an unauthorized distribution of copyrighted programming. (By the way, the pay channels [HBO, Showtime] and satellite channels [CNN, MTV, etc.] are not subject to compulsory licenses and can charge whatever they can gouge out of the cable operators.)

2. **Public Broadcasting System.**
   The PBS lobbyists did a terrific job of requiring copyright owners to license works to them at cheap rates.

3. **Jukeboxes.**
   It may surprise you to know that, until the 1976 Copyright Law, jukeboxes paid nothing for the right to use music. They were considered 'toys' in the 1909 Copyright Act (really). Now they pay set license fees, the details of which have never been relevant to me, and so I don't know them.

4. **Digital performance of records.**
   This baby was added in 1995, then modified in 1998, and it requires the owners of recordings to allow performances on digital radio, which also includes **webcasting** (radio shows on the Internet). We'll discuss this in more detail on page 308.

5. **Digital distribution of records.**
   This covers the downloading of records over the Internet, telephone lines, satellites, etc. (we touched on this on page 166). The compulsory license requires the owner of the song to allow its use in this way. As you can tell from the subject matter, this compulsory license was also recently created (in 1995). More of this on page 307.

6. **Phonorecords of non-dramatic musical compositions.**
   This is the biggie in today's music business, so we'll discuss it in detail. It's called a **compulsory mechanical license.**

COMPULSORY MECHANICAL LICENSES

To understand this area, you first need to know about mechanical royalties.

Mechanical Royalties

The term **mechanical royalties** (or **mechanicals** to its friends) developed in the 1909 Copyright Law, and referred to payments for devices 'serving to mechanically reproduce sound.' Even though devices haven't reproduced sound 'mechanically' since the 1940s, the name has stuck and the monies paid to copyright owners for the manufacture and distribution of records are still called *mechanical royalties*. And the rights to reproduce songs in records are known as **mechanical rights.**

The concept of a *compulsory* license for these *mechanical rights* grew out of a concern in Congress that the music industry was going to develop into a gigantic monopoly (we may still make it). This desire to keep copyright owners from controlling the world resulted in the compulsory license for records, which accomplishes its mission nicely. It says that, once a work has been recorded, the publisher is *required* to license it to anyone else who wants to use it in records. (The old law had a number of ambiguities and problems with it, but there's no point in discussing them because they were cured in the 1976 law. You get off easy—I had to study the damn stuff.) Let's take a closer look at what the law says:

Compulsory Mechanical Licenses

The compulsory copyright royalty provision for records is in Section 115 of the Copyright Act. It provides that, once a song has been recorded, a copyright owner must license it: (a) to anyone else that wants to use it in a *phonorecord* (which is a defined term in the Copyright Act); and (b) for a specific payment established by the law (more on this later). You can get a compulsory license *only if:*

1. The song is a non-dramatic musical work; *and*
2. It has been previously recorded; *and*
3. The previous recording has been distributed publicly in phonorecords; *and*
4. Your use of the recording will be in phonorecords only.

All of these conditions must exist before you get a compulsory license. Let's look at them separately.

Non-dramatic Musical Work.   Before you can get a compulsory license, the song must be a *non-dramatic musical composition*. It's not clear what a 'dramatic' musical composition is, but it's probably a song used in an opera or musical—i.e., a song that helps tell the story. No one knows whether or not the term includes a 'story song,' such as 'Ode to Billy Joe' or any of Harry Chapin's works. My guess is that it doesn't, but it's just a guess.

Previously Recorded.   You can't get a compulsory license for the very first recording of a work. The law allows the owner to control who gets it the first time, which is known as a **first use.** Once it's recorded, however, anyone can get a compulsory license if the first recording was *authorized by the copyright owner.* The fact that someone sneaks off and records the composition without consent doesn't trigger the compulsory license.

Public Distribution.   The first recording must have been *distributed to the public.* This closes a loophole from the prior law, and is of course eminently logical. It's not enough that the publisher allowed a recording to be made if it wasn't released.

Phonorecord Use.   A compulsory license is available only for **phonorecords,** which are defined in the Copyright Law to mean *audio only* recordings. This definition was the publishers' finest lobbying accomplishment in the 1976 Copyright Act, because it excluded home video devices from the definition of *phonorecords.* This means there's no compulsory license for home videos, and the result has been that motion picture companies must now negotiate with every copyright owner (publisher) for home video usage of each song, and that the owners are free to charge whatever rate they choose. More on how this is done when we get to publishing (on page 235).

If all of the above conditions exist, then anyone who wants to use a song in phonorecords can do so merely by filing certain notices and paying a set fee per record. This fee is called the **statutory rate** (because it's a rate set by the Copyright Statute), and has had a rather bizarre history. The rate was 2¢ from 1909 to 1976 (inflation didn't exist in those years, but record company lobbyists did). The 1976 Copyright Act raised it to 2.75¢, with provisions for further adjustments by a Copyright Royalty Tribunal, which is a committee that meets periodically and reviews the rate. It is currently the larger of (a) 8¢, or (b) 1.55¢ per minute of playing time or a fraction thereof. Thus, if a song runs five minutes or less, the rate is 8¢. However, if it's over five minutes (even by a second or two), but not over six minutes, the rate is 9.3¢ (1.55¢ × 6 = 9.3¢). If a song is over six minutes but not more than seven minutes, the rate is 10.85¢ (1.55¢ × 7 = 10.85¢), and so forth.

There's also a schedule of increases over the coming years that looks like this:

Date	Rate for 5 Minutes or Less	Rate per Minute or Fraction
1/1/04	8.5¢	1.65¢
1/1/06	9.1¢	1.75¢

To its credit, Congress did a thorough job of research in working out the compulsory licensing legislation. There are specific accounting provisions (monthly), limits for the amount of reserves (see page 80 for a definition of reserves) that can be withheld, and requirements when the reserves must be liquidated (paid out). Also, in perhaps its most sophisticated move, the royalty is payable on all records 'made and distributed' (as opposed to 'made and sold'), which means the compulsory royalties are payable on 'free goods' (see page 75 for a discussion of free goods).

Back to Real Life

Having told you how this works, I will now tell you that the compulsory license is almost never used. Record companies hate to use it because the monthly accounting provisions are too burdensome. The copyright owners (publishers) would rather give a direct license because they can keep track of it easier. (Would you want a Washington bureaucrat to handle your licensing?) However, it's still very significant because the 'statutory rate' is the benchmark for setting mechanical rates in the industry. The reason is that, once a musical composition is recorded, the 'statutory rate' is the maximum mechanical royalty anyone is willing to pay for it (if a publisher refuses to license it at that rate, the manufacturer just gets a compulsory license). Whether the rate for a particular song is less than statutory is a subject of negotiation (see page 225).

First Use

Implicit in the above (which I'll now make explicit) is the fact that the compulsory license section does not apply to a **first use** (the first recording of a song). In other words, until a song has been recorded under authorization of the copyright owner (until a *first use* has been made), the publisher can charge anything it wants. Customarily, the publisher doesn't charge more than the statutory rate, but there's no reason why it can't, other than industry custom (and the refusal of the user to pay more).

There's no concept of a compulsory mechanical licence in the U.K. Thus, whether it's the second or fiftieth recording, the publisher is not required to issue a licence.

Since there is no compulsory licence, there is no statutory rate. Instead, the rate is set by negotiation. One side of the negotiation is between the **British Phonographic Industry** (known as **BPI** to its friends), which is an industry organization of record companies. And in the other corner we have the **Mechanical Copyright Protection Society** (known as **MCPS**), which represents the owners and creators of musical compositions. MCPS makes deals with publishing companies to represent them, and then issues mechanical licences on their behalf. (By the way, most major publishers have appointed MCPS as their exclusive agent for licensing mechanical rights, and unless they go through a procedure of notifying MCPS to the contrary, it will automatically issue a licence to anyone requesting it (other than a first licence). Thus, a sort of compulsory licence exists as a practical matter, but not as a legal matter.)

Unlike U.S. mechanicals, U.K. mechanicals are a percentage of the record's price. Currently, they're 8.5% of PPD. MCPS defines PPD as the highest amount that retailers pay the record company for the record involved. (If there is no PPD, there's a secondary rate of 6.5% of retail, ex-VAT.) There's no packaging deduction (see page 73 for what that is), and the only free goods allowed are 'real' free goods that are given out for promotion (to DJ's, reviewers, etc.). These freebies have to be marked (on both the package and the device) as 'PROMOTIONAL COPY—NOT FOR SALE' or 'THIS IS FREE AND WE REALLY MEAN IT' (Okay, so I made up the second one).

The percentage of PPD covers *all* songs on the record. Thus, the *total* mechanical rate has nothing to do with the number of songs—the same amount of mechanicals is paid for an album containing eight compositions as is paid for one with fourteen. However, the amount you get per song is of course affected by the number of songs, because the more songs there are, the less everyone gets when the fixed amount is divided up. Under MCPS rules, mechanicals are whacked up on the basis of the playing time of each song. For example, if your song is three minutes out of sixty minutes of music, you'd get ³⁄₆₀, or 5%, of the mechanicals.

This same percentage of PPD system applies throughout Europe, courtesy of an organization known as **BIEM (Bureau International des Sociétés Gérant les Droits d'Enregistrement et de Reproduction Mécanique**; is that a mouthful, or what?). BIEM is an organization of agencies which, like MCPS, collect mechanical royalties for their territory. BIEM helps its members by giving them the clout of an overall organization when dealing with treaties and other frontiers where the rights of artists need defending. Also, if the members get into a squabble with each other, BIEM acts like Mom and Dad to settle the dispute.

By the way, BIEM itself doesn't issue licenses—the mechanical rights society members in each territory do that. However, the BIEM members cross-license each other's repertoire, meaning each member can license everyone else's songs. Currently, the BIEM mechanical rate is 9.009% of PPD.

Foreign Mechanicals

For contrast, it's interesting to note that, other than the United States and Canada, most countries of the world use an entirely different copyright royalty system. Mechanicals there are a set percentage of wholesale price, which covers all songs on the record. This means the rate has nothing to do with the length of the composition or even the number of songs. The same amount of mechanicals is paid for an album containing eight compositions as is paid for one with twelve. Also, as we'll discuss later (on page 247), the mechanicals are usually paid to a government-affiliated agency. For example, mechanicals in the U.K. are currently 8.5% of PPD (see page 155 for what PPD is), without any packaging deduction (see page 70 for what that is), and the only free goods allowed are 'real' free goods (see page 71), which are clearly marked as being 'free.' The rate in the rest of Europe is set by an organization called **BIEM (Bureau International des Sociétés Gérant les Droits d'Enregistrement et de Reproduction Mécanique;** is that a mouthful, or what?). *BIEM* (pronounced 'beam') is a group of agencies in each territory that collect mechanical royalties for their affiliates. Currently, the BIEM rate is 9.009% of PPD.

16

Publishing Companies and Major Income Sources

PUBLISHING OVERVIEW

Now that you're a maven on copyrights, understanding publishing is pretty simple. It works like this:

What Does a Publisher Do?

As a songwriter, you may be interested in business, but your talents are best spent in creating. However, someone needs to take care of business, and that's where the publishing industry came from.

A publisher makes the following speech to a songwriter:

'Sit down, kid. Nice shirt. You've got great taste.'

The publisher leans forward, rattling the gold chains on his neck. 'You're a smart guy, so you'll get this. Your strength is writing songs, and mine is taking care of business. So let's make the following deal: You assign the copyright in your song to me, and in exchange I'll take care of the business. I'll find people to use your songs, give'em licenses, and make sure they pay you. Then we'll split the dough. Simple, huh? Now sign this perfectly standard agreement. Cigar?'

Administration

Okay, so I'm being a smart aleck. But these principles are the basis of the publishing business.

The rights the publisher just described—finding users, issuing licenses, collecting money, and paying the writer—are known as **administration rights.** When a publisher makes a standard deal with a writer, it takes on the obligations to do these things (as well as all rights of the copyright owner), and thus 'administers' the compositions.

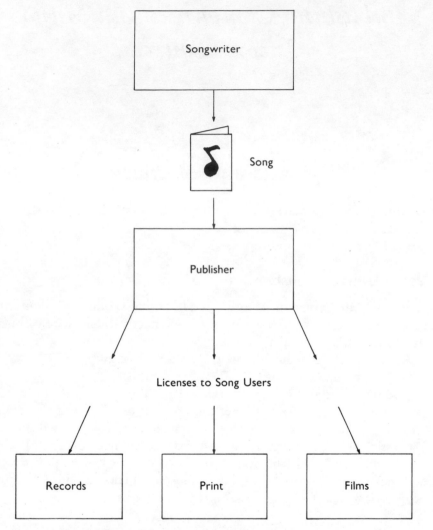

Figure 11. Publishing industry structure.

Traditionally, the publisher splits all income 50/50 with the writer (with the exception of sheet music and performance monies, which we'll discuss later). The publisher's 50% is for its overhead (office, staff, etc.) and profit. The share of money kept by the publisher from each dollar is known by a sophisticated industry term: the **publisher's**

share. The balance is just as imaginatively called the **writer's share** (see Figure 12).

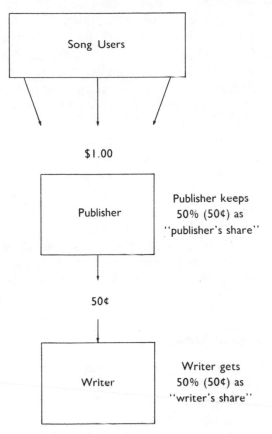

Figure 12. 'Publishers's share' and 'writer's share.'

Publishers, from the Beginning of the Universe Until Now . . .

Following the turn of the century, and well into the 1940s, publishers were the most powerful people in the music industry. (Ever heard of Tin Pan Alley? That's where the publishers were located.) Most artists didn't write their own songs in those days. Thus, because the publishers controlled the major songwriters, the artists (and therefore their companies) were at the publishers' mercy. Remember, no one can use a song for the first time without the publisher's permission (see page 215), and so the publishers would decide which artist was blessed with the right to record a major new work. Also, because of this power, it was difficult, if not impossible, for songwriters to exploit their works without a major publisher behind them.

Publishers today are still major players, but their role has changed radically. Some are 'creative' publishers, in the sense that they put their writers together with other writers, help them fine-tune their writing, match writers with artists, etc. They also use their clout to help find you a record deal, and promote your records after you have one. Other publishers are not much more than banking operations—they compute how much they expect to earn from a given deal, and pay a portion of it to obtain the rights involved. From these guys, you can't expect much more than a bet against your future income.

However you look at it, the reality is that publishers don't have as many heavy writers under contract today. This is because a lot of major songwriters keep their own publishing (i.e., they are their own publisher, retaining ownership of their copyrights and perhaps hiring someone to do the clerical function of administration). See, once a writer is well known, he or she can get to artists as easily as a publisher can, and maybe easier (artists often call important writers directly, looking for material). Also, more and more artists are writing their own songs, so there's no need for a publisher to get songs to them.

Mechanics of Publishing

A publishing company has a lot fewer moving parts than a record company. (Record company anatomy is discussed on page 63.) You only need the following (and some of these functions can be performed by the same person):

1. An administrator to take care of registering copyrights in the songs, issuing licenses, collecting money, paying writers and co-publishers, etc.
2. A 'song plugger' who runs around and gets songs recorded.
3. A creative staff person, who finds writers, works with them to improve their songs, pairs them up creatively with co-writers, etc. If the publishing company has no writers under contract to deliver newly written songs (in other words, it just administers existing songs), you don't even need this function.

Thus, unlike the record business, it takes only a small capital investment to call yourself a publisher. You don't need a large staff (until you get to be huge), and there's no need for the expensive distribution network, warehouses, inventory, etc., necessary for records (since you're dealing with intangibles). Indeed, there's an industry term, **vest-pocket publisher,** which refers to one person, with administrative help, acting as a publisher.

Types of Publishers

For this reason, there are a lot of smaller players, and the publishing business isn't nearly so dominated by the majors as is the record business, although they've been consolidating over the last few years. There are, to be sure, megaton publishing companies (such as Warner/Chappell and EMI, who have worldwide operations and generate hundreds of millions of dollars per year), but there are hundreds and hundreds of others running the gamut from a one-person show to the giants. Here's a broad-strokes view of the different types:

The 900-Pound Gorillas.　These are the major companies, most of which are affiliated with a record and/or film company. Examples are: Warner/Chappell, EMI, Universal, BMG, Sony/ATV, Famous Music (owned by Paramount Communications, Inc.), etc. Actually, the weight of these gorillas varies considerably. EMI and Warner/Chappell are clearly 900-pounders, while Universal, BMG, and Sony are closer to 600-pounders.

Major Affiliates.　There are a number of independent publishing companies, with full staffs of professionals, whose 'administration' is handled by a major. Quincy Jones Publishing, for example, is administered by Warner/Chappell. And there are hundreds of smaller examples as well. The publisher's affiliation with a major may be for the world, or it may be for only certain territories. For instance, a publisher might be affiliated with a major for the United States and have separate subpublishing deals (with other publishers) for the rest of the world.

Stand-alones.　*Stand-alone* is my term (borrowed from the cable TV business) and not an industry one. I'm using it to mean a company that's not affiliated with a major, and instead does its own administration. In other words, it collects its own money, does its own accountings, etc. It may, however, license territories outside the United States to a major. Examples of stand-alones are Peer and Bug.

Writer-Publishers.   Many writers keep their own publishing. Examples are well-established writers who don't need a publisher because people are constantly begging them for songs (such as Diane Warren), and writer/artists who record their own works. In fact, if you're a writer/artist whose material doesn't lend itself to being recorded by others (such as rap, jazz, or heavy metal), then you should only part with your publishing if you need (or want) money up front. Otherwise, you can hire people relatively cheaply to do the administration (see page 288). (If your publishing really generates a lot of money, you can even hire someone on an hourly or flat-fee basis and pay even less.)

Just because the publishing game has a low entry price doesn't mean it's an easy gig. So you have to check out your publisher thoroughly. The difference between a good publisher and an unqualified one can mean a lot to your pocketbook. For example, a good publisher knows how much to charge for various licenses and where to look for hidden monies (see, for example, page 252, discussing how foreign monies get lost when nobody claims them properly). The bad ones can lose you money just by sitting there and not doing what they're supposed to. An inexperienced publisher affiliated with a major is a quantum improvement over an unqualified publisher trying to go it alone. However, the major will not have the same incentive to take care of the independent's songs as it will to take care of its own. Also, a major owns tens of thousands of copyrights, so you can get shoved on the back shelf. On the other hand, a good independent publisher affiliated with a major can often do better for you than if you signed to the major directly. If the publisher has enough clout to become a 'squeaky wheel' on your behalf (and remember the squeaking is on its behalf as well), it can prevent you from getting lost in the shuffle.

SOURCES OF INCOME

Now let's take a look at what monies a publisher collects. I'm starting with publishing income, not songwriters' royalties, because the writer gets a percentage of the publisher's monies.

The majority of revenues come from mechanicals and performance monies. So let's examine these first.

MECHANICAL ROYALTIES

As we discussed on page 212, mechanical royalties are monies paid by a record company for the right to use a song in records. The publisher issues a license to the record company that says, for each record manufactured and distributed, that the record company will pay a royalty equal to a specified number of pennies. Often this rate is tied to the statutory rate (see page 213), and thus it increases as the statutory royalty increases. However, it may be tied only to *today's* statutory rate, meaning it's fixed in pennies and won't go up even if the statutory rate does. This is most likely when the songwriter is also an artist, for reasons we'll discuss later (on page 226).

The fixed rate can either be at the full statutory rate, or it can be a reduced percentage of that statutory rate. If reduced, it's called a **rate,** which means a mechanical royalty of less than statutory. The customary reduction is 75%, usually for lower-priced records such as midprice or budget (see pages 179 and 180 for what these are), or for compilation packages (see page 170). Record companies often request a 50% to 66.66% *rate* on budget records. Artists often ask for a rate if they have too many songs on their album to pay everyone a full shot, as we'll see later (in the discussion of controlled composition clauses).

For compilation packages, if a record company wants a 'rate,' it may offer an advance against the royalties, which means that, even though the publisher gets less, at least it gets it sooner. For example, a record company might offer to prepay on 50,000 units of a particular record in exchange for the publisher accepting 75% of the statutory rate. You'll also see, when we discuss the mechanical royalty provisions in record agreements (on page 226), that record companies routinely ask artists at all levels to issue licenses at less than the statutory rate. While they get turned down by artists at higher levels, they usually get a rate for midlevel and new artists.

There is no such thing as negotiating a 'rate' in the U.K. MCPS (see page 215 for what MCPS is) sets the price, and you either take it or leave it. This is a benefit to the publishers, since they're not subject to the whims and often staggering bargaining power of the record company on the other side. And remember, it's a percentage of PPD for all song on the album, not a number of pennies per song (see page 215).

Canada

There's no compulsory mechanical rate in Canada. Instead, there's a contractual agreement between the Canadian Record Company Association and a number of major publishers setting the 'industry royalty rate.' Currently it's 7.7¢ for the first five minutes, plus 1.54¢ for each additional minute or fraction thereof (all in Canadian pennies). This rate gets adjusted periodically for inflation, and is due to change in January 2004.

Record companies, unable to restrain themselves, try to get three-quarters of this rate as well.

Harry Fox and CMRRA

Two major organizations are delighted to issue mechanical licenses for publishers. One is the **Harry Fox Agency,** which in the United States is the largest organization of its kind, and its Canadian counterpart, **CMRRA,** standing for **Canadian Mechanical Rights Reproduction Agency.** (There have been a few competitors over the years, but none has succeeded to any real degree.) Basically, these organizations act as a publisher's agent for mechanicals. They issue mechanical licenses for the publisher, police them (i.e., make sure the users pay), and account to the publisher. For their services, *Harry Fox* and *CMRRA* currently charge 6% of the gross monies collected, although I'm told they hope to lower those fees soon.

Fox and CMRRA periodically audit record companies on behalf of all their clients, and then allocate the recovered monies among their clients in proportion to their earnings. This is particularly significant for a smaller publisher, as the cost of an audit for small earners is prohibitive. (At the time of this writing, a typical publishing audit can cost $15,000 to $25,000 or more, and unless the recovery is likely to be several times this amount, it's not economical.)

It may surprise you to know that many midsize and large publishers use this service, because the cost of hiring a staff to issue numerous licenses and police them is more expensive than the fees these organizations charge.

As we discussed on page 215, MCPS does the same things in the U.K. that Harry Fox does in the U.S. However, MCPS is much larger, and almost all publishers affiliate with it. Also, MCPS has arrangements with a number of foreign organizations, which remit monies back to it for distribution to MCPS members.

Accounting

Unlike with record deals, publishers get paid quarterly, meaning four times each year. They're usually paid sixty to ninety days after the close of each calendar quarter, meaning sixty to ninety days after each March 31, June 30, September 30, and December 31.

Reserves

In reporting mechanical royalties to publishers, record companies take substantially larger reserves than they do in accounting to artists for record royalties. And I mean *substantial*. These reserves can run anywhere from 50% to 75% of the amount due, as opposed to 30% to 50% for record royalties.

Why such a huge amount? Remember, as we discussed (on page 76), that reserves protect the record company against overshipping (i.e., shipping more records than it can sell). If a company overships and therefore overpays a publisher, the only way it can get the money back is to offset the overage against future royalties for *that specific composition*. (Once, in 1911, a publisher actually repaid an overpayment, but he was executed by his fellow publishers.) This is different from record royalty overpayments, which can be charged against royalties on *any* records.

For example, suppose a publisher issues two licenses to the same record company, one for Song A and the other for Song B (written by two different songwriters). If the record company overpays on Song A, it has no right to offset this amount against royalties for Song B. The reason is that, even though the overpayment was made to the same publisher, it's a different song and there are different songwriters involved. This is not the case with an artist, where, if the record company overpays on the first album, it can take the excess out of royalties payable on the second, third, fourth, and later albums (because it's dealing with the same artist and one royalty account). Accordingly, a record company can take smaller reserves in record deals than it can on publishing licenses, because it has more ways to get back an overpayment.

CONTROLLED COMPOSITION CLAUSES

Congratulations! You now know enough to talk about **controlled composition clauses** in record deals. These clauses are one of the most significant provisions in your recording arrangement, and you needed to understand both record deals and publishing to grasp the concepts. Since now you've got 'em both, let's do it.

You'll be delighted to hear that the U.K. has no need to negotiate a controlled composition clause. As we discussed (on page 215), mechanical royalties in the world outside the U.S. and Canada work completely differently (they're a percentage of PPD, regardless of the number of songs). However, you'll have to understand these provisions to get through the U.S. and Canadian portion of your record deal, and it can mean a lot of money to you.

A **controlled composition** is a song written, owned, or controlled by the artist (in whole or in part). However, it's usually defined more broadly than that, and includes:

1. Any song in which the artist has an income or other interest. This means that, even if the artist doesn't own or control it, it's a *controlled composition* if he or she wrote it or otherwise gets a piece of its earnings.
2. The definition sometimes also includes (depending on the record company) compositions owned or controlled by the producer of the recordings. You really have little, if any, control over a producer's publishing, and thus you should try hard to get this provision knocked out. (You'll see why the producer won't like it in a minute). It's hard to get rid of this, except at superstar levels, but do your best. I say this not only because it's difficult to impossible to get a producer to comply with it, but also because, with a producer of any importance, you could end up blowing your producing deal over it.

The Controlled Composition Clause

The *controlled composition clause* (also known to its buddies as a **controlled comp clause,** although it has no 'buddies' except record companies) puts a limit on how much the company has to pay for each controlled composition (i.e., mechanicals). See, unlike with artist royalties, the companies don't recoup advances, recording costs, or anything else from mechanicals. And since this is money going out before they break even, they're very touchy about the amount.

You have to be just as touchy about your mechanicals, because they may be the only money you're going to see for quite a while. As we discussed earlier, you only get artist royalties after you've recouped recording costs, video costs, etc. (which means they may never come, or if they do, it may not be for a couple of years). And as we'll discuss in Chapter 23, you won't be making any money from touring in your early stages. So take extremely good care of mechanical royalties—they may have to last you through a few cold winters.

Companies limit mechanical royalties in two ways:

1. **Rate per Song**
    The ink was hardly dry on the 1976 Copyright Law, raising the statutory rate from 2¢ to 2.75¢, when the record companies hit upon the idea that they should require their artists to license controlled compositions at 75% of the statutory rate, with further reductions (to 50%) for record club or budget records. (Controlled composition clauses existed before the 1976 Copyright Law, but they didn't reduce the rate below statutory.) To a large degree, the companies have been successful in getting these 75% and 50% rates with almost all new, and many midlevel, artists. Even the biggest superstars have some form of controlled composition clause, although the 'limit' may be 100% of statutory.

2. **Rate per Album**
    There is also a limit of ten or so times the single song rate for each album.

These issues are much more complex than they seem. So let's take an in-depth look. I promise to go slowly.

MAXIMUM RATE PER SONG

Because the maximum rate per album is a multiple of the single-song rate, we need to first look at what they do to you in connection with each song. Here's the skinny:

Percentage of Statutory.   The first argument is to see if you can get more than the standard, off-the-shelf '75% of statutory.' If you're a new artist, you probably won't. If you're midlevel or up, or if you have some bargaining power, try to get the percentage over 75%—anywhere over 75% would be nice. If you can't, one compromise is to ask for an escalation on later albums. For example, you might have a 75% rate on albums one and two, an 85% rate on albums three and four, and 100% after that. Or another possibility is an escalation based on sales: For example, you might get 75% for the first 500,000 (1,000,000) albums, 85% for the next 500,000 (1,000,000), and 100% thereafter.

Minimum Statutory Rate.   The limit per composition is based on the *minimum* statutory rate. This means that all compositions are treated as if they are five minutes or less in duration, regardless of their actual playing time—in other words, there is no additional payment for lengthy compositions. For example, the current statutory rate for a seven-minute song is 10.85¢ (see page 199 for why), but under these provisions, you're only paid 8¢ if you get 100% of statutory, or 6¢ (75% of 8¢) if you have a 75% rate.

Changes in Statutory Rate.   As we discussed, the statutory rate changes over time (see page 214). But controlled composition clauses set a rate that doesn't go up. Thus, even if you get full statutory rate in your deal, it's normally locked to the statutory rate on a particular date, and there's no change if the statutory rate later escalates. This is tough to change, even for superstars.

The companies lock into the statutory rate in effect on one of these three dates: (a) the date of recording; (b) the date the master is delivered to the company; or (c) the date of first release of the master.

The general thinking (and historically this has been correct) is that the latest possible date is best for you—the statutory rate has never gone down, and thus the longer you wait, the more likely it may go up.

Free Goods.   The controlled composition clause will say that you get no mechanicals on free goods (see page 75 for what free goods are). Actually, it's usually stated in language that's a little sneaky: It says that you only get mechanicals on records 'for which a royalty is payable under this agreement.' This means you don't get paid on free goods (because they don't bear royalties), but it isn't so obvious. As a new artist, you may have to live with this. When you begin to have some clout, you can sometimes get paid on 50% of album free goods, and superstars sometimes get paid on 100%. However, even superstars usually aren't paid on single free goods, and no one gets paid on special campaign free goods or promotional records (see page 78 for what all these things are).

Multiple Uses.   Controlled composition clauses say that, even if a particular song is used more than once on the same record, you get paid as if it were only used once.

Reduced Rates.   The company typically asks for reduced rates on record clubs (50% of your normal rate), budget (50% to 66⅔%), mid-price (66⅔% to 75%), and television-advertised packages (50%—see page 170 for what those are). Note, if you have a 75% of statutory rate on top-line product, you'll get a reduced percentage of that already reduced rate. For example, if you had a 75% rate on top line, and a 50% reduction for budget records, you'd only get 37.5 (50% of your 75% rate). These reductions are sometimes negotiable, but not very.

Public Domain Arrangements.   If a song is an arrangement of a public domain composition, the record company doesn't want to pay you for it. Your argument is that songs like 'Scarborough Fair,' 'Sloop John B,' and 'Turn, Turn, Turn' were extremely successful public domain songs, and if you're brilliant enough to have this concept, you should be paid. (Sorry to use old stuff, but I can't think of anything more current.) The typical compromise is that you get a proportionate royalty for public domain material, in the same ratio that ASCAP or BMI (more about them later) pay performance royalties for the composition involved. In other words, if ASCAP pays you 50% of normal performance monies for the song, you get 50% of the mechanical rate. Everyone routinely accepts this.

Non-controlled Songs.   This is a particularly nasty piece of business. The rate limits may be imposed not just on *controlled* compositions, but on *every* composition in the album. Not all companies do this, but many do. If you're using **outside songs** (meaning songs that aren't controlled compositions), this may be impossible to deliver—the owner will tell you to get lost. Remember, you can't force an owner to license you at all for a first use, and even if the song was used before, the owner doesn't have to take less than the full statutory rate (see page 216). The only way to pay less for *outside songs* is to either threaten ('We'll drop your song if you don't reduce the rate'), or grovel ('Please, I'm just a poor little singer'). But if you're dealing with major songwriters, you can forget it unless you sell a lot of records.

See, the problem is that, if you have to pay more than your contractual limit, the company carves the excess out of your hide. Here's an example for an eight-song album:

4 Outside Songs at Statutory (4 × 8¢)	32¢
4 Controlled Compositions (4 × 75% of 8¢)	24¢
TOTAL MECHANICALS PAYABLE	**56¢**
Maximum Allowed (8 × 75% of 8¢)	48¢
Less: Amounts Due Outside Songs	−32¢
MAXIMUM PAYABLE FOR YOUR 4 CONTROLLED COMPOSITIONS	**16¢**

As noted above, since you promised the record company that outside songs wouldn't cost more than 75% of 8¢, the excess comes out of your mechanicals on the other songs. In this example, the excess is 8¢, which is the difference between the 32¢ (4 x 8¢) due to the four outside song publishers, and the allowable 24¢ (4 × 75% of 8¢). This 8¢ excess is deducted from your 24¢ for the controlled songs, so you get only 16¢ for your four songs (24¢ less the 8¢ excess). This equates to only 4¢ per song for you (16¢ divided among four songs), which is less than 75% of statutory (75% of 8¢ is 6¢). And if you don't have enough controlled songs from which to take the excess, it comes out of your record royalties or your advances.

So now you're a master of the single song limit. You're ready to conquer:

Maximum Rate Per Album

Standard Clause. All controlled composition clauses impose a limit on the total mechanicals for each album, usually ten times 75% of the statutory rate (or ten times the full rate if your rate per song isn't reduced). This is known as a **ten times** rate, meaning you get ten times the single song rate. Note that this is in addition to, and independent of, the per-song limit. In other words, you must deliver each song at the specified single song rate, no matter what the total album limit, but you can't exceed the total album limit no matter how you license each individual song. This is to keep you from delivering, for example, fourteen songs at a 75% rate, which totals more than the company wants to pay even though you haven't exceeded your per-song limit. And remember: All of these limits are based on a multiple of the *minimum* statutory rate (the rate for songs five minutes and under), as we discussed on page 228).

Nowadays, it's common for CDs to have anywhere from eleven to fourteen songs on them. So you should always try for more than a ten-times limit. New artists, get used to *ten times*. With clout, you can edge up to eleven or twelve times, and occasionally a little more.

Wherever you end up, you can see that it's pretty easy to slide right over the limit. So lemme show you what happens when you do. Warning: It isn't pretty. Do not read this section alone at night, or while operating heavy machinery.

Just for consistency in the examples, I'm going to assume that you have a maximum album rate of ten times 75% of statutory, or 60¢. The same principles apply even if it's a different limit (e.g., eleven times 75%, or ten times full statutory, etc.), but let's use ten times 75%.

No Limit on Non-controlled Songs. As your bargaining power goes up, you may be able to get a clause with no limit on outside compositions (other than statutory rate), even if you have a 75% statutory limit on controlled compositions, as long as you don't exceed the overall limit for the album (which in our example is ten times 75% of the statutory rate). Thus, while the maximum mechanicals for the album is 60¢, you'd be allowed to pay statutory rate for each outside composition. This sounds a bit odd at first, but it's much better for you than a flat 75% of statutory limit on each composition (as in the example on page 230). The advantage is that you can now pay the outside publishers full statutory without reducing your royalties, because you're not limited on outside songs if you stay under the album limit.

Let's look at this using numbers. Here's what happens to the example on page 230 under this clause:

4 Outside Songs at Statutory (4 × 8¢)	32¢
4 Controlled Compositions (4 × 75% of 8¢)	+ 24¢
TOTAL MECHANICALS PAYABLE	**56¢**
Maximum Allowed (10 × 75% of 8¢)	60¢

Note the amount payable (56¢) is less than the maximum allowed for the album (60¢), which is ten times 75% of 8¢. So you get the full 24¢ for your songs, which is 75% of statutory. This contrasts with the result under the clause discussed on page 213, where you got less than this (only 16¢) for the exact same album. And by the way, that extra 8¢ can add up to a hefty sum if you sell millions of albums.

On the other hand, if the mechanical royalties total more than ten times 75% of statutory under this clause, the excess comes out of your royalties. So if you pay outsiders at the statutory rate, you either have to put fewer than ten songs on your album, or else take a reduced rate on your songs. For example, if there were five outside songs and five controlled compositions, you would get less than 75% of statutory for the controlled songs under this same clause. This is because the maximum per album applies to *all* of the compositions on the album, not just the controlled compositions. Thus, in a sense, the company is imposing a rate on outside compositions under this restriction, even when there is none under the maximum-rate-per-song provisions. Take a look at the numbers:

5 Outside Songs at Statutory (5 × 8¢)	40¢
5 Controlled Compositions (5 × 75% of 8¢)	+30¢
TOTAL	**70¢**
Maximum Allowed (10 × 75% of 8¢)	60¢
Less: Amounts Due Outside Songs (5 × 8¢)	–40¢
MAXIMUM PAYABLE FOR YOUR 5 CONTROLLED COMPOSITIONS	**20¢**

So, for each of your songs, you don't get 75% statutory (6¢), but rather only 4¢ (20¢ divided among five songs).

No Penalty for a Limited Number of Outside Songs. The next step up is to say that you can pay statutory rate for the outside songs, and that you're allowed to *exceed* the overall album limit in order to pay this to the outsiders. If you can get this, it's usually limited to one or two songs per album.

This concept is easier to understand with an example:

Assume your overall album limit is ten times 75% of statutory (60¢). If you have ten songs on the album, and two of them are outside songs licensed at statutory, you will exceed the maximum by the difference between the 75% limit and the full statutory amount (100%) that has to be paid for each of the two outside songs. (The difference is the 100% paid less the 75% maximum, or 25% of statutory, for each of the two songs.)

8 Controlled Compositions (8 × 75% of 8¢)	48¢
2 Outside Songs at Statutory (2 × 8¢)	16¢
TOTAL	64¢
Maximum Allowed (10 × 75% of 8¢)	60¢
EXCESS	**4¢**

If your clause allows up to two outside songs at full statutory, the company will pay the excess to the outsiders and won't take it back from you. Another way to look at it would be to say that the overall album limit is eight times 75% of statutory plus two times statutory, or 64¢. But this isn't really the case, because you only get the extra amount if you use two outside songs. If there was only one outside song, the maximum would be 62¢ (nine times 75% of statutory plus one times statutory), and if all ten songs on the album were yours, the rate would drop back to ten times 75% of statutory (60¢).

No Penalty for Any Outside Songs. With still more clout, you can get a clause that allows you an overall album limit of ten times the full statutory rate, even though controlled songs are limited to 75%. This means you're not penalized at all for the outside songs (unless you exceed ten songs on the album, and/or unless you have outside songs over five minutes). Here's an example using five outside songs under this kind of clause:

5 Outside Songs at Statutory (5 × 8¢)	40¢
5 Controlled Compositions (5 × 75% of 8¢)	+ 30¢
TOTAL MECHANICALS PAYABLE	70¢
Maximum Allowed (10 × 8¢)	80¢

Since the maximum allowed (80¢) is now more than the amount payable for both outside and controlled songs, you get the full 30¢ (five times 75% of statutory) for your songs.

The Ultimate.   The ultimate is to say that the only limit is ten (or eleven or twelve, if you can get it) times statutory, and the only per-song limit (on either outsiders or you) is statutory. However, you still have to live with the *minimum* statutory rate, as described on page 228, as well as the other provisions in the prior section on per-song rate limits (rate lock-in, multiple uses, free goods, public domain songs, reduced rates for club, etc.).

Multiple Albums.   Most form controlled composition clauses don't distinguish between normal albums and multiple albums (we discussed multiple albums on page 174). If you don't raise the issue, you'll have a ten-song mechanical limit on multiple albums that can have twenty or more songs. If you ask, you may get more than a 'ten times' limit, but it won't be 'twenty times': The companies will only increase the mechanical royalties in the same proportion that the suggested retail price increases over that of a single-disc album. If the multiple album has two CDs in the package, you will come close to twenty times. But, if it takes two CDs, it's probably more than twenty songs. If the multiple album is contained on only one CD, there is only a small (if any) increase in price, and you won't get much more for mechanicals. For example, if a single disc album is $10, and a double album is $11, you would get $^{11}/_{10}$, or 110% (the ratio that $11 for the double album bears to $10 for the single album) of the mechanical royalties payable for a single album. (This formula is very similar to the one used for your artist royalties on multiple albums, which we discussed on page 174). If there is no price increase, you won't get any more mechanicals in your contract, but you can often work it out when you start to record the multiple album (since you can't do a multiple without the company's consent anyway, this is one more thing to negotiate at the time).

This can be serious business if you have a lot of outside songs, because the outsiders will insist on getting paid (greedy pigs that they are), and it comes out of you. For example, if there are sixteen songs and six are outsiders, all six are in excess of the allowed ten and would be deducted from mechanicals (leaving only four songs' worth of mechanicals for your ten songs). And if you pay the outsiders full statutory, while your limit is ten times 75% of statutory, you're even further in the hole. So, if you have an attack of multi-album-itis, negotiate the mechanicals with your record company, and ideally with the outsiders as well, before you start.

As noted before, box-set mechanicals are specifically negotiated when the package is put together.

Videos. The first draft of almost every controlled composition clause requires you to license your songs for free use in videos, forever. This may be overreaching, but it's hard to change. Let's look at two parts of it:

1. **Promotional usage.**
   I don't think it's unreasonable to give the company a free promotional video license. When it's using the video to promote your records, it's not making any money.

2. **Commercial usage.**
   When it comes to commercial usages (primarily home video at this time, although there may be other outlets in the future), you should at least argue for some compensation. Independent publishers (those not subject to a controlled composition clause, who can charge what the market will bear) usually get in the range of 8¢ to 15¢ per song. Also, there is almost always a 10,000 to 15,000 unit guarantee, meaning, for example, if you got 12¢ per unit and a 10,000 unit guarantee, you would get a $1,200 advance (12¢ × 10,000 units). In addition, they often get something called a **fixing fee,** which is a non-recoupable payment for *fixing* the song in the video (basically, a synch license—see page 244 for what that is). These range from $250 to $500 per song.

   It's very difficult to get compensation if you're the artist, for the simple reason that companies don't like to do it. But it's worth asking. Sometimes you can get a small fee ($250 or so) if the video recoups its costs.

The U.K. copyright royalty for videocassettes (VHS) is 8.5% of PPD multiplied by a fraction, the numerator of which is the total weighted copyright music duration, and the denominator of which is the total actual programme duration, provided the rate can't exceed 7% of PPD. How about that for fancy words? Here's what it means in English: you divide the music (in minutes) by the whole programme (in minutes) and multiply by 8.5%. In adding up the minutes of music, featured songs (e.g., ones performed on camera) count at 100%, but background music (like an orchestral score) is only counted at 75% (so 10 minutes of background music counts as only 7.5 minutes). Here's an example: assume you had a 30-minute programme, with 20 minutes of background music and 5 minutes of featured music. To add up the music, the 20 minutes of background counts at only 75%, which is 15 minutes (75% of 20 minutes). The 5 minutes of featured counts as a full 5 minutes, so that's added to the 15 minutes for background to equal 20 minutes. The fraction is therefore the 20 minutes of music over the 30 minutes of the full programme, or $^{20}\!/_{30}$ ($^2\!/_3$). The $^2\!/_3$ is then multiplied by 8.5%, for a rate of 5.66% of PPD. If the programme had all been featured music (like a concert), however, the royalty would be capped at 7% of PPD.

In addition to the above, there's synchronization fee of £50 per work, which is good for up to five minutes of playing time (the fee goes up if you go over five minutes).

The rate for DVDs is still being worked out, but it seems to be either (a) 10% of PPD (similar to the 8.5% paid for mechanical royalties (see page 236 above), with an extra 1.5% because it includes a synchronization license); or (b) 1.4p per minute (or a portion of a minute) of music, with an increase if there's also a reproduction of the lyrics, or if the music is used interactively.

My understanding is that the BPI and MCPS are waiting for the Copyright Tribunal to tell them which DVD rate is going to win. Stay tuned for this exciting news.

Postscript

Now that you've read it (I didn't want to prejudice you before you did), I can tell you that controlled composition clauses are among the most complicated critters in the music business (you probably figured that out already, didn't you?). This section is packed full of numbers and weird concepts, so it may take a few times through to get the flavor. Don't feel bad if you don't get all of it the first time or two—it took me years to get a decent handle on it. But mechanicals may well be your only monies for quite a while (see page 227 for why), so it's worth an investment of time to understand these clauses.

PUBLIC-PERFORMANCE ROYALTIES

Remember, when we discussed copyrights, that one of the exclusive rights you get is the right to perform your composition in public (see page 209). These rights are known as **performing rights,** or **public performance rights,** and each user needs your permission to play the song on the radio, on television, in nightclubs, in amusement parks, at live concerts, etc.

As you can quickly see, it's impossible for every radio station, nightclub, etc., in the country (of which there are thousands) to get a separate license for every song they play (of which there are also thousands). The paperwork alone would send them off to buy that trout farm in Idaho. So out of this situation developed the **blanket license** and **performing rights societies.** Here's how the system works:

Performing Rights Societies

The major *performing rights societies* in the United States are **ASCAP** (standing for **American Society of Composers, Authors, and Publishers**), **BMI (Broadcast Music Incorporated),** and **SESAC** (standing for *SESAC*). Of the three, *ASCAP* and *BMI* are by far the largest, as SESAC has only about 1% of all performing rights. Virtually every foreign country has the equivalent for its own territory, most of which are government-affiliated, such as SACEM for France, STEMRA for Holland, PRS for the U.K., etc.

The societies go to each publisher and say, 'Please designate us as your agent for the performing rights in *all* your songs. We'll then go to the people who want to use them (radio stations, nightclubs, etc.) and give them a license to use *all* the songs of *all* the publishers we represent. For each license, we will collect fees, divide them up, and send you your share.' And this is exactly what happens. Publishers sign up with (known as 'affiliating with') ASCAP or BMI, who then issues licenses to the users, collects the monies, and pays the publishers.

The U.K. equivalent of ASCAP, BMI and SESAC is **PRS**, which stands for Performing Rights Society (clever, huh?). PRS is a non-profit organization, and it operates in exactly the same way as BMI and ASCAP.

To qualify for membership, a songwriter/composer must have written a song that's been broadcast, performed live, or had a recording of it performed publicly. Alternatively, you must have played a ukelele in the shower. (OK, I made that last one up just to see if you were paying attention). For publishers to join, you need a catalogue of fifteen or more tunes written by a PRS member or one of its affiliated performance societies around the globe.

Once you're a member of PRS, it will collect your United States performance monies under agreements it has with ASCAP, BMI and SESAC. Conversely, PRS remits U.S. writer's monies back to ASCAP, BMI or SESAC. Indeed, all performing rights societies throughout the world do this, so that you can collect everything from your local society.

Blanket Licenses

The license that ASCAP and BMI give each music user is called a **blanket license** because it 'blankets' (i.e., 'covers') all of the compositions they represent. In other words, in exchange for a fee, the user gets the right to perform *all* the compositions controlled by *all* the publishers affiliated with ASCAP and BMI. The fee can range from a few hundred dollars per year for a small nightclub, to millions of dollars per year for television networks.

Separate Writer Affiliation

It isn't just publishers who affiliate with these societies. The writers do also, and even more importantly, *the writers are paid directly by the society.* This means performance earnings are not paid to the publisher; instead, the society bypasses the publisher and sends the checks to the writer. This is designed to protect the writer (which it does nicely) from flaky publishers who might steal the money.

By the way, writers can only affiliate with one society.

Allocation of License Proceeds

So here are the societies sitting with all those millions of dollars of license fees. How do they know how much to pay each publisher and writer?

First, the monies are used to pay the operating expenses of the society. Then, everything left over is divided among the participants (ASCAP and BMI are non-profit, so everything not used for expenses gets paid out; SESAC is privately owned and operated for profit). The division is based only on (a) radio airplay; (b) television airplay; and (c) touring (sort of). (If you're an artist who constantly performs his or her own compositions in live concerts, but you're not on the radio or TV, you can sometimes make special arrangements with BMI [but not

ASCAP] to get paid.) So, you ask, how do they know how much a song is played on the radio or on television?

1. **Radio.**
    BMI requires its licensee radio stations to keep logs of all the musical compositions they play. This is done on a rotating basis, from station to station, and each station has to log for about three days (twenty-four hours per day) each year. BMI then projects from these logs to the whole country.

    ASCAP does it differently. It hires an independent statistical firm to listen to selected radio stations on a rotating, unannounced basis, writing down the compositions played. Based on this, it then makes the same extrapolations to the whole country.

    It looks as if the allocation of radio performance monies may be headed for major changes. There's a system called **BDS** (the letters stand for **Broadcast Data Systems**), which is owned by *Billboard* (the trade publication). BDS is used to determine *Billboard*'s charts, and its innovation is a computer that's learned how to listen to the radio. As I understand it, the computer is fed a number of compositions, which it digitizes. The computer then monitors radio broadcasts, matches songs played with its memory bank, and keeps track of which songs are played, the dates, and times. Should the performing rights societies have enough confidence to treat a system like this as gospel, we may have a much more accurate record of performances.

2. **Television.**
    Television stations are required to keep **cue sheets,** which are lists of every musical composition used, how long it was played, and how it was used (theme song, background, performed visually, etc.). The cue sheets are then filed with ASCAP or BMI, and there are specific dollar amounts paid for each type of use (theme, background, etc.). The amount also varies with the size of the broadcast area (local pays a lot less than network).

3. **Touring**
    Both societies now pay based on domestic live performances, but it's only for the top two hundred grossing tours as reported in a magazine called *Pollstar*. They pay based on **set lists**—lists of the songs played by the band involved—which they get from either the venues or artist's management.

4. **Muzak**
   Muzak, your source of fine music in elevators, grocery stores, and waiting rooms, is also logged separately.
5. **Webcasting**
   We'll get into this later.

BMI pays 'bonuses' for musical compositions that are performed heavily, and this can result in substantial increases in the amount of performance monies paid. ASCAP has no such concept, but its fees tend to be comparable anyway. Both societies pay quarterly (four times per year), and both societies pay about nine months to a year after the quarter in which monies are received.

PRS allocates its income on the basis of radio and television play, live concerts, and website reporting of online usage. Promoters (people who hire artists to put on concerts) doing shows at major and medium-sized concert venues submit play lists to PRS for this purpose.

Motion Picture Performance Monies

Due to some fancy footwork by the film industry a number of years ago, ASCAP and BMI are not permitted to collect public-performance monies for motion pictures shown in theaters in the United States. There is no logical reason for this (showing movies is certainly a public performance); it's just historical and political. However, foreign territories have never bought into this nonsense, and motion picture performance monies over there are significant. The fees are collected by local societies, then paid over to ASCAP and BMI.

Foreign performing rights society fees are based on a percentage of the box office receipts, which means they generate a good amount of green (or whatever color the local currency is). How much? Well, the composer of a major smash film score can earn hundreds of thousands of dollars in foreign performance monies alone.

Which Society Is the Best?

Hard to tell.

The best gauge is to look at cross-registered songs, which means a song that is registered with both ASCAP and BMI. This happens when a song is owned by an ASCAP and a BMI publisher—for example, if a song is owned 50% by a BMI publisher and 50% by an ASCAP publisher, it's registered 50% with BMI and 50% with ASCAP. (By the way, the shares of each publisher must match that of the writer; in other words, if ⅓ of a song is written by a BMI writer and ⅔ by an ASCAP writer, a BMI publisher must have ⅓ of the publishing, and an ASCAP publisher must have ⅔ of the publishing.)

With cross-registered songs, ASCAP collects its half of the song and remits to the ASCAP writer/publisher, while BMI does the same for its writer/publisher on the same song, each independent of the other so we get to see who pays more. And the result?

In the comparisons I've seen, ASCAP seems to do a bit better in general, but for some compositions, BMI beats them. Also, BMI pays more for certain usages under specific circumstances, and BMI changes its payment schedules periodically. Thus (unfortunately) there are no hard and fast rules.

17

Secondary Publishing Income

Now let's a look at other sources of publishing income: print, synchronization, and foreign monies.

PRINTED MUSIC

The majority of printed music revenues comes from **sheet music** (printed music of a single song—the kind you stuff inside your piano bench) and **folios** (which are collections of songs, such as *Greatest Hits of the Eighties, The Complete Led Zeppelin,* etc.). Collections of songs by a number of different artists and writers are called **mixed folios.** Another popular type is a **matching folio,** which has all the songs of a particular album (i.e., it 'matches' the album). *Matching folios* are usually printed with the album artwork on the cover and various posed candid shots of the artist inside.

Royalties

The royalties paid to a publisher for single-song sheet music are 20% of the marked retail price (currently about 80¢ for a $3.95 retail price). Royalties on folios are 10% to 12.5% of the marked retail price, and the current marked selling prices of most folios is $19.95. A **personality folio** is one that has the picture of the performing artist plastered all over it, such as *Tina Turner's Greatest Hits.* (A matching folio [see the prior section for what that is] is also a *personality folio.*) For a personality folio, there's an additional royalty of 5% of the marked retail selling price for use of the name and likeness of the artist, and it goes to the artist (who may or may not be the same person as the songwriter).

Unless the folio represents the selected works of a particular songwriter and only one publisher, it will contain songs written and/or published by a number of different people. Thus, the royalties are pro-rated, in exactly the same way as royalties are pro-rated for records that have recordings by different artists (see page 170). For example, if there are twenty compositions in the folio, and ten are owned by you, you would get ¹⁰⁄₂₀ (one half) of the 10% to 12.5% royalty. When you ne-gotiate a pro-ration provision, be sure to insist that the royalty can be pro-rated only on the basis of *copyrighted, royalty-bearing* works in the folio. Otherwise, your royalty gets reduced by 'Mary Had a Little Lamb' and 'The Star-Spangled Banner,' even though the printer isn't paying anyone for these songs.

In the U.K., unlike in the U.S., the royalty for single-song sheet music is lumped in with all the others, and thus is paid in the range of 10% to 15% of retail.

The balance of print music consists of things like instructional music (such as putting your songs in *How to Play the Nose Flute*), marching band arrangements, choir arrangements, dance arrangements, etc. The royalty for these is generally 10% of retail. Print rights also include reprints of lyrics in books, magazines, etc., usually for flat fees. This can run anywhere from $150 for the minor usage of a few words, to $25,000 or more for major uses (like a major print ad [meaning news-papers and magazines] or a book that's based on the lyrics of a song with pictures, which would also bear a royalty). Sometimes reprinting lyrics in books are quoted on the basis of a few hundred dollars per line, unless it's a major song and a major book, which can run into the thou-sands. Reprints of lyrics on albums are customarily free.

Term

Licenses for print music (other than lyric reprints) are for limited peri-ods of time, usually three to five years. Because of this, you have to spell out what the printer can do with the stuff at the end of the term. Cer-tainly they can't manufacture any more inventory, but can they con-tinue to sell what they have?

Normally these licenses give the printer a *non-exclusive* right (mean-ing someone else can sell the same materials at the same time) to sell their existing inventory for a period of six to twelve months after the term expires. At the end of the six to twelve months, they have to trash anything left over. For folios (because they're so much more expensive), the printers try not to have any time limit on their sell-off rights.

When you make these deals, make sure there's no **stockpiling, dumping,** or **distress** sales. *Stockpiling* is where the printer manufactures eight quadrillion units right before the end of the term, so that they have tons of your inventory to sell after the term. (Your new printer won't like it if the market is already flooded with the same books it's trying to sell.) You stop this by saying the printer can only manufacture enough to meet their reasonably anticipated needs during the term.

Dumping and *distress sale* mean the printer sells your inventory at less than customary wholesale prices. *Way* less. You don't want this because, if they end up with a ton of goods left over, they'll blow it out at whatever rock-bottom price they can get. (Since they have to destroy everything they don't sell, they use the age-old theory that it's better to get something than nothing.) This practice, shall we say, 'perturbs' your new printer, who is trying to sell the same stuff at full price. You solve this by saying your materials can be sold only through normal retail channels, at normal wholesale prices.

SYNCHRONIZATION AND TRANSCRIPTION LICENSES

A **synchronization license** (also called a **synch** [pronounced 'sink'] license) is a license to use music in 'timed synchronization' with visual images. A classic example is a song in a motion picture, where the song is synchronized with the action on the screen. It also includes, however, television commercials, home video devices, etc., although interestingly it doesn't include radio commercials (since they're not synchronized with visuals). Radio commercial licenses are called **transcription licenses.**

Fees

The fees for *synchronization licenses* are really all over the board, and they vary with the usage and the importance of the song. An example of the lowest end would be a ten-second background use of an unknown song in a television show (maybe being played on a jukebox while the actors are talking and ignoring it). A high-end example would be an on-camera, full-length performance of a well-known song in a major studio's high-budget film, like the use of 'Unchained Melody' in *Ghost*. And when we get into the realm of commercials, the fees go even higher.

Here's an idea of the range:

1. **Motion picture:**

   Major Studios. Motion picture synch licenses for a major studio film generally run in the range of $15,000 to $50,000, which buys out all rights in perpetuity. The fees are generally higher if you're giving them the right to use the song in advertising and trailers (previews) as well as in the film. **Main title** usages (meaning over the opening credits) run $50,000 to $150,000, and **end title** usages are more like $35,000 to $100,000 (why pay as much for a song when everybody's walking out of the theater?) The *end title* songs will be at the lower end if there is more than one over the credits, which happens these days. Of course, when there's an incredibly hot, recent song, and the film company is salivating over it, these figures can get very high into six figures.

   Independent Films. For low-budget, independent films, the deals get much more creative. Funny how things always get more creative when someone doesn't have any money.

   Most of these are **step deals,** meaning the money comes in steps. For example, the initial license might be $2,500 to $7,500, plus an equal amount on release of the film in home video. Then there might be **kickers** (additional fees) if the film achieves certain success. One deal for a very low-budget film paid amounts equal to the original license if the film had worldwide box office gross of $3,000,000, and additional *kickers* at every $3,000,000 increment, up to a maximum of four times the original fee. Other deals don't have a maximum, so the publisher can make out nicely if the film does well.

2. **Television:**

   Television quotes are based on the rights granted, with a commitment to the minimal rights needed and options for the rest. The usual bundles are:

   Free, Basic Cable, and Satellite. *Free television,* as you might guess, is over-the-air broadcast TV that you can receive free. *Basic cable* and *satellite* mean stations you get free when you're a cable or satellite subscriber (like CNN, MTV, VH-1, etc.); they have commercials and are advertiser supported. For worldwide free and basic cable rights, the range is around $2,500 to $5,000 for a five-year license on episodic television (*episodic* means it's on weekly, like *ER* or *Friends*.) If they want a license in perpetuity, the cost is about $6,000 to $7,500.

Pay TV.   *Pay television* is a service for which you pay a separate monthly fee, such as HBO, Showtime, etc. The fee for this is usually the same as the free/basic cable license.

Foreign Theatrical.   Movies shown on television in our country are often released in theaters outside the United States. The company may ask for an option to do this, and the fee is usually about $15,000, depending on the use. Note this could be more than the original fee.

Home Video.   If the television program is ever released in home video, there's an additional payment of about $6,500 to $8,500. Try to limit the user's right to exercise its home video option to the first two years of the primary television license.

Television Theme Songs.   Television theme songs are licensed on a per-episode basis, often with a guarantee of a minimum number (say thirteen episodes). The range is all over the place, and of course depends on whether the license is for five years or perpetuity, but the general range is about $4,000 to $10,000 per episode.

Common Carriers.   This is the right to exploit the television show on airplanes, ships, bicycles, etc. The price is about $1,000 to $3,000 for a five-year license, or $2,000 to $3,000 for perpetuity.

Performance License.   Typically, television licenses (and film licenses too) require that all broadcasters must have a valid performing rights license (see page 236 for what that means). That assures that the publisher will get paid not just the synch fee, but also the performance monies.

Television Promotions. $500 to $3,500 per week, sometimes even more, to use the song in ads for the licensed show.

3. **Commercials:** For commercials, a song can get anywhere from $75,000 to $500,000 for a one-year national usage in the United States, on television and radio. Really well-known songs in major campaigns can get into the millions, though the typical range for a well-known song is $150,000 to $350,000. These figures get

scaled down for regional or local usages, and for periods of less than a year.

If you're on the *Fast Track*
go to the Bonus Section on page 255.
Everyone else, onward . . .

FOREIGN SUBPUBLISHING

Barring the worldwide conglomerates, publishers don't have branch offices in all territories. So how do they collect their monies when your records sell in Abu Dhabi? Well, they do it by making agreements with local publishers in each territory to collect on their behalf. The local publisher is called a **subpublisher.**

Foreign Mechanicals

Before we talk about deals with the local publishers, you should know about an unusual creature that lives in most territories outside the United States. This is the *mandatory* mechanical rights collection society, and it works like this:

Most countries have a mechanical rights collection organization (usually government owned) that licenses *all* musical compositions (regardless of who owns them) used by *any* record company in that territory. It's like the Harry Fox Agency (see page 224), except that it's mandatory. The society collects mechanical royalties from the record companies, holds them for as long as they can get away with it (they can earn interest on these monies and not have to pay it to anybody), and finally sends them out to the appropriate publisher. (As noted on page 216, mechanical licenses are not issued on a per-song basis outside the United States and Canada. Rather, the entire record is licensed for a percentage of the wholesale or retail price, regardless of the number of compositions. This greatly simplifies the centralization process of putting all the monies through one organization.)

How do the societies know which publisher to pay? Under this system, each local publisher files a claim with the organization, saying it owns a particular composition. It can either be a claim for the entire song, or a percentage share if the rights are split among several publishers in that territory. If a claim is contested (and in some territories even if it isn't), the publisher is required to file proof of its claim, such as a copy of the contract with the U.S. publisher.

Foreign Performances

All foreign territories have some sort of performance rights society, usually government owned, and these societies pay the *publisher's share* of performance monies to local subpublishers. The foreign performing rights societies pay the *writer's share* to ASCAP/BMI/SESAC (which in turn pays the writer), again keeping these monies out of the publishers' hands (as we discussed on page 238). If there's no foreign subpublisher, the publisher's share will ultimately wind its way back to the U.S. publisher through the U.S. society. However, it takes substantially longer, and it's worth paying the subpublisher a piece so you can get it earlier. How much? Well . . .

Subpublisher Charges

The range of deals for subpublishing allows the *subpublisher* to retain anywhere from 10% to 50% of the monies earned, with the vast majority of deals being from 15% to 25%. The contracts are actually written the opposite way, stating that the subpublisher collects all monies and remits 75% to 85% of it to the U.S. publisher. The shorthand industry expression of these deals is '75/25' or '85/15' (referring to the percentages kept by each party). By the way, I heard of one deal where the local subpublisher kept no percentage whatsoever of the earnings (i.e., they remitted 100%). Can you figure out why anyone would do this? See page 254 for the answer.

Covers

It is customary for the local publisher to get an increased percentage for **cover records.** A *cover record*, also called a **cover,** is a recording of a U.S. composition by a local artist in the local territory. The subpublisher usually gets 40% to 50% of the earnings from cover recordings (meaning it remits 60% to 50%). When you make a subpublishing deal, be sure to limit the subpublisher's increased percentage to the cover recordings' earnings only, or else you'll decrease your money on the U.S. version if the local publisher's nephew records the song.

Performance Monies

A number of subpublishers try to charge a bigger percentage of performance royalties than they do for other monies. For example, they may keep 25% of all monies except performances, and 50% of performances. Here is their argument:

Assuming the subpublisher gets 25% of all earnings other than performances, for every dollar of earnings it gets 25¢. The 75¢ paid back to the U.S. publisher includes both the publisher's share and the writer's share (as did of course the dollar paid to them in the first place), and thus their percentage applied to the total writer/publisher combination. On performances, however, remember that the writer's share is paid to the U.S. performing rights society, and not to the local subpublisher (see page 247). This means that, instead of getting the full $1 of performance monies, the subpublisher only gets 50¢ (the publisher's share).

Here's a chart:

	Mechanicals	Performances
Total Writer/Publisher Earnings	$1.00	$1.00
Amount Paid to Subpublisher	$1.00	$ .50
		(other $.50 paid to writer directly by society)
Subpublisher's 25% Share	$ .25	$ .125
Percentage of Dollar Earned	25%	12.5%

Accordingly, subpublishers argue, they're really only getting 12.5% of the performance dollar. Thus, they want 50% of performance monies, so they can get 25% of the full performance dollar and be in the same position as they are with other monies. This 50% equals 25¢ (50% of the 50¢ publisher's share of performance monies), or 25% of the total writer/publisher performance dollar.

This reasoning, while clever and not without merit, usually gives way to sheer bargaining power. If the subpublisher has enough bargaining power, they'll pull it off. Otherwise, the U.S. publisher simply says no.

Printed Music

For printed music, if the subpublisher actually manufactures and sells the stuff, it pays the U.S. publisher from 10% to 15% of the marked retail selling price, the norm being 10% to 12½%. If the print music is licensed out by the subpublisher, the subpublisher keeps the same percentage as all other monies (15% to 25% of licensing income) and remits the balance.

Advances

It's customary for subpublishers to pay the U.S. publisher an advance against their ultimate earnings. This is basically a banking transaction—if the U.S. publisher's catalog has a track record, the subpublisher pays an advance based on historical earnings. It will vary, of course, with the size of the territory and size of catalog. The range is anywhere from zero (for a new artist or a so-so older catalog) to millions of dollars for major catalogs in major territories. Again, as with all other rules, there are exceptions. For example, if the publisher controls a new artist whose record is doing extremely well in the U.S., the advance can get driven up despite the lack of historical base.

A deal with no advance is known as a **collection deal,** meaning the subpublisher merely collects on behalf of the U.S. publisher. Also, if there is no advance, the percentage kept by the subpublisher is often lower, usually in the 10% to 15% range.

Advances are also affected by the currency exchange rates. When the dollar is weak, high U.S. dollar advances are relatively easy to come by; the opposite is true, of course, when the dollar gets stronger. In other words, the same number of English pounds equals more or fewer dollars at any given time, depending on the current exchange rate. When it equals more, you can get a larger dollar advance.

'At Source'

One of the most important points to have in your subpublishing agreement is a requirement that all monies be computed **'at source.'** This means the percentage remitted to you must be based on the earnings in the country *where earned,* which is the *source.* So if you have an 85/15 deal at source in Germany, and $1 is earned there, you get 85¢. If you don't require this, you'll pay 15% in Germany, then another percentage to your U.S. publisher. An extreme example is this scam, which was around for many years:

A subpublisher in the United Kingdom makes a 75/25 deal with a U.S. publisher for all the territories of Europe. The subpublisher in Germany (owned by the U.K. publisher) collects a dollar, keeps 50¢ as its collection fee, and pays 50¢ to the U.K. publisher. The 50¢ received in the U.K. is then split between the U.S. publisher and the U.K. publisher. Here's a play-by-play:

Earnings in Germany	$.100
Less: German Company's 50% Share	– .50
Amount Remitted to U.K.	$.50
Less: U.K. Company's 25% Share	– .125
AMOUNT REMITTED TO U.S. PUBLISHER	**$.375**

It doesn't take a genius to see that the $1 earned at source (in this case, Germany, where the actual earnings were generated) gets dwindled radically before it finds its way into your pocket. And the 75% deal you thought you had becomes 37.5% (you only got 37.5¢ out of the $1 earned in Germany).

This scam is no longer played in the shadows, but right up front. If you don't say the deal is 'at source,' the publisher will take both the local share and its share. Of course, ultimately, it's only a matter of dollars: how much do you get, and how much does the publisher keep. But be sure the issue is out in the open. Either the deal is 'at source' or it's not; say so from the get-go.

If the publisher doesn't own the foreign affiliate, the local publisher's share doesn't go into their pocket, so you don't have the same argument. But you can argue that the U.S. publisher's share has to include the foreign publisher's fee. In other words, if the U.S. publisher gets 25%, it could pay 15% to a local publisher, and keep the other 10%, so in effect you're getting 75% 'at source.' If you can't do that, then try to limit what the subpublishers can charge. For example, say they can't deduct more than say 15% to 25% before sending the dough back to the U.S. The result of this push-pull depends on bargaining power. But however you dress it up, it's just a way of computing how much of each dollar you and they get.

Translation/Adaptation Shares

One particularly interesting aspect of subpublishing deals is that of a **translator** or **adaptor**. If your song is a popular one, many territories want to release a version with lyrics in the language of that territory. This all sounds innocent enough, but it creates some problems:

1. First of all, the local lyricist automatically gets a share of royalties, which is paid by the local societies. Most societies require

that the lyricist receive about one-sixth of gross (meaning combined writer and publisher shares) for mechanicals, and one-sixth of the writer's share only for performance royalties.

2. Subpublishers, naturally, want to charge you for this share. If you have sufficient bargaining power, you may be able to muscle them into absorbing it out of their percentage. As their percentage decreases, however, so does the likelihood of your making them eat it. So, more commonly, the translator's percentage comes off the top, which means you pay your share of it. In other words, if you get 60% of the earnings from covers, you are absorbing 60% of the *translator's* share, and the subpublisher absorbs the other 40%.

3. Always require that the translation is registered separately with the society (since it will have a foreign title, this isn't so difficult), and that the publisher makes sure the translator doesn't get paid on the English-language version. This can be done in most territories, but some (notably Germany) insist on paying the translator on the original composition no matter what you do (in the case of Germany, however, the translator gets only a piece of mechanicals and not other income).

The upshot of all this is that you should have the absolute right to approve whether the subpublisher can authorize a local translation. Apart from its taking money out of your pocket, you want to be sure you like what they're doing. Make them send you an English version of the translated lyrics for approval before they can record. If you don't, your ballad may find itself associated with a number of perverse sexual practices, drugs, Republicans, etc.

The Black Box

Remember, the societies collect mechanicals of *all* songs, not just those registered, but they only pay out for the songs that are registered (see page 247). By now your sharp eye has probably figured out that there may be some songs not claimed by any local publisher. And you're right—there are always unclaimed songs. For example, through sheer inadvertence, a U.S. publisher may not have a subpublishing deal in a particular territory. Or maybe the rights are disputed in the U.S. and no foreign publisher has been given the rights.

These unclaimed monies are called **black box** monies. In some countries (notably Germany, Italy, Spain, France, and Holland), if the funds aren't claimed after a set period of time (usually three years), they're paid to the local publishers. Each publisher gets a portion of them based on the ratio that its earnings bear to the total earnings of the society, and also based on seniority. So if a publisher earned 100,000 drapkes and the society collected 1,000,000 drapkes, it might receive 100,000/1,000,000, or 10%, of the black box monies, and perhaps another 3% because it has been around for twenty years. This can be a substantial source of additional revenue, and the local publisher keeps it all because the monies aren't earned by any particular compositions.

If you get into the 'major leagues' of publishers, you may be able to get a portion of the black box money. The usual formula is to take a proportionate amount, based on the ratio that your earnings for the subpublisher bears to the total earnings of that subpublisher. For example, if your songs earned a total of $200,000 for the subpublisher, and its total earnings were $1 million, you would get 20% of the black box monies, because your $200,000 is 20% of its $1 million total.

DART MONIES (AUDIO HOME RECORDING ACT OF 1992)

Congress passed the Audio Home Recording Act of 1992, not surprisingly, in 1992. This act is the DART (Digital Audio Recorders and Tape) Bill we touched on before, and it did two things:

1. It said that consumers who copy records at home for their private, non-commercial use are not committing copyright infringement. I'll bet you're sleeping much better now. Actually, this wasn't such a big deal. The legislative history accompanying the 1976 Copyright Act made it clear that home copying was not copyright infringement.
2. It imposed a tax on digital audio recorders and digital audiotapes.

In other countries of the world (most notably Germany), there has been a tax on blank tape and recorders for a number of years. It's paid to the record companies, musicians, and songwriters who are deprived of income because of home taping, and it amounts to substantial sums of money. The DART bill was a step in that direction, but it applies only to digital audio recorders and tapes. In a gigantic 'OOPS,' the tax on digital recorders does not apply to computers. This is because the act only applies to machines made *solely* for the purpose of duplicating audio, and therefore blank CDs, CD burners, and the like (which do much more than copy audio) have skated past, thumbing their noses at the musicians. This isn't likely to change easily, because computer companies (who now rule the world) don't like anybody telling them what to do. They figure, if consumers are willing to pay a few more bucks (the tax) for their products, those bucks should go in their pockets. The only exception so far is Germany, which has recently started taxing CD burners and blank CDs.

The DART taxes get paid out in various percentages to the record companies, featured artists, unions, songwriters, and publishers, all separately. This would be a great thing if digital audiotapes weren't D.O.A. Or if blank CDs and burners ever got roped in.

At present, the U.K. doesn't have any tax on blank tapes or recording equipment, but other EU countries do, and this may arrive in the not too distant future. The reason you don't have the tax is because, unlike the United States and other EU countries, the U.K. doesn't allow copying for private, non-commercial use. (I'm sure that's real easy to enforce—I have this vision of bobbies bursting into a bedroom to arrest some teenager making a copy of his CD.) In countries where personal copying is allowed, the EU Directive on Copyright requires member states to provide for 'adequate compensation' to the rights holders, which is usually a tax or levy on blank tapes or recorders.

Answer to question on page 248:

While it was a stupid business deal, the subpublisher's thinking was that (a) it would enjoy a certain amount of prestige from having landed a major catalog (which prestige of course immediately vanished when everyone found out what an idiotic deal they made); and (b) even though the subpublisher kept no piece, it collected the monies locally and held them for a period of six months, which meant the company could earn interest on them. If you find someone ready to make a deal like this, give me a call because I still have that land in Florida for sale.

Bonus Section!

HOW TO SET UP A PUBLISHING COMPANY

I am now about to save you an enormous amount of time and frustration in setting up a publishing company. The tips I'm giving you here, revealed in print for the first time, were gained by yours truly through a series of hard knocks and bruises that will become obvious as you see the proper way to do it.

The Absolute First Thing to Do

Before you do anything, and I mean before you do anything, you positively must take this first step: *Affiliate your company with ASCAP or BMI*. The reason you have to do this first is that these societies won't let you use a name that's the same (or similar to) the name of an existing company. They don't want to accidentally pay the wrong party, and so they're tough about the name you can use. And you don't want to have label copy, printed music, copyright registrations, and everything else in the name of a company that can't collect performance royalties.

You can affiliate and secure your name by completing an application and giving the society three name choices, ranked in order. That way, at least one of the names should clear. If you're also a songwriter and haven't yet affiliated, you should affiliate as a writer with one of the two societies at the same time (they won't let you affiliate with both). You'll have to affiliate as a publisher with the same society that you affiliate as a songwriter. This is because, as we discussed on page 241, the societies insist on having a song's publisher affiliated with the same society as the song's writer. And for this same reason, if you're going to be a 'real' publisher (meaning you're going to publish other people's songs, as opposed to only your own), you'll need to have two companies, one for ASCAP and one for BMI.

The publishing company affiliation forms are pretty straightforward; they ask you who owns the company, the address, and similar exciting, provocative questions. You also need to give them information about all songs in your catalog (writers, publishers, foreign deals, recordings, etc.), so they can put the info into their system and make sure you're properly credited (read 'paid'). You can get affiliation applications by contacting ASCAP or BMI at the following addresses and telephone numbers:

BMI	ASCAP
www.bmi.com	www.ascap.com
320 West 57th St.	One Lincoln Plaza
New York, New York 10019	New York, New York 10023
(212) 586-2000	(212) 621-6000
FAX (212) 489-2368	FAX (212) 724-9064
10 Music Square East	2 Music Square West
Nashville, Tennessee 37203	Nashville, Tennessee 37203
(615) 401-2000	(615) 742-5000
FAX (615) 401-2702	FAX (615) 742-5020
8730 Sunset Blvd.	7920 Sunset Blvd.
3rd Floor West	Suite 300
Hollywood, California 90069	Los Angeles, California 90046
(310) 659-9109	(323) 883-1000
FAX (310) 657-6947	FAX (323) 883-1049

And get started early—it can take about five weeks to get an approval.

Here's a tip in picking a name. The more common your name, the less likely you're going to get it. So steer clear of names like 'Hit Music' and similar choices that, because they're obnoxiously obvious, won't clear. Names using just initials, such as 'J.B. Music' and the like, also seem to have a hard time clearing (so save that concept for your license plates). For some reason, many of my clients enjoy naming their publishing companies after their children or their streets, and these seem to clear routinely. (For the record, I once owned a publishing company, 'Holly Kelly Music,' that I named after my dogs.)

In the U.K., you would of course affiliate with PRS, whose address and telephone number are listed in the back of this book. However, the same warnings apply: if your name is too close to that of an existing company, they may refuse your affiliation. So do it first.

As publishers get bigger, you may want to directly affiliate with performing rights societies in other territories, rather than using a subpublisher who will charge you a percentage. You may still need a subpublisher to collect mechanicals, try to get local recordings, etc.

Setting Up Business

If you're not a corporation using the corporate name, the next step is to file what, in California, is known as a 'fictitious business-name statement.' This is a document filed with a county recorder and published in a newspaper, and it has its counterpart in most states. It tells the world you're doing business under a name that isn't your own and makes it legal to do so. At least in California, you need this statement to open a bank account and, even more importantly, to cash checks made out to that name. You can imagine the screaming phone call I got as a young lawyer when I learned this lesson.

Copyright Registration

Next, register the songs with the Copyright Office in the name of your publishing entity (see page 322). If the songs were previously copyrighted in your name, you need to file an assignment transferring them to the publisher's name.

Society Registration

To the extent you didn't do so when you originally affiliated, you must register all your songs with the performing rights society. The societies will send you the forms, which are self-explanatory. You only have to register the songs as either the writer or the publisher, not both.

After that, you're in business. You can begin to issue licenses to record companies and other users, as well as make foreign subpublishing agreements, print deals, and so forth. However, there's no particular need to rush into these deals, nor will anybody be interested in making them, until you have a record released. In fact, unless you've got a record coming out (or some other exploitation, like a film or TV show using your songs), the societies won't even let you affiliate, and frankly there's not much point in doing any of this. You'll just be all dressed up with no place to go.

18

Songwriter Deals

Now let's look at the terms of the agreement between the songwriter and the publisher. Remember, as we discussed, the songwriter signs a contract transferring ownership of the copyright in the musical composition to the publisher. In exchange for this, the publisher agrees to handle the business and pay royalties to the writer.

SONGWRITER ROYALTIES

The reason we discussed publishers' receipts first was because a songwriter gets a piece of the publisher's collections (with the exception of performance monies, DART, and webcasting monies, which are paid directly to the writer). This is almost invariably 50% (except for print music). Just to remind you, the monies kept by the publisher are called the *publisher's share,* while the monies that the writer gets are called the *writer's share.*

STANDARD CONTRACTS

For some reason, all songwriter contracts seem to be labeled 'Standard Songwriter Agreement.' However, I've never seen any two Standard Songwriter Contracts that looked like they were even distant cousins, much less twins. So don't take any comfort in the words at the top of the page. Here's really what to look for:

'Catch All.' Some contracts say the songwriter gets 50% of the publisher's receipts from 'mechanical, synchronization, and transcription income,' or words to similar effect. The problem is that the language is sometimes a *limited list* of monies from which the songwriter is paid. This means that the publisher could be collecting monies that it

doesn't share with the writer, and this is definitely something to avoid (if you're a songwriter).

This problem isn't cured by adding everything you can think of to the list. For example, even the most complete list of income sources anyone could put together in the 1950s would have omitted income from home video, since it didn't exist. The same would be true of arcade games that play music, computer software that reproduces copyrighted songs, Internet transmissions, and so forth, which not only didn't exist but weren't even contemplated. What you really need, at the end of the list of items, is a **catch-all**. This is a phrase that says the writer gets 50% of 'all other monies not referred to in this agreement.' Often, you'll find the contract states just the opposite: the writer is only entitled to a share of monies *specifically* set forth in the contract. So cross this out, and add your *catch-all*. (Tell them I said you have to have it.)

Share of Advances. Most contracts also say you don't share in any advances the publisher may get. Most of the time, this is fine—if the publisher gets an advance for its entire catalog of songs (of which you're only a part), you really have no right to share in that advance until your song has earnings that are used toward recoupment. There's no way to know whose songs will earn back the advance, and so there's no reasonable way to allocate the advance to a particular song until royalties are earned.

The exception is an advance paid specifically for your composition. One example is when a publisher issues a license at less than the statutory rate and gets an advance (or guaranteed payment for a certain number of units), for one particular song. (We touched on this on page 223.) Since this advance or guarantee is recoupable only from your song's earnings (and doesn't have to be repaid if there are no earnings), you should get your share when the advance/guarantee is paid to the publisher. So add language saying you *do* share in advances and guarantees which are specifically for your composition.

No Playing Footsie. If the publishing company is affiliated with your record company, you want to make sure they don't issue 'sweetheart' licenses (i.e., licenses at less than customary rates) to their own record company. In other words, you don't want them playing footsie with their sister companies at your expense. For example, they might license your songs to their company at half of the statutory rate. Sure, their publishing company makes less (it only gets its share of a smaller amount), but the record company more than makes up the loss, and you don't. This would also apply if they own a film company or any other potential user. So add a provision saying that licenses to their affiliated companies must be on an arm's length, customary basis.

'At Source.' It's also important (and cheap insurance) to make sure your *publisher's deals* with its subpublishers are all 'at source' (see page 250), so that the publisher's income (in which you share) is the largest possible amount. Also, you should limit what the subpublishers can charge, to say 15% or 25%, particularly when the publisher owns a number of publishing companies around the world.

It's possible (although extremely difficult, and takes a lot of clout) to have your *writer's share* computed 'at source.' In these deals as well, you should limit what the subpublisher can charge.

PERFORMANCE MONIES

As we discussed on page 238, the performing rights societies pay songwriters directly (that is, they don't pay the publisher, who in turn accounts to the writer). In fact, the societies are so protective of a writer being paid directly that they won't honor an assignment of performance royalties by the writer. In other words, if the writer tries to sell his or her performance monies, the society will simply refuse to pay the buyer and continue paying the writer. (There is an exception for assignments of performance monies to a publisher who has paid the writer an advance, and for assignments to a bank securing a loan, but these assignments are limited to the amount of the advance or loan.)

Because the writer is paid directly, all songwriter contracts say the writer doesn't share in any performance monies received by the publisher. Without this language, the writer would get all of the writer's share (from the society), and a part of the publisher's share as well. It's a good idea, however, to provide that, if a society no longer pays writers directly, the publisher must share its receipts. And try to get the publisher to agree not to cross-collateralize these monies with advances under your deal, on the theory that the publisher never expected to have performance monies for recoupment in the first place.

PRINTED MUSIC ROYALTIES

As we discussed on page 242, printed music consists primarily of single-song sheet music and multi-song folio books.

Structure of Business

There are only three major manufacturers of secular printed music in the United States these days, namely Warner/Chappell, Hal Leonard, and Music Sales. This means that, unless your publisher is one of these companies, it will be licensing print rights to one of them. Thus, in songwriter deals with publishers who license out these rights to a printer, it would be eminently logical for the writer to get 50% of the publisher's licensing receipts. Logic, however, has never been a major impediment to the music business, and for some twisted historical reason (guess who it favors), print music royalties are expressed as either a percentage of the retail or wholesale price (on folios), or in pennies (for sheet music).

Sheet Music

When we get to single-song sheet music, we really enter the Twilight Zone. For at least the past thirty years, sheet music royalties have hovered in the range of 7¢ per copy. Occasionally some superstars get as high as 10¢ to 12¢, and the publishers act as if this is removing their eyeteeth. If you recall from our earlier discussion, however (on page 223), the publisher gets 20% of the marked retail price, which today is about 80¢.

Why the songwriter still gets such a small amount of the sheet music pie bewilders me. I've been told by major publishers it's because they have **favored nations** (meaning a contract that says its rate goes up if anyone ever gets more) with a number of old writers, and that raising the pennies for the new guys would cost them a fortune on the older deals. (*Favored nations* clauses can be in any kind of agreement, not just publishing.) But whatever the reason, this practice is soundly entrenched in the business. There is some comfort in the fact that sheet music doesn't represent a significant amount of money anymore, so it's tough to get too excited about it in absolute dollar terms. Still, it's a rip-off.

Folios

With regard to folios, remember the printer pays the publisher from 10% to 12.5% of the marked retail price (see page 242). Most songwriter agreements pay the writer 10% of wholesale (you can kick it up to 12.5% with a bit of clout), which approximates 50% of the publisher's receipts. However, to my knowledge, none of the major print houses accounts to publishers on the basis of wholesale, so most publishers merely split their income and call it good. Remember to allow pro-ration only on the basis of copyrighted, royalty-bearing songs (see page 243).

Name and Likeness

In addition to the writer's portion, if you ask, most publishers will give you 5% of wholesale for use of your name and likeness in a personality folio (see page 242), which is about half of the publisher's receipts. You can often hold out for the full 5% of *retail* that the publisher gets, arguing this payment is for your name and likeness, and the publisher shouldn't share in it.

Charges Against Royalties

Often a publisher pays the costs to create a **demo** of your song or, in some deals, pays you $600 or so for each demo you make on your own. A *demo* is an informal recording made solely for the purposes of pitching a song to artists (similar to those for record deals, discussed on page 109). It's usually made by an unknown singer (or the songwriter), accompanied by one or two instruments (which, since the advent of synthesizers, can sound like the London Symphony Orchestra). The publishers try to charge 50% to 100% of the demo charges against the writer, and as your bargaining power increases, this amount decreases to as low as zero.

No songwriting agreement should charge you for anything other than the following: (1) demos; (2) collection costs (that means (a) monies spent by the publisher to collect your song's earnings, such as Harry Fox fees [see page 224]; and (b) the cost of chasing deadbeats who don't pay); and (3) subpublishing fees (see page 248).

All other costs of administration, copyrighting, advertising, etc., should be borne by the publisher. This is their cost of doing business and the reason they get 50% of the income. (When you share in publishing, you're charged with much more. We'll get to that on page 283.)

Accountings

Publishers typically account and pay within sixty to ninety days after the close of each calendar semiannual period (June 30 and December 31). Some superstar songwriters get **quarterly** accountings, but this is rare. A *quarterly* accounting comes after each calendar quarter, meaning March 31, June 30, September 30, and December 31. The advantage, of course, is that you get your money earlier.

Contracts typically limit the period in which you can object to your accounting statements, and most first drafts say you have to object within one year or you lose your right to do so. You can usually get this extended to at least two years, and often three. Beyond that is rare.

The other considerations about statements, auditing, etc., are the same as for record deals, which we discussed on page 160.

DART AND WEBCASTING MONIES

As we discussed previously, DART monies are paid to writers and publishers based on the sale of digital audiotapes and recording equipment and webcasting monies are paid for webcasts of their songs. Since ASCAP and BMI are collecting for the writers, these monies are treated like performance monies and not subject to publishers' sticky fingers (see page 240 for why performance monies don't get to the publisher).

ADVANCES

The advance for a single-song agreement is usually not very significant. It ranges anywhere from nothing (the most common) to $250 or $500, if we're talking about unknown songwriters and no unusual circumstances (such as a major artist who's committed to record the song, which of course changes the whole ball game). Major songwriters rarely sign single-song agreements other than for films (which are another story entirely, as we'll discuss in Chapter 30). If they own their own publishing, they keep the song, and if they don't, they're probably under a term songwriter's agreement. Significant advances are paid under these term songwriter agreements, which by coincidence is our next topic.

TERM SONGWRITER AGREEMENTS

A **term songwriter agreement** is just like a record deal except that, instead of making records, you agree to give the publisher all the songs you write during the term. In a sense, it's also like a bunch of single-song agreements hooked together, because it's similar to sign-ing a single-song agreement for each composition when it's created. The difference is that there's one overall contract which sets out the terms on which each song will be delivered, and of course the advances are recoupable from all of the songs on a cross-collateralized basis (see page 88 for what cross-collateralized means).

Term

The term of the agreement (the period during which you have to sign over everything you write) is usually tied to delivery of songs (which we'll discuss in more detail in a minute). Thus, it ends after delivery of the required songs (like record deal terms). Sometimes deals are for specific periods, such as one year, with the publisher having two to four additional one-year options. And some deals are tied to your recording agreement (i.e., if it's with a publisher affiliated with your record company), meaning is has the same term as the record deal (two or more deals with the same term are called **co-terminus**). Note that the term only denotes the period during which you exclusively agree to *deliver* your songs—the songs you deliver are owned by the publisher for the life of the copyright, which of course extends far beyond the term. (As we'll see on page 279, however, this is sometimes negotiable.)

Advances

Term songwriter agreements almost always require the publisher to pay advances to the songwriter. Historically, 'true songwriters' (meaning songwriters who don't come with access to someone who uses their songs, as opposed to, for example, a writer who is also an artist or pro-ducer, or someone who writes regularly with well-known performers) received weekly advances. This is still the practice in Nashville, but it's not so easy for true songwriters to get these deals in rock 'n' roll. If you do get such a deal, new writers signing to a major publisher might get an advance in the range of $18,000 to $100,000 per year, and less if they sign to a smaller publisher. The advances are paid monthly, quar-terly, or sometimes even annually, at the beginning of a contract year. (Don't get discouraged if you're a true songwriter—there's always a need for good talent. And there are true songwriters who make multi-millions of dollars per year writing hits for other people.)

If you're an established writer, the advances are based on a historical analysis of your earnings—meaning they guess your future potential based on your past—plus whatever additional gouge factor you can leverage. These advances can range from $500 to several thousand dollars per week, and up. Some superstar writers get hundreds of thousands of dollars per year.

More common these days is a deal based on songs being recorded and released. In other words, the publishers have become less interested in what I called 'true songwriters,'and more interested in people who have the ability to use songs or access someone who can use their songs. For example, if you're an unsigned artist and songwriter, a typical deal might be $25,000 to $50,000 on signing, another $25,000 to $50,000 when you secure a record deal, and another $25,000 to $50,000 on release of the album. There are often further advances at certain U.S. sales levels, such as an additional $25,000 at sales of 150,000 albums, and another $25,000 at sales of 300,000.

Under this kind of deal, if you don't get a record contract within a certain period of time (usually twelve to eighteen months), the publisher has the option to require you to deliver a minimum number of songs (around ten to twelve) over the coming year, and it pays advances for these (in the range of $15,000 to $25,000 for the year, paid quarterly). If you do get a record deal, the advance on release of the first album is the amount negotiated up front (which we just discussed).

Another scenario is for bands already signed, and is based on delivery of songs (we'll talk about the specific delivery requirements in a minute). A typical payment schedule is 50% of the agreed advance on signing (or on the publisher's exercise of its option for the next period of the term), 25% when you deliver half of that period's commitment, and the remaining 25% on delivery of the balance. So if the deal was $400,000 and you promised to deliver ten songs, you'd get $200,000 on signing, $100,000 on delivery of the first five songs, and $100,000 on delivery of the second five songs.

If you ask, you can often get a **formula** for advances on release of future albums. The *formula* is similar to those used in record deals, but based on your earnings during the prior twelve months (as opposed to the prior album). (See page 102 for a discussion of formulas in record deals.) Here's a recent deal where the advance for the second album was ⅔ of the earnings during the first year after the release of the first album, less the unrecouped balance, and with a floor and ceiling:

Formula: ⅔ of prior year's earnings, less deficit, but not less than the floor or more than the ceiling.

	Floor	Ceiling
Album 1	$75,000	(Not applicable)
Album 2	$100,000	$200,000
Album 3	$125,000	$250,000

Under this deal, if the writer earns $60,000 during the first year, meaning only $60,000 of the $75,000 is recouped (and she is thus $15,000 unrecouped), the advance for the second album would be $25,000: ⅔ of $60,000 (which is $40,000) less the unrecouped balance ($15,000) equals $25,000. However, there's a floor of $100,000, so she gets a $100,000 advance (because the formula result is lower than the floor). If the earnings are $240,000 (and thus the writer recoups) during the year, there's no deficit to be deducted from the ⅔ of earnings formula, and she gets ⅔ of the $240,000 earned, or $160,000. If she earns $600,000 in the year, she'd only get the ceiling of $200,000 for album two, because ⅔ of $600,000 ($400,000) exceeds the maximum ($200,000).

As we discussed in the record section, new artists for whom there is a bidding frenzy can get deals that used to be reserved only for artists with a sales history. The same is true for publishing. For example, when a writer is the fox with a pack of hounds snapping at their tail, you can get bids of $150,000 to $700,000 per album, and sometimes even more. With that much heat, the deal won't just be a songwriter deal—it will be a copublishing deal, or maybe even an administration deal (none of which means anything to you, because we haven't discussed them yet. Hang on 'til the next chapter).

Delivery Requirements

There are two aspects to delivery requirements:

1. **What you must deliver to move the term of the deal forward.** Since term deals require you to deliver a minimum number of songs during each period, you have to negotiate how many that is. Until you deliver them, you can't move to the next period of the deal's term.
2. **What you must deliver to get your advance.** When advances are based on your delivering a minimum number of songs, that number is not always the same as the number required to move past the current period of the term.

Let's consider these separately:

Moving the Term Forward. Like record deals, the term of a song-writer contract continues until you deliver a minimum number of songs. If you're a songwriter with a track record of hits, you may be able to simply say you'll give the publisher ten or so songs during each period of the term. Of those ten, some minimum number (say at least three) might have to be commercially released on a major label.

You can sometimes (if you have clout) get the publisher to move the term forward if you're recouped, even if you haven't delivered all the songs you promised. Your argument is that they've gotten back their advance and should therefore be happy and shut up. They don't always shut up.

If you're a **self-contained artist,** meaning you both write songs and record them, the term of your deal will usually be geared to the release of an album containing your songs. The publishers will want you to write 100% of the songs on each album, so those songs can be 100% owned by them. Which is fine if you always write all your own songs. But if you write with others, or might at some time in the future write with others, or if you ever want to record songs written by someone else, you have to scale that back. You can easily reduce the 100% to 90%, and with some pushing, you can sometimes get it down as low as 50%. In other words, if there were ten songs on your album, only five would have to be yours to move the term forward. However, if you routinely write your songs with someone who isn't a party to your songwriting deal, then you have to cut those percentages by whatever the other person takes. For example, if you only expect to write 60% of the album (because co-writers normally write the other 40%), then you should only agree to deliver half of that 60% (30%) in order to move the term forward.

If you deliver less than the agreed minimum, the publisher will thank you very kindly, gobble up what you've given them, then take the next songs without paying any additional advance (i.e., no more than what is due for the first album). That's because the deal won't move forward to the next period of the term (and therefore won't entitle you to the next album's advance) until you deliver what you're supposed to for this period. So when you deliver the second album, you'll only get the advance due for the first, which means the publisher will get two albums for the price of one. Have a look with numbers:

Suppose you had to deliver five songs on your first album to move the term, and were entitled to a $100,000 advance when the album was released. If the first album only contained four of your songs, the initial period of your songwriting deal would continue until you re-leased one more song on one of your albums. Since that can't happen until your next album comes out, the first term continues until you've released that fifth song on the second album. And even if that second album contains five of your songs, the publisher only owes you the $100,000 due on delivery of the first album, despite the fact that they got nine songs.

In addition to the number of songs, there may also be a requirement that you deliver a minimum percentage of statutory rate for each one. If your record deal isn't done when you make your publishing deal, the publisher will want you to deliver 100% of statutory rate, with a cap of say ten or eleven songs, and payment on 50% of free goods (see page 228 for what all that means). With some pushing, you can get them down to 75% of statutory (with the same cap and free goods). If your record deal is already made, the publisher will want whatever is in your deal (which may be better than 75%). The higher the rate you deliver, the bigger advance you'll get. That's because the more mechanicals a publisher can collect, the more they're willing to guarantee you up front.

The problem with song delivery deals is that they can go on forever, because you might never satisfy the delivery requirements. For example, if you committed to deliver songs that you've recorded and released, and your record deal comes to an end, you're hosed. Or if you're not an artist, but agreed that a certain number of your songs must be released on a major label, you could be stuck in the first period despite giving the publisher hundreds of un-recorded songs.

You should try for some way to move the term under these circumstances. For example, some publishers will agree you can move the term forward if you're recouped (as we discussed above). Or if the deal is based on your recording the songs as an artist, some publishers will agree that if you're out of a record deal for two years, you can split.

If there's nothing in your contract to cover this, you'll have to come begging. However, the publishers aren't always that sympathetic, particularly if you got a lot of money when you signed the deal.

Advance Delivery Requirements.   A similar requirement is that you must deliver a certain number of songs in order to get your advance. If you're self-contained, they'll want whatever *maximum* percentage of the album you normally write (in other words, without the cushion we just discussed to allow the term to move forward). So if you normally write all of your own material, you'll only get your advance if you deliver 100% of the songs on your album, even if the term moves forward when you deliver 50%. (If the deal was made knowing that you normally write less than 100%, that smaller percentage would be the criteria.)

You should build in protections for falling short. Otherwise, your advance will be 'all or nothing' if you don't hit the target. For example, if you're supposed to deliver 100% of the album, and you only deliver 75%, you should get 75% of the advance, not zero. The publishers will normally agree to this, but they'll insist on a minimum delivery requirement (usually 50% of the target) below which they won't pay anything. So if you normally write 75% of your albums, you'll get all your advance if you deliver 75%. If you deliver 37.5%, you'd get half. But if you only wrote 30%, you'd get nothing until you delivered more songs. (If you got money on signing, or at the beginning of the term, you would keep that. You just wouldn't get any more.)

As with the term delivery requirements, the advance may also be based on your delivering a minimum percentage of the statutory rate. For example, you not only have to deliver five songs, but they must be licensed for at least 75% of the statutory rate. A new wrinkle in this area is the New and Developing Artist Pricing we discussed earlier (see page 181). This is the practice of releasing new artists at mid-price or even budget levels. As we discussed in the controlled composition section (see page 226), you only get 50% of your mechanical rate for these low-priced records. So putting these concepts together, if your songwriting deal has a 75% of statutory requirement, and your company only pays 50% of that because your new-artist-priced album is released at a budget price, publishers sometimes say they don't have to pay the advance, or move the term forward, for delivery of those songs. Not so cool.

The publishers will of course count the songs against your advance and delivery requirement when the album is raised to full price. But the problem is, if it doesn't sell very well at the introductory price, the record company may never raise it to full price, and you'll end up stuck in the first period of your publishing deal (meaning they'll get another album for the same advance).

In all these deals, be sure to add a formula saying that fractional compositions count toward the delivery requirement in proportion to your ownership. For example, if you deliver half the publishing of a composition (because you only wrote half the song; see page 272 for an in-depth discussion of this), it should count as one-half of a song for your delivery requirements. Most forms don't provide this, and the net effect is that you get no credit whatsoever for fractional songs. Since these little guys earn money just like the others, there's no reason you shouldn't.

Prior Songs

Most 'standard' term agreements have an innocuous-looking provision that quietly picks up all of the songs you have written before the term of the deal. Language like, all songs 'written during or prior to the term hereof.' Unless this is something the publisher specifically negotiated for, resist such a clause, or at least get paid for these songs with an additional advance.

The other way to handle pre-term songs is to say that the publisher can administer them during the term of your deal (we'll discuss 'administration' in the next chapter, but basically it means the publisher can control the rights for a period of time without owning them). You should also argue that the prior songs' earnings should not be cross-collateralized with the newly-written songs, and that the prior songs come back to you at the end of the deal if they're not recorded during the term.

Record Deal Tie-ins

As noted on page 89, independent production entities like to grab your publishing when they sign you to a record deal. If there's any possible way to resist this, I strongly urge you to lash yourself to the mast and hang on. Most of the time these entities aren't real publishers, but are rather just looking for another way to make money from you. If you're going to give up your publishing, it should ideally be to a fully staffed publisher (see page 221). These folks can add real value to your songs, by teaming you up with creative co-writers, helping you write for existing artists, and otherwise forwarding your career as a songwriter. In fact, they can even help you get a record deal. On the other hand, the independent label publisher often just makes a deal with a major publisher, under which the major administers your songs (something you could do directly, and for which the independent takes a nice chunk of change by being in the middle), or worse yet, they sometimes do nothing but sloppily collect your money. This scenario isn't always the case—sometimes the independent advances you its own money, helps you creatively, professionally administers your songs, and thus brings a real benefit to the party. But unfortunately this is the exception.

If you must give your publishing to an independent, then, in addition to the normal publishing deal points we're discussing in this chapter, ask for these:

1. Try to keep control of your publishing, and merely pay them a piece of the income. (You'll lose this; they won't trust you to pay them. Also, publishing isn't as valuable for them to sell if they haven't got the administration rights.)
2. Try to limit their participation to mechanical royalties from your recordings. This means they wouldn't share in performance monies, print, etc., and they wouldn't share in any money (even mechanicals) from recordings of your songs by other artists. Your argument is that they're getting publishing only because they're the record company, and are thus involved only in generating mechanicals. This is very hard to get.
3. If you lose point 2, agree to let them share in all earnings (not just mechanicals), but only of those songs recorded by you as an artist. Ideally, you should also limit them to the *earnings of your recordings* of the songs. In other words, if you record a song that becomes a hit, and it's then recorded by three other artists, they would share in the earnings from your version but not the other artists. (There are some allocation problems connected with this, as we'll discuss on page 292.) If you can't get this, at least try to exclude the earnings of songs not recorded by you.
4. No matter how you do with the above, try for all the points in paragraphs 1 through 4 of the next section.

Sometimes you may make a deal with a major and at the same time make a deal with its affiliated publisher. The majors almost never require you to do this, so you make the deal only because you think it's good for your writing career. The following points deal with these kinds of arrangements, but they're applicable to independent record/publishing situations as well:

1. Try to get advances for your publishing in addition to your record advances.
2. Since they share in publishing, ask them not to reduce the mechanical rate they pay you (as a record company) for your songs (see page 226). You should get this from a major, but the independents will argue that the distributing record company forces this reduced rate on them, and they want the maximum mechanicals just like you. Both of these arguments are true, but try it anyway.
3. Be sure they can't exercise an option under your publishing deal without also picking you up as an artist. The argument is

that you're only giving them publishing because they're making you a record deal, and if that's no longer true, they should get their hands off your songs. (Unless you're getting fat advances under the publishing deal, you probably don't care if they pick up your record option and drop the publishing deal.)

4. *Never* let them cross-collateralize your record and publishing deals (see page 88 for what cross-collateralization is). This is not customary, but it's done. Remember the language about cross-collateralizing 'this or any other agreement' between you and the record company (see page 89)? It could pick up a publishing deal as well, because often it's the same parties to both contracts.

Bluntly, if you're dealing with independents who can muscle your publishing, it means your bargaining power is close to zip. So there's not a lot of room. But at least give 'em a good fight, and *never* give up points 3 and 4. **NEVER.**

POP QUIZ

Now that you have carefully digested all of the above, here's a pop quiz: What is a major source of money that a publisher can't (normally) use to recoup its advances? (Answer on page 281.)

If you're on the *Fast Track*,
go to Chapter 19 on page 282.
Everyone else, keep movin'.

COLLABORATION (TWO OR MORE SONGWRITERS)

One provision that needs special care and feeding is the one that concerns your writing with other people (people you write with are called **collaborators**).

Most of the older term songwriter agreements, and a good number of the ones currently used, take the strong position that the publisher gets 100% of the copyright and publishing (meaning both your share and the *collaborator*'s share) of compositions you write with other writers. This is virtually impossible for you to do. It requires you to deliver rights from somebody you have no control over, and who may not want to be delivered. Even worse, it may be someone you can't deliver because they already gave these rights to another publisher. In fact, if your collaborator has this same requirement in their term deal, *they* are obligated to deliver 100% of the composition (including your share) to *their publisher.*

Obviously two people can't each own 100% of the same horse. So as a practical matter, this gets worked out between the two publishers, usually by splitting the copyright and administration between them (see page 282). Sometimes, if there are going to be a number of songs written by the same two people, the publishers alternate administration rights. In other words, one publisher gets administration of the first song, the other publisher gets to administer the second, and so forth. But since neither one wants to draw a turkey when the other gets a hit, the more common solution is to split 'em all.

Many of the new forms take a compromise position, requiring you to deliver no less than 25% of the song to your publisher. That works fine if you've written 25% or more of the composition, but it's not so hot if you've written less than 25%. In that situation, your publisher takes part of your *writer's* royalties to make up the difference in income between the publishing they actually get and 25%. For example, if you wrote 12.5% of a song and delivered 12.5% of the publishing to your publisher, your publisher would take *all* of your songwriter royalties. This is because 12.5% of the publishing, plus your entire 12.5% of the songwriting royalties, equals the same dollars the publisher would get if it had 25% of publishing at the outset.

This is easier to see using money: For every dollar received, 50¢ belongs to songwriters (the songwriter's share) and the remaining 50¢ belongs to the publishers (the publisher's share). Since your publisher has only 12.5% of the 50¢ publisher's share, it only gets 6¼¢. Your 12.5% of the writer's 50¢ is of course also 6¼¢. However, the contract says your publisher must get at least 25% of the publishing (which equals 25% of the entire 50¢ publisher's share, or 12½¢). Since it only has 6¼¢ (12.5% of the publisher's 50¢ share), the publisher takes all of your writer's share (which is also 6¼¢), to equal the 12½¢ (25% of the publisher's 50¢ share) that you promised. This means you will make little (or nothing, in this example) for your collaborative efforts. Such a situation does not make for a healthy career, and it certainly turns you off collaborating.

Because of all this, the most you should do is agree to deliver that percentage of publishing that equals your percentage of the writer's share. In other words, if you write 10% of a song, you should only agree to deliver 10% of the publishing; if you write one-fifth, 20% of the publishing, etc.

How Are Songs Divided?

Historically, 50% of a song went to the writer of the music, and 50% to the lyricist. No muss, no fuss. So if one person wrote all of the melody, and one person wrote all the lyrics, they each got 50% of the song. If two people equally wrote the lyrics, and one person wrote the melody, then the lyricists each got 25% of the song, and the melody writer got 50%. You get the idea.

Over the last few years, this has gotten fuzzed up considerably. The reason is that rap, hip-hop, and similar music are as dependent on the **track** as they are on the melody and lyrics. The *track* is the background rhythm and instrumentation, on which the melody and lyrics are laid. So people creating the tracks are also getting pieces of songs.

Unfortunately, there are no hard and fast rules about how a track gets treated. It's usually negotiated by the parties at the time, depending on their sense of who contributed what to the song. I've seen deals where the track gets one-third, with the melody and lyrics each getting one-third, and I've also seen deals where the track merely becomes part of the music/melody side of the equation. And if the track contribution is minimal, sometimes it gets little or nothing.

There's an added twist when tracks contain **samples** (we'll discuss sampling in detail later, but basically it means the track incorporates somebody else's song along with your material). In this case, the sample owner gets a piece of the publishing, and that has to come out of someone's share. It's not a given that it all comes out of the track's share—the person creating the track argues that it should come out of everybody's earnings, on the theory that everyone benefits from the use of the sample. (The same issue comes up if the melody or lyric writer 'borrows' from someone else.) Results vary in direct proportion to bargaining power.

So sit down, slug it out, and have the survivor call me.

Writing Teams

If you write with a partner on a continual basis, and your publisher is signing both of you, there are some special points of concern. (If you don't regularly write with a partner, you can skip to the section on creative controls on page 276). The writing team issues are:

Advances. Despite what your first thought might be, the advances don't double for a writing team. The reason is rather simple—even though there are two of you, you're each only writing one-half of a song, and so the total output is about the same as for one person.

Delivery Requirements. By the same token, if you have a song delivery requirement, that shouldn't be increased either.

Cross-Collateralization. If the publisher hands you one contract for both of you to sign, listen up. You want to make *absolutely certain* that you each have a separate account for your earnings and advances, and that your two accounts are not cross-collateralized (see page 88 for a discussion of cross-collateralization). If you always split the songs 50/50, and get equal advances, this point doesn't make any difference—your earnings are going to be identical, as are your advances. But since that almost never happens, look at the result of cross-collateralization in the following instances:

1. One or both of you may occasionally write songs without the other (in which case you'll want to be sure those earnings aren't used to recoup the other guy's advances).
2. You might stop writing in the same ratio that you get advances (e.g., you take the advances 50/50, but on some songs you split the earnings 60/40 or 75/25). This means the advances get recouped unevenly (see the example below).
3. You may break up as a team completely, and begin writing on your own, in which case you absolutely don't want the other person's advances charged to your account.

Here's an example: Suppose you and your co-writer, Louise, are each getting $10,000 a year under a songwriting agreement. At the end of year one you have written a number of songs on a 50/50 basis that have earned a total of $5,000, and each of you has been credited with $2,500 in royalties. This means you are each $7,500 unrecouped. Now, you write a song by yourself, which earns $20,000 in royalties. If your accounts are not cross-collateralized, the $20,000 earnings recoup your $7,500 deficit, and the publisher pays you $12,500. *If your accounts are cross-collateralized, the publisher will deduct not only your*

$7,500 deficit but also Louise's $7,500 deficit. Thus, out of the $20,000 your song earned, you'd only get $5,000 ($20,000 less your $7,500 deficit and less your partner's $7,500 deficit). Since you didn't get the other $7,500 (your collaborator did), you will not be a happy camper. So separate your accounts.

Separate Obligations.   Another problem with signing one agreement is that you have to be sure your obligations are separate, and that you're not responsible for a breach by the other guy. For example, if your partner wrongfully terminates his or her agreement and walks out, you don't want to find your royalties being used to pay for the publisher's damages and/or legal fees in a fight with your co-writer.

Separate Contracts.   On the other side of the fence, suppose the publisher hands you two separate contracts. The odds are they won't be cross-collateralized (although you should always make certain they aren't). But does that solve everything? Not really. The problem with two contracts is that, at option time, the publisher may decide to drop one of you and keep the other, effectively breaking up your team. So be careful to provide that the publisher can't do this. If the publisher continues with one agreement, it must continue with both.

These problems are easy to fix if you ask up front, but can be an enormous pain if you forget. So don't.

CREATIVE CONTROL

Moral Rights

In a number of countries outside the United States, there is a legal concept known as **moral rights,** or by the snooty term *droit moral* (which in French means 'moral rights,' and in Czech means 'no parking'). The concept is that an author can stop any mutilation of his or her work, even though they may have parted with it long ago. For example, the creator of a painting (even though it has been sold four or five times) could stop someone from cutting it into smaller paintings, drawing mustaches on it, etc. Similarly, the author of a musical work can stop substantial changes in the music or lyrics.

The U.K. has a concept of moral rights. They basically consist of:

1. the right to be identified as the author;
2. the right to object to derogatory treatment;
3. the right not to be falsely attributed; and
4. the right to privacy of some photographs and films.

Thus, for example, you could object to the fact that your name was left off a song, or that you were falsely listed as the composer of a particularly horrible or nasty song.

The rights in the U.K. are not as extensive as those in other territories and, unlike some countries, they can be *waived*. 'Waived' simply means that you can give them up by contract. However, the moral rights can't be given to another person to exercise, as they are considered personal to the author. For example, you couldn't transfer them to your mum and let her decide whether or not your song has been mangled beyond recognition. The exception is when you die— your moral rights go to your heirs—but I doubt if you'll care much at that point.

Moral rights now extend not only to the authors of a copyright, but also to the directors of films (including videos).

In addition to moral rights, the U.K. has something called **performers' rights**. This is the right of a *performer* to stop their performances being recorded, and to stop the recordings (whether sound, video or otherwise) being used without authorization. Note that this is a separate right for just the performer, and is in addition to the rights of the recording owner.

If someone makes an illegal recording, you can sue them for money (similar to those remedies you get for copyright infringement, which are discussed on page 324). It's also a crime, so you can send them to jail.

The right to be paid for performers' rights is called the right to receive **equitable remuneration,** meaning a 'fair price'. Your equitable remuneration right can't be waived (given up) or assigned away (except to a collection society, so they can pick up the money for you). However, these rights are inheritable, meaning that you can leave them to your kids or significant others after you go to that Great Performers' Gathering in the Sky.

Under the Copyright and Related Rights Regulations 1996 (you Brits sure know how to put a jazzy title on things), performers got a new set of rights: a **reproduction right**, a **distribution right**, a **rental right**, and a **lending right**. You're allowed to assign these rights away by contract, similar to copyrights, except that if you transfer the rental right in a sound recording or a film, the law says the performer must get equitable remuneration for rentals. So contracts dealing with the transfer of rental rights confirm that whatever money you're getting is 'equitable remuneration'. If there's a dispute, it's referred to the Copyright Tribunal. (By the way, you're not allowed to transfer your rental monies to anyone else, except a society who collects the money for you.)

Now if that 1996 extravaganza wasn't enough for you, come see what your folks did with the Copyright and Related Rights Regulations of 2003. Performers now have something called a **making available** right (sounds sexy, huh?). It means the artist gets paid when their recordings are used in electronic transmissions that are available whenever the public wants them (as opposed to scheduled webcasts and simulcasts). In other words, performers have a right to get paid for the 'on demand' Internet services.

Contractual Approvals

The United States has never recognized a moral rights concept for music (although there is a limited one for paintings and fine art). Accordingly, to the extent you want any protection, you must put it in your songwriter/publisher contract. You do this by saying the publisher needs your approval before it can do certain things, like:

1. **Make changes in the music.**
    The publisher will normally say that's fine as long as they don't have to ask about simple changes merely to conform to the mood or style of a particular artist.
2. **Make changes in the English lyrics.**
    Again, this approval right usually excludes minor changes for mood or style.
3. **Add foreign lyrics.**
    If you have enough clout, you may be able to approve translations. This is much harder to come by, but it's worth fighting for because it's also a financial issue–remember, translations reduce your royalties (see page 251).
4. **Make changes in the title (in English).**
    Usually no sweat—just ask for this and you'll get it.

5. **Grant synch licenses.**

   If you have some bargaining power, you may be able to get consent to all motion picture synchronization licenses. (These are defined on page 244). If you have a lot of bargaining power, you might also control television synch licensing, but this is much harder to get. The reason is that publishers often have to give a yes or no answer to TV studios within twenty-four hours, and don't want to lose the opportunity because you're off sipping lemonade on your yacht. If you can't get approval rights, a compromise is to say the song can't be licensed for NC-17 or X-rated films, or for a scene in a film involving illicit drugs, sex, violence, or anything else that rings your particular bell.

6. **Use the song in commercials and print ads.**

   At best, you should have the right to approve any usage of your song in commercials and print ads (newspapers, magazines, etc.). (If you have approval of synch licenses, you automatically control TV commercials. But this doesn't cover radio commercials because radio recordings aren't made under synch licenses, as we discussed on page 244, and it doesn't cover using your lyrics in print ads.) If you haven't got enough clout to control commercials entirely, you can compromise by requiring your consent to certain categories, such as alcohol, tobacco, firearms, political candidates, and my personal favorite, sexual hygiene products.

REVERSION OF COPYRIGHT

Smile whenever you hear the words **reversion of copyright,** because this will always be good for you (unless you're a publisher, in which case you can scowl). This is different from the termination of copyrights under the Copyright Law, which we'll discuss later, on page 302, because *reversion* is a *contractual* provision, negotiated specifically. It means the publisher must give your song (copyright and all) back to you at some point in the future.

Conditions of Reversion

What should trigger reassignment? The best (short of the automatic reversions discussed below) is that the song reverts to you if it's not recorded and commercially released. If you really have bargaining power, you can say you get the song back unless the recording is by a major artist (or at least on a major label) and/or achieves a certain chart position (say Top 50). Another compromise is to say you get the song back if it doesn't achieve a certain earnings level. The higher that level, of course, the better for you, since you have a better chance of recapturing the song. However, you may have to settle for something pretty modest, such as $2,500 or so.

In these clauses, be sure to require that the recording/release must happen within some time frame. Otherwise, the publisher can keep each song for the life of copyright, telling you every week that a recording is just around the corner. If it's a single-song agreement (rather than a term deal), the publisher customarily has from six months to two years after signing within which to get the song recorded and released. Try to break this into two parts—it must be recorded within six months (or twelve months) after signing the deal, and released within six months (or twelve months) after that. This is better for you, because it comes back sooner if nothing happens. For term deals, this period usually begins at the close of the deal, although songs delivered in the later years sometimes have longer time periods (because the publisher hasn't had time to work them). A typical provision is two or so years after the end of the deal, but no less than two or three years from delivery of a song.

The smaller your bargaining power, the less likely you'll be able to pull off a reversion. However, even at the most modest levels, you should be able to get a publisher to give your song back at some point (say four or five years after the term) if it hasn't been exploited. The theory is that the song is of no value to him or her on the shelf, but potentially could be to you in a new situation. This gets more difficult if the publisher has paid you an advance, particularly one that hasn't been recouped (which is probable if the song is unexploited). However, you may be able to negotiate an option to get the song back by repaying the advance (be sure to say you don't have to pay back an advance that has been recouped). The publisher will want to put a time limit on this right to repay (say a year or two after the first date the song can revert), but even with this limit, the option is a plus.

Be certain it's your *option* to pay the money back. You don't want to be obligated to buy back your losers, because all that does is guarantee the publisher against a loss.

Reversion of copyright for non-exploitation is something you should *always* ask for. You may not always get it, but you should *always* ask for it. Is it clear I mean *always*? Did I say *always*?

Automatic Reversion

When you move into the super leagues, or if you are in a bidding war, you can ask for a reassignment of all compositions, whether or not they're recorded. Time frames on these usually run something like five to fifteen years after the close of the exclusive term, with the majority in the seven-to-twelve-year range. Also, this is sometimes tied to recoupment—for example, ten years after the term, the publisher will reassign only if you're recouped. In this case, (1) take the right to pay the unrecouped balance (remember to keep it at your option), in which case you get the songs back sooner; and (2) be sure you get the songs back if and when you do eventually recoup, even if it's five or ten years later. Don't assume the contract will say either of these if you don't ask, because it usually won't.

If they give you the right to repay and get back songs, publishers now ask for more than 100% of the unrecouped advance. For example, they want 125% of the balance; if you were $10,000 unrecouped, you'd have to pay the $12,500. Their reasoning is that, if they kept the song, they'd get the money needed to recoup your account *plus* their own share of those monies. So if they let you go early, they want their piece. Sometimes you can get his percentage down, to say 110% or so, but it's getting increasingly harder to get a straight 100%.

Answer to quiz on page 272:

Performance monies. (See page 238 for why), DART (see page 253), and Webcasting monies (see page 263).

19

Copublishing and Administration Deals

This chapter discusses deals under which two or more people share the publishing of a song. The variables are:

1. Who owns a piece of the copyright (some may just have a right to income, with no ownership);
2. Whether there is a sharing of the administration rights (the rights to issue licenses, collect monies, etc., which we discussed on page 217); and
3. How long the deal lasts (life of copyright, or something less).

The most common deals are:

1. Copublishing agreements coupled with songwriter agreements (we discussed songwriter agreements in the last chapter). In other words, a deal under which you not only get your songwriter's share, but also a portion (usually 50%) of the publishing income as well. This is the most common copublishing deal for songwriter/artists.
2. A situation where songwriters who are signed to different publishers (or songwriters who own their own publishing) write a song together. This kind of copublishing agreement sets out how the money gets divided, and how the song is going to be administered. As we'll see in a minute, the administration can be done by only one party, or shared by two or more of them. If more than one party administers, this is sometimes called a **co-administration agreement.**
3. A publisher who is too small to hire a staff enters into an agreement for a larger publisher to administer their songs.
4. A publisher hires a subpublisher in foreign territories (the sub-publishing agreements we discussed in Chapter 17).

Unfortunately, the industry definitions in this area aren't very precise. So for our purposes, I'm going to use the term **copublishing agreement** to mean a deal that shares copyright ownership, regardless of how long the deal lasts. If the deal is for someone to administer a copyright wholly owned by someone else, then I'm calling it an **administration agreement,** even if it lasts for the life of the copyright.

Because the labels are fuzzy, these are not universal terms. Some people refer to life of copyright deals as *copublishing agreements* even if they involve no copyright ownership, and others call co-owned deals that last only a few years *administration agreements*. However, we gotta start somewhere, so I'm using these terms only to make the distinction of ownership. This will keep us from getting lost in overlapping labels.

Let's start with copublishing (shared ownership).

COPUBLISHING DEALS

Net Publisher's Share

One of the first things to decide, of course, is how the money gets whacked up. Usually it's the same as the percentage of the song written by each writer (for example, if Fred wrote half the song, and Sharon wrote the other half, their publishers would share the money equally. If Fred only wrote one-third, his publisher would have one-third. You get the idea). However, if one party has more clout than another, or if one pays money for the privilege, they can get a disproportionate share. For example, even if Fred wrote only 50% of the song, his publisher might demand (or buy) 75% of the publishing.

What gets divided up is called the **net publisher's share.** It's defined as **gross income** (which is everything the publisher receives, meaning writer's and publisher's shares combined), less the following deductions:

1. An administration fee,
2. Songwriter royalties, and
3. Expenses.

Let's look at them separately:

Administration Fee. The first deduction is an administration fee, which is a percentage of the *gross income* (writer's and publisher's shares combined), usually from 10% to 20%. It's always deducted first, because it's a percentage. (Let's repeat our golden rule: 'One who gets a percentage applies it to the largest possible number.')

Sometimes the administration fee is based on the gross monies after deducting the songwriter's royalties (meaning it's applied against our old friend, the publisher's share). For example, 10% of $1 gross income is 10¢, but 10% of the publisher's share (gross income less the writer's 50%) is 10% of 50¢, or 5¢. This practice, however, is really just playing word games. It's the same as cutting the percentage in half (10% of the publisher's share is the same as 5% of gross), but cosmetically it makes the publisher feel like they're getting more. So it persists.

An administration fee is, in theory, designed to reimburse the publisher for its indirect expenses of operation—rent, secretarial help, telephone, utilities, executive salaries, etc. In reality, it's just a function of leverage, because it disappears as soon as the other party has any appreciable bargaining power.

Writer's Royalties. The next amounts deducted are the songwriter's royalties. These were discussed in Chapter 18.

Expenses. Finally, the administrating publisher deducts its **direct expenses,** which are usually spelled out in a list that ends with something like 'and anything else we can think of.' *Direct* means the expense is a specific item relating only to this song, as opposed to a general, unallocated overhead cost (like rent, secretarial, etc.). To my mind, there are only a few legitimate direct expense deductions, and none of them amount to substantial monies. They are:

1. Copyright Office **registration fees.**
2. The cost of making **demos**—informal recordings, not for commercial release, made to promote the song (as discussed on page 262).
3. **Collection costs,** such as charges by the Harry Fox Agency, subpublishers' fees, and legal expenses to chase deadbeats.
4. The preparation of **lead sheets.** A *lead sheet* (pronounced 'leed' sheet) is a piece of paper with the words and musical melody line of a song. It's used for copyright registration and promotion. The use of lead sheets has diminished radically over the last few years. Until the 1976 Copyright Act, the U.S. gov-

ernment required lead sheets to be deposited with the Library of Congress in connection with registering a copyright (see page 322). Since then, the Library accepts cassette or CD copies of songs, and publishers have stopped going to the expense of lead sheets.

Beyond these, I don't think anything should be deducted, and I've been pretty successful in limiting costs to the above. The other items publishers try to charge you for are advertising, promotion, legal fees for contracts to exploit the songs, and 'all other expenses concerning the composition.' Hold firm against these, and don't wimp out.

Who Administers?

The next question is 'Who administers the song?' When there's only one copyright owner, it's clear who has these rights. But when there's more than one, everyone's role has to be defined. (We'll talk later about what happens when there's no agreement.) It's customary to handle administration in one of several ways:

1. **One administrator**
   One party has the exclusive right to administer on behalf of all, and the other parties only have the passive right to be paid a share of income from the administrator, with no control. This, and point 2 below, are the most common arrangements for songwriter/copublishing agreements. In these deals, the publisher controls administration rights (just like a songwriter deal), and you get your songwriter royalties *plus* copublishing royalties (meaning you get the full songwriter share plus a piece [usually half] of the net publisher's share).
2. **One administrator with restrictions**
   One party has the exclusive administration rights, but can't license certain usages without the other party's consent. This could mean that consent is necessary for every usage, or it could mean only that consent is required for certain licenses (for example, there could be no usages in commercials without consent). We discussed examples of restrictions on page 276, in the context of songwriter deals, and they apply here as well.
   As noted above, this and point 1 are the most common arrangements for songwriter/copublishing agreements.

3. **One administrator with direct payments to other parties**

One party has the exclusive administration rights, but certain monies are paid directly to the other parties. For example, performance royalties are paid directly by the performing rights society to each copublisher, or mechanical royalties are paid directly by the record company to each party. Other monies, such as foreign, print, etc., are usually paid to the administrating publisher. While the non-administrating parties have no control, these arrangements save them time (they don't have to wait for the administrator to collect and disburse), and it assures that they will in fact get paid (i.e., they needn't worry that the administrating publisher will go bankrupt, use the money to buy a duck farm, etc.).

4. **True co-administration**

All parties have the right to administer their own share of the composition. This and the deals discussed in point 5 are the most common arrangements for songs co-owned by publishers of approximately equal status.

The mechanics of co-administration work like this: Assume you and I are 50/50 owners of a song. Under a typical co-administration deal, I can issue a license for my 50%, but not for yours, and vice versa. This means that no one can use the song without getting a license from both you and me.

5. **Co-administration with exceptions**

All parties co-administer (as in point 4 above), but one party acting alone can issue certain licenses. This is common where one of the writers has recorded the song and needs to deliver certain rights to the record company.

The usual exceptions include:

(a) **Controlled compositions**

If one of the parties is a performing artist, he or she will have a controlled composition clause in the record deal requiring such things as a mechanical license at less than statutory rate, a free license for promotional videos, and several other goodies that will affect the copublisher (see page 226). These clauses are usually spelled out in the copublishing agreement, along with a requirement that the copublisher must go along with them.

If the non-artist party has substantial bargaining power, this can be a source of friction. They sometimes insist on being paid more than the controlled comp clause allows, and the only way this can happen is for the extra monies to come out of the artist's pocket (see page 230).

(b) **Statutory rate licenses**

Either party can issue a mechanical license for the whole song (both publishers' shares) at the statutory rate (see page 199 for what that means). As long as it's not a first-use license (see page 200), this is something the publishers both have to do anyway (remember, the user can get a compulsory license whether the copyright owners like it or not, as discussed on page 197). Thus, some agreements say that either party alone can issue these licenses, but that the record company must pay each party its respective shares. So, for example, one copublisher could give a license to Warner Bros. Records without the other's consent, but in that license, it must require Warner to pay the money to each party.

I usually object to this clause, on the basis that the other party may never know about the license, and thus it's hard to keep track of the earnings. I think it's better for each publisher to issue its own license.

(c) **Print**

One of the publishers might have an exclusive agreement for print music, while the other may not. In this case, it's not uncommon to license print rights only under that person's exclusive print deal. However, the deal should require the print company to pay each party directly, and of course not allow them to charge costs or advances unrelated to the song.

Expenses, Fees, and Writer Royalties in Co-Administration Deals

Co-administration deals present some peculiarities in handling expenses. When one party administers the entire song, it simply deducts each party's share of costs from monies due the others. In co-administration deals, however, everybody is collecting their own money, which means there's nothing to deduct from. Accordingly, there is no administration fee, because no publisher touches any other publisher's share, and there's nothing from which to deduct the fee (taking it from yourself isn't much fun). Also in these situations, the writer's share isn't usually deducted. Instead, the full publisher/songwriter royalties are paid over to each publisher in proportion to their ownership of the song, and each publisher pays its own writer directly. (This isn't always true; sometimes one publisher collects its share of publishing plus the full writers' share, and that publisher pays the writers.)

As to expenses (the copyright registration fees, demos, etc., we discussed a minute ago), the one who pays the costs sends a bill to the other publisher(s) for their respective share(s). For example, if a 50% publisher pays $400 for a demo, it sends a bill for $200 (50% of the $400) to the other 50% publisher. It's a good idea to require that costs can't exceed a certain dollar amount (say $500) without the consent of the other party, and be *absolutely sure* that the publisher isn't taking these costs twice. I say this because, as we discussed on page 262, demo costs (and every once in a while, other costs) are sometimes charged against songwriter royalties. If so, they shouldn't also be charged against copublishing royalties. Observe: If a publisher pays $500 for a demo and charges it against the songwriter, it should not also charge it to a copublisher in computing the net publisher's share. However, many agreements would allow the publisher to do exactly this, which means it not only charges $500 against the writer, but also charges $250 against a 50% copublisher. Thus they would collect $750 for a $500 expenditure. A bit hard to justify on the grounds of fairness, but a good business to be in.

Shhh . . .

And now, an Industry Secret: Most of the time there is no agreement signed by the major publishers when they co-own a song with other publishers. Some years ago, they found that writing and negotiating these deals was so burdensome that they decided to rely on their rights as co-owners of the copyright as a matter of law (which we'll discuss in the next chapter) and industry custom (which is true co-administration). But between writers who own their own publishing, these deals are pretty common.

ADMINISTRATION AGREEMENTS

With enough clout, you can go to a publisher, not give them any ownership, but merely give them the right to administer your songs, which is what I'm calling an **administration agreement.** The party getting the administration rights is called the **administrator,** and I'm going to refer to the party granting these rights as the **original publisher** (not an industry term).

This is a common deal for small publishers (or writers who own their own publishing) that don't have a staff to handle their songs—they make an administration deal with a larger publisher. The subpublishing deals we discussed in Chapter 17 are also administration deals.

The administration rights under these deals are handled in one of the five ways we just discussed (on page 285). Usually these contracts are for a short period of time (three to five years or so, often with extensions if you're unrecouped). And because the publisher gets only a small piece, and only for a limited time, these deals have more modest advances (or no advance at all).

Administrator's Share

Under an administration deal, the administrator takes an administration fee, reimburses itself for any direct expenses, and pays 100% of the balance to the original publisher. The administrator customarily (but not always) takes care of accounting and paying the songwriters and any other participating publishers. These monies are of course deducted before remitting to the original publisher.

Administration fees range from 10% to 25% of the *gross* dollars (writer's and publisher's shares combined). Note (as we discussed on page 284) that a percentage based on the gross dollars is equal to double that percentage of the publisher's share alone. This means that an administrator taking a 20% administration fee is in reality getting 40% of the publisher's share of income. In other words, if a dollar comes in (including writer and publisher money), the administrator gets 20¢, which equals 40% of the 50¢ publisher's share. The original publisher gets the balance, less the songwriter royalties. It looks like this:

Gross	$1.00
Less: Administration Fee (20%)	−.20
Less: Writer's Share (50% of the $1.00)	−.50
ORIGINAL PUBLISHER'S SHARE	**$ .30**

Here's another way to look at what everybody gets out of the $1 in this same example:

Each Party's Share

	Administrator	Publisher	Writer
Original Dollar Amount	20¢	30¢	50¢
% of Gross	20%	30%	50%
% of Publisher's Share	40%	60%	0%

As noted above, any direct costs are deducted 'off the top' and are therefore borne by the administrator and original publisher in proportion to their share of publishing (60%/40%). Of course, neither of them bears costs that are recouped from the writer's royalties.

Also, as discussed in subpublishing deals (on page 248), the administration fee on performance monies is often doubled.

Cover Records

Often administration deals have an incentive for **covers.** A *cover* is a recording obtained by the administrator, and the incentives can be one of several:

1. **The administrator gets an increased percentage on covers.**
   For example, if the administrator has a 15% administration fee, this might increase to a 25% fee on income from cover recordings. This is the fairest approach, because it rewards the administrator's efforts directly. But it's not as simple as it looks if the cover isn't the first recording of a work. The problem is that you can't always tell which version of the song is generating the money. It's easy enough for mechanical royalties—the royalty statements list the company and record number. But when it comes to performances, the songs are only listed by title, and there's no way to know which version was played on the radio (the original or the cover?).

   One way to deal with the performance issue is by using a formula based on the ratio that the mechanical royalties from the cover version bear to the mechanical royalties from other versions. For example, if the cover version earned $100 in mechanical royalties and all other versions earned $200 in a particular period (total of $300), then one-third (100/300) of the performance monies are treated as being earned by the cover. This works reasonably well, but it's subject to aberrations under circumstances where (1) the cover version was not a single, and thus generated very little airplay even though it was on a successful album (singles get substantial airplay, while album cuts usually don't, and little airplay means there's little performance money generated by that recording); or (2) the song generated enormous amounts of airplay (meaning lots of performance monies) but didn't sell records particularly well, which would skew the formula the other way. So I have sometimes written into deals that we would use the mechanical royalty formula unless it generates an unreasonable result, in which case the parties would negotiate in good faith as to an appropriate allocation.

2. **The administrator gets an increased percentage of all income.**

   Another possibility (although I don't like to agree to this) is that, if the administrator gets a cover, it gets an increased percentage of *all* earnings of the composition, not just those from the cover version. This eliminates the allocation problem, but it gashes your pocketbook.

3. **The administrator retains administration rights to the covered song for an additional period of time.**

   For example, if the administration term is three years, the publisher might continue to administer covered compositions for a period of five years from a particular date (the start of the deal, the date of the cover recording, the end of the deal, your mom's birthday, etc.). I don't particularly like this, because it breaks up your catalog and makes it difficult to move the songs away. This is of course precisely why publishers like such a clause (as well as the fact that it gives them a longer period to participate in the money).

4. **The administrator gets copyright ownership for covers.**

   Getting a cover may even mean the administrator gets copyright ownership (usually 50%). If you do this, try to make sure it's an extraordinarily successful cover record. For example, require that it reach a certain level on a major chart. (See the next section for more on this.)

5. **Any combination of 1, 2, 3, and/or 4.**

6. **None of the above.**

What's Really a Cover?   You want to be very careful about how a 'cover record' is defined, because, as you just saw, the consequences are significant. If the only result is an increased percentage of income from the cover itself, it's not such a big deal—either it's successful and you both make a lot of money, or it's a flop and forgotten. However, if a cover means the publisher gets copyright ownership or an increase on non-cover earnings of the song, you must be very tough about how a cover is defined. Certainly you don't want the publisher's Aunt Esmerelda singing to a tape recorder to be considered a cover. But under many definitions, it would be, because the contract simply says 'a recording.' (Aunt Esmerelda's recordings are available over the Home Shopping Network, between the cubic zirconia and the porcelain carousels that play 'Somewhere My Love.') At a very minimum, you want the recording to be a commercial one, and it must be released (it's amazing how many people neglect these simple criteria). If possible, you should add that the release has to be on a major record company label, and you should try to require that (a) the recording features a major artist (which you should define as an artist whose last album was gold, platinum, or better); and/or (b) the release itself must achieve some chart position, or else the song comes back to you. As to chart positions, the higher you get, the better—Top 5 or 10 is ideal, but even the Top 30 or 40 isn't bad. Make sure this is on a national chart such as *Billboard,* and not some schlock local station chart. Ideally it should be a singles chart (which means airplay), but album charts are second best. And it should be on a mainstream chart, not country, gospel, etc.

NOW LOOK WHERE YOU ARE!

Here you are, only partway through the book and you already know enough to answer the final homework assignment I gave after my nine-week music business class at USC Law School. Very impressive! So try your hand at it:

You are a record company and have just been delivered an album by Freddy London, produced by Marvin Lester. Freddy is signed exclusively to Warner/Chappell Music as a songwriter, and he wrote eight of the ten songs on the album. The other two were written by Marvin, who owns his own publishing under the name Marvelous Music.

1. Each time the album is sold, who is entitled to a payment from the record company? (Ignore any recoupment.) Clue: There are five parties, but you won't know the last one if you're not on the Expert Track.
2. Freddy makes a promotional video of his single. Who gets paid when the video is played on television?

Answers to quiz:

1. Artist; producer; publisher (Warner/Chappell), which includes Freddy's songwriter royalties; publisher (Marvelous Music),

which includes Marvin's songwriter royalties; and unions (see page 156).

2. The publisher and writer get public performance monies. (The record company may get a fee from MTV for the right to use all the company's videos, but this fee isn't broken down by video. Also, I never told you that, so you couldn't know.)

If you're on the *Fast Track,* and if you're in a group,
go to Part IV (Chapter 22) on page 329.
If you're on the *Fast Track,* and you're not in a group,
got to Part V (Chapter 23) on page 353.
Everyone else, read on . . .

20

Advanced Copyright Concepts

WHO OWNS THE COPYRIGHT?

Copyright ownership is pretty easy to figure out if you sit down at the piano and knock out a little ditty by yourself. You, of course, are the owner, since you created it. But we lawyers wouldn't have much to do if it were all that simple, so let me show you how we've managed to fuzz it up over the years.

How About Two People Writing a Song Together?

Suppose you and your cousin Louie sit down and write a brilliant work together. Which one of you owns it?

As you probably guessed, both of you own it. But there's more to it than appears at first glance:

Who Controls the Song?   Suppose you want to put it on your next album, and Louie wants to save it until he gets a record deal. Can he stop you?

The Copyright Law, in Section 201(a) of the Copyright Act, spells this out pretty clearly. It says that you and Louie have created a **joint work** (keep the puns to yourself), meaning it was created jointly by the efforts of two or more people. When you have a *joint work*, either of the authors/owners can deal *non-exclusively* with the *entire* composition, subject to the obligation to pay the other person his or her share of the proceeds. That means you can give all the non-exclusive licenses you want to record companies, film companies, etc., subject to paying Louie for his share of the song. And Louie can do the same. (In practice, there's often a written agreement that spells out exactly what everyone can do, as we discussed in Chapter 19. But now we're talking about what the Copyright Law says, without such an agreement.)

What Do You Own?

How about this one: You and Louie sit down together to write a composition, and you write only the music while Louie writes only the lyrics. Suppose you don't like Louie's lyrics and want to take your music and write with somebody else. Can you?

My mentor and partner Payson Wolff once told me that creating a joint work is like adding water to a ball of clay and squishing it; it's not so easy to separate the two afterward. My partner Bruce Ramer uses the analogy of scrambling the white and the yolk of the egg together. So as you may be starting to guess, the law isn't what you would intuitively think. It says that, even though two people create separate, distinct parts, they each own an interest in the *whole work*, not just their own contribution. Thus, Louie owns half the music and half the lyrics, and so do you. So you can't just pick up and leave him. Even if you add new lyrics, he has a percentage of the song.

Does this sound like an absurd result? To some extent, yes; but if you get into dividing up works where the contributions aren't so easily defined as music and lyrics (which is 99% of the time), the alternative is even more impossible. Think, for example, about all the elements that go into making a film. What part is the screenwriter's? The director's? The producer's? The wardrobe designer's? Or what about a song where three people work on the lyrics, while two work on both music and lyrics?

What Makes a Joint Work 'Joint'?

By now you're beginning to see that this is more complex than it first appears. Which it is. But we're just getting warm—try this one: A songwriting team consists of one person who lives in California and writes only music, and another who lives in New York and writes only lyrics. The California writer, totally on her own, writes a piece of music and mails it to her friend in New York. The guy in New York gets it several days later, sits down, and writes the lyrics. Is this a joint work? Did these two people create the composition together?

The law says, to have a joint work, you only need an author who *intends,* at the time of creation, to merge his or her work with someone's else's. In other words, when the musician wrote the music in California, did she intend to have lyrics written for it? That certainly is the case in our example, even though the lyricist never physically got together with the melody writer. (It's almost always true that a lyricist intends to merge the words with music, since he or she probably has little call for poetry readings.) So, to have a joint work, you don't need to be in the same room (or on the same planet), and you don't even have to know each other, as long as there is an intent to merge the work at the time of creation.

If you want to see how this can get carried to the ultimate, get a load of the 'Melancholy Baby' case (*Shapiro Bernstein v. Vogel*, 161 F.2nd 406 [1947]). In that case, a guy named Ernie Barnett wrote a song with his wife Maybelle. Ernie wrote the music and Maybelle wrote the lyrics, and they sold the song to a publisher. Well, Maybelle's lyrics were apparently pretty awful (a lot of 'moon' and 'June,' I'll bet), so the publisher tossed them out and had a new set written by a total stranger, George Norton. The result was 'Melancholy Baby.'

Based on these facts, the court held that 'Melancholy Baby' was a 'joint work' because, when Ernie wrote it, he had the intent to merge lyrics with it. The fact that the lyrics were ultimately written by someone he never met was irrelevant. And this result also meant the new lyricist held an interest in the music too (although the case didn't deal with that issue). Nice coconuts, eh?

The law in the U.K. about 'joint works' is somewhat different. Specifically:

1. In the U.K., the music to a song has a separate copyright (as a 'musical work'), and the lyrics are separately copyrighted as a 'literary work'. You can have joint authorship if several people write the music (which would make the music a joint work) or several write the lyrics (which would make the lyrics a joint work). However, unlike the U.S., the whole song can't be a joint work even if the same people write the music and lyrics together.

In practice, writers can agree by contract to share the copyright in both music and lyrics.

2. If a work is a joint work, *both* copyright owners must consent to any usage, whether exclusive or not. This contrasts sharply with the U.S., where either joint author may issue a non-exclusive licence for the whole work (as discussed on page 340).

WORKS FOR HIRE

Remember that Teddy Kennedy hired someone to take an exam for him at Harvard? Well, the Copyright Law is one place where this is perfectly legal. It's done with **works for hire** (technically known as a **work made for hire** in the Copyright Law). A *work for hire* is a situation where you hire someone else to create for you, and if you observe the technical formalities, you actually become the author of the work insofar as the Copyright Law is concerned. And when I say 'the author,' I really mean *the* author. It's as if the person you hired doesn't even exist (in the eyes of the Copyright Law), and indeed he or she needn't even be mentioned on the copyright registration form.

I suspect (but I really don't know, and would hate to disillusion myself by researching it) that 'works for hire' developed to cover such things as fabric companies that printed copyrighted designs on their cloth, and wanted to be sure that the company (not the dork who actually designed the pattern) was the owner of the copyright. Seems reasonable enough.

Application to the Entertainment Industry

Here's an example of how it works in show biz. Suppose you are Walt Disney Pictures and you hire someone to write the theme for *Snow White* (I picked the example of a motion picture for a particular reason, as you'll see on page 298.) In this situation, Walt Disney Pictures (the corporation) becomes the author of the work, and the person hired to write it disappears. Does this mean the writer won't get his or her name listed as the writer of the song (e.g., on sheet music, in the film, etc.)? Usually not; the real creator customarily gets credit. (But sometimes for example, with jingles written for radio and television commercials, a creator doesn't.) Also, the amount of compensation paid to the real creator is normally not affected by this type of arrangement—most of the time they're paid exactly the same whether or not the work is 'for hire.' However, a number of important rights we'll deal with later (on page 302) are drastically different, so whenever you're creating a work for hire, be alert to the consequences.

Technical Definition

A work for hire can be created under the Copyright Law in only one of two ways, which are a bit technical. They're set out in Section 101 of the Copyright Act. (You can skip to the 'Duration of Copyright' section on page 300 if technical things make you squirm. But try it first.)

1. If the work is made by an *employee* within the *scope of employment*, it is a work for hire. An example of this is the fabric designer I mentioned before.

   The test of whether there is 'employment' is not the one used for the income tax laws, or in fact for any other type laws. The cases treat it as situations where the employer is actually 'directing, or supervising the creation of the work, in a very specific way.' (The major case in this area is *Community for Creative Non-Violence v. Reid*, 490 U.S. 730 [1989], in which the Supreme Court held that a Vietnam memorial sculpture was not a 'work for hire' because the people who paid to have the work created did not exercise control over the details of the work, did not supply the tools, had no ongoing employment relationship, etc.). Normally (although not always), a songwriter is given quite a bit of latitude in his or her creation. However, if a songwriter is given very specific instructions, and is supervised during the process, he or she might be considered an employee. This would be extremely rare, and work for hire in the music area usually falls under the next section.

2. If not created by an employee within the scope of employment, a work can only be a work for hire if it meets *all* of the following criteria. The work must be (1) *'commissioned'* (meaning created at the request of someone); (2) created under a *written agreement;* and (3) created *for use in* one of the following:

   (a) **A motion picture or other audiovisual work.** This is the most common area where songs are treated as works for hire. It includes musical scores, title songs written for films, etc. Remember, these songs do not have to be written by employees. There only needs to be a written agreement saying they are works for hire, and that they are commissioned for use in an audiovisual work.

   (b) **A collective work.** A *collective work* is a collection of individual works which, independently, are capable of copyright. Examples are an anthology of short stories; a magazine containing several copyrightable articles; an encyclopedia; etc.

(c) **A compilation.** A *compilation* is a much broader term than collective work, although it's basically the same thing. The term *compilation* means a work made by compiling a bunch of things, and thus it includes collective works (where the parts are separately copyrightable). However, it also includes works where the compiled materials are not separately copyrightable, such as a reference index to the Bible.

(d) **A translation of a foreign work.** *¿Qué pasa?*

(e) **A supplementary work,** which is a work supplementing another work (clever definitions, these copyright guys, eh?), such as an introduction to a book.

For a brief period in 1999, a sound recording was included in the categories listed above (in other words, the copyright act said it could be a work for hire). However, the artist community went ballistic when this was dropped into the law, and after a Battle Royale, Congress reversed itself and took out 'masters.' Nonetheless, record companies take the position that an album is a 'collective work,' and therefore they think they have the right to treat masters as works for hire anyway. Some view otherwise.

Before we can discuss the dire consequences of something being a work for hire, you need a few more concepts. So, plug it into your memory bank (or put a Post-It on this page if your memory is like mine), and we'll get back to it later.

The U.K. has a similar 'work-for-hire' concept, but the standards are much stricter. This is not a right that can be given away contractually (as it can in the U.S., under the conditions we discused above). Rather, it requires a true, salaried employee, creating within the scope of employment. Accordingly, it's rare to non-existent in the music industry.

DURATION OF COPYRIGHT

Remember we said (on page 207) that a copyright is a *limited duration monopoly?* The next logical question is, 'How long?'

History

Prior to 1978, the United States had this bizarre copyright concept, adopted in 1909 and not changed for almost seventy years (the new law was adopted in 1976 but not effective until January 1, 1978, to give those of us who work in this area a year to study it). I tell you about it because (1) it is still relevant for older copyrights; and (2) I had to learn it, so why shouldn't you listen to it?

Anyway, the important thing you need to know is that copyrights used to last for a period of twenty-eight years from publication of the work. (I could spend an entire chapter on what *publication* means and meant, but I'd like you to finish my book awake, so I'll skip it. Basically, it means 'distributed to the public.') These copyrights were then renewable for an additional twenty-eight years (total of fifty-six years). (For you purists, I'm aware that some copyrights could be obtained without publication, but none of this stuff is the law anymore, so let's not get carried away with too much detail.) By the way, it used to be the law that, if you forgot to renew, your copyright was gone after twenty-eight years. However, in 1992, Congress passed a law stating that the renewal is now automatic, so there's no loss of copyright if you forget.

So the maximum copyright protection was fifty-six years. If you wanted to sell your copyright, you could sell the full fifty-six years' worth. You were, of course, free to sell much less, but the number of buyers dropped radically. Even if you sold the whole fifty-six, however, there was one way you could get back the second twenty-eight years. If you signed an agreement transferring all fifty-six years, you automatically got back the second twenty-eight years if you did one little thing during the first twenty-eight—die. (It's not for everyone, but it's had its fans.) If the author of the work died before the second twenty-eight years started, then the transfer was nullified and the heirs of the author got to renew the second twenty-eight years for their own benefit. If you didn't die, you were stuck with whatever agreement you made when you first sold the work.

As to works created after the effective date of the 1976 Copyright

Law (January 1, 1978), the duration of copyright was changed to the life of the author plus fifty years. It also extended the old fifty-six-year terms (for works created before January 1, 1978) by nineteen years, for a total of seventy-five years.

So much for the old stuff. In 1998, the congressional folk got to gether and, in memory of Congressman and croonster Sonny Bono, slapped on another twenty years. That extended the copyright term for pre-'78 songs (if they were still under copyright) to a total of ninety-five years, and for stuff made after January 1, 1978, to life of the author plus seventy years (we'll get more into this later).

Now this new system (life of the author plus seventy years) sounds a lot simpler than that old system of renewals, publication, etc., huh? Well, how about:

1. A work written by two people. Whose life do you use to measure the copyright duration?
2. A work written anonymously or under a phony name (called a 'pseudonymous work'). How do you know whose life to check on?
3. Works for hire. Remember, the author is the employer, who could be a corporation. And some of those suckers live forever.

Well, rest comfortably, because all of these have been taken care of. They work like this:

1. In the case of a joint work, the copyright lasts until seventy years after the death of the last survivor. So write all your songs with your five-year-old son.
2. Anonymous (no name) or pseudonymous (phony name) works last the sooner of ninety-five years from publication, or one hundred twenty years from creation. *Creation* means the first time it's fixed in tangible form (written down or recorded). *Publication*, as I said, is a tricky little devil, but for our purposes just take it to mean the distribution of copies to the public.
3. Works for hire. Same as anonymous.

Once the copyright expires, the work goes into the **public domain** (also called **p.d.**), which means anyone can use it for free.

Similar to the U.S., the U.K. term of copyright is seventy years from the end of the calendar year in which the author sheds their mortal coil. Sound recording copyrights (which we'll discuss on page 319) have a term equal to the later of: (a) fifty years from the end of the calendar year in which the work was made, or (b) fifty years from the end of the calendar year in which it was released, but only if it was released within fifty years after it was made (it if wasn't, it's probably a serious dog).

By the way, if a work (other than a sound recording) is first published outside the EEA, and the author is NOT an EEA national, the copyright term in the country of origin may apply, but with a minimum period of life of the author plus fifty years, and a maximum of the life of the author plus seventy years. This gets to be technical stuff, undoubtedly beyond your pain tolerance level, so consult a pro if it applies to you.

RIGHT OF TERMINATION

One of the best goodies given to authors in the 1976 Copyright Law is the **right of termination.** This concept, together with the concept of measuring copyrights by the life of the author plus some period of time, has existed in other countries for many years. (Heaven forbid we should do anything like the rest of the world, at least until sixty or seventy years later. But we finally caught on to it—and we'll no doubt keep it long after the other territories have abandoned it.) So putting aside my sarcasm, the termination provisions say that, even if you make a stupid deal, the copyright law will give you a second shot—thirty-five years later. In other words, thirty-five years after a transfer, you can get your copyright back. And under the new law, you don't even have to die.

The exact mechanics get a bit technical, so I've stuck them back on page 313, in a section for the real die-hards.

Termination and Works for Hire

Now you know enough to understand the consequences of something being a *work for hire* (see page 297 for what that is). With works for hire, there are *no* termination rights, because there has been no transfer to terminate. Remember, the creator never existed in the eyes of the Copyright Law—the person or company commissioning the work owns it as if they had created it themselves. So with no transfer to be terminated, there's no copyright coming back to you and your kiddies. Bummer.

Be very aware of this consequence when you create a work for hire.

Until 1956, the U.K. had a similar right of transfer termination. However, that's gone (except for works first assigned between 1 July 1912 and 1 July 1957 by authors who were the first owners of the copyright of those works). Accordingly, unless you're one of the lucky shlumps who fit in the preceding exception, transfers in the U.K. are for life of copyright. [There's also an exception for some works prior to 1 July 1912, but if you're old enough to be thinking about it, you're probably not reading this book.]

By the way, a U.K. author is entitled to terminate transfers made in the U.S., even for U.K.-created copyrights. This means that the U.S. rights could be held by one party, while the U.K. rights are held by another. The same split of rights happens to U.S. authors, who are permitted to terminate the U.S. transfer in the U.S. but not in the U.K.

DIGITAL PERFORMANCE OF MASTERS, DIGITAL DELIVERY OF MASTERS, AND WEBCASTING

Public performance of masters was first covered by the **Digital Performance Right and Sound Recordings Act of 1995.** Those folks in Washington sure know how to put a sexy title on something, huh?

The Digital Performance Act did two things that are interesting to the music business:

1. For the first time in U.S. history, it created a right for the *artist* and *record companies* to be paid when records are performed. That's the good news. The bad news is that the right was so narrow that you'd need a pair of tweezers to get any money out of it. (This has gotten better recently, which we'll discuss a little later).

2. The Act extended the compulsory mechanical copyright license (see page 212 for what that is) to include the digital distribution of records. In other words, when records are sold by trans-

mission over the Internet, telephone lines, satellite, waffle irons, etc., the Act makes sure that the companies selling these transmissions have the right to use the *songs* (not the masters) in exchange for a compulsory license fee.

Let's look at these areas one at a time:

Public Performance Right for Masters

Until 1995, the United States had no public performance right for *masters.* Quite the contrary, when it passed the anti-piracy law in 1972, Congress specifically said that it *wasn't* creating a right for the artist or record company to be paid when the recordings were played on the radio or TV, or otherwise publicly performed (like at a disco). This was true even though the owner of the *song* is paid for all of these.

Other countries of the world have routinely paid artists and record companies for the performance of their records (see page 184), and they earn substantial money from it. Because the United States had no such right, these other countries felt no need to pay Americans for overseas performances of their records, under the age-old government theory of 'Why should I pay foreigners when I can have more money for my citizens?'

The United States first put its toe in the water of master public performance by amending Section 106 of the Copyright Act in 1995. Actually, it was only the tip of its little toenail, because the following were the only performances for which record companies and artists got paid:

1. It must be a *digital* public performance. And what's digital? Digital is music made by computers, as opposed to *analog,* which is FM and AM radio, over-the-air TV, and most everything else that makes up the mainstream. The only digital performances today are on the Internet, satellite radio, and satellite TV.

2. It must be an *audio-only* sound recording that's performed (meaning the artist doesn't get paid for performances of a master in films or TV shows).

3. You only get paid for *subscription transmissions,* which sounds like you have to be reading a magazine while AAMCO works on your car's transmission. Actually, a subscription transmission means the listener pays for the right to hear the station, as op-

posed to hearing it for free—such as radio in your car, over-the-air television, etc.

So after all those fancy words, artists and companies only got money from digital radio transmissions of their audio-only records, and then only if the listener paid to get the signal. Subscription radios are trying to build into a business, but at the moment you can make more money opening a soft-drink stand. (This law has been expanded recently, but I won't ruin the surprise by telling you about it just yet. Can you feel the suspense building?)

People get paid for these performances one of two ways:

1. There's a compulsory license, which means that, under certain conditions, the owner of the recording *must* allow its performance for a set fee. (Remember, as we discussed on page 210, that without a compulsory license, the copyright owner can prevent someone from using their work.) This license works exactly the same way as the other compulsory licenses (see page 211).
2. If the transmission falls within the parameters of 1, 2, and 3. above, but it doesn't qualify for a compulsory license, then you get paid whatever you can gouge out of the user, or you can stop them from using your master.

Compulsory License. How does a broadcaster qualify for a compulsory license? Under the amended Section 114 of the Copyright Act, it has to act like a radio station, as opposed to anything that remotely resembles a transmission for the purpose of the listener's copying it. For example, it can't be interactive (you can't request certain songs and hear them whenever you want them), they can't publish the titles in advance, etc. The idea is to exclude transmissions that are intended to be copied by the user, which will of course be another way to buy records. (Transmissions intended for the user to copy are discussed in the next section.)

If the broadcaster qualifies for a compulsory license, it pays statutory license fees. These are set by voluntary industry negotiations, or, if the two sides look like they're going to strangle each other, it's decided by something called the Copyright Arbitration Royalty Panel. The monies paid are allocated 50% to the record companies, 45% to the featured artist, 2.5% to the American Federation of Musicians for non-featured musicians, and 2.5% to AFTRA for non-featured vocalists (see page 54 for who AFM and AFTRA are).

Voluntary Licenses. If the performance doesn't fall within the statutory license, then the record company doesn't have to allow the song to be performed. This is a good thing if you're a record company, because it means you can charge whatever the traffic will bear.

What kinds of uses fall within this? Subscription transmissions (see page 304 for what those are) that don't meet the requirements for a statutory license, such as interactive transmissions (meaning you can get specific music you want whenever you want it). Also, broadcasts on every other Tuesday in Tanzania.

With voluntary licenses, note that the record company (the owner of the master) holds the rights and makes the deal. So, unlike the compulsory license, the law doesn't require the artist and non-featured musicians to be paid anything. This means the record company will keep all the money unless you have a provision in your recording contract that says you get a piece. So it's time to start adding one.

In the U.K., artists and companies have for years been paid for the public performance of records. However, the only artists who can collect are those resident in the EEA or other 'qualifying territories', which includes such places as Canada, Australia and Japan. (If you're a Yank who pinched a copy of this book, it doesn't include the U.S., so don't get excited.) These payments come courtesy of your friends at **Phonographic Performance Limited**, also known as **PPL**. 50% of PPL's income is distributed to record company members, and the balance goes to performers (both featured and session). Monies are paid once each year, based on logs kept by broadcasters and a sampling of concert venues.

The U.K. also pays companies and artists for the broadcast of videos. Video broadcast money is paid by **VPL**, which stands for **Video Performance Limited**.

Over the last few years, PPL got some competition. Specifically, **PAMRA** (standing for Performing Artists' Media Rights Association) and **AURA** (standing for Association of United Recording Artists) sprang up to collect performance monies for masters.

Recently, PPL, AURA, PAMRA, the Music Producers Guild, and the Musicians Union all got together and formed the **Performers Forum**, which is a trade group that represents all their interests to outsiders, and settles squabbles among the members. While things are still in flux at the time of this writing, it looks like PPL will be solely responsible for making deals with overseas collecting societies, and therefore collecting foreign performance income. However, at least for now, AURA and PAMRA are still grabbing money for their members.

Digital Pizza Man

The second section of the 1995 Digital Performance Act dealt with the delivery of music that is intended to be copied by the consumer. This is in Section 115 of the Copyright Act, and it provides a compulsory mechanical license for recordings of non-dramatic musical works (see page 212). Note that this is a *mechanical* license, for the *song* (not the master). The rate is set under a procedure that is basically identical to the procedure Congress uses for setting the statutory rate for digital public performances (see page 305).

The Digital Millennium Copyright Act

If you liked the 1995 Digital Performance Act, you're gonna love the encore. So come on over and grab a front-row seat for 1998's very own **Digital Millennium Copyright Act (DMCA).**

Here's what your tax dollars have done for you:

1. Made a few changes necessary for the U.S. to ratify the WIPO Copyright Treaty, and the WIPO Performances and Phonograms Treaties (WIPO is pronounced 'wipe-oh,' and even though it sounds like a sixties surf tune, it stands for 'World Intellectual Property Organization'). These provisions make it illegal to sell black boxes that defeat the electronic 'locks' protecting copyrighted material;
2. Laid out certain circumstances under which online providers aren't liable for copyright infringement. Basically, it says that someone providing space on their server, who has no input on the content, isn't liable for copyright infringement. There is also a procedure for removal of the material after someone gives them notice that it's infringing;
3. Added some junk about union residual obligations for people buying movie copyrights (yawn); and
4. Provided a compulsory license for webcasting of masters. That's our baby.

Webcasting.   The DMCA first says that 'non-subscription transmissions' are exempt from public performance royalties only if conducted by an FCC-licensed broadcaster (like over-the-air radio and TV stations). That means webcasters aren't exempt, and therefore need a license to webcast masters. The law then goes on to add another compulsory license (like we didn't have enough already), which requires the record companies to license their masters for webcasting, in exchange for fees to be set by the Copyright Arbitration Royalty Panel. To get this license, you need to meet twelve specific conditions, the details of which are beyond your pain tolerance level. Essentially, they make it difficult for you to know about the music in advance and copy it (the webcaster can't announce the play list in advance, the transmissions can't be interactive, etc.).

The more minutiae-minded of you will be interested to know that the act allows websites to make **ephemeral recordings,** which basically means non-permanent recordings. You can't directly put a CD on the Internet, so the music first has to be recorded on the website's hard drive. And, as you now know, every copy of a copyrighted work has to be authorized, so Congress had to add this provision. (If you want to look up any of this scintillating material, it's in the amendments to Sections 112 and 114 of the Copyright Act.)

By the way, the owners of *songs* have always had a right to get paid for using their music on the Internet, and there is no compulsory license (other than for digital transmissions that are in essence sales of records, which are covered in the 1995 Act and discussed in the prior section). The scuffle that's going on now is over who's going to collect the dough: The public performance societies say every digital packet that goes over the wires is a 'performance,' while the mechanical rights collection folks (Harry Fox, CMRRA; see page 224) believe it's a 'distribution' of music, like the sale of a record. Now it's true that a transmission isn't a 'performance' in the traditional sense, because it isn't being played in a form to which you could listen. (Actually, you could listen, but it sounds like a parakeet in a blender.) On the other hand, it's obviously not the sale of a tangible record either, so it's not clear the distribution triggers a mechanical royalty (other than transmissions that really are sales of records in the form of downloads, which were specifically covered in the 1995 Act).

Whichever way you come out on this argument, everyone knows that the owners of songs have to get paid for these newfangled transmissions. The real fight is only about who gets a piece of the money for the privilege of picking it up, and this is a very hotly fought issue. Stay tuned for updates.

If you're on the *Advanced Overview Track*
and are in a group, go to
Part IV (Chapter 22) on page 329.
If you're on the *Advanced Overview Track* and you're not in a group,
go to Part V (Chapter 23) on page 353.
Experts, keep rollin'.

'FIRST SALE' DOCTRINE

Remember how a copyright owner has the right to control the *distribution* of his or her work (see page 209)? One reason is that, if this right didn't exist, I could buy unauthorized, pirated copies of a motion picture and freely distribute them to the public. Since I wouldn't be duplicating the picture (my seller presumably did that), if the film company couldn't control the right to distribute copies, it couldn't stop me. So the scope of a copyright includes the exclusive right of distribution.

Now suppose I decide to have a garage sale and sell all of my college textbooks (which are all copyrighted). Can the book publishers stop me because I'm infringing their right of distribution?

Under the literal terms of the Copyright Law, the copyright owners could do exactly that. But section 109 carves out an exception. It says the owner of a lawfully made copy of a work can, without the authority of the copyright owner, sell or otherwise dispose of the work. This is known as the **first-sale doctrine** because, once the copyright owner sells a copy of something (after the 'first sale'), it can't control further distribution of that particular copy. Note this means I can't duplicate the books, or do anything else that would infringe on their copyrights. But I can sell them. So feel free to have a garage sale without guilt.

This provision also allows stores to sell used CDs, which generated a lot of heat a few years ago because some artists and companies don't like it (since they don't get paid).

Right to Rent

The first-sale doctrine is the entire basis for the video rental industry. This is because, once a DVD or videocassette has been sold to the dealer, he or she is free to sell it or rent it, without any further obligations to the film company that owns the copyright in the movie itself.

Record Rental

If this applies to movies, how about records? Can I set up a store and advertise: 'Never Buy Another Record! Just come in and rent ours! And we'll even sell you a blank CD at the same time!' It doesn't take a rocket scientist to figure out people can save lots of money by renting a CD for $3.00, taking it home and copying it, and returning it to the store the next day. Under the terms of the first-sale doctrine, this was totally legitimate, and indeed beginning to burgeon as an industry. (In fact, it's a big business in Japan.) But you know it couldn't last here.

Enter the Anti-rental Bill of 1984, which states that records can't be rented. End of the record rental industry overnight.

A terrific story goes with this legislation. (I don't know firsthand whether it's true, and I'd hate to spoil it by finding out it's not.) Apparently Senator Howard Nielson of Utah was instrumental in seeing the anti-rental legislation through. Walter Yetnikoff, then chairman of CBS Records, grew rather close to Senator Nielson in the process and, when it passed, Walter sent the senator a copy of the album *We Are the World* as a thank you. It was Walter's feeling that the senator truly understood the threat that copying of records presented, and was an industry friend. I'm told Senator Nielson wrote Walter a letter afterward, thanking him profusely for *We Are the World,* and saying he liked it so much he had duplicated numerous copies and given the cassettes to his staff.

21

Even More Advanced Copyright Concepts

I GOT YOU TWENTY, BABE

In 1998, Congress passed the **Sonny Bono Copyright Term Extension Act,** in memory of the late Sonny Bono. Basically, this added twenty more years to the term of a copyright—it now lasts for the life of the author plus seventy years for works created after January 1, 1978, and ninety-five years for earlier works.

This 'life plus seventy' stuff brings the United States in line with the European Union, whose copyrights have lasted this long for quite a while. Without ol' Sonny's bill, U.S. copyrights would drop out of European protection much sooner, because of something called **the rule of the shorter term.** This *shorter term rule* means that, even though U.S. copyrights were protected in Europe for life plus seventy, if they went into the public domain earlier in the U.S., the European copyright disappeared at the same time. For example, if an author died in 1970, her copyright could last until 2040 in Europe. However, if the work went into the public domain in the U.S. in 2010, the European protection would also end that year.

But now that's all behind us, and we're one big harmonious family. The Act also:

1. Gave libraries and archives the right to make copies of works during the last twenty years of protection (under certain restrictions);
2. Created a new termination of transfer right, as well as expanded the old one (these are discussed on page 313); and
3. Strongly suggested that motion picture studios and talent

ought to agree how to divide money earned by films and TV programs during the twenty-year term extension. I'm sure they're already at it.

The Act only applies to works still protected by copyright on October 27, 1998. In other words, it doesn't go back and re-protect works already in the public domain. So works first published between 1904 and 1922 still belong to you and me.

This copyright extension didn't come without a hefty price tag. The lobbyists for stores, restaurants, and bars got together and persuaded Congress to pass the **Fairness In Music Licensing Act of 1998,** in exchange for supporting the twenty-year extension. Just hearing the name lets you know this isn't going to be good for the music biz, huh? I mean, anybody who has to tell you how 'fair' they're going to be . . .

Anyway, this new little piece of handiwork says that stores, restaurants, and bars smaller than a certain size (2,000 square feet for stores, and 3,750 square feet for restaurants and bars) don't need a license to perform music. So they can use your songs for free. Now for quite a while we've had an exemption from performing rights licenses for single apparatus stereos, and for stores that play music in order to sell records. But this has now been expanded: on the store/restaurant/bar side, the only test now is the size of the store, regardless of how much music they pump out, or how they use it. And on the 'record sale' side, the exception was expanded to include the sale of home video and CD players.

An interesting twist is that the World Trade Organization (known to its friends as the WTO) recently determined that this U.S. small business exemption violated an international treaty. (For technical folks, it violated Article 11 of the Berne Convention, which was made enforceable by Article 9 of the TRIPS agreement.) The Europeans cried foul because the small businesses were no longer paying for their songs, and they asked the WTO to fix it. To the U.S.'s surprise, the WTO agreed with the Europeans and said the treaty didn't allow us to exempt the little fellas. So the American government coughed up money to make a short-term deal, in essence paying the Europeans' lost earnings with your tax dollars. At the time of this writing, no one has worked out a long-term solution.

As you can see by how the Europeans reacted, the small business exemption is serious stuff, and will cost copyright owners a fair chunk of change over the years. Hopefully the extra twenty years will make it up.

Now speaking of those extra twenty years . . .

Recently, a lawsuit went all the way to the U.S. Supreme Court, challenging the constitutionality of the extra twenty years. As you might remember, we talked about the Constitution authorizing a 'limited duration monopoly' for copyrights. Well, this lawsuit argued that the latest extension went beyond any reasonable definition of 'limited duration' that was contemplated by our founding fathers. And the Supreme Court found the question interesting enough to take the case.

Under the surface were a lot of political issues. On one side were the free speech folk, who believe things should dump into the public domain as quickly as possible. On the other were (1) the creators (or more likely their heirs, since this is old stuff) arguing for their livelihood, (2) the millions of dollars that the United States collects in taxes on copyright royalties, and (3) monies that come from overseas based on uses during these extended periods (which would disappear along with the U.S. copyright, under the rule of the shorter term we just discussed).

Anyway, the Supreme Court ruled that the twenty years were okay—basically, they said Congress was being reasonable when it extended the term. So your copyrights are safe. For now. If you want to look up the case, it's *Eric Eldred v. John Ashcroft,* 537 U.S. [page number citations not available at time of publication] (2003).

And the beat goes on . . .

TERMINATION RIGHT MECHANICS

As noted on page 302, the 1976 Copyright Law lets you undo any deal thirty-five years later. For example, if you sell your song to a publisher, you can get it back after thirty-five years by merely sending a notice. Here's how to do it.

You can give a notice of termination no less than two years, nor more than ten years, before it is to be effective, and the effective date must fall within five years after the end of the thirty-five-year period. To be more precise, if the grant of the work covers publication, which it almost always does, the right to terminate is effective on the sooner of forty years from the grant, or thirty-five years from publication. This protects you even if the work is never published.

This is easier to understand if we use some actual years. For example, if a copyright was transferred and published in 1980:

Year of Publication	Years in Which Termination Can Be Effective (5 Years After 35 Years from Publication)
1980	2015 to 2020
First Year That Notice Can Be Sent (10 Years Before First Possible Effective Date)	Last Year That Notice Can Be Sent (2 Years Before Last Possible Effective Date)
2005	2018

If you really want to know the details of how this works, take a look at Sections 203 and 304 of the Copyright Act.

The Sonny Bono Term Extension Act, which we discussed in the prior section, added some frills to this. They are:

1. Previously, only a living author, surviving spouse, or surviving children or grandchildren could exercise the right of termination. Now, if none of them are alive, the author's estate can do the honors.
2. There's a second bite at termination rights for pre-1978 copyrights, which we'll discuss in a minute.

By the way, this termination only applies to United States rights. If you sold off your copyright in foreign territories, you're stuck with the deal.

Attempts to Avoid Termination

So what have the publishers done in response to these rights of termination? Well, they've tried putting in fancy clauses asking you to assign over the right to terminate, to give it up, to let them have the first chance to buy it, and several other creative solutions that haven't yet come down the pike. However, Uncle Sam anticipated all of these, and the Copyright Law says that nothing you do with the termination rights is valid until you actually have the rights back. The only exception is that you can deal with the guy who has the rights about to be terminated (but no one else) after you've sent the notice, but before you get the rights back. This gives him or her a head start.

EXTENSION RIGHTS

Extension Recapture

So Congress took care of folks who wrote songs after 1978, by giving them this nice little right to get out of a stupid deal after thirty-five years. But what about the oldsters?

There's a little transitional quirk thrown into the 1976 Copyright Act that takes care of the pre-'78 copyrights. (If you weren't writing prior to 1978, or aren't the heir of such a writer, you can skip to the Digital Samples section on page 295. This isn't mandatory; feel free to read this for your general education or if you need help sleeping.)

The Copyright Law said that the fifty-six year duration of pre-1978 copyrights (remember the twenty-eight plus twenty-eight discussed on page 300) was extended to a period of seventy-five years. (As noted above, this has now been extended to ninety-five years. But for now, let's just look at the 1976 act.) In other words, the 1976 Act added nineteen years to the fifty-six years that already existed. More importantly, however, it gave the author (or his or her heirs) the right to take back these new nineteen years. The recapture procedure is similar to that for termination rights of newer copyrights (the right to terminate after thirty-five years, which we just discussed in the prior section). It's done by a notice given no less than two years, and not more than ten years, before the beginning of the nineteen years (i.e., before the end of the fifty-sixth year).

Here's an example: If a song was first published in 1960, the fifty-six years expire in 2016. This means that, beginning in 2006 (ten years before the end of the fifty-six years), and no later than 2014 (two years before), you can give a notice to be effective in 2016. After the effective date of the notice, the new nineteen years added to the copyright (2016 to 2035) belong to the author, or his or her heirs.

A few years ago, publishers began scurrying around to buy these extended terms from the authors or their heirs, and it looked like it was going to be a nice business. However, Congress gave the original owners (i.e., the original publishers) a nice perk, which is similar to the termination rights provision. The law says that, before the extended term actually comes into effect, but after giving a termination notice, the person to whom the original grant was made can make a new deal for the extra years. However, no one else can buy that term until it actually starts. Thus, because the original publisher has the ability to buy the rights at least two years before any outsider, it has an enormous advantage in getting them. So, unless the publisher has really been a jerk during the first fifty-six years (which is no small 'unless'), it can usually keep the copyrights. And this business dried up.

Now enter the Sonny Bono Term Extension Act of 1998, which added twenty years to the copyright term, and made the extension period thirty-nine years. They also threw in (at no extra charge) an added bonus: If your right to recapture came up before October 27, 1998, and you forgot to send the notice, you got another bite. At any time within five years after expiration of the first seventy-five years (the old fifty-six, plus the nineteen you blew), you can get back the newly added twenty years.

The Mills Music Case

Another quirk of the termination/extension rights is that the original publisher can continue exploiting derivative works (see page 210 for a definition), but it can't create any new works. This derivative work exception is shaping up to be a loophole you can drive a truck through, based on a U.S. Supreme Court case involving the appropriately entitled song 'Who's Sorry Now.' (If you want to look it up, it's *Mills Music v. Snyder,* 105 SCT 638 [1985].) In this case, the publisher (Mills Music) acquired the rights to 'Who's Sorry Now' from Ted Snyder and two other writers. Snyder went to that Great Songbook in the Sky, and in 1978, his heirs exercised their right to terminate the last nineteen years. (So much for my theory that the initial publisher can hang on to the songs.)

After termination, Mills Music argued that all of the *records* it had licensed were derivative works, and therefore it had the right to collect mechanical royalties for sales of these records after termination. As you can imagine, Mr. Snyder's heirs took a contrary view. They felt these rights should come back to them, so they could then license the record companies (and get all the money). The decision flipped back and forth until it came to the U.S. Supreme Court (known to its friends as 'the Supremes'). In a closely divided decision (five of the nine justices in favor, four opposing), the Supreme Court found that indeed the records were derivative works, and that the money from them went to Mills Music, the terminated publisher. Mr. Snyder's heirs had the right to money from future recordings, but not the existing ones.

After *Mills Music,* two other cases have defined the scope of a publisher's right to hang on to derivative works. The first was *Woods v.*

Bourne Co., 603 F.2d 978 (2d Cir. 1995), where the terminated publisher argued that every piece of printed music was based on the original lead sheet, and therefore the right to put out sheet music forever belonged to the old publisher (see page 284 for what a lead sheet is). The court kicked their butts on that one, holding that new versions of printed music weren't derivative works, and therefore belonged to the new publisher. Next was *Fred Ahlert Music Corp. v. Warner/Chappell Music, Inc.,* 155 F.3rd 17 (2d Cir. 1998), where the court made the derivative work exception even narrower by saying that the reissue of a master recording with a different record number was not a derivative work, even though it was the same recording made earlier, and therefore the new publisher of the song could issue the mechanical license (and get the dough).

So, as you can see, the sentiment in the later cases is to expand the rights of the person getting back their copyrights. Stay tuned to this channel; as the older copyrights tick on and terminations become more prevalent, there may be some more interesting law.

DIGITAL SAMPLES

A **digital sampler** is a device capable of taking any guitar sound, drum sound, voice, etc., and making a perfect digital copy. It can then be played on a keyboard, edited, etc. Unless you've been living in a cave for the last few years, you know that every rapper on the planet samples freely from other people's works. What started out as a minor practice of taking great drum sounds, unusual squeaks and groans (James Brown was and remains a special favorite of the samplers) has turned into a wholesale lifting of rhythm tracks, melodies, etc. For example, M.C. Hammer's 'Can't Touch This' was a very close copy of Rick James's 'Super Freak,' and Eminem sampled Dido's 'Thank You' in his song 'Stan.'

As with any new practice, everyone started out groping around for what kind of deals to make. In the early days, a lot of sampled records were released before anybody even tried to clear the rights, and the artists and companies often had an attitude along the lines of 'If they catch me, I'll make a deal.' And when they did catch them, the deals consisted mostly of throwing around a few bucks and buying out the rights.

Can you guess whose rights had to be bought out? The obvious one is the record company owning the sampled recording. But they aren't the only one whose rights you need. The publisher of the sampled musical composition must also be taken care of.

This 'catch me if you can' attitude came to an abrupt halt after the case of *Grand Upright Music Limited v. Warner Bros. Records, Inc.*, 780 F.Supp. 182 (S.D.N.Y. 1991), which involved the rapper Biz Markie sampling Gilbert O'Sullivan's 'Alone Again (Naturally).' See if you can guess how the judge ruled in this case by reading the first line of his opinion:

'Thou shalt not steal.'

The Honorable Kevin Thomas Duffy of the New York Federal Court not only slapped the hands of the sampler, but referred the matter to the U.S. Attorney's Office for possible *criminal* prosecution! (As you'll see on page 325, intentional copyright infringement is a criminal offense.) End of the days of casual sampling.

Because of this case, everyone now treats sampling with the utmost care and respect. Record companies won't release a record containing samples without assurances that the samples have been cleared, and you as an artist should want the same thing. Clearing samples is a major pain in the rear end, because there's nothing in the law that requires anyone to let you use a sample, and thus any record company or publisher is free to make you pull it off your record. Moreover, you can't clear the sample until you finish the track—the publisher and record company want to hear exactly how the sample is used before they'll tell you how much they want to charge—which puts you in the position of having to record the sample before you know whether you can use it. And if you're on a tight schedule and/or if it ruins your song to take it out, you won't be a happy camper.

Suppose you don't actually sample, but just duplicate the track by playing it in the studio. Does that solve your problems? Well, only half. You've just created what we call a **replay.** *Replays* eliminate the need to license the master, but you still need to license the song.

Since there's no compulsory license for samples, you have to make whatever deal the rights owners decide to bless you with. If the usage is minor, and it's a little-known song, you *might* be able to buy out all of the rights for a flat fee (buyouts are very rare these days). If you can get one, the range is usually from $5,000 to $15,000 for the record company, and about the same for the publisher. If the usage is more significant and/or the song is well-known, or you happen to hit an ornery rights owner, record companies may still give you a buyout, but the price can go up radically—I've seen fees of $50,000 and more. If there's no buyout, the record company will want an advance against a royalty, which is usually in pennies and payable on worldwide sales. The range is around 8¢ to 10¢. Sometimes their fee is a **rolling payment,** meaning a flat amount based on a certain number of sales. For example, they might get $8,000 for every 100,000 units sold. This is sort of like a 8¢ royalty, but it's better for you because if you only sell 199,999 units, you don't owe them anything beyond the first 100,000.

Publishers rarely give a buyout, and in fact will almost always insist on owning a piece of the songwriting/publishing. The percentage varies with how significant the sample is in the work, and it's settled after the publisher listens to the song and negotiates a deal. If you've lifted an entire melody line, or their track is the bed of your song, they might take 50% or more; for less significant uses, the range is 10% to 20%.

Another fun thing happens with multiple samples. I've seen more than one situation like this: a song has three samples, and Publisher X wants 40%, Publisher Y wants 40%, Publisher Z wants 30%. If you do some quick math, you'll see that's 110%! So every time you sell a record, you get to write a check out of your pocket. And by the way, don't assume the publishers will be the least bit sympathetic. Their attitude is usually something like, 'Those other publishers are pigs. But my share is really worth 40%, so go squeeze the other guy.'

Even when you get past all these hurdles, the publishers (and some record companies) will often limit the usage of their sample to your records and promo videos. Also, the publishers will usually ask to co-administer their portion of the composition (see pages 286–87 for discussion of co-administration agreements). This means they have the right to stop you from granting a particular license—for example, you couldn't license the song in a commercial without going back to the record company and publisher (and paying them for it). So when you sample, you can lose control of your own song.

The lesson in all this is that putting a sample in your record is serious business. So think carefully about what it means. A moment of pleasure can mean a lifetime of pain.

SOUND RECORDING COPYRIGHTS

It may surprise you to know that, prior to 1972, the United States had no copyright protection for a sound recording itself. I'm now talking about the physical *sound recording* (not the musical composition). Here's what happened:

The Age of the 'Lawful Duplicators'

As I said, prior to 1972, nothing in the United States Copyright Law made it illegal to duplicate a master recording (other than the fact that permission was required from the owner of the musical composition, who was almost never the owner of the sound recording.) Thus, to take an easy example, suppose a group made a recording on Elektra Records of 'My Country 'Tis of Thee' (or 'God Save the Queen,' if you're British), which is, of course, a public domain song (see page 302 for what public domain is). Prior to 1972 it was perfectly legal to set up a machine in your garage and begin manufacturing records from that recording without anyone's permission, and more importantly, without paying the artist or the record company who invested the money to create the recording. (As a note for you purists, I am of course assuming that the group making the original recording did not create such an unusual arrangement of 'My Country 'Tis of Thee' to be copyrightable as a derivative work [we discussed derivative works on page 210]. If this were the case, then the composition would have to be licensed from the publisher. Also, I'm assuming there's no trademark infringement, such as knocking off the Elektra Records name or logo.)

Avoiding the Wrath of Publishers

However, as you can imagine, there wasn't much demand for knockoff recordings of public domain songs—people were much more interested in the Beatles, the Rolling Stones, and other best-selling groups of the day. So how did the pirates get around infringing the copyrights in the songs? Since the artist often controlled the publishing and wasn't getting any royalties from the sale of these rip-offs, they certainly wouldn't give the pirates a mechanical license. So the duplicators used our old friend the compulsory copyright license (see page 212).

Remember, once a composition has been recorded, the publisher *must* issue a license to anybody who wants to use it in phonograph records. So the pirates went to the publishers, asked for a mechanical license for their unauthorized duplications, and, when they were turned down (which was the case with legitimate publishers), they simply got a compulsory license and proceeded to pay the publisher. Under this guise, and seeking to slip through a loophole in the Copyright Law, the pirates blossomed into a multi-million-dollar industry at the expense of the recording artists and record companies who had invested substantial monies in making the recordings. Many of these sleazebags used names like Pirate Records, or had a logo with a skull and crossbones, a pirate with a patch and a cutlass in his teeth, etc. Real class. (If you were going to give the music business an enema, this would have been the place.)

Anti-piracy Legislation

This smelled like thievery (which it was), and the courts were stretching to stop the pirates, usually under state laws. However, it ultimately took an amendment to the Copyright Law to nail the coffin shut. In 1972, Congress enacted a full-fledged, legitimate Copyright Law provision dealing with piracy (which is now Section 114 of the Copyright Act). This prohibits the unauthorized duplication or dubbing of the *sound recording* itself, by creating a copyright in the actual recording. (This is in addition to a separate copyright in the musical composition.) It is imaginatively called a **sound recording copyright,** and is represented by the symbol℗. Look for it on records in your collection.

One of the most interesting aspects of this sound recording copyright involves what it did *not* protect. While it's clear you can no longer duplicate records without consent, the sound recording copyright doesn't prohibit a 'sound-alike' recording, no matter how closely you duplicate the original. In other words, nothing in the sound recording copyright stops you from hiring a singer to imitate the original artist, or hiring a band that sounds just like the original recording, regardless of how close you come. Of course, you must license the song, and you must disclose that the recording is not the original. If you didn't label your record as an imitation, you would run afoul of various trademark and unfair practices acts, which deal with the proper labeling of goods (and thus stop you from defrauding the public into thinking they're getting the original when they're not). These are the same laws that stop you from calling a cereal Grape Nuts if it's not made by Post, even if it has exactly the same ingredients.

THE COPYRIGHT NOTICE

Let me say a couple of words about the copyright notice. The notice itself is the © followed by the year of copyright (which is the year the work was first fixed in tangible form).

The copyright notice is much less significant under the 1976 Copyright Law than it was under the old law, because the consequences of leaving it off or making a mistake in it are no longer very serious. (Under the old law, you could lose your copyright.) It's not worth getting into all the niceties, but you should know a few things:

1. In music, the copyright notice is significant primarily for printed music. This is because the law only requires notices on 'visibly perceptible copies.' Since you can't 'see' a song by looking at a CD, there's no need to put a copyright notice on the song.
2. So why do you see copyright notices on albums? Good question! The reasons are:
   (a) sometimes the lyrics are printed inside, and since they are 'visually perceptible,' you need a copyright notice;
   (b) there is a copyright in the album cover artwork; and
   (c) there is the sound recording copyright ℗ notice we just discussed.

The U.K. requires no copyright notice whatsoever. However, there are several international copyright treaties to which the U.K. is party, some of which require a notice for copyright protection in other nations. And people usually include the notice even if it's not legally required. Thus, you often see a copyright notice.

REGISTRATION AND DEPOSIT

The U.S. has a concept of registration and deposit which does not exist in the U.K. So you can skip this section unless you're riveted by minutiae.

The Myth

As we discussed, the myth that you get a copyright by sending something to the Copyright Office is just that—a myth. You get a copyright by fixing the work in tangible form, and nothing more.

The act of registration gives you certain remedies you don't otherwise have, and so you should always do it if you're going to commercially exploit your work. However, the failure to register doesn't affect the validity of your copyright and, if you're a beginning songwriter, it's probably not worth the money until someone bites.

The old trick of mailing a copy of the work to yourself actually does work. It has nothing to do with securing a copyright, but it clearly establishes a date on which you had created your work. If you're going to do this, send it by certified mail and don't get excited and open it when it arrives; store it in a safe place, and let a judge open it if someone ever gets cute.

Penalties for Failure to Register

On the other hand, if your work is being commercially exploited (recorded on records, used in a film, commercial, etc.), you should register with the Copyright Office. If you don't, the following penalties apply:

1. You can't collect compulsory license royalties (see page 211).
2. You can't file an infringement action to recover damages or stop someone from using your copyright (see page 324). You can wait and register just before you file the action, but it's a better idea to take care of it as soon as you know there's going to be a recording.
3. If you don't register within five years after first publication, you lose the legal presumption that everything in the registration is valid. This legal mumbo jumbo basically means that if you do register within the five years, a court will assume everything in your registration is correct, and the infringer has the burden of proving it's not. If you don't, you have to prove it is.
4. You can't recover attorneys' fees, nor can you get statutory damages (see page 324).

You get the forms you need to register by writing the Copyright Office at:

Information and Publications
Section LM-455
Copyright Office
Library of Congress
Washington, D.C. 20559

You can also reach them online at www.lcweb.loc.gov/copyright, unless that's now become a porno site.

Deposit

A separate requirement from registration is the obligation to deposit copies of your work within three months after publication. If you don't, there's no loss of copyright, but there are penalties and fines. The purpose of this is to keep the Library of Congress overflowing with tons of crap that nobody has ever heard of, and the system works quite well. You can deposit either tapes, CDs, or sheet music for songs.

WHAT YOU GET WHEN SOMEONE RIPS OFF YOUR COPYRIGHT

When someone steals your song, they have **infringed** your copyright (meaning they've used it without your permission). What you can get is in many ways peculiar to the copyright (and also trademark) world, and works like this:

1. **You get the fair market value**
    of the use they made. For example, if they rip off your song in a commercial, and the song would be worth $25,000 if they had gotten a license, you can get $25,000.
2. **You can recover the infringer's profits.**
    This is not a common remedy and is extremely valuable. It means that if the sleaze made a profit using your work, you can recover his profits, which may be more than the fair market value of the usage. (If you pick this remedy, you don't also get fair market value.)
3. **You can get an injunction,**
    which means the court **enjoins** (prohibits the infringer from

using) the infringing work. If they continue to use it anyway, they're subject to substantial fines, and sometimes even jail.

4. **You can recover statutory damages,**
   which is a real copyright original. This is where you can't prove actual damages—for example, your infringer was not only a thief, but also a moron in business and he lost money on your rip-off. Or maybe his profits are so well hidden that you can't find them. In this case, the court can give you anywhere from $750 to $30,000 for a single infringement (this is per act of infringement, not the number of copies actually made; for example, putting out 100,000 records with your song is still only one act of infringement). The judge can raise this to $150,000 if it's a willful (intentional) infringement, and can lower it to $200 for an 'innocent' infringement.

5. **The court can order the destruction or seizure**
   of any infringing copies. This is also not a common remedy.

6. **If the infringement is willful, there are criminal penalties.**
   An interesting bit of history is that the Marx Brothers stole some poor schlub's copyright for a radio show and were convicted of criminal copyright infringement.

7. **You can get your court costs**
   and, to a limited extent, recover your **attorneys' fees.** The latter is unusual, because you normally don't get attorneys' fees when you win a lawsuit.

PART IV

Group Issues

22

Groups

If you're a member of a group, everything in this book applies to you. But you also get a whole set of goodies that don't concern individual artists. Let's take a look at them.

GROUP PROVISIONS IN RECORD DEALS

When you're a group, there's a whole section in your record deal that isn't in an individual artist's contract. It deals with what happens when the group is no longer a group, or when one individual (a prima donna or the only rational member, depending on the side of the fence where you sit) decides he or she no longer wants to play with the others.

Key Members

First of all, most agreements will say that a breach of the record deal by one member of the group is treated as a breach by all members of the group. This, in effect, means that if one of the members refuses to record with the others, the entire group is in breach. This is not such an unreasonable position if we're talking about the lead singer or main songwriter or key instrumentalist, but it's much less so if we're talking about a percussionist who neither sings, writes, nor knows what state he lives in.

To handle our percussionist friend, we who represent artists gave birth to the concept of a **key member.** Under this system, certain individuals are designated as *key members.* If a key member leaves the group or otherwise breaches the agreement, the company can treat the event as a breach by the whole group and exercise its various options (which we'll discuss in a minute). If anyone else does, it can't.

This is something you have to ask for—no company uses a key member concept in its form agreements. Also, as you might imagine, working this out has been known to break up groups, because the people not named as key members tend to get their noses out of joint. And it also puts the lawyer/manager in the position that non-key members may feel their representatives are 'playing favorites.' However, as you'll see, it isn't always so great to be a key member.

The Company's Rights to Leaving Members

What can the company do if a member (key or not) leaves the group?

1. All companies provide that, if a member leaves a group, the company has the option to his or her services as a solo artist (and of course as a member of any other group). This is reasonable enough—without it, you could get out of your record deal just by leaving the group.

   Even when you have a key member concept, the company may want the right to pick up any (even non-key) leaving members. However, I like to argue the company really has no business (or usually interest in) keeping the services of non-key members, such as our percussionist. (This is also how you sell the percussionist on not being a key member—if he decides to leave the group, he can split from the record company and make his own deal, while the key member can't. But if the company insists on the right to pick him up as a soloist even if he's not a key member, it scraps this argument.)

2. The company also gets the option to keep the remaining members as a group (assuming, of course, there's not a total breakup).

3. The company has the option to terminate the remaining members, since the group is no longer the one they signed. Note this means if they don't exercise their option for the leaving member, the deal is over. So make sure that only a key member's leaving can trigger this right.

Leaving Member Deals

The person leaving the group is cleverly called a **leaving member.** The terms of a *leaving member*'s solo agreement are spelled out in the group's deal, and are almost always much less favorable than the deal for the group. The record company's position, which is understandable, is that the soloist is an unknown quantity, whereas the group was the reason for making the deal. Success is by no means assured—there are many cases of soloists who have left groups to fall flat on their faces (as well as those who have been more successful than the groups they came from). If the group is important enough, the soloist's royalty may be close to or the same as the group's, but the advance is always substantially less, and the commitment is usually for one album at most (sometimes only demos). As your bargaining power increases, so does your ability to negotiate these clauses, particularly if a member of a group has been emerging as the star, or had an earlier solo career.

TRIVIA QUIZ

Name the lead singers who have had solo careers after leaving the following groups:

1. The Police
2. Genesis
3. Destiny's Child
4. Wham

Name the groups from which the following soloists came:

1. Don Henley
2. Lauryn Hill
3. Neil Young (*not* Crosby, Stills, Nash & Young)
4. Eric Clapton
5. Ice Cube
6. Ricky Martin
   (Answers on page 349.)

Deficits

Intimately related to all of this is the question of what happens to the group's deficit (unrecouped balance) when a soloist sets out on his or her own (see page 85 for what a deficit is). For example, suppose a group breaks up and is $500,000 unrecouped. The company then picks up one member as a soloist, who sells millions of albums. Can the company take his or her solo royalties to recoup the group's $500,000 deficit? Conversely, if the group was recouped but the soloist is a flop, can the company use the group's royalties to recoup the soloist's deficit?

Many companies, at least in their first contract draft, take the right to do both these things. If you ask, however, they will generally agree that only a pro-rata share of the group's deficit can be charged to the soloist. For example, if there are five members of the group, only one-fifth of the deficit ($100,000 of the $500,000 in the above example) can be carried over to a solo deal. Conversely, if you ask, they'll also agree only to charge the soloist's pro-rata share of *group* royalties with the *soloist's* deficit. The company will sometimes agree not to charge the soloist's share of group royalties with the deficit under the solo agreement, but this takes more bargaining power.

You should be careful to provide that, if the group continues to record without the soloist, no *future* group deficits can affect the soloist's new account. Also, make sure this deficit can't affect his or her share of group royalties. It's not uncommon for a successful group, after a key member has left, to record several dud albums, which then eat up all the old, successful albums' royalties. If they also eat up the ex-member's royalties on the successful albums, he or she will be, shall we say, perturbed.

For example, suppose Harvey leaves the group after making four successful albums. Because the group did well, it's fully recouped, and Harvey retires to that dream house in Elk Snout, expecting to live on his royalties from future sales of these four albums. The group, without Harvey, then goes into the studio and runs up $2,000,000 trying to make the next *Sgt. Pepper's Lonely Hearts Club Band,* which sells three hundred copies. If you don't change the form, the company will take Harvey's royalties from the four successful albums and use them to get back the $2,000,000 it spent on the flop. Harvey will not be pleased.

Most companies will agree not to charge future costs against a person who has left, because the leaving member doesn't participate in the future records' royalties and thus shouldn't bear the costs. But you gotta ask.

INTERNAL GROUP DEALS

Why You Need an Internal Contract

When two plumbers in Pacoima decide to go into business together, they know enough to have a lawyer write them a partnership agreement. Or at least they go to the supermarket and buy a printed form. On the other hand, groups earning tens of millions of dollars sometimes never get around to formalizing their relationship. And, every once in a while, this neglect bites them in the butt.

The time to make an agreement among yourselves is *now,* when everybody is all friendly and kissy-face. When you're fighting with each other, particularly if there's a lot of money on the table, you may find yourself killing the goose that lays the golden eggs, as well as supporting the Retirement Fund for Entertainment Lawyers.

One of my early experiences as a music lawyer was trying to solve the problems of a major group who had never formalized their relationship. One of the members got pumped up by a relative, who told him he was the real star of the group (even though he didn't sing or write). So he started a fight to stop the others from using the group name, and both sides got so angry they couldn't agree on anything. Because they were set up as a corporation, and were so deadlocked that they couldn't agree to pay the phone bill, we had to have the court appoint a neutral third director to break the tie. The court appointed a crusty ex-judge, who wore a three-piece suit with a watch chain. He'd done this for many bitterly fighting corporations and was supposed to be the tie breaker that allowed the corporation to finally move forward. Well, His Honor lasted about three months, saying he had 'Never in my days seen anything as nasty as this,' before disappearing into the sunset and leaving behind a large bill.

The upshot was that the litigation lasted over nine years, and cost the parties over $1 million in legal fees. The group of course was killed early in the process, and the fellow who started the fight ended up broke. All of which could have been avoided with a simple agreement and a couple of hours of planning.

So pay attention and take care of it now. I know, nobody likes to talk about anything negative (like breakups) when everything is working well. But, believe me, when everything is going well is *exactly* the time to discuss it, because you can do it in a friendly way. It's like insurance—you may never need it, but you'll sure be glad you have it if you do. Find a third party (like a lawyer) to blame for raising the issue, so you don't have to take the heat. (I routinely say that I'm the jerk insisting on this, so you can be a good guy.)

But enough brotherly advice. On to the practical aspects of what to do.

Corporation Versus Partnership

The major differences between having a partnership and a corporation are the tax-planning aspects (which could be a book in itself), the liability limitations, and the fact that corporations are more expensive to set up and run; otherwise, it doesn't make much difference whether you're a corporation or a partnership. By *liability limitations,* I mean that corporations limit what assets someone suing you can grab. In a corporation, they can only get the assets of the corporation. With a partnership, however, they can grab both the partnership's assets *and* the personal assets of *every partner* (that means you). While these are nice benefits of corporations, they're offset by the increased cost of setting up and running the suckers, so it's marginal in your early stages.

Most states now have something called a **Limited Liability Company,** or **LLC.** *LLCs* are basically partnerships, but they provide the limited liability of a corporation. Because they're as cheap and easy to use as partnerships, they're the vehicle *du jour* for many groups.

The mechanical difference between these entities is that, if you want a partnership, you need a written partnership agreement, and if you want a corporation or LLC, you need both a written shareholders' agreement (meaning an agreement among the shareholders of a corporation, or the owners of the LLC, who are called *members*), and employment agreements between yourselves and the corporation or the LLC.

For purposes of these discussions, I'm going to use partnerships because they're simpler. But all these principles can be built into a corporate or LLC structure.

The Most Important Asset

Can you guess what your most important asset is?

Apart from your good looks, charm, and talent, your most important asset is the group name. So, whatever else you do, by all means figure out what to do with your group name if there's a fight. In fact, if you only deal with your name in a written agreement, I will be happy (but not ecstatic; to get me there, you have to deal with everything).

You have to think through everything about the group name, such as what happens if:

- The lead singer and songwriter leave the group.
- The drummer who doesn't write music or sing leaves the group.
- Three out of five members leave to form another group.
- The group breaks up totally and everybody goes back to Waxahachie.

Obviously, there are about ten thousand other possibilities, but all of them can be covered with a few general rules. While you can do anything you want, the most common solutions run along these lines:

1. No one can use the name if the group breaks up, regardless of how many of you are still performing together (short of all of you, of course).
2. Any majority of the group members performing together can use the name. For example, if there are seven people in a group that breaks up, any four of them together can use the name.
3. Only the lead singer, Sylvia, can use the name, regardless of who she's performing with.
4. Only George, the songwriter who founded the group and thought of the name, can use the name, regardless of who he's performing with.
5. George and Sylvia can use the name as long as they perform together, but if they don't, no one can use the name.

If one or two people really created the unique sound of the group, I've always thought they should have the right to use the name, because the others alone wouldn't truly represent the group to the public. On the other hand, many groups operate on a 'majority rule' principle, regardless of that spirit. So anything you can imagine is okay as long as everyone agrees, and it has some rational basis that a judge can understand. Just do *something*.

What happens if you don't do anything? As you can gather from my previous horror story, the law is not very helpful. In fact, there is very little law on the subject (surprising as that sounds). This is because most disputes are settled privately, even though they may start as a lawsuit. The cases that have gone the distance turn on the question of whether the performing members are deceiving the public. The argument is that one or more key people are the 'essence' of the group, and anyone using the name without them misleads and defrauds the public. And that gets decided by a judge whose favorite music is probably Wayne Newton.

If you think this sounds messy and expensive to resolve, you're right. So solve it yourself. *Now!*

Percentages

Now that we've raised the subject of an agreement, the next important thing to decide is everybody's percentages. It may surprise you to learn that there are many bands who, despite laughing, giggling, and grabbing each other's tushies on stage, are in fact owned or controlled by one or two people, and everybody else is merely a hired hand. Being a hired hand doesn't necessarily mean you're on a salary—you can be a hired hand and get both a salary and a percentage of the profits. It does, however, mean you serve at the will and pleasure of the employer, which actually makes for a rather pleasant band atmosphere— somehow the knowledge that they could be out on the street tomorrow keeps people's attitudes a lot healthier than if they think they have life tenure. (Hiring people usually isn't practical for new artists, because you have no money to pay them a salary. So everyone works for a percentage of the future pie.)

Assuming you're all going to be partners, how should the profits be shared? Again, there are no rules, and you can do it any way that makes you happy. The easiest way, of course, is to split things equally—if there are five of you, everyone gets one-fifth, or 20%. This is common in new bands, but it can become a source of irritation if some members work harder or contribute more than others. Another approach I've seen (with a band that was built on a core of two people who were together for a number of years before the others joined) gave the two founders bigger percentages than the others. And frankly, even when everyone has been together from the beginning, there may be one or two key members who deserve more than the others.

By the way, nothing says you have to use the same percentage for records that you use for other areas. Sometimes bands split evenly on concert monies (on the theory that everyone is out there sweating together), but have different splits for phonograph records, merchandising, television performances, etc.

Control

Just as ownership doesn't need to be equal, neither does control of the band's business decisions. Normally you vote in proportion to your percentage of profits, but this is not carved in stone. Thus, even if your percentages are equal, one or two key members may control the vote— for example, they may have two votes where everybody else has one. Or it can be set up so that the group can't act without one of the key members agreeing, regardless of how many people want to do it. The possibilities are again endless, depending only on your creativity and desires, but they need to be thought out carefully. For example, try not to have an even number of votes, because this allows a **deadlock** (meaning an equally divided vote where nothing can be done). At worst, have a third party like your manager break the tie, but better still, try to have a mechanism to do it inside the group.

Other Issues

Here are the other major issues to deal with in your partnership agreement:

Firing. What kind of vote does it take to fire a member? Majority? Unanimous of everyone else? (Unanimous of everyone doesn't work, since the guy being fired usually votes the other way).

Hiring. What kind of vote do you need to take in a new partner? Or to hire a lawyer, agent, or manager? Majority? Unanimous? When my son Danny was twelve, we came back from vacation to discover that his band had hired a manager and keyboard player without even asking him. It ultimately broke up the band, and yours could be next.

Quitting. Is everyone free to quit at will? Note that this only concerns leaving the other band members. You're not free to quit under your record deal (see page 330), and if you're in the middle of a tour, you're not free to walk out on the concert promoters without getting the teeth sued out of your mouth.

Since slavery was abolished in this country, there's no way to force someone to continue working with a group. But it is possible to stop him or her from working as a musical artist after quitting, or to require the member to pay his or her solo earnings to the partnership (meaning the other group members get a piece). These are the real means to enforce such a provision. On the other hand, I've always been in favor of letting people go if they're unhappy, as long as they don't walk out in the middle of a tour or otherwise leave some third party hanging.

Contributions. What kind of vote do you need to make partners contribute to the partnership (translation: put in money)? For example, if the group needs dough to buy equipment, cover unexpected expenses, etc.?

Incurring Expenses. What kind of vote do you need for the group to spend money?

Amendment of Partnership Agreement.   What kind of vote does it take to change the terms of the partnership deal? For example, can a majority vote reduce your percentage? Or does it take your consent?

Death or Disability.   What happens in the event of your death or disability? The one sure thing is that your partners don't want your surviving spouse or parents voting on partnership matters (not likely they'll get on stage and sing). For this reason, there is normally a **buyout** (see the next section), and you're treated as if you had quit the partnership or were terminated.

Ex-Partners.   What happens after you're terminated as a partner, or after you quit? Do you keep your same percentage level for past activities (almost always 'yes')? For future activities (almost always 'no')? Do you get bought out of your share of assets of the group (called a *buyout*), and if so, at what price and over what period of time? Funny you should ask . . .

Buyouts

So speaking of buyouts, here's one used by one of my clients:

Price.   The price of the buyout equals the leaving partners' percentage of all 'hard' assets owned by the partnership. 'Hard' assets mean goods that you can touch and feel (sound equipment, instruments, cash, etc.), as opposed to 'intangibles' (such as the group name, recording contracts, television shows, etc.). Thus, if the assets are worth $100,000, and the partner had a 25% interest, his or her value of the assets would be $25,000. This is usually done on a 'value' as opposed to 'cost' basis, because used equipment is generally worth less than the cost. It can also be done on something called **book value,** which is an accounting concept meaning the 'value' on the books of the partnership. *Book value* is typically the original cost minus some scheduled factor of depreciation that is worked out by your accountant. Of these three methods, book value is likely to be the lowest, although it's possible the real value could be less. Cost is the least accurate measure of anything.

I specifically provide that there is no value given to any intangible rights. First of all, I think they're impossible to value, and second, the value may be different after someone leaves the group (for example, if the lead singer/songwriter goes, the group name and record deal may be worthless). Finally, I think the leaving member's contingent payout (discussed in the Contingent Payout section below) covers this.

You should know that not everyone agrees with this approach to intangibles. There are certainly situations where a name is worth a lot of money after the group has broken up. For example, the Beatles, the Doors, and Led Zeppelin still generate tons of dough from the use of their names in merchandising, and it's not illogical to give an ex-member some reduced piece of materials created after the member has left. (Note that if the band breaks up, everyone continues to own their shares of the name.) Despite all that, and despite the fact that it could arguably create an unfair result, I still like my way. You can't know in advance what a particular member will really contribute to the value of the name, or how much value will be added after that member leaves. And figuring it out after the fact makes lawyers rich.

Cash Payout. The value of hard assets is paid out over a period of two years, at the rate of 25% each six months. Thus, in our $25,000 example, $6,250 would be paid six months after termination, $6,250 paid twelve months after, and so forth. Because the total isn't paid up front, a leaving partner gets interest (in this deal, 6%) on the unpaid balance.

The reason for structuring a payout over time is to protect the remaining members from having to come up with a big chunk of cash (which they may not have) all at once. Also, it's not uncommon to provide that the terminated partner can look only to the assets of the partnership for his or her buyout payments. That means the other individual partners aren't responsible if the partnership tanks and has no money to pay.

Contingent Payout. The leaving member(s) get their continuing percentage from activities of the partnership in which they participated. This means royalties from records they played on, monies from merchandise using their names or likeness, concerts and TV shows they performed, etc. (Remember, there are special record contract provisions about leaving members, which may affect their continuing royalties. See page 330.) The leaving member(s) don't get any portion of group earnings from activities after they leave.

Legal Ethics

You should be aware of a common ethical problem groups have. A lawyer that represents a group and draws up a partnership agreement has a built-in **conflict of interest.** A conflict of interest or **conflict** means the lawyer represents two clients whose interests are adverse to each other. (We also discussed *conflicts* on page 52). So if a lawyer represents the partnership, he or she can't take sides and represent any one of you against any other of you. However, this is exactly what making a partnership agreement requires, because your best interests aren't the same. For example, extra chunks of money or control going to Sylvia have to come from the other members, whose best interests are to keep them. (A manager, business manager, or agent who counsels you about group matters also has the same conflict.)

This of course happens every day, and all ethical lawyers will advise you of its existence. You can do one of two things:

1. Each member can get independent counsel (which may or may not be affordable) to negotiate the agreement among yourselves. This also takes a long time and can be destructive if anyone decides to be a hero. However, it's the best way to do it.
2. Far more commonly, the lawyer explains all the issues to you openly, and then lets you decide among yourselves how you want to resolve them. In this case, the lawyer doesn't represent any of you, but rather just acts as a 'secretary,' writing down whatever agreement you reach on your own. If you use this route, your lawyer will ask you to sign a **conflict waiver,** which says he or she has explained the conflict to you, and you're going ahead anyway.

WHAT'S IN A NAME?

We talked before (on page 334) about group members' rights in your name. Now let's talk about how to protect your name from people outside the group.

Rights in a Name

A few years back, a band named Green Jellö changed its name to Green Jellÿ to avoid a dispute with the owners of the Jell-O trademark. While the group ultimately got terrific publicity from all the flap, having a name that steps on somebody else's toes can be a serious problem. The most common problems don't come from naming your band after snack foods, vacuum cleaners, etc., but rather from another group that used the name before you did.

Your group name is protected by a **service mark,** which is similar to a **trademark**—a *trademark* is a name used for *goods* (like Heinz ketchup, Kleenex tissues, etc.) and a *service mark* is a name used for *services* (like airlines, dry cleaners, and musical groups). The rule is that you get rights in a mark by actually using the name and having it associated with you in the mind of the public. So if the fans think of you when they hear the group name, it's yours and no one else's.

In fact, you can even stop names that are different from yours but are similar enough to confuse the public. For example, there's a famous case from the 1920s where Charlie Chaplin stopped someone from using the name 'Charles Aplin,' and there's an even more fun case where the Dallas Cowboy Cheerleaders stopped the porno film *Debbie Does Dallas* from calling its star an 'X Dallas Cheerleader.' (For you research freaks, the case cites are *Chaplin v. Amador,* 93 Cal. App. 358 [1928]; and *Dallas Cowboy Cheerleaders, Inc. v. Pussycat Cinema, Ltd.,* 604 F.2d 200 [2d Cir. 1979].)

By the way, your association with the group name doesn't have to be nationwide—it can be only in your hometown. Let's take an example: Suppose you live in Tulsa, Oklahoma, and like the name Pukeheads. Using this name, you start playing locally in August 2000, and build up a major buzz and fan base. Then one day in 2003, you walk into the record store and find an album by a group from New York called Pukeheads. What can you do?

Actually, you may be able to do quite a bit. If you were a Pukehead in Tulsa before the New York guys used the name in Tulsa (the date you started using it is key—you have to be first), you can stop them from distributing records in Tulsa. Even if they used the name first in New York, if you were first in Tulsa, that town is yours. (They could, however, stop you from using the name in New York if they used it there first; and if they used it nationally before you, they might even stop you in Tulsa. This gets pretty complicated and depends on the specific facts in each case, including the genre or kind of music each group performs. But let's assume you own Tulsa.) Since it's impossible for a record company to skip a specific market when it runs a national distribution system, if you own the name in Tulsa, you can effectively block them from using it on records in the U.S. This is a joyful result if you're the band from Tulsa, but nose-dive downer if you're a Puke-head from New York.

Note that your rights come from using the name, *not* from register-ing it. (Registration means filing a public notice that tells the world you claim a particular name.) When you use a name, the public begins to associate it with you. And if someone else uses the same name, the pub-lic could be fooled into thinking it's you or a spin-off group, which is a no-no. So your most important rights are from usage, even though you do get some important rights from registering, including the fact that filing an Intent to Use a federal trademark puts you first in line, even if you started to use the mark later (as we'll discuss in a minute).

An important new area in trademark is something called **dilution.** Until recently, you only got trademark protection in the specific area where you did business. In other words, if you were a phone company named Presto, you probably couldn't stop a massage parlor from using that name, since people wouldn't likely think their massages were com-ing from the operators. With *dilution,* there's an argument that using a well-known name in another area dilutes the value of the original trademark, and it may be possible to stop the massage parlor. So, even though the Rolling Stones don't have a record label, you couldn't get away with starting up Rolling Stones Records.

Check It Out

So how do you stop from being a New York Pukehead? You have to make sure no one else used the group name before you did, which is a bit of a pain (I'll tell you how in a minute, although there's no way to ever be 100% sure). It's not too serious a problem until you get ready to release records, or at least until you start touring over a broad geo-graphic area. Up to that point, the most trouble you'll likely get is a snippy letter from someone else using the name, and you can usually work it out (see page 344 for how things get worked out). However, changing a name that has built up a local following is not a happy event, and if you really have a roll going, you may want to check out the group name even before you get a record deal.

When you get ready to make records, clearing the rights in your name becomes a very serious matter. If someone can stop your com-pany from putting out records (as in our Tulsa example), it could cost them a lot of money. And if it does, the record company will turn to you with a hand full of 'gimme,' asking you to pay for the damage—

virtually every record deal makes you guarantee that they can use your name without any legal hassles, which means you have to pay for the mess if there is one.

After being stung by a few of these situations, most record companies now check the names of new artists before they put out their records. They use several common sources and types of searches:

1. *The Billboard International Talent and Touring Directory* has an alphabetical listing of a large number of bands currently touring. You may be able to find it in your local library, or you can order it from *Billboard* (see page 18 for their address, or try www.billboard.com).

2. *The Internet* has become an excellent tool for preliminary searches.

    (a) Try looking up your name on a search engine, like Google or Yahoo, to see what comes out. Also try some of the music websites like Amazon (www.amazon.com), CD Now (www.cdnow.com), All Music Guide (www.allmusic.com), or the Ultimate Band List (www.ubl.com). Remember this is only a starting point: Finding your name doesn't mean the other band is still around using the name (bands break up regularly, in case you didn't know), and just as importantly, not finding your name doesn't mean it's clear.

    (b) Look for your name at www.whois.com by trying out combinations like [*group name*].com or [*group-name*].com or [*group-nameband*].com and so forth. This could lead you to another band with your name, and it also lets you know whether you can get a domain name registration for your website.

3. *The U.S. Patent and Trademark Office* has a website where you can search federal trademark applications and registrations (www.uspto.gov/tmdb/). The searching there can get awkward (what government procedures aren't?), but this can be a good jumping-off point.

4. If the record companies don't find anything in the above sources, they order a *trademark/service mark search* to look for registrations (both state and federal), as well as other listings (known as common-law references), of the group name and anything similar. It currently costs about $300 for a preliminary search, and about another $800 to $1,500 for an in-depth

one, which is cheap insurance in the long run. And there's an even more extensive search known as a Music Media search, which is offered by Thomson and Thomson, whose address is listed below. (Whichever search they use, it's recoupable from your royalties; see page 85 for what that means.)

These searches are conducted by independent search companies and also by lawyers that specialize in trademarks. (If you use an independent firm, it's a good idea to have the report reviewed by a trademark attorney who can advise you whether anything you find might be a problem.) Here's a few searchers:

Thomson & Thomson Copyright Group, 500 Victory Rd. North Quincy, Massachusetts 02171-3145: (800) 692-8833; www.thomson-thomson.com.

CCH Corsearch, 28 W. 23rd St., 7th Floor, New York, New York 10010; (800) 734-7241; Fax (800) 233-2986; www. corsearch.com.

Trademark Research Corporation, 300 Park Ave. S., New York, New York 10010: (800) 872-6275; www.cch-trc.com.

Fross, Zelnick, Lehrman & Zissu [a law firm], 866 United Nations Plaza, 6th Floor, New York, New York 10017: (212) 813-5900; e-mail: fzlz@frosszelnick.com.

As noted above, searches can never be 100% foolproof (for example, there may be a local band like the one in Tulsa that hasn't registered a service mark but has acquired rights in the name by performing), but it's about the best you can do.

If you find a group using your name, or using a name that's similar to yours, you have to deal with it. (If you find a name that's similar, you'll need a legal opinion as to whether or not it's too close—the test is whether the public is likely to confuse the two groups.) Most of the time you can contact the other group and work out a deal. If you find them and discover that they broke up or abandoned the name, they may have lost their rights and you don't need to worry about them. If they're still using the name, and if they're willing to change it, they'll want to get paid. The most common deal is the payment of a lump sum in exchange for their drifting into the sunset (usually in the range of a few thousand dollars to maybe $20,000 or so, though it can get into six figures if they smell blood).

If you do make a deal, you'll need a knowledgeable lawyer to draw it up because this is a very tricky area. *Never* try to handle this kind of deal by yourself. And by the way, making a deal doesn't assure yourself of total peace. For example, you might buy out the Tulsa Pukeheads, only to find there were Pukeheads in Seattle that you never knew about, and they came before the ones in Tulsa. Or, in our worldwide business, Pukeheads in Düsseldorf or Abu Dabi. In that case, you're back to square one (minus several thousand bucks).

Sometimes, bands in this position think they've got you by the squeezable parts, and they hold out for enormous sums of money. When you get one of these, or if you come across a band that simply won't sell the name, you have to change yours. Sometimes you can keep part of the name by adding something to it, but you need to add something distinctive that clearly separates you from the others. For example, if you were using the name Silver and found that it was taken, you might call yourself Denver Silver. (I always think of that great scene in the movie *Spinal Tap* where they talk about having been called the Originals, only to find another group had that name, so they called themselves the New Originals.) But this procedure is tricky, and you'll need legal help.

Registration

At some point in your career you want to file a **registration** of your service mark. Registration tells the world that you're using a particular name (or more accurately, it tells everyone in the United States; foreign protection is a different story, as we'll discuss on page 347). Registration also establishes a date on which you are using the name, and creates a **legal presumption** that you own it. (A *legal presumption* means the other group has the burden of proving you *don't* own it; without the presumption, you have to prove you do own it.) Also, in addition to this basket of legal goodies, a registration makes sure that you will show up in any search that somebody else does (see point 4 on page 343).

If you're operating only in one state, you're only allowed to register in that state. If you're operating in more than one state, you can (and should) register with the federal government, so that you have a national notice. You can get federal applications by writing to the United States Patent & Trademark Office, 2021 S. Clark Pl., Suite 2C02, Crystal Plaza 3, Arlington, Virginia 22202. You could also call them at (800) 786-9199, or check out their incredibly sexy website at www.uspto.gov/tmdb/. And while I hate to tell you this, you can file an application online. I really don't recommend it; this area is very tricky and technical. I strongly suggest that anything having to do with these rights be run through a trademark lawyer—even with my experience in music law, I wouldn't do it myself.

You're on your own to find out where to file in each state. Try the governmental listings in your capital city.

Do You Have a Reservation? Since 1989, it's been possible to reserve a name before you actually use it. This was a major change from the prior law, which said you could only get rights by using the mark. You reserve the name by filing something cleverly called an **Intent to Use** federal service mark application, and all you need is a serious desire to use the name in the not-too-distant future. If you're the first one to file with your name, then even if someone else uses the name before you do (but after you file), you can stop them after your registration is issued.

You can turn the Intent to Use into a real, live service mark application for registration by filing evidence that you've actually started using the name. The evidence only needs to be something that shows you've used your name in interstate commerce (meaning across state lines). If you don't file this evidence within three years after the government okays your application, then your application is declared invalid, turns into a frog, and you have to start all over.

This 'interstate commerce' requirement is pretty easy to pull off. For example, it's enough if your performance under the name has been advertised in a newspaper that crosses state lines; if you send a flyer about your performance through the mails to another state; or if you play in a club where out-of-staters like to hang.

After filing your application, it can take a year or more to get the registration. And that's if everything goes smoothly (your tax dollars at work). First, the guys in the federal Patent Office check around to see if someone already has a registered mark that they think is too close to yours. If they do, your application gets bounced, and you can start squabbling with them. If you get past these guys, they will then publish your name in the *U.S. Official Gazette* (so if you haven't made it anywhere else, at least you can happen there). This is so that anybody who reads the *Gazette* (don't you and all your friends?) can object to registering your name because it's too close to theirs.

Once you're registered, you have to continue using the name in order to keep up your rights. In fact, there's a legal presumption that you've abandoned the name if you haven't used it for three years. (A *presumption* means that in court you have to prove you didn't abandon it, as opposed to the other guy having to prove you did.) However, if you use a name continuously for five years after your registration is issued, you can file something called an 'Affidavit of Incontestability,' which is fancy talk for saying that no one else can ever come along and claim they had the name before you did (actually, they can still give you a hard time, but it's really tough for them). If you're happening bigtime, this is a good idea.

Foreign Registration. Many countries of the world have a registration system similar to the United States, but I doubt you could stay awake through a discussion of different territories' intricacies. This is only meaningful when you're having success on an international scale, but at that point you should start registering in foreign places (at least in the major territories such as Australia, Canada, Japan, and something called a **CTM registration,** which is a single registration that covers all fifteen countries of the European Comunity, which includes the U.K. and Germany).

Unlike the U.S., some countries even have a **first to file** rule, which means that someone could rip off your name, beat you to filing it in that territory, then stop you from performing there. Since only a moron would rip off the name of a dud group, this isn't usually important until you're having some success. But when you do, you ought to start registering pretty quickly.

U.K. trademark rules are generally similar to those in the U.S., although the U.K. Trade Mark Office no longer makes any distinction between trade and service marks.

Like the U.S. 'Intent to Use', you can file in the U.K. if you have a genuine intention to use a mark within five years. If you don't use it by that time, someone else may be able to take it from you. Unfortunately, there's no Affidavit of Incontestability in the U.K.

If you register in the U.K., you can stop people using your mark not only on the same kinds of goods or services, but also on ones that are similar. Additionally, you can keep well-known registered marks from being used even on *dissimilar* goods or services, if the use would take an unfair advantage or be detrimental to the character of the famous mark. For example, you couldn't open a fast-food restaurant called 'The Beatles', even though the Beatles have never been in the fast-food business (at least as far as I know).

Personality rights aren't protected in the U.K. in the same way as they are in the U.S., so it's much harder to stop someone like a T-shirt pirate using your image. If you plan to use a particular picture for more than just publicity purposes (e.g. on merchandise), you should register it as a trademark, to keep anyone from ripping it off.

If you don't register, you will most likely get protection for only the exact usages you have actually made, and this will be very expensive to enforce. So get registered as soon as you have success.

While it's not related to trademark, another way to protect yourself is to get copyrights in your photos, album cover artwork (although, as we discussed, the company may want to own the copyright in those), logo designs, and so forth. This gives you the ability to go after pirates for copyright infringement, even if your trademark rights are weak.

Domain Name Registration. Once you're committed to a name, it's a good idea to check if anyone else owns that domain name. (See the discussion of using www.whois.com on page 343.) Be sure to check '.net' and '.org' as well as '.com.' If the name is clear, it's usually worth the money to register it as a domain name, so you can set up a website at some point in your career.

Owning a domain name is nothing like a federal trademark registration, and doesn't give you any trademark rights. It's more like a telephone number—useful to have, but without the other protections, not much more than a locator.

As in the U.S., you should register any internet domain names using the band's name. There have been several high-profile cases involving pop and film stars trying to recover registrations of their names by others. The U.K. has recognized some unregistered (called 'common law') trademark rights—for example, Madonna and Julia Roberts squashed their cyber squatters—but Sting lost out, partly because he couldn't show that his name was ever used as a trademark. And the less famous you are, the harder it is to prove you have rights without a trademark and domain name registration.

Group names are a very complicated legal area, requiring careful analysis of your specific facts. If you have any problems with your name, no matter how small you think they are, you MUST get a lawyer. Do not ignore the problem—it will only lie there

sleeping until you're successful, at which point it will wake up and chomp a large gash out of your rear end.

Answers to quiz on page 331:

Groups:
1. The Police—Sting
2. Genesis—Phil Collins; Peter Gabriel
3. Destiny's Child—Beyonce Knowles
4. Wham—George Michael

Soloists:
1. Don Henley—Eagles
2. Lauryn Hill—Fugees
3. Neil Young—Buffalo Springfield
4. Eric Clapton—Cream; Derek & the Dominoes
5. Ice Cube—NWA
6. Ricky Martin—Menudo

PART V

Touring

23

Personal Appearances—Touring

Now let's see what happens when you hit the road to get up close and personal with your fans.

ROLES OF TEAM MEMBERS

Here's what the various players on your team do when you tour:

Personal Manager

As the chief executive officer of your professional team, the personal manager is in charge of the tour. He or she is the one who gets you onto the right tour in the first place; ensures that your agent is making the best possible deals for you (read 'hounding the agent on a regular basis'); and once the tour is set up, mechanically makes it happen. He or she has to coordinate (and supervise people hired to coordinate):

1. Transportation of people and equipment.
2. Hiring and smooth functioning of crews.
3. Booking hotels.
4. Collecting money on the road.
5. Dealing with and supervising the **promoters** (the people who hire you, rent the hall, advertise the event, etc.; see page 356 for more about *promoters*).
6. Putting out whatever fires crop up (such as missing equipment, improper advertising, dates that aren't selling well, lapses in security, etc.).

With bigger artists, many of these duties are delegated to a tour manager and/or tour accountant. But the personal manager is ultimately responsible, and the buck stops with him or her.

Agent

The agent, in conjunction with your manager, books the tour. He or she makes the deals with the promoters (which includes the job of picking promoters that will put on the show professionally and not disappear with your money). At the early stages of your career, they will be pounding promoters to book you. At the later stages of your career, they will be pounded by promoters to book you.

Your agent and personal manager also make the following decisions about your tour:

Itinerary. Your **itinerary** is the route your tour takes and the halls you play in. If you're the opening act for a major tour, setting the itinerary means you show up when you're told. If you're headlining, the *itinerary* becomes critical. Proper routing can save or lose you a bundle of money. While it may seem obvious, the tour has to be planned so you don't end up going from New York to Oregon to Florida in a four-day period. However, concert halls are not available at all times (due to circuses, hockey games, etc., as well as other rockers), and the juggling act is quite a sight to behold.

Image. How does the tour work with your image? This is twofold:

1. If you're an opening act, is the headliner compatible with your audience? If you're a heavy metal band, for example, you won't want to be the opening act for the Osmond Family Reunion tour.
2. What venues are you playing? It says one thing if you play a brand-new 5,000-seat amphitheater in a high-end neighborhood, and it says something else if you play an older, 3,500-capacity hall with no seats, on the funkier side of town.

Skating Through the 'Radio Promotion' Jungle. Ever noticed how many radio stations either 'present' a concert, or else have concert tie-ins, ticket giveaways, live reports, etc.? That of course never happens by chance; it's always very carefully planned. And apart from just picking the right station, it has to be done in a way that doesn't upset the other stations in the market (who will promptly drop your record).

When to Put the Tickets on Sale.   This is something that can vary from market to market. Some markets will buy tickets way in advance, while others are mainly **walk up** (meaning the bulk of the attendance 'walks up' the night of the show and buys the tickets). Also, it's crucial to put tickets on sale the right amount of time before the show—not too late and not too soon. You also have to be careful you're not going on sale the same day as a major tour that's blitzing the market (or maybe they have to be careful of you!).

Pricing of Tickets.   Although your first reaction may be to 'grab all the gusto you can' by charging the highest ticket prices the market will bear, this decision isn't so black and white. Many managers and agents are squarely within this camp, and their thinking is persuasive: Nobody knows how long things will last, make hay while the sun shines, get 'em while you're hot, etc. On the other hand, many respected managers and agents take a different view, feeling a lower-priced ticket draws more people, creates a bigger 'hype,' makes the show accessible to people who couldn't otherwise afford to go, and in the long run is a better career-building move. Also, some bands intentionally keep a low ticket price because they feel it maintains their commitment to artistry before business, or because they want to attract a younger audience who can't afford expensive tickets.

This debate is not only endless, but also related to what sort of audience you appeal to—for example, young kids have more trouble with an expensive ticket than an older audience. And the answer also varies with where you are in your career—if you're an established artist, you needn't worry as much about building for the long term. So feel free to join the debate, because your guess is as good as anybody else's. (We'll discuss more details of ticket pricing on page 360.)

Deposits.   Agents are also responsible for collecting **deposits,** which are amounts paid in advance by the promoters. In order to hold you for a particular date, the promoters historically paid 50% of the total price, about thirty days ahead of the performance. It's a way of ensuring that you don't get stiffed (at least completely). So, for example, if your deal is $10,000 for a show, the promoter would pay $5,000 in advance. Currently, promoters are trying to pay much less (10% or so), and only three to five days before the date. This obviously increases your risk of getting stiffed.

Deposits are held by the agent and paid to you when you perform the gig (after deducting their commission).

Promoter

Promoters are the people in each market who hire you for the evening. *Promoters* are the entrepreneurs who take the full risk of the concert. They can be 'local' (meaning they work only in one city or area), regional (several states), national (covering the entire U.S.), or international. (National promoters will also book regionally as well as nationally.) Promoters book the hall (which means they owe the rent even if nobody shows up), pay for advertising the concert, and supervise the overall running of the show for maximum efficiency.

Promoters actually have a tough time. If they lose, they can lose big, but as acts get more successful they squeeze them and limit the promoter's upside (as discussed below). The result is a friendly game of 'hide the pickle' that promoters routinely play in rendering statements of how much has been earned. But I'm getting ahead of myself, because we're going to talk about this later (on page 363).

A company called Clear Channel now owns the vast majority of local promoters. They, as well as other national promoters, now routinely purchase entire tours. In other words, they make a deal to promote every date. These deals have their own complexities, which we'll discuss when we get to promoter deals on page 364.

Over the last couple of years, **venues** (meaning the owners of the physical buildings—the amphitheaters, arenas, etc.) have begun buying shows themselves. As we discussed above, promoters traditionally rent the buildings from the owners, then turn around and make the deals with the artists. Under *venue* deals, the building owners directly contract with the artists, in effect acting as promoters themselves, and in fact competing with the promoters who rent from them. Sometimes these venues will pay more than promoters will pay. This is partly because they've eliminated the middleman, but more importantly, it's because they have income from parking, food, beverage sales, and other areas that promoters don't share.

Business Manager

The business manager is in charge of all financial aspects of the tour. This job begins way before the tour starts by forecasting (a fancy accounting word for predicting the future) the likely income and expenses, and projecting how much you're going to make or lose. If you're a new band, this information lets you go to the record company and beat them up for tour support (see page 153). At all levels, it helps avoid unhappy surprises.

When the tour gets going, all your road personnel (the people that set up the equipment, supervise your crew, etc.) are on payroll, and the business manager is in charge of keeping everyone paid. He or she also makes sure your performance fees are collected from the promoters (which is physically done by a tour manager if you have one), and that all bills (travel, hotels, food, etc.) are paid. And it's their responsibility to make sure the tour doesn't run over budget without an alarm being sounded in advance, while there's still a chance to fix it.

Tour Manager

If you have a tour manager (and if not, your personal manager should be doing the job), he or she will make sure everything runs smoothly on the road. This means that the hotel reservations are in fact there, that your airline tickets are where they should be, that the bus is where it's supposed to be, that you are on the bus or plane when you're supposed to be, that only certain groupies get through security, etc. It's the tour manager who's responsible for collecting the money due after each show, reviewing the promoter's accounting on the night of the show (called **settling the box office** or, as a noun, the **settlement**), and depositing the dough in the right place. (As you move up the ladder, you'll have a tour accountant doing the money part of the job.)

PERSONAL APPEARANCE DEALS

It's difficult to make much money touring until you're a major star. In the traditional music biz, you don't put a lot of tushies into concert seats until you sell a lot of records, so until then, you're touring to create a buzz, get a deal, and sell records, so you can tour profitably. (There are of course exceptions to this rule. Some artists sell relatively few records, but pack concert halls. Conversely, some artists sell millions of records but can't fill an auditorium).

There's a fairly recent phenomenon of bands touring locally and regionally, building a base of 500 to 1,000 people per night, sometimes even filling 3,500 seat theaters, all without a record deal. This seems to work best for rockers and jam bands ('jam bands' being the Grateful Dead heirs, such as Phish, String Cheese Incident, etc.). They build a local base and spread it by word of mouth, particularly over the Internet (through people who go *Hey, Dude, check this out!*, then e-mail the bands' MP3 files to all their friends). Groups like this can make money and develop a cult following, which can lead to a record deal.

In the beginning, unless you're one of these phenoms, you will most likely lose money on touring. You'll also get stuck in uncomfortable dressing rooms, with food left over from last night's headliner. And you'll be regularly humiliated, playing to concert audiences who are there to see someone else, still arriving and buying beer while you're performing, talking loudly during your ballads, and chanting the headliner's name if they don't like your show. Did I sugar-coat it too much?

Well, let's look at what the deals are:

NEW ARTISTS

As a new artist, your choices are to play in clubs (100 to 1,500 people or so) as a headliner, or to be the opening act on a big tour. How you get to be the opening act on a major tour is very political. If your album is only doing so-so, and there are several other groups in your position, then it depends on the political clout of your manager and agent—it's that simple and cold. If you're selling a lot of albums, or generating a lot of interest in some other way (like a hot single or MTV video), you'll have an edge in the political process, but it's still political. The exception is the situation where you're really exploding out of the box. In this case, the headliners may be clamoring for you. For example, a well-known artist may not be selling tickets very well and wants a hot new opening act to bring people in.

The major touring season, not surprisingly, is May through September, primarily the summer months when kids are out of school and can go to concerts every night. While superstars tour throughout the year, new artists have traditionally toured only in the summer months (unless they were opening for a major artist who was touring at some other time). Recently, however, newer bands have taken to hitting the road in the fall or even winter, when there is less competition for concertgoers' dollars. This is especially true for college/alternative acts who want college radio blasting while they tour, and who want school to be in session when they get to town.

Fees

If your record is beginning to make some noise, or you've got a local following, you can get fees in the range of $250 to $1,500 per night, either from clubs or opening slots. If you're really big in the local/regional scene (like we discussed above for jam bands), and can draw

1,000 or so per show, you can get $5,000 to $6,000 or even more per night.

Splits/Guarantees

Some clubs will pay you no front money, but will give you a **split** of the gate (meaning the money charged for admission). The *splits* run from 20% to 60%, depending on your stature and the number of other acts. For example, if there are three acts, you might divide up 60% of the gate. If your band is the biggest **draw** (meaning you draw in the biggest crowds) you can ask for more than an equal share. Sometimes you can get up to 100% of the gross after the promoter gets back his or her expenses for the evening (advertising, sound, lights, etc.). This is most common when the promoter is also the club owner and is happy to break even on the door charge just to get thirsty mouths into the seats. As to the accuracy of the club's count, you'll have to rely on the club's reputation or else have Bruno, your 300-pound roadie, stand at the door and check.

If you're really hot locally, and have a following, you might get a minimum guarantee of $100 to $250 or so against your share of the gate. Or you may just take a higher fee, of say $500 to $800 per night (with no share of the gate). (I'm basing the numbers in this section on the club scene in L.A., because it's the one I'm most familiar with. These are also based on a ticket price of $5 to $7. I'm told the basic pattern holds true for most major cities.)

Expenses

The *minimum* cost of putting yourself on the road is the money to rent a van you can use to carry equipment and sleep in, plus three meals a day at McDonald's. And you'd better get along really well with each other, or else expect some violent crimes.

The next step up (three or four to a room in cheapie motels, slightly better meals, and perhaps someone to help move the equipment) gets into more expense, as you can readily see. But if you watch it carefully, you can get by cheap enough to play the independent circuit and make a few bucks. If you're headlining larger clubs or doing the opening act on a tour, the minimum cost of putting a four-piece band on the road can run around $10,000 per week, broken down roughly as $1,000 for crew, $2,000 for food and hotels, $2,500 for equipment and personnel costs, and $4,500 for insurance, commissions to managers and agents, equipment repairs, etc. With travel, setup, etc., you can't really do more than five shows per week, and you don't need to be a math genius to see that you're going to lose money doing this. Five nights at even $1,500 per night is only $7,500, which is $2,500 per week less than it costs you to be there. And the longer you stay out the more you're going to lose.

So where does this lost money come from? (See page 153 for the answer.)

MIDLEVEL ARTISTS

Let's assume you're now past the new artist level, and are selling 750,000 to 1,000,000 copies of your albums. You now have the option, in addition to opening for a major artist or playing clubs, of headlining small venues, such as 1,500 to 2,500 seaters.

At this point, you should at least be able to break even, and you may be able to take home a nice profit. If you're playing small venues (1,500 to 2,500 seaters), or if you're going out as an opening act, you should be able to make about $5,000 per night. If you're headlining amphitheaters (meaning venues of about 5,000 seats), you can get $7,500 to $50,000 or more per night, depending on the ticket pricing.

Let's elaborate on the ticket pricing: Many artists, for their credibility and/or the fact that nobody will come if they raise their prices, like to keep their tickets cheap (in the range of $10 to $15 per ticket). If this is you, because of the expense of being on the road, you'll break even or make a small profit. However, if you're able and willing to charge $20 to $25 per ticket, you can make a tidy profit. And if you can command a $50 to $60 or higher ticket price, you could get $250,000 or more per night! Note also that, because your expenses are fixed, the first $10 to $15 per ticket covers them. Thus, almost every dollar of increase (which isn't exactly true because the promoter, manager, and agent take a part, as we'll discuss in more detail in a minute) is profit and goes directly to your bottom line (meaning into your pocket).

At midlevel you can also get into **splits.** (*Splits* are discussed under superstars, so I won't ruin the surprise. But see the next section if you like ruining surprises.) The only difference is that the guarantees against splits at this level are of course lower than the superstars' (midlevel artist guarantees are in the range of $7,500 to $25,000 per show, or more if you raise your ticket price).

SUPERSTAR TOURING

Now we get into some real fun and money. This is where you make the really big bucks in touring. (And if you pay close attention, I'll tell you how to put a lot more of them in your pocket. If you choose not to listen, don't get mad at me when your agent, personal manager, and other team members have more money than you at the end of the tour.)

Splits

First let's look at the money you can earn. Here's how the deals work when you're a superstar: Instead of being paid flat fees, you get a **guarantee** against a percentage of the **net profits** or **gross** of the show. (Your share is also called a **split,** because you split the money with the promoter.) The *guarantee* works exactly the same way as an advance against your record royalties (see page 85); if you don't make any profits, you still keep the guarantee. If you do make profits, the promoter deducts the guarantee and pays the balance to you.

And these numbers are not chopped liver. Major artists in **arenas** (meaning venues of 12,000 to 20,000) get guarantees in the range of $100,000 to $500,000 plus per night. And major artists can sell multiple nights in the same venue, which can be a substantial savings of costs—you don't have to move the equipment, yourself, or your crew every night, and you can make a better rental rate for the concert hall.

The usual split is **85/15 to 90/10,** meaning the artist gets 85% to 90% of the net profits of the show, and the promoter gets 10% to 15%. Superstars push promoters even farther (e.g., 95/5), but that takes a lot of clout and it only kicks in after the promoter has gotten back all their money. For example, there might be an *85/15* split until the promoter breaks even, *90/10* to a certain level above break even, then 95/5 after that. (There are also deals based on *gross,* which we'll discuss on page 364.)

Here's an example. If a date has gross ticket sales of $250,000 and the promoter's expenses are $150,000, there will be $100,000 in net profits ($250,000 income less $150,000 expenses). 85% of this, or $85,000, is paid to the artist. If the artist got a $60,000 guarantee, this is deducted from the artist's share. Thus, the artist gets an additional $25,000 (the $85,000 share of profits less the $60,000 guarantee):

Gross Ticket Sales	$250,000
Less: Promoter Expenses	−$150,000
Net Profits	$100,000
Times: 85%	× 85%
Artist Share:	$85,000
Less: Guarantee	−$60,000
PAYABLE ON NIGHT OF SHOW	**$25,000**

The sensitivity of profits to ticket pricing, which we covered in the previous section for midlevel artists, is even more dramatic when you get to the superstar level. As we discussed, once you've covered expenses, most of the increase goes directly into your pocket. Accordingly, adult-oriented acts sometimes charge as high as $250 per ticket and occasionally even more (though the norm is $75 to $125). At this level, especially when they're playing large venues, the artists can walk away with truckloads of money each night.

Computation of Net Profits

Let's look at some of the finer points in computing **net profits.** *Net profits* are defined as 'gross receipts less the promoter's expenses,' and are determined as follows:

Gross Receipts.   Gross receipts means gross monies from ticket sales, less selling costs (such as ticket agencies), taxes, and facilities charges. That's pretty straightforward, but your team should go to great lengths to make sure you get an accurate accounting. For example, some of my clients have their tour accountant 'count the house'(meaning they actually count the number of seats and people in them) and/or (especially in 'festival' dates where there are no seats) stand at the door with 'clickers' and count the number of people that come in (in response to which one promoter opened three other entrance doors without telling us).

Expenses.   From the gross, the promoter deducts every expense he or she can possibly think of. The major ones are:

1. Advertising. It's obvious when you think about it, but not until then, that the more important an artist you are, the less advertising money the promoter has to spend. One or two an-

nouncements of a major show usually does it. So watch this expense. On the other hand, major stars don't want to let the promoter underspend either. Advertising can be a cross-promotion for a current album, and your tour should be perceived as an 'event.'

2. Rent for the facility
3. Personnel (box office, cleanup, ushers, ticket takers, doormen, etc.)
4. Rental of equipment (P.A. [public address system], lights, pianos, etc.)
5. Insurance
6. Security
7. Stage crew
8. Ground transportation for the artist and entourage
9. Catering for artist and crew
10. Public-performance license for the music (see page 236 for what this is)
11. Medical
12. Elvis impersonators (just seeing if you're paying attention)

Over the years, as promoters became more and more squeezed (or in some cases more and more greedy), they developed systematic ways of 'adding' to the expenses. Crasser promoters have been known simply to create phony invoices for various items. A more sophisticated example might be that the promoter advertises so much in the local newspaper or radio station that they get a rebate at the end of the year. In other words, if they spend $100,000 for ads on a radio station, the station gives them back $5,000 at year end. This doesn't show up on each individual invoice, and thus the shows are charged for the full amount. Another example is a rebate that promoters get from Ticketmaster and certain venues, which they also don't share.

The interesting part is that everyone knows pretty much what the promoters are doing, and thus there is this little 'waltz of the toreadors' while your agent negotiates how much the promoter can steal from you (using much more civilized terms, of course). Because everyone knows what expenses really are, there are accepted amounts of stealing, and it's bad form for (a) the promoter to steal more than is customary; or (b) the artist to 'catch' the promoter and not allow the accepted level. So in this bizarre netherland, everyone reaches a happy compromise.

Promoter's Profit as an Expense

Some promoters also ask for a profit to be added as an expense, which has the effect of delaying your split of proceeds until after they get a negotiated amount of money. For example, if the gross from a particular evening is $100,000 and the expenses are $60,000, the net profits would be $40,000 ($100,000 minus $60,000). If your deal is 85/15, you would get 85% of $40,000, or $34,000. However, if the promoter negotiated for a profit of $10,000 to be added as an expense, the net profits would only be $30,000, because the expenses are now $70,000 (the $60,000 actual expenses plus the promoter's $10,000 profit). Thus, you would only get 85% of $30,000, or $25,500, instead of $34,000. (In other words, you got $8,500 less because you are paying 85% of the $10,000 profit.) As your bargaining power increases, the promoter's ability to add a profit disappears.

Splits Based on Gross

For superstar acts, there has been a trend over the last few years to get a percentage of gross income. (In these deals, the expenses are of course irrelevant.) The range is 65% to 70% of gross, and the artist can get even more when the ticket prices are high. Remember, the expenses are fixed, so that as gross income (i.e., ticket price) goes up, the expenses become a smaller percentage of the gross. Which means the artist can get a bigger and bigger piece of it. For example, if the expenses were $50,000 and the gross was $100,000, the expenses are 50% of the gross. But if the gross was $200,000, the $50,000 expenses would only be 25%. So the higher the ticket price, the bigger the artist's share of gross.

HALL FEES

Over the last few years, agents have become responsible for negotiating **hall fees**. A *hall fee* is the amount charged by the building for selling merchandise (T-shirts, posters, etc.), and it's a percentage of the gross sales. This is discussed in detail in the next chapter, so hang loose 'till then.

RIDERS

The actual contracts for each appearance are customarily handled by the agency. At lower levels, they're merely AFM standard printed forms. As you hit midlevel to superstar, they're the same printed forms with an attached **rider** (an addendum that *rides* on another contract). Your attorney (together with your manager and agent) puts the rider together for you, and it's the guts of the deal. The contract itself is only one or two pages, spelling out the specific terms (dates, guarantee, hall size, splits, etc.). But riders typically run thirty pages or more.

Here are the major points covered in your rider:

Expenses. If your deal involves a split of profits, the promoter's expenses should be listed separately, with *maximum* amounts for each category. (Sometimes this list is in the contract itself.) In other words, the rider says you can only be charged for the actual expense, or the maximum in the contract, whichever is *less*. The rider should also spell out your right to verify expenses by examining invoices, checks, etc.

Tickets. The rider should have very strict procedures concerning the tickets, such as security for the tickets, how unsold ticket stubs must be retained, etc. The penalty for violating these requirements is customarily that all tickets are treated as if they had been sold at the highest price.

Free tickets. You want to have a certain number of free tickets (called **comps,** an abbreviation of **complimentary**) to each performance for yourself (usually fifty to one hundred), and you want to limit the amount the promoter can give away without your consent (usually twenty-five or so). If you have a tour sponsor, you may have to give and/or sell tickets to them, and the rider must cover this as well. (Remember, most of the revenue lost to free tickets comes out of your pocket, because 85% of the lost ticket money would have been yours.)

Free tickets are usually a minimal item, and not a big deal. However, some artists may not do so well in certain cities, and the promoter sometimes gives away as many tickets as humanly possible, to make the house look full. This is called **papering the house,** and is done very quietly. (If you find a lot of policemen, firemen, city council people, and similar folks boogying and/or holding their ears in your audience, there's a good chance you've been papered.)

I use an interesting clause that says the promoter's free tickets can't be in the first ten rows. Can you guess why? (Answer on page 370.)

Billing. You of course want 100% headline billing, and you should have the right to approve the presence and size of anybody else's name in the same advertising, publicity, or sign.

Recording.   The rider should have strict prohibitions against recording your performance in any way, either audio and/or visual. A poor-quality (or even worse, a good-quality) bootleg tape is a serious rip-off of your professional life, not to mention a possible violation of your record deal. I normally put in extraordinarily tough language, including high damages for a violation.

Merchandising.   Your merchandiser will require you to include specific language giving them the exclusive right to sell merchandise at your concert. (Merchandising is discussed in Chapter 24.)

Interviews/Promos.   Be sure the promoter can't commit you to any interviews or local sponsors without your consent.

Catering.   I have so much fun reading the catering requirements of riders that I've made it a hobby. Many riders have three or more full pages of food and drink that the promoter has to provide for the artist and the crew. They range from mundane foods for the crew to true exotica for the headliner. (I always get a kick out of artists who require whole-grain macrobiotic food, together with six cases of beer and two gallons of tequila.) Here are some of the better items, actually lifted from various riders over the years:

> Turkey (white meat only; never rolled or pressed)
> Gourmet-grade coffee—no canteen type
> Lactaid non-fat milk
> Shelled red pistachios
> M&Ms, with the brown ones removed

Technical.   You need to have very specific technical specifications for your show, such as size of stage, what equipment the promoter must supply, power requirements, exact security needs, dressing room facilities, sound check requests (meaning a time you can come into the actual venue and set the levels of your sound equipment), etc. Sometimes this is in a separate tech rider.

Legal.   Riders have a lot of legal sections regarding cancellation, bad weather, riots, mechanics of payment, etc.

I'LL TAKE THE WHOLE THING . . .

As I said earlier, a number of artists are selling their entire tours to one promoter. These deals look very similar to single night deals, except of course they cover all the dates. The major economic difference is that all the dates are *cross-collateralized* (we discussed this concept in record deals on page 88), meaning the promoter gets back their losses on turkeys from successful shows. This of course isn't good for you as an artist—without cross-collateralization, you'd get paid on the good dates, and the promoters would eat the bad ones. On the other hand, you can usually get a larger overall guarantee in these deals, because the promoter is hedging their risk. And sometimes you can get a limited cross-collateralization. For example, the six major market dates are crossed with each other, but not the other dates; the eight secondary market dates are crossed with each other, etc. Also, these deals are easier administratively, in the sense that you only have to do one contract and negotiate one rider for the entire tour, as opposed to separate negotiations for each date. But since you're dealing with a huge promoter, and gargantuans like to flex their muscles, you don't have as much leverage.

There's a lot of controversy over what these deals mean for the agents. Some people argue that, since you only have to make one deal (instead of the usual multiple deals for a tour with different promoters), maybe you don't need an agent. On the other hand, someone needs to supervise the national promoter, making sure you get an honest count, that the promoter is making the best deals with the venues (in fact, some of these promoters own the venues, so you have to be especially careful how they deal with themselves), etc. So arguably these national players need even more supervision—you're dealing with one powerful source, rather than a number of smaller players.

Good, bad, or ugly, these deals are becoming the norm for major acts. However, as the promoters consolidate into bigger and bigger chunks, more plants wind their way to sunlight through the cracks. What I mean is that alternatives to the big players are starting to grow up as real forces in the marketplace. These are things like fairs (it may surprise you to hear that fairs pay big money for artists, because it brings people in to see their prize cows and to spend money throwing darts at balloons), casinos (similar idea of luring in spenders), and performing arts centers, which are theaters of about 3,000 to 4,000 seats that traditionally put on classical symphonies but have found they can make money booking pop artists, particularly those with an older demographic.

LINING YOUR POCKETS WITH MORE GOLD

And now to my promised method of making you more money. Let me first say a couple of words about money in general.

More Income Versus Cutting Expenses

It's more expensive to put another dollar of income in your pocket than it is to put a dollar of cost savings in your pocket. This may sound a bit weird, so let me explain.

For every dollar of income you make, you have to pay your manager, agent, and perhaps business manager and/or lawyer (if they're on a percentage) out of it. This will leave, for example, only about 65¢ to 75¢ to go into your pocket. On the other hand, for every dollar of expense you save, the whole dollar goes in your pocket because you've already paid the professionals on the money that would have been used to pay the expense.

Let's look at an example: Suppose your tour grosses $1,000,000, and your professional team fees total 35% ($350,000). This means that you have $650,000 after commissions, out of which you must pay $400,000 in expenses. Thus, your net after everything is $250,000 (I'm ignoring income taxes).

Had you earned another $100,000 on the tour, 35% would have gone off the top to your professional team, leaving you $65,000. Since your expenses are already covered, however, the full $65,000 would be in your pocket. Thus your net after everything is $315,000 ($250,000 plus the $65,000). On the other hand, if you didn't earn another $100,000, but instead saved $100,000 in expenses, the picture looks quite different: Instead of deducting $400,000 in expenses, you'd deduct only $300,000, and your net after everything would be $350,000. You thus keep the *full $100,000* by cutting expenses, *which is almost 60% more than the $65,000 you would put in your pocket by earning another $100,000.*

Here's a chart:

	Example	EARN $100,000 more income	SAVE $100,000 expenses
Earnings	$1,000,000	$1,100,000	$1,000,000
Less Commissions (35%)	−$350,000	−$385,000	−$350,000
Subtotal	$650,000	$715,000	$650,000
Less Expenses:	−$400,000	−$400,000	−$300,000
NET	$250,000	$315,000 ($65,000 more in your pocket)	$350,000 ($100,000 more in your pocket)

And as you add another zero or two to these numbers, they get even more impressive.

What to Do

How do you pull off this minor miracle? It's pretty simple, but you may not like the answer:

Spend less on yourself.

Here are the biggest areas of abuse:

Salaries. Watch carefully how much you're paying your band and crew, and really think through how many of them you need. This is primarily your manager or tour manager's area of expertise, and you obviously don't want to scrimp on essential personnel. But you don't always need to carry as many people as you think, or to pay them as much as they demand. And be extra careful with friends and relatives. Hiring 'pals' with little or nothing to do is wasteful and demoralizing to the people who really work.

Stage, Sound, and Lights. Your stage, sound, and lighting systems have to be up to your level; anything less cheats your audiences. On the other hand, these expenses can eat up a large chunk of your profits. And the costs aren't just the obvious ones of building fancier sets. Larger staging means you need to hire more trucks to haul the stuff around, hire more folks to drive those trucks, and hire more crew to load, unload, set up and tear down.

Remember, your fans are there to see you perform, and if you need an array of trapeze artists and rocket ships to keep their attention, either something is wrong with your show or you're being insecure and hiding behind the hoopla. (You're better than that—you wouldn't be where you are if you weren't.) Of course you should do something innovative and spectacular, but be practical as well.

Travel. You can save a lot by traveling light. This means two things:

1. Almost nothing I know of (except non-income-producing real estate and owning a restaurant) eats money like chartering (or heaven forbid, owning) your own jet. As you reach a certain level, it makes economic sense (or at least not a significant difference) to begin chartering planes. But for the most part, flying commercial is feasible and substantially less expensive. I know it's more inconvenient—the hassles of the public in the

airport and on the plane, delayed fights, oversleeping and missing flights, etc.—but every major celebrity and political figure has at one time or another flown commercial, and all survived the experience. Remember, it's *your* money.

2. Try not to **hub**. *Hubbing* means you base yourself in a central location (say, Dallas–Forth Worth) while you play venues within a short flight from that city (other parts of Texas, Oklahoma, and Arkansas). When you stay in one place like this, you double your mileage—every day you not only fly to the gig, but you have to fly back. And most artists like to hub out of expensive cities, which increases your hotel/lodging bills.

Catering.   Some artists are particularly notorious for having lavish spreads backstage, much of which is never eaten by them (or even touched by human hands). Or, worse yet, it's eaten by the hangers-on who show up to see what they can scam. (I said that to make you mad; but it's true.) Because these goodies are supplied by the promoter as part of your deal, it feels like the promoter is paying for them. But the truth is that 85% of this expense is yours. Remember, as you get into the major leagues, you make only a portion of your money from the guarantee. A nice chunk of it comes from the profit split, which is usually 85/15 (see page 361 for a description of profit splits). Thus, every dollar spent on food for scavengers is 85¢ less you put in your pocket. So ditch the imported caviar and order in from Burger King.

Just Watch It.   The above isn't exhaustive; there are many other ways to cut expenses (and I'm always surprised that people find even more innovative ways to spend money). I know the road is a hassle and you want to be comfortable. There's nothing wrong with that. But be mindful of your expenses and keep them down. You'll be glad you did when you get home and count your take.

Answer to question on page 365:

Nothing is as much fun as playing your heart out to a standing, screaming audience, only to have a bunch of zombies in three-piece suits sitting in the first ten rows looking at their watches.

PART VI

Merchandising

24

Tour Merchandising

So now you're famous, and kids can't wait to plaster your face on their backs, fronts, bedroom walls, etc. And bootleggers can't wait to rip off your name and likeness with illegal merchandise (more about bootleggers later).

So how do you make money from your face? Selling products (posters, T-shirts, bumper stickers, etc.) with your name or likeness on it is called **merchandising,** and there are two basic kinds:

1. **Tour Merchandising.** This is the stuff sold at concert venues, for prices you would never pay anywhere else, so you can prove you were there.
2. **Retail Merchandising.** This is basically the same stuff (without tour names or dates), but it's sold everywhere *except* concerts, like retail stores, Internet, mail order, through fan clubs, etc.

Of the two types, tour merchandise is by far the more significant (assuming, of course, that you're touring; otherwise, it doesn't mean much). While *retail merchandising* may be more visible, it doesn't create the same intense sales frenzy as concerts do, for the obvious reasons—people are all pumped up by the show, they want a souvenir, etc.

So let's discuss tour merchandising first, and we'll deal with retail in the next chapter.

MERCHANDISERS

Merchandising at concerts (and also at retail) is handled by licensing the right to use your name and likeness to a **merchandiser.** A *mer-*

chandiser, very much like a record company, manufactures the goods, oversees the sales at your concerts, and pays you a royalty for each sale.

ROYALTIES

The computation of merchandising royalties is a lot easier than record royalties. For the most part, they're just a percentage of the **gross sales.** *Gross sales* is a term of art, meaning the selling price to the public, less only taxes (sales tax, Value Added Tax, excise, and similar taxes), and credit card fees. **Value Added Tax,** or **VAT** to its pals, is something we don't have (yet) in the United States, but is common in other countries. It's a tax on goods at each stage of creation, based on the "value added" at that point. For example, there's a tax on the lumber mill as it cuts down a tree and turns it into lumber (adding value); a tax on the furniture manufacturer when it turns the lumber into furniture (more value added); a tax when the upholsterer does its thing, etc. The tax gets bigger at each stage, but through a system of crediting back (which I have never had any need to fully understand, so I don't) each guy gets a credit for the tax paid by the previous guy. But it pumps up the price to the consumer.

The range of royalties, for sales at concerts in the United States and Canada, is generally 30% to 40% of gross sales (though recently, Canada has been running 3% or so less than the U.S.). There are higher deals for superstars. It's not uncommon to escalate your royalties based on sales, which can either be on a per-night basis, or a cumulative basis for the entire tour. This is a good thing to remember if you're getting stuck with a low royalty.

Foreign royalties run somewhere around 80% of the U.S. rate, but if your United States royalty isn't that high, you can try for the same foreign royalty. However, you're probably going to end up around 80%.

More and more, foreign deals are moving toward a split of net profits. In other words, the merchandiser takes the gross selling price, deducts the cost of the goods, etc., and divides up what's left. The usual split is somewhere between 75/25 and 85/15.

Stadiums and festivals are also starting to be profit splits. This is because stadiums are more expensive to set up and service, and festivals don't sell as much individual artist merchandise (because people want an "event" T-shirt—for example, a Family Values Tour shirt, as opposed to the specific performers). The split on stadiums is usually 80/20 to 85/15, and on festivals, 70/30 to 75/25.

The souvenir programs sold at concerts are also based on a percentage of net profits, regardless of how everything else is calculated. This is because the merchandisers finally figured out they weren't making much (or any) money on programs, but were paying the artists a lot of royalties. (Programs are expensive—they have to be designed, laid out, set up for printing, etc. Thus the profit split evolved, and it's now the norm.)

Artists of major status will sometimes have **designer goods,** such as an expensive (sixty dollars plus) sweatshirt. Because a designer is paid a fee (or royalty) on these goods, your royalty is negotiated separately and is lower. Usually it's around 70% of net profits.

HALL FEES

Over the last few years, as artists have pushed royalties higher, the merchandisers built in limits on **hall fees.** We touched briefly on *hall fees* in the last chapter (on page 364), but now let's take a more detailed look.

Your merchandiser doesn't actually hire people to sell products in each of the venues. Instead, they make a deal with the hall to supply the personnel, display racks, etc. (Actually, as we noted in the prior chapter, it's the artist's agent who makes the deal with the hall, although the merchandiser may assist.) It works like this:

The merchandiser pulls up its truck early in the day, checks in a certain quantity of merchandise to the hall personnel, and at the end of the evening gets back the unsold merchandise plus cash for what's been sold or otherwise disappeared. From the money that's turned over, the venue keeps a percentage, and this is the hall fee. It covers the cost of hiring the people who actually sell and the venue's profit, and often includes a charge for bootleg security (more about that in a minute). (By the way, not all venues actually supply the merchandise personnel themselves. There are a couple of companies that contract with venues to supply these people, pay the hall a percentage, and keep the difference as profit.)

A standard hall fee is from 30% to 35% of the gross monies collected for the merchandise, and superstars can knock it down to about 25% (or even lower in rare instances). So if you sold $10,000 of merchandise, the hall would keep 30% to 35% ($3,000 to $3,500) and pay the balance to the merchandiser. (These are U.S. numbers; you can sometimes get lower fees in foreign markets.)

Historically, the royalties paid by merchandisers to the artist were based on gross sales without regard to hall fees. So the hall fees never affected the artist. However, as artists demanded higher and higher merchandising royalties, the merchandisers finally had their profits squeezed so tightly that they began making artists responsible for hall fees above a certain percentage. So today's deals almost always set a limit on the hall fees, and if you go over it, the excess comes out of your royalties. For example, a merchandise deal might say that you have a royalty of 37% and that the hall fee cannot exceed 30%. Under this deal, if your hall fee for a particular date was 35% (i.e., 5% more than the allowed 30%), the extra 5% would come out of your royalty, and instead of 37% you would only get 32%.

By the way, unless you ask, you won't get any part of the savings from keeping hall fees below the maximum level. If you do ask, you can usually get a percentage (50% to 75%) of the savings. In the above example, if you got 50% of the hall savings below 30%, and if you pushed the hall fee down to 25% (i.e., you saved 5% below the 30% maximum), your royalty would increase from 37% to 39.5% (the 37% royalty plus 2.5% for 50% of the 5% hall fee reduction). Your argument to win this point is that if you don't share in the decrease, you don't have any incentive to do it.

Another deal that's becoming more common is simply to pay the artist a combined royalty/hall fee percentage of, say, 65% to 70%. Under a 65% deal, for example, if the hall fee was 30%, the artist would get a 35% royalty; if the hall fee was 25%, the artist would get 40%; etc. In other words, the artist gets 100% of the hall fee savings, as well as 100% of the burden for higher fees.

As noted above, hall fees are negotiated by the agent (at the same time they make the overall deal for the guarantee, splits, etc.). Ironically, the agent doesn't get paid for this—the agent's commission is based on the earnings of the artist from the performance only, and not from merchandising. So the agent is in the position of negotiating a part of the deal that gives him or her no benefit. However, their incentive goes way up when the artist glares daggers at them, and so they have gotten quite good at muscling down the hall percentages.

ADVANCES

As you learned from record and publishing deals, where there are royalties, there are advances. And merchandising is just such a place. Unfortunately, they're not nearly as favorable as record and publishing advances, because they're almost always returnable, and they sometimes bear interest. We'll discuss these conditions in a minute.

Merchandising advances are usually paid over the course of a tour. For example, if your merchandising advance is $250,000, you might get $50,000 when you sign the deal, $100,000 one-third of the way through the tour, and the balance two-thirds of the way through. As your bargaining power goes up, you get more of the advance sooner.

When you get an advance, the merchandisers require you to perform for a minimum number of people, and at a minimum number of shows and/or cities (this is discussed on detail on page 379). They also want the tour to start within a reasonable period after signing (say ninety days), or else they can get out of the deal and/or charge you interest on the advance. And if they decide to get out, they want back the money they gave you plus interest. (There are other things that trigger paybacks, which we'll discuss in a minute.)

The size of the advance is based on a projection of your gross sales times your royalty rate. It will also vary with the size of the tour—the more bodies you play in front of, the more merchandise you can sell. Advances will also be higher if the deal includes retail merchandising (which we'll discuss in the next chapter). Because they are so deal-specific, it's hard to give you any hard and fast numbers. The broad range is anywhere from nothing to $10,000 or $20,000 for a baby act, to several million for a superstar.

TERM

The term of most merchandising agreements is one album cycle, or until the advance is recouped, whichever is *longer* (note this means the deal could go on forever). An album cycle is usually defined as beginning on the date of release of your album, and ending sixty days prior to release of the next album. If you have this kind of deal, you'll want to add an outside date of say three years, in case there never is a 'next album.' (The three years would also be extended if you're unrecouped.) If the deal isn't based on an album cycle, it'll be based on your tour cycle, which means it continues until the end of the tour (or until recoupment, if longer).

When you're negotiating, try to get the right to repay the advance and terminate the deal during extensions for non-recoupment, so that you don't find yourself with a perpetual merchandiser. For example, if you have a tour cycle term with an extension until recoupment, and at the end of the cycle you have recouped all but $10,000 of a $200,000 advance, it means you've done pretty well. However, if you don't have the right to repay, the term would continue until you recoup. Thus, the merchandiser would get your next tour automatically and for no advance. If you have the right to repay, however, you can write them a check for $10,000 (which would be more than covered by the advance you get for your next tour), and move on. Or more commonly, you rattle your saber by threatening to repay the advance, which brings the merchandiser to the negotiating table and gets them to pay you an additional advance and make a new deal. (Note this payback right can only be good for you. If the unrecouped amount is very large, it means something is seriously wrong and you won't leave because no one else wants you; if it's a small amount, you want the ability to pay them off and renegotiate the deal for the next tour. For this very reason, this provision is also getting harder to come by.)

ADVANCE REPAYMENT

As noted above, unlike record and publishing deals, tour merchandise contracts require repayment of the advance, generally with interest, under circumstances like:

- The tour doesn't start on time.
- You're disabled or otherwise unable to perform all or part of the tour. This is based on the same theory as the tour not starting on time, and also protects them from the possibility that you might not tour for years, after which the public has forgotten you exist.
- You don't meet a **performance minimum** (which is discussed in the next section). This means you agreed to play before a certain number of people and fell short.

Most companies want back the entire advance if you fall short of your *performance minimum,* but you should try to get a pro-rata formula based on how many people you actually played for. For example, if you agreed to play before 200,000 people, but only played before 100,000, you would only want to pay back one-half (100,000/200,000) of the advance.

A compromise is that the merchandiser agrees to pro-rate if you hit a certain percentage of your performance guarantee. In other words, if you only played for 10% of the people, they may not be willing to give you any credit whatsoever. The usual requirement is that you must hit 50% to 90% (depending on bargaining power) of the performance minimum before you get the benefit of pro-rating the advance. For example, if you agreed to perform before 200,000 people and you had to hit 50% before you could pro-rate your advance repayment, you would need to perform before at least 100,000. If you didn't, then you would have to pay back the entire advance (though see the next paragraph). If you did, then you'd only have to pay 50% of the advance (because you played to 50% of the people). If you played to 150,000 people (which is 75% of the 200,000), you'd only have to pay back 25% of the advance.

When you negotiate all of these, it is *absolutely imperative* to make sure you don't have to pay back any more than your unrecouped balance. For example, if you only hit half your performance criteria and owe back half the advance, but you're recouped, you shouldn't owe the merchandiser anything—the company shouldn't have the right to get its money back more than once. However, I have yet to see a form that gives this to you if you don't ask.

PERFORMANCE MINIMUM

The requirement to perform for a minimum number of people (called the **performance minimum** or **performance requirement**) isn't nearly as simple as it sounds, and over the years has gotten pretty complex. Let's first look at why it's important.

How successful you are in selling merchandise is calculated in terms of **per-head** amounts, meaning the average money spent by every head that attends the concert. For example, if 10,000 people attend a show, and your merchandising gross revenue is $30,000, you did $3 *per head*. Since this is how merchandisers measure sales, you can see why they want you to guarantee how many warm bodies will pass before their merchandising stands. Thus, merchandising deals require a minimum number of people to attend your shows.

So, figuring out how many people attended your shows (to meet your performance criteria) should be pretty simple—just count heads, right? *Wrong.*

Paid Attendees. First, the only people who count are those who *paid* to see your show. The theory is that people who get freebies are lousy merchandise buyers, so they're excluded from the count.

Adjustments. Second, there are two important adjustments to the paid attendee number:

1. **Stadium Shows.**

(meaning venues of roughly 20,000 plus) are treated differently, because the per-head amounts tend to be lower at these shows. This is logical; since there are so many people, they can't all be die-hard fans. This effect is magnified if there are a number of headlining acts (like a festival), because a lot of people came to see another artist. And at festivals, a lot of people buy event T-shirts instead of the individual artists'. Thus, stadium per-head figures are usually less.

Some contracts try to exclude stadium shows altogether, meaning the attendees don't count against your performance guarantee. This isn't fair, because you will sell merchandise, even if it's less per head than other shows. The usual compromise is to count a negotiated portion of the people at stadium shows (like one person counts only as one-half or two-thirds of a paid attendee). I prefer, however, tying the reduction to the per-head figures at the stadium show over the average per-head figures for other shows, which may mean little or no adjustment. For example, if your tour averages $3 per head in merchandising for normal shows, and you have two stadium shows where you average $2 per head, then two-thirds of the stadium paid attendees (the $2 per head stadium figure over the $3 per head average) count toward your *performance minimum*. Thus, if 30,000 people showed up at the stadium, 20,000 would count.

2. **Foreign.**

The second adjustment is for performances outside the United States. This is again either a negotiated fraction (one-half, two-thirds, etc.), or else a reduction based on the per-head figures in the territory involved versus the United States per-head figures. For example, if your United States merchandising averages $2 per head, but in England your average is only $1 per head, then each person in England would count as one-half ($1/$2) of a paid attendee for purposes of meeting your requirement.

If you're a major international act, you can negotiate specific attendance figures for each territory (e.g., you agree to play for 50,000 people in Germany), and then there is none of this adjusting (except for stadium shows). This is really just saying the same thing in different words: A 50,000-person requirement that counts people as one-half each is the same as agreeing to play for 25,000 people.

EXCLUSIVITY

Tour merchandise deals require some exclusivity, which is normally a statement that you can't sell your merchandise within twenty miles of a concert site, within forty-eight hours prior to the show. Be sure you exclude retail sales from this (you might find yourself in breach of both your concert and your retail sales agreements if you don't), and you should also exclude any record company promotions (such as a T-shirt or poster giveaways to promote your album). If you have a tour sponsor or have done a commercial, and they have the right to give away or sell merchandise, you have to deal with this specifically in your merchandising agreement—and your merchandiser isn't going to like it very much. So be extremely careful in giving these rights to a commercial sponsor. The usual compromise is to limit the amount of merchandise the sponsor can give away within a few days before the concert, which is in both your and the merchandiser's interest. (If the sponsor gives all your fans a T-shirt just before the show, your concert sales won't be so hot.)

CREATIVE CONTROL

You should have the right to approve the design, artwork, photos, drawings, layout, etc., used in all merchandise, as well as the quality of the goods themselves.

For the most part, merchandising companies give you creative approval without much of a fight (in stark contrast to the wrestling match you have with your record company over these same issues).

If you have a federally registered service mark for your name, you need to approve the quality in order to preserve your mark's legal status. (As we discussed on page 341, a service mark is like a trademark; it's your group's or individual professional name.) Even if you haven't registered your mark, however, you should still insist on approving quality for purposes of maintaining your claims in the name, as well as keeping your image up.

SELL-OFF RIGHTS

At the end of the term, the merchandiser wants the right to sell off any remaining merchandise. This is usually for a period of six months, and they should have no right to *manufacture,* only to sell whatever is on hand. They will ask for the right to sell it through wholesale (meaning retail) outlets, since there won't be any concerts. You get a royalty for these sales, which is the same as if they were sold under a retail deal (see the discussion of retail royalties on page 385).

Here are some other things to ask for, which are very similar to the sell-off rights under print music deals which we discussed on page 243:

1. The right to sell off must be totally non-exclusive, so you can have another merchandiser in place.
2. The merchandiser can't **stockpile** goods. This means it can't manufacture a ton of goods right before the end, so that the company has a lot of leftovers to sell. You should get language that restricts manufacturing to 'only such quantity of goods as is necessary to meet reasonably anticipated sales requirements.'
3. Merchandisers can't have **distress sales,** meaning they can't sell your goods at low prices just to get rid of them. (This practice is also called **dumping.**) Otherwise, you'll be adorning a lot of Kmart shoppers and swap-meet fans. It also perturbs your new merchandiser, who is trying to sell your stuff at full price. However, this has become extremely hard to get over the years, as merchandisers' profits have been squeezed, and their tolerance for dining on left-over goods has been stretched to the regurgitation point.
4. You should have the right to purchase, at cost, the merchandise at the end of the term. And if you buy it, the merchandiser has no sell-off rights at all. (If you don't, the merchandiser gets a six-month sell-off period, and at the end of that you should have a second right to purchase the leftovers.) *Never* take the *obligation* to repurchase; if they can't sell this crap, why would you think you can? But always take the *option*—if you're successful, your next merchandiser may want it.
5. At the end of the sell-off period, they have to destroy anything you don't buy, or else donate it to a charity.

BOOTLEGGERS

Merchandisers want the right, and you should encourage them, to chase **bootleggers.** *Bootleggers* (as the name implies from its original usage during Prohibition, where bootleggers sold illegal booze) are people who, without any authority, manufacture merchandise with your name and/or likeness on it, and sell it outside the venues. Legitimate merchandisers are always inside the facility; bootleggers are the guys who hit you on the street or in the parking lot approaching the building. (One of their better tricks is to hire college students for $100 or so per night, so the vendors look wholesome, clean-cut, and somewhat innocent, while the manufacturers stay out of sight.) Not only are these people costing you money because you don't get paid for the merchandise, but their goods are usually of inferior quality. And guess who gets the complaint letters when some Schenectady fan's T-shirt shrinks to fit her Barbie doll?

The legitimate merchandisers have been relatively successful in dealing with these pieces of slime, and have discovered that in many cases they are large, sophisticated operations (one even owned its own T-shirt factory). Through means I'm not free to tell you, the merchandisers have been able to track the bootleggers down, and then get the courts to stop them. Thus, over the last few years, at least in the United States, this practice has decreased. (The laws abroad aren't always so hospitable.) The merchandisers will ask you to pay part of the money to chase the pirates, but if you have some clout, they'll front it and have you bear a percentage out of either the recovery and/or your other royalties.

25

Retail Merchandising

Retail merchandising means all the non-concert ways of selling merchandise—retail stores (poster shops, Wal-Mart, Gucci, etc.), mail order, Internet, fan clubs, etc.

The *retail merchandiser* acts not only as a manufacturer/distributor (as you would expect), but also as a middleman between you and other merchandisers. Since there are tons of small companies that specialize in particular areas (posters, buttons, belt buckles, stickers, patches, trading cards, condoms, etc.), it's better to license some of these rights to an expert. Also, it's not economical for the merchandisers to engage in all these areas, since they're not great profit centers compared to clothing. Thus, retail merchandisers are only apparel manufacturers, and they sublicense these smaller rights (meaning they license out the rights to someone else). The merchandisers keep a percentage of the license income, ranging generally from 15% to 25%. In other words, they make a deal with a bumper-sticker company to manufacture and sell bumper stickers with your name, then pay you 75% to 85% of the royalties and advances they get from the sticker company. In exchange for their percentage, they negotiate and sign the license agreement, and afterward 'police' it (read: 'make sure you get paid'). Because entering into a number of these licensing agreements yourself is best described as a 'pain in the butt for small money,' paying this percentage is usually worth it. As you move further into the superstar realm, you may want to make some of these deals directly, but only as the numbers get pretty big.

ROYALTIES

The royalties merchandisers pay you when they manufacture the goods themselves (as well as the royalties they get when they license someone else to manufacture) are generally in the following range (for the United States):

1. **Sales through retail stores:** 15% to 25% of the wholesale price. This includes T-shirts, sweatshirts, hats, posters, buttons, cards, bumper stickers, belt buckles, etc. These rates are for top-line retailers. For the midlevel stores (JCPenney, Sears, etc.) you'll get 75% of these rates, and for mass-marketers (KMart, Wal-Mart, Target) you'll get 50%. The reason for lower royalties is simple: Stores that push out tons of merchandise have a lot of clout, and they beat up the merchandise distributor to give them lower prices. So in that great schoolyard tradition, he who is beaten up, beats up the next smaller person (you).

2. **Mail-order sales:** 25% of the price charged. This is higher because they are, in this case, the actual retailers selling directly to the public, and there is no distributor taking a profit in the middle. Thus, they get more for the goods than when they sell them to a wholesaler.

3. **Internet sales:** Internet sales (such as ArtistDirect and Music-Today) are treated just like retail sales. This is because the Internet company buys finished goods from your merchandiser (since your deals are exclusive, you're not allowed to create your own) and then resells them just like a store. So you get the normal royalty set out in items 1 and 2 above. However, some of these sites also make deals directly with artists, so they can present that artist's 'experience' online. In that case, they pay you an additional royalty (usually around 10% of retail) for these sales—so you get paid twice.

Foreign royalties are roughly 80% of the U.S. rates.

OTHER DEAL POINTS

When you make a retail merchandise deal, many of the considerations are exactly the same as tour merchandising deals, such as:

1. Approval of the merchandise items
2. Approval of your likeness
3. Approval of the designs and layout
4. Restrictions on sell-off rights
5. Right to purchase merchandise at the end

In addition, there are a couple of points peculiar to retail:

Approval of Sublicenses.   You want the right to approve all agreements they make with sublicensees concerning your product.

Cross-Collateralization.   If your retail agreement is with the same company that has your tour merchandise (which it almost always is), you have to deal with whether the advance under the tour agreement is cross-collateralized with the retail deal (and vice versa). (For a discussion of cross-collateralization, see page 88.) Cross-collateralization is never good for you; allow it only if they offer you a humongous amount of money that you can't get any other way.

If you're on the *Fast Track* and
you're interested in Classical Music, go to Chapter 26 on page 389.
If you hate Classical and want to explore Music and New Technologies, go to Chapter 27 on page 395.
If both of those sound boring, saunter on over to Motion Picture Music in Chapter 28 on page 407.
If you answered 'None of the above,' *Fast Track* to the Conclusion on page 451.

CAUTION

Before you tackle the rest of the book, be sure you have a pretty good understanding of record and publishing basics in Chapters 7, 8, 15, 16, and 18. If you skipped ahead and don't already know this stuff, I suggest you go back. Even if you're reading straight through, you might want to review these chapters quickly. The areas we're about to discuss are a bit complex, so be sure you have a solid grasp of the basics before attempting them.

Now hang on to the safety bar and keep your arms and legs inside the car.

PART VII

Classical Music

26

Classical Music

I shall now tap my baton on the music stand to politely engage your attention, as we move into the world of classical music. Please do not applaud between movements, and speak only in quiet, mellifluous tones for the duration of this chapter.

• • •

The principles of royalty, advance, etc. are the same for classical as for rock and all other kinds of music. In particular, **cross-over** artists like Andrea Bocelli (*cross-over* meaning their appeal extends beyond the classical market) have deals that are virtually identical to the contracts we've discussed for pop artists. At the other end of the equation are the older, traditional, pure classical deals, which look quite different. These 'classical classical' deals have become rare over the last few years for one simple reason: Their economics suck. Classical records are very expensive to make and have limited sales potential. So unless you're a major-name classical artist, the deals are very hard to come by, and when they do get made, they have very modest terms.

TERM AND PRODUCT

Because classical artists don't generally compose the material they record, and because their recordings are in essence 'live performances,' they can make records much faster and more often than pop artists. Also, since the compositions already exist, the recordings can be planned very far in advance, which is not generally possible in the pop world. So for both of these reasons, classical artists can record several albums per year. And in fact, historically, classical deals would commit the company and artist to two or three albums per year, and the terms would be for several years firm. However, as the classical market continues to shrink (or at least not grow), while costs continue to rise, multi-album deals have dropped off radically, and are rare except for very significant artists. Instead, similar to pop deals, the record company has options for one year at a time, and one album at a time.

ROYALTIES

As noted above, the economics of classical music are quite different because the potential sales are so much smaller, and the costs of recording can be quite large. For example, the cost of recording with a full orchestra can run $150,000 to $400,000, and typical album sales are in the 5,000 to 10,000 unit range *worldwide* (the sales levels that we've been using for pop artists are only for the United States). In fact, a 'big seller' is 50,000 or more worldwide.

In light of the low sales levels, you won't be surprised to hear that royalties in the classical world are also lower. The good news, however, is that you're paid on every record sold, meaning the company eats all of the recording costs. In other words, the only thing recouped is the advance you put in your pocket. This is a radical difference from the pop world, where the company will recoup anything it can get its hands on (remember, in this section, we're talking about the traditional classical deal, not the cross-over artists whose recording costs are recouped just like pop artists).

How much lower are the royalties? A typical deal is in the range of 7.5% to 10% of SRLP (pop music royalty ranges are on page 93). However, classical artist's royalties aren't 'all-in' (see page 98), which means you aren't responsible for a producer, and thus you keep all of the royalties (though you often have to share them, as noted in the next paragraph).

In classical, unlike pop, albums are often amalgamations of several different artists. This means that the royalties get spread around. Important guest soloists get a royalty, and so do major conductors and very successful orchestras. In fact, it's sometimes difficult to tell whose album it is. For example, is an album on which Leonard Wheezebottom, violin virtuoso, performs with the Tarzana Symphony (Jay-Z conducting), a Jay-Z, Tarzana, or Wheezebottom album?

Just like joint recordings on the pop side (see page 171 for what those are), the royalties are allocated in an agreed manner among the participants. While there's no hard and fast rule, a principal soloist might get 4% to 5% of SRLP, a conductor 1% to 2%, a guest soloist 2% to 3%, and a well-known orchestra 1% to 2%.

ADVANCES

As noted above, a typical classical release sells far less units than a typical pop release (or at least less than what the pop company hopes to sell). So because of this, advances are much smaller, typically in the range of $5,000 to $10,000 per album. If an artist has 'marquee value,' meaning that his or her name is recognizable (e.g., Yo-Yo Ma, Luciano Pavarotti, John Williams, etc.), the advance is generally from $15,000 to $50,000.

The size of an advance also depends on:

1. The extent you participate in the recording. If you're only guesting, for example, your advance will be lower than if you're the principal soloist.
2. The type of work being recorded. If you're the principal piano soloist on a recording, for example, you'll get a lower advance for an orchestral recording (which is expensive) than you will for a recording of piano solo works (where they just set up a microphone and drop a few bucks in your brandy snifter).
3. And lastly, your advance depends on that common denominator of all business: clout and leverage.

MECHANICAL ROYALTIES

Much of classical music is in the public domain, which means that no mechanical royalties are paid for the music (see page 312 for a discussion of public domain, and page 212 for a discussion of mechanical royalties). However, some of the compositions may be more recent, or even contemporary, and thus mechanical royalties have to be paid to the publishers of these works. Also, arrangements of public domain works are copyrightable if they have enough originality, and mechanical royalties have to be paid for the arrangement.

When mechanical royalties are paid, there is often a reduction of your royalty. You are usually charged about half of the burden, although this is negotiable, and it's not always as simple as I've just stated. For example, sometimes the contract just says that your royalty rate goes down a point or two if the company has to pay mechanicals. By an amazing coincidence, this also results in your eating about half of the mechanicals.

MARKETING TIE-INS

Because of the limited market for classical recordings, the companies have been looking for alternative ways to market their albums. For example, a great way to move product is for you to appear in a public television special, perform a concert tour, etc. If you have some clout, you can get the company to commit money to these ventures. For example, you might get tour support (which we discussed on page 153). Or get some help with a PBS special. While these TV shows move records nicely, they're very expensive—public television only pays $50,000 to $100,000 for their programs, while the costs can easily run $500,000 to $700,000 or more. (You might get some money back from selling the show to foreign television, but it's not usually much.) So the rest has to come from somewhere—guess where? And if the record company picks up the shortfall, what they spend (or only 50% of it, if you push them) will be recoupable from your record royalties.

If you're on the *Fast Track,* and you're interested in
Music and New Technologies, go to Chapter 27 on page 395.
If you're interested in Motion Picture Music, go to Chapter 28 on page 407.
Otherwise, *Fast Track* to the Conclusion on page 451.

PART VIII

Music and New Technologies

27

Music and New Technologies

Boy, oh boy, oh boy. Is this chapter a challenge . . .

Basically, I've torched the last edition's new technology chapter, which was embarrassingly out of date. This one may soon be as well, but I'll do the best I can and try to stick to general principles. You'll also get my predictions for the future—a completely stupid thing for me to do, because no one has guessed correctly so far—but I can always ditch them in the following edition and try again.

The good news is that things are changing so rapidly that the laws and customs haven't hardened into stone (or even soft rock). So those of us who've been in the music business for years don't have much more expertise than you do. Maybe we have even less, because a lot of old-timers have trouble working microwave ovens, much less computers.

Let's start out with a peek at where we are (at the time of this writing anyway):

WHAT'S GOING ON TODAY?

I'm told that music is the second-most popular thing on the Internet. (Can you guess the first? If not, see the answer at the end of this chapter on page 403.)

The current musical activities are:

1. **Promotional websites,** which have information available for reading and downloading (meaning copying onto your personal computer), such as publicity materials, photos of artists, tour schedules, and sound samples. A lot of record companies have these kind of websites, as do a large number of artists (many artists have more than one, and a lot of them are unauthorized, created by fans).

2. **Chat rooms,** where you can connect with a bunch of other people interested in the same subject and talk back and forth through your keyboards. There are a number of music chat lines around, where fans can trade information and gossip, and you can find them on any search engine. There's also an 'insiders' industry chat line, the location of which is pretty well guarded, and in fact I've never seen it. I'm told that record company executives go in there under phony names and trash each other.

3. **Bulletin boards,** which are places to read electronic messages, and also where you can leave messages for other people to read. A lot of artists have bulletin boards devoted to them.

4. **Webcasters,** which are basically radio stations that play music on the Internet in **real time** (which means you get it almost at the same instant they're sending it). As of this writing, the sound quality is nowhere near that of CDs. (We discussed webcasting on page 307.)

5. **Authorized commercial sites,** which consist of two distinct catagories:
   (a) **Packaged goods.** Sites such as Amazon and CDNOW sell traditional packaged goods by taking orders online and shipping them to the consumer.
   (b) **Electronic sites,** which deliver music electronically. Examples are Apple's iTunes Music Store, MusicNet and Press-Play (both owned by combinations of the major record companies), Listen.com, and EMusic. MusicNet and PressPlay sell both streaming-on-demand, tethered downloads, and permanent (untethered) downloads (we discussed all of these on page 167).

6. **Unauthorized file sharing sites,** such as KaZaA, Morpheus, Napster, and their spawn, which allow people to copy music off each other's computers for free. Basically, these sites help people hook up with each other, so they can swap files. I'm sure you've never heard of this before . . .

THE LAWS OF THE ELECTRONIC FRONTIER

The laws here are still evolving (and will be for years), as they try mightily to adapt themselves to new technologies that arrive hourly. And any time you have a concept created in 1909 being applied to things that weren't even conceived at the time, you create a healthy fund to put lawyers' children through college. See, Internet usages aren't quite records, aren't quite radio, and aren't quite television. Or maybe they're all of them.

So far, pirates have run rampant (though they're slowing down a little, as we'll discuss in a minute). And everyone owning intellectual property is at jeopardy in this new world. Films, television, books, you name it. Music is getting it first, because (1) there's a lot less digital information on a CD than, for example, a DVD of a movie, which means that music moves around the Net a lot faster than films (you can get plenty of movies online, usually within days after (and sometimes before) they hit the theaters, but it takes all night to download them); (2) the demographics of Internet users match those of music lovers pretty closely; and (3) college students with lots of time and free, high-speed Internet connections love to thumb their noses at the establishment (although a recent study showed that most of the downloading through university computers was done by non-students! They were outsiders looking for the fastest connections, which are university high-speed lines).

Until recently, the courts protected the rights of owners pretty well. In a pioneer case, *Playboy* sued an outfit that was putting up centerfolds and allowing people to download them. *Playboy* annihilated these shlumps in court, and won a judgment that the site infringed *Playboy*'s right to distribute and to display the pictures and violated *Playboy*'s trademark (see page 340). They also won on two other legal theories. (For you lawyers, the other theories were (a) unfair competition and passing off, by not attributing ownership of the photos to *Playboy*; and (b) the decision that these activities weren't a 'fair use.' The case is *Playboy Enterprises v. Frena,* 839 F. Supp. 1552 [1993].)

The major cases in the music area are MyMP3 (*UMG Recordings et al. v. MP3.com, Inc.,* 92 F. Supp 2d 349 [2000]), Napster (*A&M Records Inc., et al. v. Napster, Inc.,* 239 F.3d 1004 [2001]), and Farm Club (*Rodgers and Hammerstein Organization, et al. v. UMG Recordings, Inc. and the Farm Club Online, Inc.,* (60 U.S. P.Q. 2D [BNA] 1354 [2001]). Though the facts and legal theories varied in each of these, the bottom line is that putting music online without permission is a no-no, and the courts slap your hand (or some other vital part).

However, in April 2003, one federal court took an abrupt left turn on the music and film biz. In this case, the music and film folk sued Grokster and Morpheus, distributors of software that allows people to search and swap music and video files. But unlike Napster, there was no central server to hook them up (the central server was a major reason why the court shut down Napster).

While the decision was pretty technical, the gist was that the software distributors were like the manufacturers of copying machines and video recorders, and couldn't be held responsible for people using their software to steal copyrights (I'm oversimplifying a very complex decision). The judge said this was true even though the software distributors made a lot of money by zapping ads at their users, and even though they could technologically prevent infringement of copyrighted works.

Not surprisingly, the music and film companies are appealing, and it may have been decided by the time this book gets into your hands. (I can't give you a case cite because there is none as I write this.) To my mind, this is a wrong decision. However you whack it up, the primary purpose of this software is to help people steal copyrighted works, as I seriously doubt there's a lot of folks swapping Shakespeare and Mother Goose. And the idea that someone can profit from this, and escape any responsibility, shouldn't fly.

By the way, I get that some of you think this is very cool. And that free speech means unchaining things from copyright. The problem is that it will be impossible to make a living as a musician if this becomes the law. And I have an example from history to prove it:

In 1789, France had themselves a little revolutionary party. Not only did they lop off the heads of Louis and Marie Antoinette, they also lopped off their copyright laws—in the same spirit of freeing intellectual property for the people. What happened was that about thirty percent of the publishers went broke, because everybody printed up the popular works. The ones who survived took to publishing current news and getting it out fast, before anybody else could copy it (a concept that obviously wouldn't work in today's Internet world of the fast jam). Under these conditions, there was no reason for publishers to invest money in something everybody else could take for free, so writers had no reason to spend the time or energy to create anything of importance. And this could be you . . .

What ultimately happened in France? About three years later, they reinstated the copyright law.

And now, back to the twenty-first century. The Grokster decision isn't as totally bleak for intellectual property rights as the French musketeers. Specifically, the ruling refers to the fact that a lot of people are using the software to *infringe copyrights*. Which means that, while the court didn't think the software folks were guilty of infringement, it didn't say the *users* of their software were exempt. In fact, the RIAA has sued the most flagrant of these users—people who put up thousands of songs for others to copy—and they recently settled the first of these suits against college kids who were "sharing" huge numbers of files (for about $17,000 per kid). So if the Grokster decision stands, it forces the record companies to go after consumers. Not great for publicity, but the only legal choice left them.

While going to court works as a matter of law—and works even better if Grokster is overturned—it's essentially a game of 'Whack the Mole,' meaning other pirates pop up as soon as you squash the ones you can find. But there's an even bigger problem: what if the pirate isn't in the United States, but in some evil empire where copyrights are used for cocktail napkins? As I write this, KaZaA is hopping around islands in the South Pacific (lying in the shade of laid-back Vanuatu copyright laws, to be exact), trying to stay away from record company lawsuits. So even though U.S. law has protected the rights holders, other countries may not be so hospitable.

Despite these difficulties, the record companies are making progress on the piracy front. As I'm sure you've noticed, a lot of the biggest pirates (Napster, Audiogalaxy, Morpheus) have gone away. This was based on lawsuits, or the threat of lawsuits. In addition, some of the companies have taken more practical measures. For example, some have been 'spoofing,' which means they take a popular download target (this was done with Eminem's singles, for example), loop a small part of it over and over, then put up thousands of files on the Internet. So when people try to copy the real song, they end up with the continuous loops.

Piracy is really serious business. I know it seems like innocent fun— downloading a few (hundred) music files in the privacy of your own room—but in essence, it's no different from sticking some CDs under your coat and walking out of a record store without paying. And if you want to make a living as a musician or executive in the music business, it's difficult to lower your prices enough to compete with 'free' and still eat.

NOW WHAT?

Industry Strategy

All of this has finally shaken up the record companies, who'd grown complacent after years of success and had ignored the problem until recently. The bad news is that it's happening at a time when the economy is shaky and the record companies are hemorrhaging money. Still, while downturns are painful in the short term, they're always healthy in the long term (assuming, of course, you believe there's a long term). That's because bad times weed out sloppy business practices and force people to come up with innovative ideas.

So the record companies are buckling down. In addition to cost-cutting and belt-tightening, the industry has adopted the following strategy for the digital age:

1. Make piracy more difficult (as we just discussed);
2. Put on an educational campaign to tell consumers that piracy is stealing (reminiscent of Nancy Reagan's 'Just Say No' to drugs campaign that was so successful); and
3. To my mind, the most important: inching toward an author-ized online service that maybe somebody wants.

At the time of this writing, they're doing better at 1 and 2 than they are at 3.

The current mess is a situation where a technology has outrun the intellectual property holder's rights to control their works. Past exam-ples are VCRs (if you didn't know, a film studio sued, and went all the way to the Supreme Court, to keep VCRs off the market—and ironi-cally, home video is now one of the studios' largest income sources), pay TV (the movie people feared uncut movies at home would keep folks out of theaters), and photocopy machines (people were upset over the unrestrained copying of copyrighted materials).

It seems to me—and I'm going off into personal opinion here (al-though much of it comes from friends' opinions that I'm pilfering to make myself look smarter)—that while it's useful to make piracy more difficult, that's only a leapfrog game, meaning pirates find new ways to outwit the protections, then the rights holders find new ways to pro-tect, which the pirates figure out how to defeat, and so on ad nauseam. I think the real answer is for the industry to provide an alternative which is of better quality and easier to use than the crude pirate sites, as I believe people will pay a reasonable amount for that. Of course there will always be stealing; there's stealing in every business. But most peo-ple are honest if given the alternative, especially if it's a better-quality product.

One analogy is the pornography business. You can get all the free porno you want on the Internet (or so I'm told . . .), yet people pay billions to get it through pay sites. Why? To have it organized, easy to use, and presumably better quality. So, on the music side, I believe if we build it, they will come. The industry is certainly moving in this direction, although at the time of this writing the legitimate services are cumbersome and incomplete. Hopefully by the time you read this, they'll be (most of the way) there. In fact, as I write this, Apple just launched a download service that looks like it might work.

In fairness, none of us in the industry have made this an easy go. For years, record companies were precious about putting their music online without some kind of **DRM** (**Digital Rights Management,** meaning copy-protections and the like), while pirates delivered exactly what the companies held back. Folks in the artist and publishing community were (and remain) afraid to give long-term licenses, because no one knows what the business and economics are going to look like. And historically, with the introduction of each new format (cassettes and compact discs, for example), artists got less than a fair share at the outset. It took years to move artist compensation up, and we don't want to repeat the same mistakes here. So artists and publishers haven't been terribly cooperative in allowing these things to go forward, and the creative community is as much to blame as the companies for not solving this.

At least now the pain is so intense that people have to deal with it. Which they're starting to do. Sl . . . ow . . . ly. And if creators and companies don't get their act together privately, there's rumblings that the government may do it for us. In other words, Uncle Sam may force a compulsory license. Now while that's rarely a great solution for anybody, this may be one of the few situations where it becomes a necessity. For example, take a look at the webcasting situation (we discussed webcasting on page 285). The publishers, record companies, and webcasters couldn't agree on a rate to charge webcasters for the use of masters and songs, so everyone went to a Copyright Arbitration Royalty Panel (a governmental committee, run by the Copyright Office). After passionate arguments, and a lot of legal fees, the CARP set a rate that nobody liked, and currently both sides are appealing the decision. See what I mean?

So what's the solution? Who the hell knows. But here's a radical idea, just to stir things up:

One possibility is to make the music feel like it's cheap or even free, but indirectly compensate the creators (this comes from my friend Jim Griffin). The concept is a tax on blank CDs (as we previously discussed, there's been a tax on blank tapes in other countries for many years, to compensate musicians for lost earnings, and Germany recently enacted a similar tax on blank CDs and burners). The problem of course is that blank discs are used for things other than music, and the computer industry, which is very powerful in Congress, won't easily support something that could slow their sales.

Another possibility is a tax on Internet Service Providers (Earth Link, AOL, etc. who connect you to the Internet), so that everyone pays a few dollars each month as an 'entertainment charge' or something like that. Most people wouldn't get too out of joint for, say, three bucks a month, and this could make up hundreds of millions in lost revenue. That way, the online music services could charge very little, and make up the difference with the tax.

Still another thought is a tax added to cell-phone bills, as there's no doubt that cell phones will be delivering music in the future—you'll be able to call up any song you want on demand, and play it through your phone (which will have a jack for earphones), or even through a stereo. You already have some small, odd charges on your cell phone bill that I'll bet you've never noticed (take a look and see if I'm right), so another three dollars or so could go down more smoothly than you think. Ditto maybe for the cable and satellite TV industry, as music will be delivered that way as well.

While none of these would be particularly popular, and may not even be practical, the idea is to get folks thinking about how we can make this work for both consumers and the industry.

Other Fallout

What else might come out of the current storm? Well, possibly the death, or at least serious disabling, of the album format. Record companies like to sell albums, even if the consumer only wants one or two of the songs, because of the large profit margin. However, I'm convinced that a lot of people who won't shell out the expense of an album just to get one or two songs might well buy those songs separately. The idea would be to sell enough single songs to make up for what's lost on albums, which I think is very do-able.

Another advantage is that you, as an artist, wouldn't have to wait until you had twelve or thirteen songs before releasing an album, since you could put out a song or two anytime you're ready. Just because we haven't done it that way doesn't mean it wouldn't work (in fact, in the fifties and sixties, artists routinely put out singles without albums, because singles were a profit center back in those prehistoric times).

There's also been a lot of talk about artists no longer needing record companies. I don't see this happening so quickly, although it may be possible for established artists, particularly if they've developed an electronic fan base, to market their own records. Young artists can certainly put their music up on the Internet without needing anyone in between, but the problem is that *every* artist can put their music up that way. And with hundreds of new bands coming along each week, how does anyone ever break through the noise? That of course is the record company's job, since it's expensive and takes a lot of expertise. So while the record company of the future may look different from today's, I don't think it will disappear.

Good News?

So where's the good news? Well, we're learning there's still a very strong desire for music. We just haven't figured out how to harness it for the forces of good instead of evil. Another positive is that, once these technologies develop, we'll have a much more intimate relationship between the creator and the consumer. Right now, record companies don't really know who is buying their records. But when it's done electronically, while details would have to be anonymous out of respect for consumer privacy, at least you'd know if the buyer is living in a particular city, is male or female, and maybe an age demographic. And even if you couldn't get that info, you'd know what kind of music that buyer has ordered, which makes it easy to suggest similar artists as a marketing tool (like Amazon does now).

To sum up, I think things are going to be rough until we figure out this new era, then I think they'll be better than ever. It's my sincere belief (some would say foolishly) that most people are honest, and given a legitimate, easy-to-use, high-quality alternative, they'll take it over piracy.

Then again, I'm a bit of a Pollyanna.

Hold on to your hats, sunglasses, and small children.

Answer to question on page 395:

Music is the second most popular material on the Internet, behind only pornography (bet you suspected that, huh?)

PART IX

Motion Picture Music

28

Overview of Motion Picture Music

Congratulations again! You are now in graduate school. To understand music in films, you need a complete knowledge of the music business (records, copyrights, and publishing), as well as a knowledge of the film business. I couldn't have put this chapter earlier in the book, because you wouldn't have been ready for it. But now you are, so let's go.

INTRODUCTION

I have seen music screw up more motion pictures than bad directors. This is because music is a stepchild in movies. It's a small item compared to the budget of the film, and as you'll see, music in films is quite complicated. It is normally left to the last minute, at which point there's a massive panic and very little time to get it together properly. Often this is for good cause—it may not be possible to record the music until the studio knows exactly what the picture looks like—but many times it's simply a matter of neglect. As music supervisors become more important in the industry (more about who they are later), this seems to be changing (a little). However, there are always panicked emergencies, no matter what.

ONE SONG—SIX DEALS

One of the main difficulties is that film people, by and large, don't fully understand music (not that they should—their expertise is in making films). And it doesn't help that film music is complicated. For example, for every song going into a film, there are always deals to be made with at least three, and often up to six, entities:

1. The performer (singer/instrumental)
2. The songwriter
3. The publisher to whom the songwriter is signed
4. The record producer
5. The record company to whom the performer is signed
6. The record company putting out the soundtrack album

And if you have several songwriters signed to different publishers, several performers signed to different record companies, and a number of samples, you can get up to fifteen or twenty deals for one song!

If any of the above balls drop while you're juggling, or if any of the rights under one agreement don't match those required by another, the song may have to be trashed. And film producers on a tight delivery schedule with a multimillion-dollar film at stake don't like to be told a song is holding up their picture (would you?).

For all these reasons, the music supervisors/business affairs/lawyers/studio executives in charge of film music have extraordinarily difficult jobs. If they deliver the music and pull off minor miracles by balancing all the competing interests, it was expected and they're lucky to get a thanks. However, if something goes wrong and the film producer can't use a song, they're the villains. Wanna sign up?

All in all, if I were going to sum up clearing music for films, I'd describe it (as we say in Texas) like being a one-legged man in an ass-kicking contest. But it's fun and satisfying when it works, and if you're strong of heart, come along and I'll show you this side of the business.

THE RIGHTS INVOLVED

Film music rights fall into two categories:

Acquisition of rights for the picture.   These are deals to put music in the film, meaning deals with:

1. Performing artists
2. Songwriters, composers, publishers
3. Record producers
4. Record companies (both for using existing masters or samples in the film, and for clearing the right to put new recordings of their artists in the film)

Licenses of rights from the picture company to others. Once the film company acquires the rights, these are the deals to let other people use them:

1. A deal with a record company to release a soundtrack album
2. Licensing film clips for music videos
3. Possibly a publishing administration deal

Category 1 will be our focus, since it's the main area that will concern you. But I want to give you a feel for the second area as well, so it's sprinkled throughout the discussion, and dealt with in depth in Chapter 34.

29

Performer Deals

OVERVIEW

The deal for an artist to perform in a film consists of two distinct parts. One is to perform in the picture itself (which is pretty simple and straightforward), and the other is to use the performance on a sound-track album and/or single (which can be horrendous).

PERFORMANCE IN THE FILM (NO RECORD RIGHTS)

The deal for an artist to perform a song in a picture is usually for a flat fee. No muss, no fuss, no complications. Remember, as we discussed on page 143, that most record deals say that the record company owns all 'recordings' made during the term, which is broad enough to include film recordings. Also, home video devices of the film require the record company's consent, because these devices are treated as 'records,' as discussed on page 69. So the record company becomes a cozy partner in these deals, usually wanting a nice chunk of the fee. Often they'll want all of it, but will graciously apply half against your account. However, this is negotiable.

Fees

The artist's fee can range anywhere from union scale (see page 87 for what that is) up to $100,000 plus for a major artist. The norm is about $5,000 to $10,000 for a minor artist, escalating to perhaps $15,000 to $25,000 for a midlevel artist. Superstars tend to be in the $50,000 to $75,000 range, with some occasionally going higher if the film company is hot for them and the star is playing hard to get. Title songs (i.e., songs played over the opening or closing credits) usually pay better than background music.

Featured instrumentalists get fees in the range of $10,000 to $20,000 or so for lesser-knowns, and sometimes as high as $50,000 for big names.

There is a recent trend to bring in vocalists the same way that featured instrumentalists are brought in—sort of like being a 'vocal instrumental.' Usually it's someone well-known in their particular genre, like opera, Native American chanting, fraternity songs, etc. These folks usually get a fee of about $10,000 or so per track; more if they're well-known and their vocal might help sell albums.

Larger fees are often all or partly an advance against royalties (we'll discuss royalties in a minute).

All-in Deals

Some artists prefer to negotiate an all-in type deal with the film company. For example, for a total of $75,000, they will record and deliver a completed track. In this case, the artist pays the recording costs out of the $75,000, then keeps the difference as a fee.

Unless the fee is extraordinarily high, and the artist produces himself or herself, I generally don't like to do this. Directors are fussy about what goes into their films, and you don't want to be in the position of having to re-record it several times at your expense. Also, if the artist is not the producer of the recording, you have to pay a producer's fee to someone else, which can be an unknown quantity. I much prefer just having the artist show up, sing, and leave.

Credit

The other major negotiating point is credit. Unless you have the main title song (which I'll talk about in a minute), you won't have much to say about credit. Just make sure your credit is no less prominent than any other artist's, both as to size and placement in the film. In reality, this means you'll be included in the **crawl,** which is the credits resembling an eye chart that roll by at the end of the film after everyone's left the theater. (Everyone except me, that is, because I always stay to see who did the music. And half the time I can't read it because it goes by too fast.)

If you do the **main title song** (meaning the song at the beginning of the picture, as opposed to the **end title song,** which is, not surprisingly, the song played over the credits at the end), you can sometimes negotiate a credit in the **main titles.** *Main titles* are where the director, writer, and stars are credited, and are usually, but not always, at the beginning of the picture. Whether or not you get main-title placement, a title song performer should be able to get a **single card** credit (meaning no other credit is on the screen at the same time as yours), or at least a card shared only with the songwriter. Other folks who may want to be on the card are your music producer and your record company. You should also ask for your credit to be the same size as the director's, writer's, and (film) producer's credit.

RECORD RIGHTS TO FILM PERFORMANCES

When we move into records, things get much more complicated. First of all, before you even start negotiating, *you must clear the deal with your record company.* In case you didn't hear me, let me say it again: *Before you start negotiating, you must clear the deal with your record company.* Failure to do this has caused some of the biggest disasters in film music. And don't think you're immune because you're a big name—it happened to Michael Jackson on the *E.T.* album, and his record company actually went to court and stopped MCA Records from distributing the record until they made a deal. Record companies take it very seriously if you don't follow this rule, because they see it as a violation of their exclusive rights to your recording services. Which it is.

Today, the major film companies have been stung enough to make sure the artist's record company has blessed the deal. But minor and independent film companies may not be so careful, and in the rush of the moment, anyone can drop something. Also, there are sometimes missed signals and miscommunications. For example, a manager might think he's cleared the rights with the record company, and indeed he has (sort of). He may have discussed it with the company, and the company said it 'sounds OK.' However, the record company people meant their approval was subject to working out a deal to compensate them, while the manager genuinely believed they had approved without qualification. So the moral is: Have the film company talk directly to the record company.

Of course, if you can build an exclusion for soundtrack albums into your record deal at the outset (see page 143), you don't have to worry about this. But most of the time you can't. And even if you have an exclusion, you may not want to use it for this film. (If the company agrees you can do a particular soundtrack, you might want to save the exclusion for a time when they don't.) Or you may have already used the exclusion—exclusions usually allow only one cut every album cycle or so, and there may be a second film you want to take. Or the film company may require more rights (like singles) than your exclusion allows. So be sure everyone knows what everyone else is doing.

Assuming you get your record company to go along, you must now negotiate a deal both for the use of your recording in the film (remember, your record company may try to grab a part of your fee, as we discussed on page 410), and to use your recording on the soundtrack album. There are six aspects to the album part of this:

1. What's your royalty?
2. Is your royalty paid to you (rarely) or to your record company?
3. What can the company distributing the soundtrack album recoup against your royalty?
4. What can your record company recoup against your royalty?
5. Exactly what record rights does the film company get?
6. Who is responsible for what in connection with music videos?

Let's take these in order:

Royalty

Artists' royalties on soundtrack albums generally hover in the range of 12% to 14%, all-in (i.e., including the producer), and if you're a new artist, you may even get less. If you're midlevel and up, this is lower than you would get in the marketplace (because the film company takes part of the royalties). And remember this is pro-rata (see page 159), which means you only get a small piece of the royalty (because you will only have one or two cuts out of the twelve or more on the album).

If there are a number of artists on the album at about the same level, the 12% to 14% pro-rata is about right. However, if you're the only star on the record (such as an album whose other cuts are minor artists or underscore ['underscore' is defined on page 420], or where you're the only superstar among a bunch of midlevel artists), you should definitely get more because the other cuts bear lower royalties. In these cases, you're justified in asking for a much higher royalty, say in the 16% to 18% range—sometimes more if you've really got clout. You might also ask for a **floor,** meaning that no matter how many tracks are on the album, your royalty will be no less than, say ¹⁄₁₀ (or ¹⁄₁₁ or ¹⁄₁₂, depending on your bargaining power). For example, if you had a 10% royalty and a floor of ¹⁄₁₀, you'd get 1% on the album even if there were fourteen masters. Still another technique is to get a non-pro-rated royalty, of say 1% to 1.5% on the entire album. The companies will kick and scream, but if you have enough clout you can pull it off.

It's also possible to get escalations based on sales of the album.

An exception to all this is where the soundtrack album is on your own label. In that case, you should get no less than the royalty you get under your record deal.

For a featured instrumentalist or a featured vocalist (which we discussed on page 411), royalties are in the range of 9% to 10% of retail, pro-rated based on the number of album cuts, and further pro-rated if you're performing with another royalty artist (for example, if you sing with an orchestra that gets a royalty). In other words, where there are two or more royalty artists on a track, it's treated as a joint recording (which we discussed on page 171.

The Record Company Piece

Record companies want to collect all the royalties you get from sound-track albums and singles. They normally keep 50%, as a cost of waiving your exclusivity and allowing your recording to be released on somebody else's label. If you have an enormous amount of bargaining power, you may be able to beat them down below 50%, but it's getting tougher to pull this off. However, if your company happens to be distributing the soundtrack album, you should ask for 100% of the royalty, because you're not being released from any exclusivity.

The companies normally treat your share of royalties exactly the same as all other royalties under your deal. That means they use your share to recoup your deficit, or else pay it to you on your next accounting statement if you're recouped. Sometimes you can get half or all of your share paid to you even if you're unrecouped. The ability to do this varies directly with your bargaining power.

If you get an advance against your royalties, the record company will also want a piece of that.

Recoupment

Unlike record deals, where everything is recoupable, in films you can often knock out a good portion (sometimes even all) of the costs. Let's look at them individually:

Recording Costs.   You can sometimes make all or a portion of the recording costs nonrecoupable. The way to do this is to argue that the costs of recording are really costs of the film, which they would incur even if there were no album, and thus it's not fair to charge them against record royalties. If you're a superstar, you can pull it off; if you're not, you'll end up with anywhere from 50% to 100% of the costs being recoupable.

Artist's Performance Fee.   Another question is whether any of your fee to record for the film is recoupable from your royalties. Again, you can take the position that this is a fee to perform for the film, not on records, and so they shouldn't recoup it. If you have some bargaining power, you can pull this off; otherwise, a part of it may be recoupable. (As a negotiating ploy, if you want to increase your fee and are getting nowhere, try making a portion of the increase recoupable. But use this as a last resort.)

More and more often these days, soundtrack albums are being financed by a record company who pays for the music and gets the right to put out the album (we'll discuss these deals in Chapter 34). The monies paid by the record company are advances against the soundtrack album royalties, and because the film performers' fees come out of these advances, all or a portion of the fee is often treated as an advance against the artist's royalties.

Conversion Costs.   As good as all this news sounds, there are other costs recouped under film deals that aren't chargeable under record deals (because they don't exist). These are known as **conversion costs,** a name I take credit for inventing. (I'm really a pretty modest guy, but every once in a while something gets the better of me.) *Conversion costs* are the costs of converting a film recording to a master that can be used in a record. For example, the recording for the film might only be thirty seconds, but you need a four-minute version for the album. The conversion costs are the costs to do this, and include those costs you would expect, such as remixing, editing, overdubbing additional instruments (called **sweetening**), and sometimes even totally re-recording the song. But they also include something you haven't seen before, called:

Re-use Fees. Whenever you use a recording made for one medium (in this case, a motion picture) in another (in this case, records), the union charges you a fee. These fees are called **re-use fees** or **new-use fees** because they are charges to *re-use* an existing recording in a different way (a *new use*). (Re-use fees are also payable when you go the other way around—taking a recording made for records and using it in a film—and in other situations like going from television to records, records to television, records to commercials, etc.) The reasoning is that, when you use an existing recording, you don't have to hire the musicians you would have needed to re-record the composition. Since you're putting union members out of work, the union allows you to do this only if you pay them an amount listed on a schedule (which is close to union scale for the missed sessions).

The re-use fees payable for a particular recording are directly proportionate to the number of musicians on the track. Thus, a three-piece band is cheap, and the Los Angeles Philharmonic Orchestra is not. Indeed, for a fully instrumental, orchestral soundtrack album, the re-use fees can run $90,000 or more.

Conversion costs are almost always recoupable from your royalties.

What Rights Are Granted

If you can help it, you don't want to give the film company any more than the right to use your master in the film, on the soundtrack album, and on a single. This means you're excluding things such as compilation albums, licenses for commercials, licenses for other films, etc. You and your record company should control these other rights, although they're often restricted (as we'll discuss in a minute).

Unless you have very little bargaining power and are up against an obnoxious film company, none of this should be a serious problem (although the usual form contract gives them all rights unless you change it). The usual restriction required by the film company is that you can't issue a synchronization license for the master (to another film or television show, or a commercial) for at least a number of years, if not forever. The theory is that they don't want someone else getting the goodwill of a song closely identified with their picture. The other kicker is that some film companies require the right to use your recording in sequels, remakes, etc. You almost always have to give up these rights, but sometimes you can get an additional fee for the uses. Either it's a set fee per use, which the film company pays according to a schedule, or sometimes, with a lot of clout, you can leave it to be negotiated in good faith at the time of the use (with the provision that you can't stop them from using it; you just get to argue about the size of the fee).

Another issue that's come up over the last few years is **co-promotions.** That's where the film company ties into an advertiser (such as McDonald's, Pizza Hut, Burger King, etc.) who gives away plastic cups and toys to promote the movie, hangs posters in its stores, hypes the film in its advertising, writes the film's name on its men's room walls, etc. The film company will want the rights to use your master in radio and TV commercials that promote both the advertiser and the film, and that's a source of negotiation. You may well object to having your voice on a commercial for something besides the film—certainly without getting paid, and maybe altogether if it's inconsistent with your image. Also, if you're a superstar, the right to use your voice in a commercial is a serious exploitation of your persona. This is often resolved by bludgeoning you into submission, since the film companies fight hard for these rights—*co-promotions* can mean millions in advertising for the film. If you have clout, you may be able to get a prenegotiated additional payment, or even prohibit some or all co-promotions without your consent (which means you can make a deal later, if you're willing to allow it).

Use on Artist's Own Record.

One nice goodie you can sometimes get is the right to use the recording on your own records. If the film company allows this, they'll limit it to one album, or maybe one studio album plus one Greatest Hits. They'll also say you can't put it on your record for a period of somewhere between six months (if you've really got clout) to two years, with the norm being around nine to twelve months. This period before you can release is called a **hold-back.** The time period may start at release of the picture, release of the soundtrack album, or release of your recording as a single. Whatever you do, be sure the date someday arrives. For example, if you measure your period from release of the soundtrack album, and the album is never released, you could never use it. If you ask, the film company will usually agree to an outside date after which you can use it no matter what.

The *hold-back* effectively means the soundtrack recording will end up on a Greatest Hits album, because it's going to be stale by the time they let you use it (especially if it's released as a single in conjunction with the film). And that's not a coincidence; the film company wants people buying the soundtrack album (not your record) to get the song. Sometimes your record company wants to put the cut on your own album at the same time as the soundtrack album is out (no hold-back). The film company (and especially the record company with the sound-track album) won't like this at all. But if you're important enough, and it's the only way they can get you, they may go along.

Also, there's a trend these days for some pictures not to have a soundtrack album at all, so the only records with the soundtrack cut are the artist's own. Obviously there's no hold-back in these situations.

The film company may ask for a piece of your royalty if you use it on your record, and my response is to tell them to stuff it. So far, they've generally stuffed it.

Re-recording Restriction.   Just like your record deal, soundtrack deals include a re-recording restriction (see page 142). The period is generally five years, but the date can be from recording, from release of the picture, or release of an album or single. If the date is measured from anything except the date of recording, be sure the restriction period someday expires.

Singles.   Another major point of contention is the question of whether there will be a single, and if so, who can put out a single with your performances on it. (We touched on this on page 144.)

The 'whether' question depends on scheduling. If you've got your own single on the radio, your record company won't want a competing single out there fighting for airplay.

Assuming there's going to be a single, the next question is which company can put it out. Historically, the company with the artist's exclusive agreement never parted with single rights. However, in recent years there is a trend to the contrary. As singles sell less and less, and, as we discussed, many aren't even manufactured for sale (they're just promoted on the radio), most companies have come to the conclusion that it's not such a big deal for somebody else to put out a single and pay all the marketing and promotion costs.

The film company wants a single about six weeks before the picture. They want the radio and video airplay to hit its peak around release of the film, so they can get maximum promotional value for the picture.

Music Videos

If there is going to be a music video, the record and film company usually share the cost 50/50. The film company customarily supplies footage from the film (at no cost) to be included in the video. Normally the film company only commits to the first video from the album, and any others are decided at the time.

In the beginning, film companies turned these videos into long previews of the movies. This worked terrifically until MTV and the other broadcasters figured out they were giving away free advertising for the film, at which point the practice came to an abrupt halt. Now the videos are allowed to have only limited footage from the film, and otherwise must consist of visual performances of the artist or other materials.

When the film company supplies footage, they need some control over the exploitation of the video. This is because improper usage can trigger union problems. As long as the video is shown in close proximity to the release of the film (including television release, home video release, etc.), there should be no union problems; it's considered a promotion of the film. However, if it's exploited at other times, the film unions may require a payment to use footage with their members in it (actors, musicians, singers, etc.), and the film company may also need the consent of union members performing in the clip. This has become less of an issue in recent years, as films stay in continual home video release, and thus the videos can be considered 'promotional' at virtually any stage of a film's life.

The record company will want to recoup some portion of the video costs from your royalties. Remember, in normal record deals, 50% of the video costs are recoupable (see page 178). In this case, however, the record company is only paying 50% of the costs, and thus there is a strong argument that none of it should be recoupable. The outcome depends on your bargaining power.

30

Film Songwriter Deals

TERMINOLOGY

Let's now look at film songwriter deals. By songwriter deals, I mean deals for *songs* (both music and lyrics, or sometimes instrumental only) written for the film, as opposed to what's known as the **score** or **underscore,** which is the background music used underneath dialogue, action, etc. (We'll deal with underscore in Chapter 31.) Also, this chapter deals with *creating* a song for the film, as opposed to licensing an existing song (not written for the film). (Licensing existing songs is covered in Chapter 32.)

DEAL POINTS

The payment for writing a film song is a fee plus songwriter royalties. And if you're a songwriter with even modest stature, you may also be able to keep a piece of the publishing.

Fees

The range of fees is anywhere from zero to $50,000 plus for established writers. There are occasionally deals even higher in the stratosphere, but they're rare. Zero is even rarer; usually a low-budget film with no music budget, and the songwriter keeps all the publishing (see page 240, dealing with the fact that songs in films can earn substantial performance monies in foreign territories, as well as on television here). The vast majority fall in the range of $25,000 to $50,000 for major studio films. Whether or not the writer gets a part of the publishing also affects the size of the fee. Some deals also have additional monies (called **kickers**) based on the success of the film. For example, you might get more dough if the film does $100 million U.S. box office gross; another *kicker* at $150 million, etc. (By the way, the film company will never obligate itself to use a song. The most it will do is agree to pay the fee, which is known as **pay or play** because it can either use you [play] or pay you to go away. *Pay-or-play* provisions in record deals were discussed on page 107.)

Step Deals

Songwriter deals are sometimes done on a **step** basis, meaning the deal is done over a series of 'steps.' The steps are:

1. The writer creates the song and gives the company an informal demo recording for a small amount of money.
2. If the film company doesn't like it, the company either passes or goes to step two, which requires the writer to rewrite the song for a small additional fee (or maybe no more money). If the company then likes it, it's a firm deal; if not, the deal is off.
3. Once the film company people are happy, it goes forward on a pre-negotiated deal to use the song. At this point, the deal is the same as the songwriter deals we just discussed, although I like to ask for more money because we've covered their downside.

All of this is a fancy way of saying the writer does it **on spec** (meaning 'on speculation'; i.e., he or she writes the song without a commitment from the film company to pay a full fee). The deal may be completely *on spec,* meaning a film company pays nothing or perhaps a small amount for the cost of a demo. Or the film company may pay a smaller fee (usually in the range of $2,500 to $5,000, sometimes as high as one-half the normal fee) for writing the song, and then have the option to go forward if it likes it (by paying the rest of the full fee).

If you're a major songwriter, you should do very little on spec, because you don't want to spend your time working on a project that will pay you half your normal fee. Also, rejection is not good for your self-image unless you get your full fee. (It's not great even then, but at least you didn't totally waste your time.)

Rights Granted

The film company wants the right to use your song not just in this film, but also in sequels, **prequels** (the same characters in an adventure that takes place before the one in your film), and **out-of-context uses.** *Out-*

of-context means advertising for the film, **trailers** (the short previews you see in theaters), co-promotions (we discussed co-promotions on page 417), and anything else besides the film itself (or clips from the film)—in other words, a use outside the original context (i.e., outside the specific scene for which it was created). Over the last several years, film companies have radically expanded the list of things they can do with your song, all without paying you: studio tours, theme parks, live entertainment (like Broadway shows, ice shows, etc.), storyteller and sing-along records, and merchandising.

You usually have to give up these rights, but with some clout, you can get more money for them—either by increasing your original fee, or getting additional monies if the song is used in one of these categories (you get a prenegotiated amount, or a requirement to pay you a 'customary fee' that you can argue about later). If you have a *lot* of clout, you can sometimes prohibit some or all co-promotions.

As we'll discuss in more detail in the next chapter, there are also some categories for which the film company might get paid by third parties, but don't pay you. In other words, they treat your fee as having 'bought out' these usages, even if they get paid.

Publishing

Until the last several years, writers got no share of publishing on film songs. Now, with some clout, you can get from 25% to 50% of the publishing income, and usually the same percentage of copyright ownership. If the song is based on music in the underscore (see the discussion of score on page 424), and if the song can be separately identified from the underscore (in other words, it has a distinct name, has lyrics, etc.), you can sometimes get publishing on that as well. (However, the underscore composer whose theme is used may or may not get publishing in the identifiable song. As you'll see in the next chapter, people who compose underscore don't get a share of the publishing in the score, and since this song is taken from underscore music, the composer may not be able to get a share of the publishing. On the other hand, if the composer writes a song which is *not* based on a theme in the underscore, he or she may—if they have enough clout—be able to get a percentage of that publishing.)

The studios want the exclusive administration rights (see page 217) for a discussion of administration), but if you've got clout you may be able to keep co-administration (unless it's the title song, where the studio feels it's so identified with the film that they have to keep control).

(Co-administration is discussed on page 285.) Even with co-adminis-tration, however, there will be restrictions on synch licenses, as we dis-cussed in connection with masters on page 416. If you don't get administration, you may still be able to approve certain types of synch licenses (such as commercials), just like in any other songwriter deal (see page 278), but this takes muscle. At a minimum, try for consulta-tion rights on commercials, which means they have to discuss proposed usages with you even though they can make the final decision alone. Also, try to get paid directly by the record company (for mechanical royalties) and by your performing rights society, so you don't have to wait for the money to go through the film company.

Some small-budget films will license songs for very little and let the composer keep all ownership, administration, and income from the songs. However, they will restrict synchronization licenses, as we've discussed.

Credit

The other provision negotiated in a songwriter deal is credit. Normally, unless you write the title song, you get a credit in the 'crawl' (see page 411). If this is the case, there's not much to say except that your credit shouldn't be any less prominent than anyone else's. If you write the main title song, you may be able to get credit on a single card (mean-ing no one else's is on the screen at the same time), or on a card shared only with the artist performing the song. Possibly you can get your card in the main titles (meaning those listing the stars, director, etc.) and, if so, you should ask for the size to be no less than that of the writer, director, or producer.

Unless you're the performer as well as the writer, you don't usually get a single card—at best, you share credit with the performer, in a form such as 'Title song performed by *X*, written by *Y*.' If you're a really major writer, you may be able to get credit in the **billing block** of paid ads for the film but this is extraordinarily hard to come by. (The *billing block* is that microscopic list of credits down at the bottom of movie ads.) If you do get the credit, it will only be in ads where the writer, producer, and director are credited, since some ads only have the title and stars. A compromise is to get credit in full-page ads in New York and Los Angeles only (which is great, unless your mother lives in Des Moines). You may also be able to get credit in full-page trade ads (meaning entertainment industry ads, such as *Variety, Hollywood Re-porter,* etc.), so at least people in the industry know what you did.

31

Composer Agreements

Composers are the guys and gals who write the **underscore.** *Underscore,* also called **score,** is the music underneath the dialogue, action, transitions, etc., that you're not supposed to notice but that enhances the mood of the story. If you've ever seen a film without music, you know how stark and empty it feels. A good underscore can radically increase the impact of a movie, just as a bad one can make a movie feel weird and cheap. (For an example of a bad underscore, rent any porno movie at your local video store.)

DEAL POINTS

Deals for composers are similar to those for songwriters, except that a composer almost never gets any share of the publishing. The fee for writing and conducting a major studio theatrical motion picture underscore ranges anywhere from a low of $50,000 to a high of $1,000,000 plus for the superstars. The normal range is from $200,000 to $700,000. These amounts are just the fees; the film company pays the recording costs on top. Independent companies pay less, and often do 'package' deals, as we'll discuss in a bit. Start-up composers rarely do fee deals; they're almost always packages.

Most of the issues we discussed in Chapter 30 concerning songwriters also apply to composers. But here are additional points to cover in composer deals:

Delivery Date. The delivery date of the score is a critical point of negotiation. You would expect the fuss to be over your having to deliver by a set date, but surprisingly this isn't the case. In fact, form composer deals don't even have a set date unless you insist on one.

For years, the studios simply had a phrase that said the composer would start and finish whenever the film company decided they wanted him or her to do so. This resulted in composers sometimes being tied up on a film for years at a time, all for a relatively minor fee. As the composers got more sophisticated, they began limiting the time a film company could require their services, and if the company wanted them longer, it would have to pay additional amounts. Typically, these terms are in the range of ten to twelve weeks, if the companies will give any term at all. Some companies still refuse, especially at the higher prices.

Exclusivity.   Composer deals used to be exclusive throughout the term (meaning you couldn't do anything else during that time), but now are more commonly **first priority,** which means you can take other work as long as you don't short-change this film while you're doing it. In fact, some are even **non-exclusive** (which means you can do anything else you want, as long as you perform on time). However, even the most liberal deals require composers to be exclusive at some point. For big money deals, they want exclusivity from **spotting** through recording. *Spotting* means there has been a final cut of the film, and the composer and director have sat down and determined precisely which 'spots' need music, as well as the exact length of each piece needed (measured in tenths of seconds). (I was surprised to learn that a change of even one second in a scene may require a total rewrite of the music. This is because a well-written score moves precisely with the action on screen, and even a slight variation throws everything out of whack. It's like a marching band doing an extra half step between beats.) If the deal is more moderate, or not with a major studio, the exclusivity may only be from start of recording.

Payment Schedule.   Before you get any money, the studios want you to sign something called a **Certificate of Authorship,** also known to its friends as a **C of A.** This is a one-page document that says they own everything you do, under the terms of your (still being negotiated) composer deal. Once that's done, composers normally get their fees in either thirds or fourths. If it's in thirds, you usually get one-third on spotting, one-third on commencement of recording, and one-third on completion of services. If you're paid in fourths, expect one-fourth upon spotting, one-fourth on commencement of recording, one-fourth on completion of recording, and the balance on completion of services. Completion of recording is almost always the same as completion of services, but occasionally you have to stick around and help with dubbing the recording into the picture, editing for the sound-track album, sweeping the floor, etc.

Major composers can speed up the payment schedule a bit. One recent deal was as follows (it's in thirds and sixths, but it could also be fourths as well): One-third on commencement of services and execution of the *C of A,* one-third on commencement of recording, one-sixth on delivery of the score, and one-sixth on completion of all services.

All studios hold back money until signature of an agreement, which may be well after the services have started (or finished). The range is from ten percent to one-third.

Orchestrations.   It may surprise you to know that many composers don't have the ability to write musical parts for each instrument in their orchestras. (In fact, some composers don't even read music, although this is rare. These guys are known in the trade as 'hummers.') Most of us think of composers as being like John Williams, who is obviously a premier orchestral conductor and arranger, and who understands the subtleties of every instrument. However, many composers are musicians who write only the melody line for the underscore. This melody line is given to an **orchestrator,** who writes out the parts for the trumpets, oboes, clarinets, violins, etc. Next time you see a film, look for the orchestrator's credit buried among the assistants, makeup people, grips, and gaffers (whatever they are).

Orchestrators aren't used only by composers incapable of writing their own instrumental parts. Quite the contrary, virtually all composers use orchestrators, if for no other reason than to save the time and/or tedium of mechanically doing it themselves. Often, however, classically trained composers sketch out the parts pretty thoroughly, and the orchestrator then becomes more of a copyist. (By the way, I know of one situation where a composer, under extreme time pressure to finish a film before its release date, hired three orchestrators at the same time to crank out the parts.)

The orchestrator is of course paid for his or her services. The composer and primary orchestrator get a negotiated fee, usually in the range of $80 to $85 per page. Second and third orchestrators are generally paid at union scale, but the better known ones can get more. Scale for orchestrators varies with the size of the orchestra and number of pages of music. As a rough guideline, at the time of this writing, the price for *simple* orchestrations is roughly $400 per minute of music (e.g., thirty minutes is $12,000). Complex orchestrations can exceed $30,000 for a film.

An important part of the deal is whether or not your composer's fee includes orchestrations. Even if the film company knows you aren't capable of doing this job, you may be responsible for paying the orchestrator out of your fee. Conversely, you may be perfectly capable of doing orchestrations but (a) your time doesn't permit it; or (b) you want to do the orchestrations only if you're paid additional money for the trouble. You should make sure the orchestrations are on top of your fee (if you don't raise this issue, the film company may try to deduct the cost of orchestrations from your money), unless of course you're doing a package, which includes everything (as we'll discuss in a minute).

Record Royalties. A film composer, being a songwriter and not a performer, doesn't automatically get record royalties. The only royalties for underscore are paid for (a) conducting the orchestra; and/or (b) producing the recordings. And these services may or may not be performed by the composer. Let's look at them separately:

Conducting Royalties. When conducting, the composer becomes (in a sense) a recording artist by leading the orchestra. The customary range of these royalties is 6% to 10% of retail (though some studios won't go beyond 9%), pro-rated on the number of cuts (see page 159 for a discussion of pro-ration), and further pro-rated for royalty artists on any particular cut (see page 171 for a discussion of joint recordings).

In actuality, many composers don't really conduct. Instead, they hire a conductor and 'buy out' all royalties for a fee. Thus, the composer steps into their shoes and gets the 'artist' royalty.

Producing Royalties. If you produce the recordings (see page 125 for what producing is), you can get 3% to 4% of retail. (Note that this is independent of conducting royalties; you can produce even if you don't conduct, or vice versa.) Like other producer royalties, these are usually retroactive to record one after recoupment (see page 127 for a discussion of retroactivity).

You can usually insist on producing the underscore for records, but composers have had singularly bad luck imposing themselves as producers of songs. This is because artists may simply refuse to work with them. The best you can do is say that the film company must use you as the producer of all songs if the artist and record company approve. Sounds great, eh? Unfortunately, it's almost meaningless, because most artists don't want a film composer producing them. (If a composer is a producer of note in his own right, that's of course a different story.)

The studios will insist on reducing your royalty if another producer reworks your cuts. Try to have this only happen with your permission, and in any event try not to go below 50% of your normal producing royalty.

Floors. Major composers can sometimes get a **floor,** meaning that if you do absolutely nothing on the record, you still get a royalty. Usually it's a guarantee of one or two cuts on the album, although they don't really guarantee to include your cuts, but rather only to pay you as if they were included. In other words, if you have a 10% royalty, and there are ten masters on the album, you would be guaranteed 1% or 2%, even if you don't have any recordings on it. This point is relatively easy to get when the album is mostly underscore, but it gets difficult to impossible if you're working on a 'music picture,' meaning a film with a number of pop songs, such as *Moulin Rouge; O Brother, Where Art Thou?; The Bodyguard;* etc. The reason is obvious—the company has to pay royalties to a lot of expensive outside artists, and there's no assurance as to how many score selections you'll have on the album (if any). That means your floor royalties come out of the studio's pocket.

Some major composers can even get a guarantee that there will be a score album released (many films don't release score albums, even if they release song albums).

Recoupment. With composers, the record company normally recoups only conversion costs. (Conversion costs are discussed on page 415.) The issue becomes what they're recouped from, and the larger the royalty rate, the faster you'll get paid. The best is the gross royalty payable to all participants, and the worst is your artist/conductor royalty. On the other hand, most deals say you won't get paid until the film producer has recouped everything charged against their total royalty, which could be huge advances and therefore slow you down quite a bit. When they do recoup, your royalties will be payable from the time the conversion costs are recouped—in other words, once they're recouped, you'll get paid on all sales after those used to recoup conversion costs (this is similar to the concept of retroactive producer's royalties, which we discussed on page 127).

Try to get the *record* company to pay your royalties directly to you once the conversion costs have been recouped. The studios don't like to do this, so you'll have to fight. Your argument is that most of the studio's advances were used to pay artist advances and recording costs, and therefore the studio will be able to recoup those costs from the artists' royalties. Accordingly, it's not fair for them to take these advances and costs out of the overall royalties before paying you. Sometimes you can pull this off, and sometimes the studio will agree only if the record company agrees.

Credit

- *Credit in the Film.* Composers normally get main title, single-card credit. (See page 412 for a discussion of film credits.)
- *Paid Ads.* All composers can get credit in paid ads where the full billing block of film credits appear. Midlevel to major composers can get credit in ads where the writer, film producer, and director are credited. (See page 423 about paid ads.)
- *Soundtrack Album Credit.* Composer credit on soundtrack albums is a hot issue. As we discussed, the composer isn't really an 'artist'—he or she only wrote the music, and maybe conducted it or produced the record. So it's not a foregone conclusion that the composer will get credit on the soundtrack album. Which means you gotta ask.

Ideally, you want credit on the front cover of the soundtrack album. The film company will argue (correctly) that it doesn't control this; it's up to the soundtrack album record company. So you'll probably end up with a commitment for the film company to use its 'reasonable efforts' to get you front-cover credit.

Whether you get front-cover credit also depends on the nature of the album. If it's a compilation of songs by major artists, you're not likely to get credit on the front cover—bluntly, your name won't sell as many records as the names of the artists. However, if it's a 50% or more score album, front-cover credit shouldn't be too difficult. If you do get it, insist on tying your credit to the size of the title of the film (100% or 50% of the title size, for example).

You should always insist (and the film company should have no trouble agreeing) that you get credit on the back cover of the album.

Other Uses. As we discussed earlier, film companies take the right to use music in more than just the film for which you're hired. As the composer, you pretty much have to go along, but the question is whether you can get some more money for any other uses.

As noted in the last chapter, you can often get paid for sequels and prequels. However, composers normally don't get additional monies for anything else, even in situations where the film company gets money. For example, one of the biggest current fights is over the use of your score in video games. The majority of studios argue this is a 'related use' of the score, just like a co-promotion (which we discussed previously), and therefore they owe you zippo. They say this even though they get a flat fee or even a royalty from the video game company.

The other area coming down the pike is the whole business of streaming and downloadable motion pictures. What if anything will composers get? Stay tuned. . . .

Travel Expenses.   It's not uncommon for composers to have to travel (for example, to England, Ireland, Germany, or Canada, where it may be cheaper to record). In this case, you should negotiate for reimbursement of your expenses. On a high-class, big-budget picture, this should be first-class travel, plus something in the neighborhood of $2,000 to $3,500 per week for New York or London. Otherwise it's first-class accommodations plus $100 to $150 per day for all expenses besides the hotel. For low-budget flicks, you'll get Greyhound tickets and Motel 6 vouchers. If you're going to a foreign country, it's important to get your expense money in the local currency, as you don't want to be in the business of speculating whether the dollar is going to be worth more or less than the peso. For example, suppose your London hotel room costs £100 per night, which at the time of your deal is $160. If your deal is $160 per night in dollars, and if the dollar drops against the pound so that your $160 only equals £90, you're in trouble. The room is £100, but you only get £90 for your $160. So you'll be coming up £10 short. But if instead your deal says you get £100, you're covered.

PACKAGE DEALS

There is a trend in recent years for some composers to do **package** deals, especially in television. A 'package' is very much like a 'fund' in record deals (see page 99 for a discussion of funds). In other words, the composer agrees to deliver a completed score for a set fee, and the fee includes both the compensation for the composer's services and the costs of the score.

Not surprisingly, most package deals are done by composers who create electronic scores. In other words, a small number of musicians (sometimes only the composer) create the music on a synthesizer (which of course these days can sound like the Academy of St. Martin in the Field).

There are some pure orchestral score package deals, but they tend to be very large (we'll discuss how large in a minute). In these deals, the composer gets the film's entire music budget, less only an amount the studio thinks it'll need to license existing songs and recordings, and/or to create new songs and recordings.

There is also a relatively new hybrid package, which consists of synthesizer recordings mixed with orchestral recordings.

Package Prices

The price of packages can be anywhere from $50,000 for a low-budget film up to $1,000,000 plus for a mainstream feature. Pure electronic scores (or electronic scores with up to maybe ten musicians in a package) run around $100,000 to $400,000, sometimes a bit higher for top-level folk. The hybrid packages described above (both synthesizer and score) have funds of $150,000 to $250,000 for the synthesizer portion, on top of which the composer receives a market rate fee for conducting the orchestra. The costs of the orchestra are paid in addition by the studio—in other words, they're not part of the package.

At the other end of the scale, I've seen starving composers do low-budget film scores for a $5,000 to $10,000 package price. In this case I always try to keep the publishing, and sometimes we can keep the soundtrack album as well. At the very least, you should get a nice chunk of the income from publishing and records, since you're taking so little up front.

Exclusions

If you're going to make a package deal, you have to worry about exactly what's in the package. Most contracts just require you to deliver 'all music,' and the trick becomes negotiating what *isn't* included. This turns out to be more complicated than you'd think, and by the courtesy of my friend Michael Gorfaine (one of the most experienced film music agents in the business), I bring you the following list of exclusions:

Licensing of Outside Music (i.e., songs not written by the composer).   Since most contracts say you must provide 'all music,' I've seen film companies license an expensive outside tune and expect the composer to pay for it. You can't control the costs of outside songs (indeed, one license could eat half your package fee), so never agree to this.

Recording Costs of Outside Music.   If the sessions for outside music can't be scheduled during the normal scoring sessions, their costs shouldn't be included in the package.

Re-use Fees.   (See page 416 for a discussion of these babies.) Not your problem.

Re-scoring.   This is one of the most important and trickiest areas. The concept is to save your rear end in situations where the director tells you he wants bands of angels accompanying his scene, which you record and deliver, only to have him decide later that he really meant heavy metal. In other words, if the film people require you to re-record for reasons totally beyond your control (as opposed to your screw-up), it should be on them.

Lyricist Expenses.   If the producer wants to hire a lyricist to write words to your music, it should be on his or her nickel.

Vocalist Expenses.   As with lyricists, if the company wants somebody to croon your newly created song, they should pay.

Music Editor Fees.   The music editor's fee should be a film cost, not a package cost. A **music editor** is to film music what a film editor is to film. In other words, he or she is the technical person responsible for getting all the music in the right places. They will create the **spotting notes** (which are detailed notes, down to a tenth of a second, as to where music goes), help with any technical difficulties, edit music to fit a scene if the film has been cut, etc.

Mag Stock and Transfer Costs.   **Mag stock** is the actual soundtrack imprinted on the film, and **transfer costs** are the costs of transferring the music from the recording studio to the film. The purpose of this exclusion is to clarify that you only have to deliver a standard audio recording, and that the cost of putting this music into the film is a motion picture, and not a package, cost.

Pre-records. This is music recorded before shooting, to be lip-synched and/or danced to in the film. (We'll discuss this further on page 442.) Include the cost of pre-records only if it's specifically negotiated up front.

Sidelining. This is a situation where a musician either gets on camera and pretends to perform, or actually performs. Film companies have been known to charge the cost of this against the package, which again is a matter of negotiation. It's usually easy to exclude if you ask, because the musician is paid through SAG (Screen Actor's Guild) as an actor, and this isn't a music cost.

Excess Musicians. It's a great idea to limit the number of musicians you're required to supply. For a television package, this is usually small—in the range of four or five at the most—and the limit gives you ammunition to ask for more money if the director has a sudden attack of orchestra-itis.

Of course, any of the above exclusions may be included in your package if it's negotiated up front and you budget for it. But be sure they're only in there when you expect them, or you may be paying the film company for the privilege of using your music.

CREATIVE FINANCING

A recent trend is something known loosely as 'creative financing' (not really an industry term). That's where an independent studio (or a major studio for that matter) doesn't have the budget to hire the composer they want, and instead comes up with creative ways to snag their dream person for a lower fee. These are things like:

Back-end Participation. The composer gets a piece of the film's profits, or built-in bonuses at certain box-office levels (the 'kickers' we discussed earlier). If it's a piece of profits, it's usually tied to the director's or producer's computation. For example, you might get 1% of the film's profits, as defined in the director's deal. If it's a bonus, it might be $50,000 for every $25 million of box-office gross, as reported in *Variety*. Usually this is only based on U.S. box office, but major composers (or international films) can be based on worldwide.

Percentage of Publishing.   As we discussed, film companies normally own all the publishing on underscore. In these creative deals, the composer might get ownership and/or administration. Or if not, certainly a share of the publishing income. Sometimes the composer gets a large percentage until they make a certain sum, then a lesser amount thereafter, maybe dropping to zero if the composer makes enough money.

Soundtrack Record Goodies.   The composer gets a higher than normal record royalty, or higher guaranteed number of cuts, or sometimes the right to own the soundtrack album itself, subject to paying the film company a small royalty.

Adding the Advance.   The composer's fee or package price is increased by the amount of the advance (less conversion costs) that the film company gets for the soundtrack album, or for its publishing. In this event, the additional monies are almost always recoupable from the composer's record royalties, and sometimes even the mechanicals.

If the composer gets several of these, there's often a ceiling on the above, so that, for example, once the composer has made $1 million from all sources (including the fee), the participations drop out. However, the improved record provisions usually go on forever.

TELEVISION COMPOSERS

Television composers live in a different world from film composers. The time to compose and deliver is shorter because, as I'm sure you know, television programs are knocked out like pancakes right before they go on the air. Also, the budgets to produce TV shows are substantially lower than those of motion pictures, so the music budgets (being a piece of this smaller pie) get squashed down along with everything else. Thus, the composer's fees and the money available for recording costs are much less than those for theatrical films.

The good news is that, even though the fees are low, the performance monies generated by television programs can be substantial—much more than for films—because programs may be shown over and over, forever. And remember (from page 236) that you get performance monies each time your music is played on television. (By the way, when I say shown 'forever,' I really mean 'forever.' My kids watch some of the same shows I did when I was a kid, although they think the old *Superman* half hours are stupid. I loved them.)

Background Score

Because of the short time frame and lower budgets, television music is tailor-made for electronic score packagers (the folks who get an all-in amount that includes both their fee and the recording costs, as we discussed on page 430). And in fact, almost all television deals are packages. Typical package fees (which include recording costs) are around $8,000 to $15,000 for a half-hour television episode, $9,000 to $40,000 for a one-hour program (with the average being $16,000 to $25,000), and $10,000 to $60,000 for a two-hour movie of the week. **Pilots** (the show produced in an attempt to sell a series) are usually a little higher, because they need a theme song written and require more music.

Some composers have started hiring their own music editors. In this case, they include the cost in their package, and typically raise the per-episode fee by $3,500 to $4,000.

If you want to give somebody a good chuckle, just ask the TV people if you can have a piece of the publishing. In the television industry, the producer's commandment to hold on to publishing isn't just carved in stone, it's tattooed across their foreheads. (Remember all that lovely performance money? The TV guys figured that out too.) The only exceptions are a few non-studio shows (mini-series, HBO, TNT), where you can sometimes get a piece of the publishing, though usually not administration.

And if you think it's bad enough that the television people want to take your publishing, get a load of how some of the smaller producers, including cable networks that produce their own shows, are not only getting publishing, but also taking your *writer's* share of royalties. This means you don't get the performance monies I talked about in the previous section, or in fact any money for *any* use of the song (besides your fee). And the fees for these deals aren't any higher than the fees for deals where you keep your writer's royalties!

Be very wary of this. Sometimes you don't find out that's what they want until the contract arrives, so you have to be clear up front that you expect writer's royalties. If you can't get them, it may be worthwhile to give up writer's royalties when you first get started (to get credits under your belt), but as soon as you have enough clout, fight hard to hang on.

Assuming you're getting songwriter royalties, you need to negotiate what they are (as we discussed previously). Other deal points are the payment schedule (usually all the money is paid on completion), record royalties (unless the producer knows in advance there will be a record, the royalties are usually left to good faith negotiations), and credit (half-hour shows are usually separate card, end titles, shared only with the theme composer; one hour or more are a main title or Act 1 credit, also shared only with the theme composer. See page 411 for what all this means).

Over recent years, television soundtrack albums have become a bigger deal. For example, shows such as *The X-Files* have had very successful albums. Accordingly, it's a good idea to get a royalty rate specified in your contract. These tend to be slightly lower than film—instead of the figures we discussed on page 427, the rates are around 7% for composing/conducting and 2% to 3% for producing.

TV Themes

Composers sometimes write the main title theme for a television show. This is usually done as a package, and a typical price would be in the range of $10,000 to $25,000, sometimes up to $40,000 plus for a superstar.

Studios won't give up publishing on TV themes, but sometimes non-studio players will.

Occasionally the producers hire a Big Name Writer to compose the television theme, and someone else (cheaper) to write the weekly score. Big Name gets the high end of the scale we just discussed, plus a royalty on records close to what the film composers get (see page 427).

If you're on the *Advanced Overview Track,*
go to the Conclusion, on page 451.
Experts: Onward . . .

32

Licensing Existing Recordings and Existing Songs for Motion Pictures

This chapter deals with licensing existing masters and songs (records and songs not created for the film).

MASTER LICENSES

Record Company Masters

Most of the master licenses are, not surprisingly, from record companies. The rest are individual owners of recordings, which we'll deal with a little later. With record company masters, you'll only be involved in the deals as a secondary player. By that I mean you're not directly involved in the deal; the primary players are your record company and the film company, who make a deal with each other. The money is paid to your record company, who promptly pockets half and treats the balance as artist royalties under your deal.

If your record contract says they need your consent to license masters into films (see page 158), they'll call up and ask for your consent. If the record company doesn't need your consent, they may not even call you, although most will as a courtesy. (By the way, even if you don't have the right to consent in your record deal, but you wrote the song and control the publishing, you can block the deal—remember, the right to use the master is only the right to use the physical recording itself. The record company can't give the film company the right to use the musical composition [they don't have these rights], and so the film company has to contact both the record company and the publisher to get a full set of rights. Thus, if you're the publisher, you have the right to control the deal through the side door even if you don't have it through the front door. We'll talk more about these deals in a minute).

Because you may be asked to consent to these deals, and because you share in the income, you should know how they work. Let's take a look.

A record company–film company master license consists of three main elements:

1. How much is the fee to synchronize the master in the film?
2. If the master is also going on a soundtrack album, what's the royalty?
3. Who pays the re-use fees? (For an explanation of re-use fees, see page 416.)

Let's examine each in order:

Master License Fees

The fee varies directly with how important the song is in its own right (was it a number-one single, or an obscure album cut?), the stature of the artist, and how it's used in the film (is it in the background on a radio for ten seconds, so that you need a radar detector to even know it's in the film, or is it played in its entirety, with action on screen following the lyrics, so that it takes on a dramatic content and moves the story forward?). Obviously, there are all shades of variations in between, and sometimes it's just a question of how much the producer has fallen in love with this particular cut. The range of fees is essentially the same as what's paid for use of the song in the master, which we discussed on page 244.

You should always ask the record company to pay through your half of the fee if you're unrecouped, on the age-old theory of 'Hey, no harm in asking.' Since most of the time you won't get it, don't let it affect your self-esteem.

Royalties

If the deal also grants record rights, the range of royalties is 11% to 14% of retail, pro-rata (see page 170 for what *pro-rata* means). Again, if your master is the key master in the album (meaning, for example, it's the only song in an album of underscore, or it's the only hit in an album of otherwise minor artists or obscure songs), then your royalty should be the same as we discussed for artists (in Chapter 29). In addition, you can usually get a **favored nations** treatment for the master (meaning no one gets a higher royalty), at least insofar as other *existing* masters are concerned. (The film company usually wants the right to pay higher royalties for recordings created for the film.)

Recoupment.   Since there are no recording costs, the only things that can be recoupable are the union re-use fees (see page 416), and this too is negotiable. The fee paid to use the recording in the film or television program should *not* be recoupable under any circumstances, although a small advance may be paid for the LP use.

Other Master License Deal Points

The other deal points are about consent: the AFM (American Federation of Musicians) and you.

AFM Consent.   There is an obscure rule in the AFM labor agreement that requires not only the payment of re-use fees, but also the *consent* of the AFM to put existing masters in a motion picture or television program. The theory is that the union won't put musicians out of work (i.e., by not requiring a new recording session) unless it's such a unique master that a new recording won't do justice to the film. An example would be a Buddy Holly master, which obviously can't be duplicated, since Buddy isn't available. In actual practice, however, I've never seen the union object to any licensing—in fact, this rule is almost always ignored and no one even asks. If you do ask, their consent is a rubber stamp.

Should You Consent?   Remember, the licensing deal is between your record company and the film company, and you're not directly involved. But once the deal gets under way, the record company will call up your manager and ask if you'll consent to the use of your master in a particular film. How do you evaluate this?

   On the financial side, you should review the deal and decide if you think it's fair. The above criteria should give you a pretty good feeling for it. If that sounds OK, then proceed to the next step, which is just as important as checking the financial terms, but often overlooked: You should find out precisely what's going on in the film when your song is being played. I have avoided a number of disasters with this simple question. For example, I once found that a film company wanted to use a recording of one of my clients during a scene in which a number of kids were shooting drugs. Or perhaps it's a graphic sexual sequence (which, depending on your image, could be a plus). Remember, it's your music and your career, so be careful about the creative aspects.

Non-Record Company Masters

As we discussed in the section on record deals, artists don't usually end up owning their own masters, and when they do, they license the rights to a record company for a number of years. On the other hand, there are artists whose careers are, shall we say, 'taking a holiday'—they might have been huge in the eighties or nineties, but don't quite mean as much today. Often these artists are 'between deals' and have recorded stuff that they own. When these masters are licensed for movies, the deals are pretty much the same as those outlined above, except of course there's no record company in the middle.

Another type of license is made by composers who have built up a library of instrumental song masters that they license into small films (who then hire someone to sing over the track). These songs go for anywhere from $500 to $5,000, depending on how much of a hit the studio thinks it might be, which is often related to which artist they have lined up to record the vocals. If the composer is also doing the underscore, or if the film company guarantees a soundtrack album, then the license fee can be even lower.

LICENSING EXISTING MUSICAL COMPOSITIONS FOR FILMS

As we discussed above, the money paid to use a master goes to your record company. This means two things:

1. Right off the top, they get half of it.
2. If you're unrecouped, you never see the other half.

Not such an appetizing proposition. But remember that the film also needs a synchronization license for the *song* in the master. So if you wrote the song and own the publishing, they now need to make a deal directly with you, and this side of the equation looks very different: You keep all the money. No minor distinction.

Fees

We discussed the fees for synchronization licenses on page 244.

FILM MUSIC QUIZ

You are the representative of an independent film company, which is producing a teenage motion picture. The music supervisor called Capitol Records and got a license to use the Beatles recording 'She Loves You' in the film, for a payment of $10,000. The license is fully signed, the money has been paid to Capitol, and the master is recorded in the film.

Assuming you're now aware of everything that has been done with respect to this situation, are there any problems in going forward and distributing the film? If so, what?

Answer to quiz:

Here's what's wrong: They haven't licensed the *song* for the film, only the recording. Thus they can't use the track until they make a deal with the publisher. (See page 244 if you want a refresher.) Also, the Beatles haven't licensed anything for $10,000 since 1962.

33

Music Supervisors

ROLE

The music supervisor's job, as the title implies, is to coordinate all the music for a picture (except the underscore). He or she first sits down with the producer and director to work out the types of music needed, ideally before production. If the film is either a musical or relies heavily on music (such as a dance film), the music supervisor *must* be involved in advance. This is because songs performed on camera must be **pre-recorded,** meaning they're made in a recording studio before commencement of photography of the film (and merely lip-synched or danced to on film). As you can imagine, it's difficult to dance to a song not yet recorded.

Actually, I was once involved in a situation where the opposite happened. A dance scene had been shot to a specific composition, but after the film was finished, the writer of the song refused to make a deal with the film company, and the song had to be scrapped. A client of mine then wrote a new song for the dance sequence (obviously having to match the beat precisely), which ended up being a number-one hit.

After meeting with the director and producer, the music supervisor comes up with suggestions for artists, songwriters, etc., for the film. The director and producer make the final decisions, and the supervisor then oversees the whole process of making it happen. He or she contacts the creative people, arranges for meetings with the film personnel, negotiates and structures the deals (or oversees the negotiation and structuring, depending on the supervisor and the film company), and supervises the recording sessions.

Done properly, being a music supervisor is one of the most difficult jobs on the planet Earth. Let me count the ways:

1. Other than pre-recorded music (which we discussed above, and which is a tiny minority), most of the music can't be finalized

until the film is complete (see page 425 for why.) The studio has millions of dollars riding on a specific film release date, and music is at best considered a minor element in the overall production, even if it's a central element in the film. (The cost of a *major* music budget is maybe $2,000,000, while most major studio films easily run $40 million to $50 million, not to mention multimillions for advertising and marketing. And a more typical music budget is about $600,000 to $1,000,000).

2. Most studio executives (with a few outstanding exceptions) don't understand music nearly as well as they understand films (which is why they're film executives instead of music executives). This can make it very difficult to conclude a deal—the executives think the prices and rights demanded by the music people are outrageous (which they often are), and they have no patience for the complexity of a bunch of little deals.

3. Each piece of music in a film can represent six deals (see page 407 for what they are), and because music comes in last, complicated deals have to be made under enormous time pressure, which increases the likelihood of mistakes geometrically.

It's the music supervisor's job to keep all these diverse, competing interests satisfied, and to ensure a happy ending. And good music supervisors are worth their weight in gold (maybe platinum). They call on their relationships to get favors and smooth out difficult situations, getting music into pictures that couldn't be there any other way. Music supervisors are in a sense 'marriage brokers.' They creatively marry music and films, which is no easy process, as well as marry the two industries on a business level (which is even more difficult). For all these reasons, the top ones are paid handsomely.

FEES AND ROYALTIES

How handsomely? Music supervisors get fees of $150,000 to $300,000 per picture (sometimes even more). The top supervisors also have royalties on the soundtrack album, usually in the range of 2% to 3% of retail, non-pro-rated. There may also be escalations of ¼ or ½ percent at 500,000 and 1,000,000 units. These royalties are payable prospectively after recoupment of all costs, at the same time the film producer recoups.

In addition, there may be box-office bonuses based on the picture's gross, just like the deals for composers that we discussed on page 433.

TELEVISION SUPERVISORS

Recently, a number of television shows have licensed existing music, in part to be hip, slick, and cool, and in part to create a soundtrack album that can make a lot of money. However, because of the quick production time frame in television, and the smaller budgets, and the fact that television producers' music departments simply aren't equipped to deal with the music clearance issues we've just discussed, this is a tough thing to pull together.

Stepping in to save the day are a handful of music supervisors who work on television shows. (I don't want to make it sound like there's a lot of this happening, because at present it's pretty rare that a show can afford someone in this role.) The fees are pretty small—$3,500 or so per episode, and a royalty of maybe 1% with sales escalations.

34

Soundtrack Album Deals

As an artist, you have nothing to do with the deal to distribute a soundtrack album—not even consent or consultation. These contracts are made between the film company and a record company, and in a sense are 'none of your business.' However, they affect the types of deals you can make with the film company, so you should know about them.

Once the film company has acquired the bundle of rights we discussed in Chapters 28 through 32, they turn them over to a record company to put out a soundtrack album. There are two broadly defined types of soundtrack albums—score albums and song albums—and the type you're dealing with radically impacts the deal.

SCORE ALBUMS

A score album is an album wholly of underscore (i.e., with no songs), usually because the only music in the film is underscore. Unless there's something extraordinary about the situation (for example, the film looks like it's going to be huge, or there's a song from a major artist on the album), the soundtrack album deal is relatively modest. The reason is simple—pure underscore albums usually don't sell very well (15,000 to 30,000 copies or so). Many record companies aren't interested in this product at all, and will only put out a score album if someone forces them. (For example, a film company owned by the same parent company as the record company may force them to take an album just to satisfy the ego of a film producer or star.) However, there are a couple of companies (like Varese Sarabande) who specialize in score albums.

Assuming someone is interested, the deal for pure score albums is usually an advance equal to the re-use fees, and sometimes there is no advance at all (which means the film company has to pay the re-use fees). (For a discussion of re-use fees, see page 416.) The royalty on these albums also tends to be lower than for the song albums, usually in the range of 16% to 18% of retail, but soaring over 20% for bigger films.

Exceptions are huge films that click on all levels, like *Titanic,* which sold close to 20 million units, *Star Wars,* and so forth. And of course these sales can continue for a number of years, as long as the film is still kicking around.

SONG ALBUMS

At the other end of the spectrum is an album of songs by major artists, particularly songs that (a) are completed before the sound-track album deal (so the record company can hear them); and (b) sound like hits. For these albums, the price escalates dramatically. In fact, some soundtrack albums, if they're extraordinarily hot, can command advances up to $1,000,000 (sometimes even more) if the record company is really frothing at the mouth. More commonly, the advances are in the range of $250,000 to $1,000,000. (These prices include re-use fees.) The royalty on song albums is also higher, usually in the range of 18% to 20% of retail, and sometimes with escalations to 21% and 22% at sales levels of, say, 1 million and 2 million albums (U.S.). And on extremely rare occasions, the film company can get a piece of the record company's profits.

More commonly, these deals are made before the music is actually in existence. Depending on what everyone believes the music will be, and to a large degree depending on the reputation of the film director or producer (and the director/producer's prior history with soundtrack albums), the advances can still be quite high. In these situations, the record company may require that a certain number of 'gold' or 'platinum' artists be included on the album, and the advance may vary depending on this. Here's a deal one of my film company clients made for a major 'hot' film:

The advance for the album was $500,000, including re-use. If there was a platinum artist on the album and the company got the right to put out a single of that artist (see page 418 for a discussion of singles in soundtrack deals), the advance increased by $125,000. If there were additional platinum artists, with single rights, it increased by an additional $100,000 for each one. If there were two gold artists (one didn't do anything), the advance increased by $150,000. In no event could the total advance exceed $1,000,000 (including re-use).

COST COVERING

Another trend these days is for the record company to simply pay all or part of the music costs of the film: recording costs, synchronization licenses, master licenses, songwriter fees, artist's fees and advances, composer's fees, and so forth.

This, of course, is never a blank check, so there are pre-set parameters. The amount of money depends on the same factors we discussed above: the budget of the film, the number of songs versus score, the amount of music in the film, etc. Other variations include the record company covering the budget up to a set figure, then splitting 50-50 with the film company over that amount. And of course when the record company is paying all the monies, they'll want quite a few approvals over what music goes in the film and album. Sometimes they even insist on the right to designate some or all of the music. In these deals, there's also a discussion of what exactly is included. For example, synch fees or the music supervisor's fee are sometimes in, and sometimes out.

Of course, whatever the record company pays is recoupable from the royalties.

OTHER ISSUES

The other major issues in these deals are:

Release Timing

The record has to be released in coordination with the film. The film company wants maximum promotion for its film, and the record company wants maximum promotion for its record, all from the cross-advertising and cross-marketing of the film and album, radio play of the record, etc. Thus, both sides are extraordinarily touchy about delivery and release dates.

The film and record companies want a single out approximately six weeks ahead of the film, and they want the album released about two to four weeks ahead. This allows the single and album to gather steam by the time the film hits the theaters. The major reason for screwing up this ideal timing is the film company (or the record company, if they're controlling the music) not having the recordings ready, or the film company not having the film artwork ready, or some combination thereof. Accordingly, the release date and balancing these competing interests are all part of the negotiation.

Film Release

The record company wants a guaranteed release of the film. They argue (quite rightly) that their album isn't worth much without a film to go with it. Film companies are very reluctant to do this, since they never give it to any of their actors, producers, directors, etc. For some film companies, it's an absolute no-no. For others, they'll work out some compromise, such as a minimum number of theaters.

Who Owns the Masters?

There are obviously two choices: the film company or the record company. The film company argues that it paid for the little darlings, and thus should own them. The record company argues that the advance it pays under the soundtrack album deal pays for the masters, and thus the record company should own them. The record companies are particularly touchy when the master is recorded by one of their exclusive artists; they can't stand the idea of someone else owning that recording. So the record companies insist on owning the masters and licensing them back to the filmmaker, while film companies insist on owning them and licensing them to the record company.

Compromises run all over the map, but most often the record company owns the masters and licenses them to the film company. Occasionally, they split the ownership—the film company owns the recordings for the film and other non-record rights, while the record company owns them for phonograph records.

To me, the real issue isn't so much ownership as who controls the masters outside the area of the film, the soundtrack album, and singles. This covers such things as synchronization rights (for other films, television programs, commercials, etc.), and usages on records other than the soundtrack album and singles, like compilation packages, the artist's albums, etc. Both sides have legitimate arguments, and the answer depends solely on bargaining power. However, regardless of who ends up with the ownership and control, most film companies will insist (and most record companies will agree) that the film company has ultimate control over licensing the masters for usage in other films, television programs, etc. The record companies are sensitive to the fact that these usages could dilute the film company's right to have the song identified exclusively with their movie.

Related to the issue of control is the question of who gets the money from usages outside the film and records. If the record company ends up with the rights, then the monies are split between it and the film company (or credited to the film company's account if unrecouped). If the film company keeps the rights, then it usually keeps the money (but not always).

Videos

Who makes the videos and how are the costs recouped? Is the film company supplying footage without additional charge? Will the film company pay for part of the videos?

Credit

What type of credit will the record company have in the film? Will it be in film ads as well as on screen? What credit will the film company get on the records and in record company ads?

Advertising

Will either company guarantee advertising of the album and/or the film?

Marketing

Will the film company pay any money for marketing, promotion, etc.? Will the record company?

Conclusion

This concludes the informational portion of our program.

Congratulations! Whichever track you took through the book, you now have a better overview of the music business than 98% of your colleagues (or at least 97.63%). Despite my informal style of writing, the material in this book is very compact, and there's a lot of information. So you've learned much more than you may think. In fact, you now have everything you need to go as far as your music and drive will take you, without being pillaged and plundered along the way (or at least you can only get zapped with your eyes open).

To get the most from this book, keep it handy as a reference. It was important for you to read it through as a solid framework on which to build, but it will be even more valuable as you apply it to specific situations in your life. When you get involved in a particular deal, look up that section and read it again. Seeing it for the second time, you'll pick up things you might have missed before. And they'll be far more meaningful in practice than they were in theory. It's like reading a book on flying when you're home in bed, then reading it again just before you pilot an airplane.

Now you're ready for takeoff, so . . .

Go get 'em!

U.K. Organizations

Agents' Association (GB), 54 Keyes House, Dolphin Square, London SW1V 3NA. Tel.: 020 7834 0515. Fax: 020 7821 0261. Administrator: Carol Richards.

Arts Council of England, 14 Great Peter Street, London SW1P 3NQ. Tel.: 020 7333 0100. Fax: 020 7973 6590. Administrator: Rowan Jarvis.

ASCAP (American Society of Composers, Authors and Publishers), 8 Cork Street, London W1X 1PB. Tel.: 020 7439 0909. Fax: 020 7434 0073. Senior Dir. or Membership: Sean Devine.

Association of Independent Music (AIM), Lamb House, Church Street, London W4 2PD. Tel.: 020 8994 5599. Fax: 020 8994 5222. Chief Executive: Alison Wenham.

Association of United Recording Artists (AURA), 1 York Street, London W1U 6PA. Te.: 020 7486 6059. Contact: Peter Horrey.

BACS (British Academy of Composers and Songwriters), British Music House, 25–27 Berners Street, London W1T 3LR. Tel.: 020 7636 2929. Chief Executive: Chris Green.

Black Music Industry Association, 146 Manor Park Road, London NW10 4JP. Tel.: 020 8961 4857. Fax: 020 8453 0428. Coordinator: Alan Cuffy.

BMI (Broadcast Music Incorporated), 84 Harley House, Marylebone Road, London NW1 5HN. Tel.: 020 7486 2036. Fax: 020 7224 1046. Senior Executive, Public Relations: Brandon Bakshi.

BPI (British Phonographic Industry Ltd), Riverside Bridge, County Hall, Westminster Bridge Road, London SE1 7JA. Tel.: 020 7803 1300.

British Music Rights, British Music House, 26 Berners Street, London W1P 3DP. Tel.: 020 7306 4446. Fax: 020 7306 4449.

British Video Association (BVA), 167 Great Portland Street, London W1W 5PE. Tel.: 020 7436 0041. Fax: 020 7436 0043. Director General: Lavinia Carey.

Guild of International Songwriters and Composers, Sovereign House, 12 Trewartha Road, Praa Sands, Penzanze, Cornwall TR20 9ST. Tel.: 01736 762826. Fax. 01736 763328. Membership Secretary: Carole A. Jones.

IFPI (International Federation of Phonographic Industries), IFPI Secretariat, 54–62 Regent Street, London W1B 5RE. Tel.: 020 7878 7900. Fax: 020 7878 7950. Contact: Lucy Butler.

In the City, 8 Brewery Yard, Deva Centre, Salford M3 7BB. Tel.: 0161 839 3930. Fax: 0161 839 3940. Contact: Yvette Liversey.

ISM (The Incorporated Society of Musicians), 10 Stratford Place, London W1C 1AA. Tel.: 020 7629 4413. Fax: 020 7408 1538. Chief Executive: Neil Hoyle.

MCPS (Mechanical Copyright Protection Society), Elgar House, 41 Streatham High Road, London SW16 1ER. Tel.: 020 8769 4400. Fax: 020 8378 7300.

MPA (Music Publishers' Association). Third Floor, Strandgate, 18–20 York Buildings, London WC2N 6JU. Tel.: 020 7839 7779. Fax: 020 7839 7776. Chief Executive: Sarah Faulder.

Music Managers' Forum, 1 York Street, London W1V 6PA. Tel.: 0870 850 7800. Fax: 0870 850 7801.

Musicians' Union, 60–62 Clapham Road, London SW9 0JJ. Tel.: 020 7582 5566. Fax: 7582 9805.

National Entertainment Agents Council, PO Box 112, Seaford, East Sussex BN5 2DQ. Tel.: 0870 755 7612. Fax: 0870 755 7613. General Secretary: Chris Bray.

National Sound Archive (British Library), 96 Euston Road, London NW1 2DB. Tel.: 020 7412 7676. Fax: 020 7412 7441. Contact: Richard Fairman.

PAMRA (Performing Artists' Media Rights Association), 161 Borough High Street, London SE1 1HR. Tel.: 020 7940 0400. Fax: 020 7407 2008.

PLASA (Professional Lighting and Sound Association), 38 St Leonards Road, Eastbourne BN21 3UT. Tel.: 01323 410335. Fax: 01323 646905. Contact: Norah Phillips.

PPL (Phonographic Performance Ltd), 1 Upper James Street, London W1F 9DE. Tel.: 020 7534 1245. Fax: 020 7534 1111. Head of External Affairs: Jill Drew.

PRC (Performing Registration Centre), 1 Upper James Street, London W1F 9DE. Tel.: 020 7534 1234. Fax: 020 7534 1383.

PRS (The Performing Rights Society), 29–33 Berners Street, London W1P 4AA. Tel.: 020 7580 5544. Fax: 020 7306 4455. Chief Executive: John Hutchinson.

VPL (Video Performance Ltd), 1 Upper James Street, London W1F 9DE. Tel.: 020 7534 1400. Fax: 020 7534 1414. Business Affairs Manager: Jane Samuels.

Index

Page numbers in *italics* refer to charts.

About the Author

DONALD S. PASSMAN is a graduate of the University of Texas and Harvard Law School. He lives in Los Angeles with his wife and four children, and practices law with the firm of Gang, Tyre, Ramer & Brown, Inc.

After initially practicing tax law, Don has specialized in the music business intensively for over twenty years. His clients include major entertainers, publishers, record companies, songwriters, industry executives, film companies, managers, producers, and other participants in the music industry. Don is listed in *The Best Lawyers in America*, and has lectured extensively on the subject of the music industry, including teaching a course at the University of Southern California Law School's Advanced Professional Program, and lecturing for Harvard Law School, Yale Law School, the UCLA Entertainment Law Symposium, the American Bar Association, the Practicing Law Institute, the USC Entertainment Law Institute, and the Los Angeles Copyright Society.

Don's hobbies include real estate investment, guitar, five-string banjo, weight lifting, chess, ham radio, magic, dog training, and karate. He is a licensed real estate broker, a magician member of the Magic Castle, a dog obedience trainer with degrees in the United States and Mexico, and the highest possible amateur radio licensee (Amateur Extra), all because he is a bit weird and enjoys taking tests.

Don has also been active in community and charitable activities, including acting as president and chairman of the Music Industry Division and sitting on the national board of the City of Hope; as a trustee of the Artists' Rights Foundation; and as a Federation Chief in the YMCA Indian Guides Program (presiding over three hundred father and child Indian braves and princesses).

He is currently writing novels, which you are all required to buy.

Check out Don's website at www.donpassman.com.